Essentials of
Business Communication

Essentials of Business Communication

SECOND CANADIAN EDITION

MARY ELLEN GUFFEY

Los Angeles Pierce College

BRENDAN NAGLE

Red River Community College

I(T)P® International Thomson Publishing

The ITP logo is a trademark under licence

Published in 1997 by

I(T)P® Nelson

A division of Thomson Canada Limited
1120 Birchmount Road
Scarborough, Ontario M1K 5G4

Visit our Web site at http://www.nelson.com

Canadian Cataloguing in Publication Data

Guffey, Mary Ellen
    Essentials of business communication

2nd Canadian ed.
Includes index.
ISBN 0-17-605610-6

1. Business writing.   2. English language — Business English.   3. Business communication.   I. Nagle, Brendan, 1958–   .   II. Title

HF5718.3.G84 1997   808'.06665   C97-930154-8

Publisher and Team Leader	Michael Young
Executive Editor	Andrew Livingston
Production Editor	Tracy Bordian
Project Editors	Joanne Scattolon/Dianne Horton
Production Coordinator	Brad Horning
Art Director	Sylvia Vander Schee
Cover and Interior Design	Julie Greener
Lead Composition Analyst	Zenaida Diores

Printed and bound in Canada
  2 3 4 WC 00 99 98 97

Contents

Preface

Tell me, I forget. Show me, I remember. Involve me, I understand.
                                                    —Chinese proverb

The second Canadian edition of *Essentials of Business Communication* continues to draw upon the wisdom embodied in the above adage. This edition remains a hands-on textbook that emphasizes writing skills and reinforces those writing skills through classroom techniques that require students to *participate* in the writing process. As with the first edition, this book involves students in the learning process so that they *understand* what's being taught.

This textbook will be especially helpful to post-secondary and adult students preparing themselves for new careers, planning a change in their current careers, or wishing to upgrade their writing and speaking skills. Now more than ever, the workplace demands excellent communication skills. As the work environment and technology changes, new and demanding communication challenges present themselves. This book is designed to prepare students to meet those challenges.

The second Canadian edition of *Essentials of Business Communication* retains the structure and approach of the first Canadian edition. The aim of this edition is to incorporate more of the comments, suggestions, and insights provided by adopters over the last few years. For those new to the book, some of the most popular features include the following:

Text-Workbook Format.   The convenient text-workbook format presents an all-in-one teaching/learning package that includes concepts, workbook application exercises, writing problems, and a combination handbook/reference manual.

Four-Stage Plan.   The second Canadian edition develops communication skills in a carefully designed four-stage plan. Stage 1 lays the foundation by presenting communication theory and an optional grammar/mechanics review. Stage 2 introduces the techniques of writing and includes useful hints for writers trying to improve their skills. Stage 3 teaches effective writing strategies and helps students apply those strategies in writing letters and memos. Stage 4 challenges students to apply the effective writing strategies learned in previous stages to a variety of communications situations.

Grammar/Mechanics Emphasis.   Exercises are included at the end of each chapter to allow students to continually review the fundamentals of correct writing. Students can pursue grammar in greater detail in the Grammar/Mechanics Handbook either on their own or in class. The

Grammar/Mechanics Diagnostic Test helps students see areas of weakness in their writing. New to this edition is the Grammar/Mechanics Challenge at the end of each chapter, which provides documents for revision and editing practice.

Writing Improvement Exercises and Cases.   Prepared exercises and cases, available at the end of each chapter, help students see the writing process in simple, manageable components. Many of the case samples focus on rewriting existing business messages. By practicing editing and rewriting skills, students can focus on strategies to solve writing problems.

Examples.   This edition retains the many examples of letter models as well as carry-over exercises that require students to write a request and then respond to that request. It also provides complete examples of longer writing models for informal and formal reports, proposals, minutes, and agendas. In addition, several résumé models clearly display the correct format and style for effective résumés.

The second Canadian edition of *Essentials of Business Communication* explores the four main problem areas of communication in the workplace: writing letters and memos, writing reports, applying listening and speaking skills, and adopting successful employment strategies.

Letters and Memorandum Writing.   After laying the foundation for effective business communication in Chapters 1 to 4, students learn to write routine and good news letters and memos in Chapters 5 to 7. Letters that use the direct strategy to request information, order goods, make claims, respond to inquiries, and respond to claims are covered. In Chapter 8, students learn the indirect strategy for negative news messages and apply it in writing request and claim refusals. Students add to their persuasive skills in Chapter 9 by writing sales letters, proposals, and other persuasive messages. Chapter 10 completes letter writing with special messages such as letters of appreciation, congratulations, sympathy, and recommendation.

Report Writing.   Chapters 11 and 12 develop useful report-writing skills. Chapter 11 concentrates on planning and writing informational and analytical reports. Chapter 12 covers formal reports and includes a model formal report.

Employment Skills.   Chapter 13 helps students develop the vocabulary for successful résumé-writing, then takes them through the steps in producing effective chronological and functional résumés. Model résumés are used to illustrate the important requirements for a successful résumé. Application letters are also covered, as well an expanded discussion of interview techniques.

Listening and Speaking Skills.   Strategies for improving listening and speaking skills are covered in Chapter 14. Active listening techniques are enumerated as well as the three-step approach to oral presentations. This edition also includes a full discussion of meetings, including how to success-fully participate in a meeting, how to chair a meeting, and how to produce an agenda and minutes.

New to the Second Canadian Edition

Report Writing. For those familiar with the first Canadian edition, the report-writing chapters (Chapters 11 and 12) will look different. Chapter 11 helps students learn about the process of defining and then refining a report problem into manageable parts for study. Chapter 12 builds on the concepts in Chapter 11 and adds the structural elements so important to formal reports. Each chapter has many expanded and updated report examples, including a new long formal report in Chapter 12. An expanded section on proposals has been moved to Chapter 9 ("Persuasive Writing").

Electronic Communication. Expanded sections on electronic communica-tion include useful tips in Chapter 1 for producing high-quality electronic documents; methods for producing and examples of electronic memos in Chapter 5 and electronic letters in Chapter 6; a new discussion of presenta-tion software in Chapter 14; new information covering the Internet and its impact on the workplace in Chapter 1; a step-by-step description with exam-ples of the methods of conducting an information search of the World Wide Web in Chapter 12; and new information in Appendix 2 covering the meth-ods of citing electronic sources in reports.

Intercultural Communication. Chapter 15 from the previous edition has been condensed and repositioned in Chapter 1. Interest boxes have been added in locations where the intercultural information parallels that of the text.

Interview Techniques. Chapter 13 includes expanded coverage of the methods of interviewing and consideration for each stage of the interview process—before, during, and after.

Meetings. Chapter 14 broadens its discussion of meetings including expanded examples of minutes and agendas and helpful tips on how to run a successful meeting and maintain control.

New Grammar/Mechanics Challenge Exercises. To provide more realis-tic grammar reviews, each chapter now includes a letter, memo, or short report containing grammar and mechanics problems. Students must recog-nize the problems and rewrite the challenge exercise.

New and Updated Exercises and Examples. Many of the additional prob-lem sections at the end of the chapters now contain at least one new exercise. As well, many of the book's examples have been expanded, updated, or replaced.

Instructor Support

Essentials of Business Communication, Second Canadian Edition, includes extensive instructor support:

- A comprehensive instructor's manual (includes solutions to the grammar/mechanics questions, writing improvement exercises, cases, additional lecture material, chapter-by-chapter lesson plans, evaluation suggestions for oral presentations and reports, and transparency masters).

- A Canadian computerized test bank.

- Canadian PowerPoint presentation disks.

Please contact your local ITP Nelson sales representative for information about World Wide Web support resources.

Acknowledgments

Dr. Mary Ellen Guffey again deserves first acknowledgment in this the second Canadian edition. Her comments were interesting, helpful, and at times inspirational.

Second on the list is, as before, the many classes of students at Red River Community College who acted as test subjects—sometimes knowingly, sometimes unknowingly. As always, their suggestions were invaluable.

Reviewers comments were particularly important to this edition and as usual were comprehensive and insightful. Among the reviewers were Janice Burk, Sault College of Applied Arts and Technology; Judy O'Shea, Lethbridge Community College; Christopher Petty, Red River Community College; Alberta Smith, Algonquin College; and Tom Swankey, Simon Fraser University. Thanks also to the editors at ITP Nelson: Andrew Livingston, Joanne Scattolon, Dianne Horton, and Tracy Bordian. Finally, thanks again to Terry Klan for her judicious advice and timely beverage preparation.

Brendan Nagle
Red River Community College

UNIT 1

LAYING COMMUNICATION FOUNDATIONS

1

Communicating in Business Today

In this chapter, you will learn to do the following:

- Explain why communication skills are valuable both to employers and to employees.
- Analyze the process of communication.
- Discuss ways of improving intercultural communication.

- Describe how to produce an effective document.
- Identify five key forms of electronic communication.
- Describe how communication skills can be developed in four stages.

Communicating and the Information Age

We are now living in the information age. Our lives and our jobs revolve around information—its development, management, processing, and exchange. This book is about understanding how we communicate and learning how to improve our communication skills.

> **Government estimates show that, of all new jobs created, 95 percent will be information- or service-related. Only 5 percent will be product- or manufacturing-related. What does this situation mean for you?**

Knowing how to communicate successfully will be invaluable to you both professionally and personally. In your professional life, language skills are vital for four employment phases: in obtaining the job you want, in performing the tasks of your employment well, in securing promotions within your profession, and in moving to new professions. Aside from employment, good communication skills enable you to create a rich and satisfying personal life.

Some things about ourselves we can't change—our height, our disposition, even our intelligence. But other characteristics we can change, and proficiency in communication is one of them. Frank Carey, former board chairman of IBM, once said that the four qualities of truly successful top executives are intelligence, integrity, empathy, and the ability to communicate. Of the four, only the last, communication, is a learnable skill.

This chapter takes a broad look at communication today. First, it discusses the importance of communication skills in the workplace. Next, the chapter examines communication theory, followed by a glimpse of the effects of technology on communicating today. Finally, it outlines a plan to help you improve your communication skills.

Wanted: Good Communication Skills

Possessing effective communication skills is highly regarded in the business world. Employers, aware of the value of clear expression, increasingly identify and require oral and writing skills in job announcements. Examine the following excerpts from employment advertisements taken from two major Canadian newspapers. Notice how these ads for diverse positions in professional, managerial, technical, and secretarial fields specifically designate good communication skills.

Director of Personnel

Progressive software company seeks highly motivated, results-oriented personnel generalist. Must be a hands-on self-starter with *effective communication skills.*

Manager, Business Systems

National organization seeks project manager to develop, coordinate, and provide automated tracking and control systems ... An outgoing, congenial personality and *exceptional communication skills* essential.

Management Trainee

Leading, innovative financial organization seeks energetic, organized, detail-oriented individual to monitor programs. Candidates must have initiative, *excellent written and verbal skills,* and strong analytical ability.

Administrative Assistant

Toronto cosmetic firm seeks capable administrative assistant to work with our dynamic team. Requirements include word processing and spreadsheet experience, and *excellent communication skills.*

Classified ads reflect a growing concern for good verbal and writing skills.

Why Employers Value Good Communicators

Business needs good communicators because these employees stimulate additional business. They are able to sell ideas, services, and products. Good communicators know how to analyze, organize, and clarify information. Not only do they promote business for their organizations, but they also keep administrative costs down because their messages are not misunderstood and do not have to be repeated. Good communicators produce good will for their organizations. They project a positive image of themselves and their organizations.

Estimates indicate that more than one third of all business letters do nothing more than seek clarification of earlier correspondence.

Jonas Samons of the Alliance of Exporters and Manufacturers Canada emphasizes the importance employers in Canada attach to good communication skills. "We need individuals who possess effective oral and written communication skills, individuals who can function well in a group—individuals with people skills, able to reach consensus."[1] According to Samons, communication skills rank considerably higher than professional competence on the list of qualities that employers are looking for in prospective employees.

In locating individuals with good communication skills, some organizations require job candidates to submit a writing sample. Other employers test communication skills. All personnel officers judge a job applicant's performance in the interview. How well you answer questions, communicate your ideas, explain your qualifications, and promote yourself determine whether you will be hired. According to a report published by the Conference Board of Canada, Canadian employers look for and hire applicants who can *read, comprehend,* and *use* written materials, including graphs, charts, and displays, and *write* effectively in the languages in which business is conducted. Also highly valued by employers is the ability to *think critically, be adaptable,* and *work effectively with others*.[2] Clearly, if you can communicate well, you will get along better with others than will those who do not communicate well.

Communicating on the Job

Once you have been hired, you'll need good speaking, listening, and writing skills to get your work done. The degree of communication skills you will need depends on the profession you enter and on the stage of your career. Jobs such as selling insurance and managing investments demand excellent communication skills for entry-level positions. Other positions may not require exceptional writing and speaking skills at first.

Individuals who are promoted into supervisory and managerial positions require better communication skills than do entry-level employees.

However, as one advances into supervisory and management roles, the demand for communication skills increases. Studies show, as you might expect, that supervisors, managers, and executives spend a much higher percentage of their time writing memos, letters, and reports than do their employees. Promotions are often given to those employees who demonstrate that they are effective communicators. In a study of vice-presidents selected from *Fortune 500* corporations, 98 percent reported that effective communication skills had positively affected their advancement to top executive positions.[3]

But Not for Accountants?

"But," you may protest, "I'm going to be an accountant (or computer specialist or financial analyst or health-care specialist). In my profession, language skills are unimportant."

Even in business activities that centre on technical concepts, skill in communicating ideas is required. In an article in *CA Magazine*, Gale Cohen

Ruby, an accounting industry communications consultant, states that the products accounting firms deliver to their clients are, for the most part, written ones: audit reports, review engagement reports, management letters, and the like. "These products indicate the quality of a firm's service ..."[4] Employers value communication skills because they have a direct effect on the prosperity of the company. Ruby also points out that "writing can help to win or lose clients ... People judge professionals by the way they write."[5]

Your communication skills also influence the possibility of promotion into supervisory or managerial positions. "An accountant with excellent writing skills will be sought after by partners and managers alike ... Possessing excellent writing skills is one sure-fire way to stand out in a CA firm."[6] The move into supervisory roles also brings increased administrative responsibilities. An informal survey done by Ruby showed that senior chartered accountants can spend up to 75 percent of their time writing and rewriting documents. Since much of what professionals do requires communication skills, it is important to consider this: "Too many CAs realize the importance of good writing only when they sit down to compose a client letter and find they lack the skill to do so."[7]

> Workers in technical areas must be able to communicate their ideas to both technical and nontechnical colleagues.

On the Personal Side

Aside from professional considerations, good communication skills benefit us personally. Since we spend the better part of our lives communicating with others, it is reasonable to assume that individuals who express ideas easily and clearly are better understood and experience greater satisfaction in interpersonal relationships than do those with weak skills. Moreover, good communicators create favourable impressions. For better or worse, we all make judgments about others based on a number of factors, including the way they speak and the way they write. Our judgments, then, are influenced to a great extent by communication skills. Individuals who speak and write well convey the impression of intelligence, education, and success. They command respect, whether deserved or not. They are also happier because they are productive.

> The impressions you make on others are largely determined by the way you communicate.

What Is Communication?

Communication skills play an important part in our personal lives and in our business careers. Before we begin our plan for improving those skills, let's explore briefly the general process of communication. What does the word "communication" mean? This complex term has no single definition. *Funk & Wagnalls Canadian College Dictionary* (1989) lists at least three considerably different meanings for the word, which is derived from the Latin *communis*, meaning "common." When we communicate, we convey knowledge; that is, we share something with others, with or without a response.

1. An *act* of transmitting

2. *Information* transmitted, or the exchange of ideas by speech or writing

3. A *means of passage* by which information is exchanged between individuals

Communication is both a process and the product of that process.

To make the term less abstract, let's try to illustrate each of the preceding definitions. The act of transmitting might be as simple as voicing the word "hello" to a friend or handing a co-worker a memo. Both of these are examples of the act of transmitting. Notice that communication in this sense requires no response on the part of a receiving individual.

The second sense of the word emphasizes a product. This product might be a new work schedule announced by an office manager. It might be a business letter sent to a customer. Again, no response is required for this sense of communication.

In the third sense, however, communication is described as a means of passage or process in which information is *exchanged*. This exchange of information cannot be accomplished unless individuals, or machines, use a system of symbols or signs that both parties understand. It is with this last sense of the definition that we will be most concerned in our study of the essentials of business communication. Improving the process of communication is our goal. To achieve this goal, we need to understand better the components of the communication process.

Understanding the Communication Process

Only in comparatively recent times has the communication process been studied. In the past 50 years, theories of communication have been developed. Theories, by the way, seldom solve immediate problems. Rather, they help us view our experiences in a fresh way. Theories and models enable us to organize experiences so that relationships are simplified and more easily comprehended.

Effective communication is a *cyclic* rather than a *linear* process.

The model shown in Figure 1.1 breaks down the process of communication into its component parts and illustrates its cycle. When we consider communication to be the exchange of information, feedback becomes an important part of the cycle. Let's look more carefully at each of the five parts of the communication process.

Sender

Messages may be conveyed verbally (with spoken or written words) or nonverbally (with actions or pictures).

The communication cycle begins with a sender who has an idea to transmit to another individual. How can the sender shape that idea into a message that the receiver will understand? The sender must make choices regarding the length, emphasis, tone, and organization of the message. The words the sender selects to convert, or encode, the idea into an appropriate form require careful thought.

The sender considers the purpose, the subject, and the intended receiver of the message. The message the sender encodes will be influenced by the communication skills, attitudes, experiences, and culture of the sender. The goal of a good communicator is to create a message that is understood as he or she intended.

Figure 1.1 Communication Model

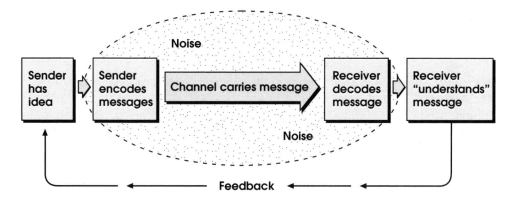

Communication barriers and noise may cause the communication cycle to break down.

To ensure understanding, the sender chooses words and concepts that are not beyond the receiver's knowledge and experience. For example, a telecommunication software sales representative presenting a new product to an office manager with little knowledge of computers would wisely avoid descriptions like "it's a file-transfer-level protocol designed for dial-up asynchronous transmission." Even though such language may be clear to the sales rep, it's probably not so clear to the office manager.

In the communication cycle, the sender may fail to communicate with the receiver when the code or symbols are not understood by both. It is the responsibility of the sender to prepare a message that is within the comprehension of the receiver. Moreover, the sender should strive for feedback, which will be discussed shortly.

Message

The message created to represent an idea may be verbal or nonverbal. A nod of the head delivers a simple message of agreement. When a smile accompanies that nod, it signifies approval as well. Nonverbal communication is often subtle and may be culture-dependent. Throughout most of the world, shaking the head back and forth indicates a negative response, but in certain regions of India it means just the opposite. Culture affects both nonverbal and verbal messages.

In this textbook, we will be most concerned with verbal messages—that is, those that are expressed with spoken or written words. The words the sender chooses, the way they are arranged, their number, their meaning, and their length all contribute to the effect a message has on the listener or reader. Consider Howard Hightower, the national sales manager for a publisher. He must tell all salespeople that declining sales necessitate reducing their commissions; however, he also wants to encourage them to increase their sales. He could make this announcement in a blunt statement of 15 words. But if he desires comprehension, compliance, and cooperation, he will probably create a message with well-considered words organized into an effective strategy. The same information delivered by a Japanese sales manager to salespeople in his or her firm might be presented quite differently. Messages, then, are determined by the sender's objective, audience, subject, communication skills, attitudes, and culture.

Channel

The medium over which the message is physically transmitted is the channel. Messages may be delivered by computer, telephone, letter, memorandum, report, announcement, picture, face-to-face exchange, fax, or through some other channel.

The selection of an appropriate channel for a message is determined by its complexity, importance, expected response, immediacy, degree of formality, audience, and cost.

How should a message be sent? Several factors determine the choice of channel, the most important of which are these:

- **Complexity of the message**. Is the information so detailed that the receiver will need to read and study it?

- **Importance of the message**. Is the content of this message such that it requires a permanent record?

- **Anticipated reaction**. Will this message create a positive or negative receiver response?

- **Immediacy of the situation**. Is a quick response needed?

- **Degree of formality**. Does a personal relationship exist between the sender and the receiver?

- **Size and location of the audience**. Is the message intended for a single receiver nearby or for hundreds of distant receivers?

- **Comparative costs**. Does the message warrant a costly channel in terms of time, equipment, and people?

Let's say, for example, that you are an executive in a large company and you are announcing a profit-sharing plan to employees. The best channel for your message would probably be a memo, rather than a personal interview with or a telephone call to each employee. If, however, you wish to convince a director of the company that certain options in the profit-sharing plan should be revised, then a personal conference, along with a report, would be most effective. If you were inviting a colleague to lunch, the most appropriate communication channel would be the telephone.

Physical transmission of a message can affect the receiver's perception of that message. If you receive a letter addressed to "Occupant," you may dismiss its contents as junk mail. The same message, however, addressed to you by name and delivered on quality stationery may command your attention. You perceive the message as important; you have a favourable attitude toward it.

Receiver

The receiver's reaction to a message is determined by a number of external and internal factors, including the following:

■ **Form and appearance of the message**. Is the channel appropriate? Is the message attractive and clear?

■ **Subject of the message**. How much does the receiver know about the subject?

■ **Attitude toward the message**. Does the receiver have an open, closed, or neutral attitude toward the message? Is the receiver in a receptive mood?

■ **Communication skills**. Does the receiver possess sufficient communication skills to comprehend the message?

■ **Physical conditions**. Is the receiver free of physical distractions so that it is possible to concentrate on the message?

Successful communication results when a receiver understands a message as the sender intended and responds as expected. To do this, the receiver must decode the symbols and ascribe to them the same general meanings as those ascribed by the sender.

Feedback

The final step in the communication cycle is the response of the receiver. Nonverbal feedback may consist of a puzzled frown if, for example, the receiver does not understand the message. Verbal feedback may be a spoken comment or a written message. Even no response to a message is, in a sense, a form of feedback.

Feedback helps the sender evaluate the effectiveness of the original message. If the desired results were not achieved, the sender selects other words organized in an alternative strategy to repeat the communication attempt.

Skilful communicators recognize the importance of feedback and consciously provide for it. In conversation they watch facial expressions and respond accordingly. They don't dominate; conversation is two-way. They encourage questions. In letters and memos that provide feedback, they conclude by asking for a specific action that indicates comprehension of the idea communicated.

To ensure that receivers comprehend their messages, skilled communicators provide opportunities for feedback during and after the delivery of the messages.

Barriers

For an infinite number of reasons, the communication cycle is not always successful. Barriers may cause the breakdown of communication in any of the encoding, transmitting, decoding, and responding stages of the process. A message sender who lacks awareness of the receiver or who possesses poor communication skills will have difficulty sending clear messages.

Barriers in transmitting messages are created by physical distractions and by long communication chains. Messages become distorted when too many people must process them. In the decoding stage, communication is disrupted if the receiver lacks interest in, or knowledge of, the topic in the message. Emotional distractions may interfere with both the encoding and the decoding of messages. These disruptions, sometimes called "noise," can create failure in any step of the communication cycle.

Communication barriers and noise prevent effective communication.

Communicating in the Global Environment

Increasing international trade and the growth of transnational corporations are making international business communication a daily occurrence. An awareness of the intricate nature of intercultural communication—and some of its pitfalls—will help you to communicate more effectively with contacts both abroad and within Canada's multicultural environment.

What Is Intercultural Communication?

As we have seen, the process of communication is a cycle that involves the sender encoding a message and choosing a channel, and the receiver decoding the message and providing feedback. In intercultural communication, the encoding and decoding is affected by the respective cultures of the sender and receiver. Each is encoding and decoding based on a different set of cultural rules. These differing sets of cultural rules create noise, or barriers to understanding.

An awareness of our own personality traits helps us communicate with people from other cultures.

Understanding Different Cultures

Culture is a code by which we see the world and by which we respond to the things we encounter. Our culture helps us decide what is important about the objects around us. Not all cultures perceive the same objects in the same way. When we look at an object, we may notice its size, price, and utility, or we may focus on its colour and smell. Minor communication problems can be aggravated by differences in cultural perception.

Every culture has a dominant set of ideas, or world view, that has consequences for how an individual or organization conducts business. Consider the example of a Hindu CEO whose company has just experienced a dramatic loss of market share. Rather than launching an aggressive ad campaign in an effort to restore the company's former market position, the CEO might choose to do nothing out of a belief that the shift in the marketplace is a matter of karma, and therefore inevitable.

Culture, world view, and values provide people with ways to perceive, so people from different cultures differ in their perceptions.

Different cultures also have different values and goals, different social and organizational structures, and different attitudes toward the role of women in the workplace. Even the concept of time varies across cultures. Western cultures tend to see time in linear terms. According to this way of thinking, the stages of a task should run in a straight line from start to finish. The attitude toward any deviation from this linear movement is summed up by the expression "Time is money." In other cultures, however, time is seen as organic and nonlinear. For these cultures, human activity may not fit easily into an environment that runs with clocklike efficiency; delays or interruptions may be a necessary part of completing a task. In business, these conflicting views of time can cause misunderstanding and frustration for both sender and receiver.

Our ability to understand another culture depends on a number of factors. The fact that North American products have found increasing acceptance in non-Western societies in recent years can lead us to falsely assume that those societies are becoming more like ours on a more profound cultural level. It is important to keep in mind that while cultures may adopt symbols from other cultures, the meaning they attach to those symbols can be quite different.

Cultures that rely heavily on nonverbal communication present special challenges when it comes to decoding messages. In Japan, for example, important information is often conveyed through a nod of the head or movement of the hand. Careful and persistent observation on the part of the outsider is a prerequisite for learning this form of communication.

Further complicating our ability to understand other cultures is the fact that each society contains within it subcultures that exist as part of the larger culture. A recent immigrant living in downtown Toronto and a newcomer living in southern Manitoba in a predominantly Mennonite community would acquire very different ideas of Canadian culture. Even Japan, which is often seen as being culturally homogeneous; has internal variations. The rules of communication that prevail in a given subculture are a mix of those adopted from the larger culture and those retained from the original culture.

In order for effective communication between cultures to occur, both sender and receiver must accept that the other has a different set of communication rules. As receivers, we must allow for cultural differences when decoding messages and avoid reacting negatively based on our own cultural assumptions. As senders, we must take into consideration what we know of the other culture when encoding messages. As both senders and receivers, we can reinforce our mutual understanding by engaging in constructive feedback and follow-up.

Familiar cultural symbols, nonverbal communication, and cultural variation present special challenges for intercultural communication.

Communicating in the 21st Century

Despite extraordinary technological advances in the field of communication today, the process of communication remains largely unchanged—that is, individuals still have ideas that must be encoded properly and transmitted through appropriate channels to receivers. However, in this information age, we are witnessing remarkable changes in the tools of communication. Advances in technology have altered the way we gather and store information, create messages, transmit ideas, and respond to those ideas.

Today, computer skills are a basic requirement for nearly all workers. As the demand for efficiency increases, office and shop-floor workers, managers, and executives will be expected to adapt to technological change. Business communicators today must be proficient in both document production and electronic communication.

The process of communication changes little, but the expectation that all workers will be proficient in their use of electronic communication tools grows as technology changes.

Document Production

When producing a document, you should perform the following tasks to ensure accuracy and readability:

1. **Plan your message**. Computers allow us to create messages quickly and revise them as we go. The downside of our unlimited ability to revise is that we may neglect the planning stage of document production. Lack of planning and organization can result in a message that lacks coherence.

2. **Edit your message**. Don't rely on spell checks to do all the work. Spell checks find only misspelled words, not misused words that are spelled correctly. For example, if you were to mistakenly type the word *than* instead of *that*, your spell check would not identify the error because both words are spelled correctly. The mere existence of spell checks, however, means that readers are less tolerant of *all* typographical errors.

3. **Ensure accuracy of information**. In addition to ensuring that your document exhibits an appropriate tone and style, you should double-check the accuracy of your facts. If possible, enlist a second reader to review the message.

Also critical to a document's success is its physical appearance. Following are some suggestions for enhancing the visual appeal of your document.

1. **Use font changes when appropriate.** Fonts can be sized and styled in a variety of ways. Bold, italic, or underline can be used to indicate different levels of headings or to create emphasis within body text.

2. **Use headers and footers to convey information and provide a visual frame.** Headers and footers can contain such information as document name, page number, and chapter title. Graphics, such as a company logo, can be incorporated into this feature.

3. **Use clip art, pictures, and symbols to enliven your document's design.** Cartoon clip art is probably too casual. Pictures and line art should be scanned from a high-quality original and saved at a high resolution. Symbols can be used effectively as bullets to set off each point in a list.*

4. **Create a template.** To ensure that the formatting of your document is consistent throughout, create a template that has the desired margin settings and other options.

When producing a document, it is important to consider the capabilities of your receiver's hardware (e.g., modem transfer rate and monitor colour capability). You should also know the platform and software in which your receivers work. Are they DOS, Macintosh, or UNIX? Do they use Microsoft, Novel, or other software products? This kind of knowledge will allow you to plan your document so that it is compatible with the receiver's personal computer.

Electronic Communication

In creating and exchanging information today, business communicators employ the following forms of electronic communication.

Voice Mail.   Voice messaging systems allow users to send and receive messages from telephones at any time or to any destination; the recipient takes the call when convenient. The effective use of voice mail is discussed in Chapter 14.

> *Planning and editing the content of a message as well as its visual appeal must not be overlooked when using technology tools.*

> *New employees, from clerks to managers, find that computer skills are necessary both for entry-level employment and for promotion.*

---

*Note: Scanned pictures, art, symbols, and other visual elements can increase the file size of your document significantly, which can be problematic if your document is to be E-mailed or saved to diskette. A file that is more than 1.44 megabytes cannot be transferred using one diskette. Large and complex files that are E-mailed can cause problems when displayed by the receiver.

Fax.   Communicating by fax is becoming as common as picking up a telephone. Fax communication is different from other forms of electronic mail in that it produces a paper duplicate of the original document.

E-mail.   Many organizations currently exchange memos and other internal documents using E-mail. They may also store much of this information in a central electronic location. See Chapter 5 for further discussion of E-mail.

In offices of the future, E-mail may one day replace most internal forms of communication—including telephone calls, meetings, and "snail mail" (paper mail).

LANs.   Local area networks (LANs) allow dissimilar computers to exchange information. LANs are required if organizations are to use E-mail services for distributing messages among employees. Organizations are now moving toward a system of internal networking called *Intranet*, which links networked computers inside a company using the protocols of the Internet (html, Java, etc.). This allows the internal network to be linked to the resources of the Internet.

GANs.   Global area networks (GANs) connect millions of computer users, providing them with an E-mail system, a source of vast amounts of information, a platform for linking with different computers, a place to buy goods and services, and a vehicle for distributing information.

On the Internet, you can talk to people, exchange mail, shop, do research, get the news, or just surf. In fact, it is probable that in the future we will be linked to the Internet in much greater ways than we are now. We will be linked whenever we turn on our computers or whenever we plug into an electrical outlet. We will no longer *choose* to "log on" as we do now. The Internet will be part of our lives. We will all be "Net Users" without even knowing.

Developing Your Communication Skills

Thus far in this chapter you've learned that communication skills are vital both in the business world and in your personal life. You've become familiar with the communication process, and you've had a brief introduction to some of the issues facing communicators in the global and technological business world of the 21st century.

What does all this mean to you? It means that to be successful, you need well-developed communication skills. But the ability to communicate effectively is not a universal trait. Most of us require instruction, practice, supervision, and feedback to develop and improve these communication skills.

Effective communication includes speaking, listening, and writing skills. All these topics will be presented in this book, along with numerous opportunities to apply the concepts presented. Many of the suggestions intended for analyzing business communication problems are equally helpful in resolving personal problems.

Emphasis on Writing

For many reasons, special emphasis will be directed to writing skills. Although data may be shared electronically and decisions arrived at in conversations, business people frequently say, "Put it in writing" or "Get it on paper."

The process of "putting it in writing" can be challenging. Writing is not easy, especially if the writer has had little instruction or supervised practice. Effective writing techniques, however, can be learned, and real skill can be developed.

Good writers are not born with their writing skills; they develop such skills through training and practice.

Four Stages of Development

Good writers learn the craft of writing in much the same way that other skilled artisans or professionals learn their trades. Each of them typically follows a four-stage plan.

The first stage involves learning how to use the *tools of the trade*. For the writer, these tools are the basic rules of language, including grammar, punctuation, and capitalization, as well as number, spelling, and syntax conventions.

In the second stage, the writer learns the *proper techniques* for efficient and coherent combination of these basic tools. These techniques involve learning how to use words skilfully and precisely, how to write effective sentences and paragraphs, and how to develop appropriate style and tone.

After learning these techniques, the writer needs a *plan of action*. The third stage, then, involves learning and applying strategies for producing the desired result.

Finally, in the fourth stage, the writer practises *applying the tools, techniques, and strategies* in varying situations. In this way writers improve their skills in producing satisfactory results.

Textbook Parallel

This textbook is organized to parallel and amplify these four stages of skill development. Stage 1 (Chapter 1 and the Grammar/Mechanics Handbook) lays a foundation for communication by introducing communication theory and concepts. Some students will need to review the basic tools of language. Your instructor may assign the Grammar/Mechanics Diagnostic Test so that you can assess your strengths and weaknesses. The Grammar/Mechanics Handbook, following the diagnostic test, provides a review of grammar and punctuation, as well as exercises to enable you to sharpen your basic skills.

Stage 2 (Chapters 2, 3, and 4) presents writing techniques, the "tricks of the trade" for authors. Stage 3 (Chapters 5 through 9) develops communication strategies. Stage 4 (Chapters 10 through 14) applies and adapts these techniques and strategies in varying communication situations.

The emphasis throughout this volume is on developing communication skills in practical business applications.

Summary

Communicating successfully in the information age will be valuable to you professionally and personally. It will help you get a job, do your job effectively, get promoted, and change careers. It will also help you personally by allowing you to create a favourable impression.

Communication is both a product and a process of exchange. The process of communication can be seen as a cycle that includes the sender encoding a message and choosing a channel, and the receiver decoding the message and providing feedback. Messages may be conveyed verbally or nonverbally. Choice of a channel depends on the complexity of the message, its importance, expected response, immediacy, degree of formality, audience, and cost. Skilled communicators provide opportunities for feedback during and after the delivery of their messages. The intercultural communication cycle is affected by the respective cultures of the sender and the receiver. In order to communicate effectively, both parties should be aware of cultural differences.

Workers at all levels of the organizational hierarchy are expected to adapt to technological change. Today's business communicators must be proficient in both document production and electronic communication.

The significance of communication cannot be overstated. It is important to remember that effective communication can be learned through instruction, practice, supervision, and feedback.

APPLICATION AND PRACTICE—1

Discussion

1. How do communication skills affect promotion to and within management?

2. Discuss whether or not managers or executives with good assistants should be concerned about their own communication skills.

3. Describe the communication cycle. Why should it be considered a cycle rather than a line?

4. What factors influence the intercultural communication cycle?

5. Discuss the impact that technology might have on you in the workplace.

Short Answers

6. Name two or more ways in which an individual with good communication skills could be valuable to an organization.

7. What are three definitions for the word *communication*?

8. Give a brief definition or explanation of the following words:
   a. encode

   b. channel

   c. decode

9. Identify four ways in which one culture might differ from another.

10. Name three concerns a business communicator might have about his or her electronic document.

11. List four stages in developing the craft of writing.

Activities

12. Select from a local or national newspaper five or more advertisements for positions that require good communication skills. Bring the ads to class for discussion.

13. Analyze the communication process for a vice-president of sales who must send an announcement to the sales staff regarding a new product. Using the communication model in Figure 1.1, discuss the components of the process. How might noise interfere with successful communication? How could the vice-president reduce or prevent such noise? How could he or she ensure feedback?

14. In small groups, role-play how you would explain to a recent immigrant to Canada the significance of common nonverbal communication devices. Use specific facial expressions, gestures, and body language in your role-play.

15. At the direction of your instructor, make an oral or written report based on an interview with a businessperson. Gather information on these topics:

   a. types and frequency of communication within the business,

   b. importance of written communication to the individual and to the business,

   c. importance of oral communication to the individual and to the business, and

   d. types and effects of technological tools.

16. Make an informal study of technology in your profession. Talk with two or more individuals who are familiar with your career choice. Ask them how communication technologies have changed in their workplace. How would they rate the effectiveness of the various technologies? What recommendations do they have for individuals training to enter the profession? Be prepared to present your findings in an oral or written report.

GRAMMAR/MECHANICS CHECKUP—1

Nouns

These checkups are designed to improve your control of grammar and mechanics. They systematically review all sections of the Grammar/Mechanics Handbook. Answers are given for odd-numbered statements; answers to even-numbered statements will be provided by your instructor.

Review Sections 1.01 through 1.06 of the Grammar/Mechanics Handbook. Then study each of the following statements. Underscore any inappropriate form, and write a correction in the space provided. Also record the appropriate G/M section and letter to illustrate the principle involved. If a sentence is correct, write C. When you finish, compare your responses with those provided. If your answers differ, study carefully the principles shown in parentheses.

companies (1.05e)   **Example:** Two surveys revealed that many companys will move to the new industrial park.

_____   1. Several attornies investigated the case and presented their opinions.

_____   2. At the counter we are busier on Saturday's, but telephone business is greater on Sundays.

_____   3. Some of the citys in Mr. Graham's report offer excellent opportunities.

_____   4. Frozen chickens and turkies are kept in the company's basement lockers.

_____   5. All secretaries were asked to check supplies and other inventorys immediately.

_____   6. Both the Finchs and the Lopezes agreed to attend the business meeting.

_____   7. In the 1980s, profits grew slowly; in the 1990's, we anticipate greater growth.

_____   8. The two father-in-laws kept silent during the civil and religious ceremonies.

_____   9. Luxury residential complexs are part of the architect's overall plan.

_____   10. Voters in three municipalitys are likely to approve increasing school taxes.

_____   11. The instructor was surprised to find three Jennifer's in one class.

_____   12. British Columbia's interior valleys become quite warm in August.

_____   13. All of the bosses of the secretarys attended the luncheon.

_____   14. The sign was difficult to read because one could not distinguish between its *o's* and *a's*.

_____   15. Two runner-ups complained that they should have won the contest.

1. attorneys (1.05d)   3. cities (1.05e)   5. inventories (1.05e)   7. 1990s (1.05g)
9. complexes (1.05b)   11. Jennifers (1.05a)   13. secretaries (1.05e)   15. runners-up
(1.05f)

GRAMMAR/MECHANICS CHALLENGE—1

Document for Revision

The following memo has faults in grammar, spelling, punctuation, capitalization, word use, and number form. Drawing upon the guidelines provided in the Grammar/Mechanics Handbook, revise the memo.

Poor Memo

TO: Tran Nguyen   DATE: May 11, 199x

FROM: Rachel Stivers, Manger

SUBJECT: WORK AT HOME GUIDELINES

Since you will be completing most f your work at home for the next 2 months. Follow these guidelines;

1. Check your message bored daily and respond promptly, to those who are trying to reach you.

2. Call the office at least twice a week to pick up any telephone messages, return these calls promptly.

3. Transmit any work you do, on the computer to Jerry Gonzalez in our computer services department, he will analyze each weeks accounts, and send it to the proper Departments.

4. Provide me with monthly reports' of your progress.

I know you will work satisfactory at home Tran. Following theses basic guidelines should help you accomplish your work, and provide the office with adequate contact with you.

Notes

1. Jonas Samons, panel discussion, Red River Community College, September 1992.

2. *Foundation Skills for Canadian Youth: Report of Findings from Meetings Commissioned by the Prosperity Secretariat*, Conference Board of Canada, National Business and Education Centre (Ottawa: Conference Board of Canada, June 1992), p. 3.

3. James C. Bennett and Robert J. Olney, "Executive Priorities for Effective Communication in an Information Society," *The Journal of Business Communication* (Spring 1986): 15.

4. Gale Cohen Ruby, "Author! Author!: Why Your Firm May Be Paying a Heavy Price for Poor Writing," *CA Magazine*, March 1993, p. 36.

5. Ruby, p. 36.

6. Ruby, p. 36.

7. Ruby, p. 36.

2

Using Words Skilfully

In this chapter, you will learn to do the following:

- Make your writing more readable by substituting familiar words for unfamiliar words.
- Recognize and avoid unnecessary jargon, legalese, non-English expressions, and slang.
- Achieve a forceful style by using precise verbs, concrete nouns,

vivid adjectives, and other specific forms.
- Avoid clichés, buzz words, repetitious words, and redundancies.
- Identify and employ idiomatic expressions.

Most of us seldom choose our words carefully.

We usually take the words we use for granted, seldom thinking consciously about choosing them carefully. We use whatever words come to mind. In this chapter, we will ask you to become more aware of the words that you write.

Writers are totally dependent on their words to convey meaning. If the speaker's words are misunderstood, the listener will signal that more information is needed to clarify an idea. If a writer's words are unclear, the reader cannot immediately seek clarification.

Because words have different meanings for different individuals, the communicator must be judicious in selecting and using words. We can never be certain that our words will have the exact effect intended. We can improve our chances for successful communication by following specific word-selection and writing techniques. The techniques presented here include practical suggestions encouraging the use of familiar and vivid words. We'll also show you how to avoid overworked, redundant, and improper words.

Familiar Words

Familiar words are more meaningful to readers.

Clear messages contain words that are familiar and meaningful to the reader. How can we know what is meaningful to a given reader? Although we can't know with certainty, we can avoid certain groups of words that are likely to create misunderstanding.

Avoid long, difficult, unfamiliar words. Substitute short, simple, common words. Here are some examples:

Difficult, Unfamiliar Words	Simple Alternatives
ascertain	find out
conceptualize	see
encompass	include
hypothesize	guess
monitor	check
operational	working
perpetuate	continue
perplexing	troubling
reciprocate	return
stipulate	require
terminate	end
utilize	use

Jargon

Jargon is special terminology that is used by a particular group or profession. For example, geologists speak knowingly of *exfoliation, calcareous ooze,* and *siliceous particles.* Aerospace engineers are familiar with phrases like *infrared processing flags, output latches,* and *movable symbology.* Telecommunication experts use such words and phrases as *protocol, mode,* and *asynchronous transmission.*

Every profession has its own special vocabulary. Using that vocabulary within the profession is acceptable and even necessary for accurate communication. Don't use special terms, however, if you believe that your reader may misunderstand them.

Jargon, which is terminology unique to a certain profession, should be reserved for individuals who understand it.

Plain Language

Good writers use plain language to express clear meaning. They don't use overly complicated words and ambiguous expressions in an effort to dazzle or confuse readers. They write to express ideas, not to impress others.

Some business, legal, and government documents are written in an inflated style that obscures meaning. This style of writing has been given various terms, such as *legalese, bureaucratese, doublespeak,* and *the official style.* It may be used intentionally to mask meaning, or it may simply be an attempt to show off the

Inflated, unnatural writing that is intended to impress readers more often confuses them.

writer's vocabulary. What do you think one manager meant by the following message? "Personnel assigned vehicular space in the adjacent areas are hereby advised that utilization will be suspended temporarily Friday morning." It no doubt took several readings before employees understood they were being asked not to park in the next-door lot on Friday morning.

Legal documents and contracts often suffer from this same inflated, ambiguous style. One Toronto company actually specializes in producing "dejargonized" reports for private- and public-sector clients.

What does plain English mean? Although it's difficult to define precisely, it generally means writing that is clear, simple, and understandable. It suggests writing that is easy to follow, well organized, and appropriately divided. A plain English document should include many of the writing techniques you are about to study (active voice, positive form, parallel construction, use of headings).

Don't be impressed by high-sounding language and legalese, such as *herein, thereafter, hereinafter, whereas,* and similar expressions. Your writing will be better understood if you use plain expressions.

Non-English Expressions

To many readers, non-English expressions are like a code; they hold secret meanings known only to the select few. Writers who use these expressions risk offending readers who cannot decipher the code. Although such expressions as *pro bono, prima facie,* or *ipso facto* may be acceptable for specific applications (especially legal documents), they have little justification in business messages.

Slang

Slang sounds fashionable, but it lacks precise meaning and should be avoided in business writing.

Like jargon and non-English expressions, slang usually has precise meaning for only a favoured few. Slang is composed of informal words with arbitrary and extravagantly changed meanings. Slang words quickly go out of fashion because they are no longer appealing when everyone begins to understand them. Government officials often flavour their messages with slang terms. They may refer to *fallout* (consequences), *withinputs* (contributions), or *spin* (interpretation). All of us use slang expressions in informal daily conversation. Here are some common examples: *hassle* (bother), *gross* (disgusting), *cool* (appealing), and *loonie* (Canadian dollar coin). Good communicators avoid unintelligible or overly intimate slang.

Forceful Words

Effective writing creates meaningful images in the mind of the reader. Such writing is sparked by robust, concrete, and descriptive words. Ineffective writing is often dulled by insipid, abstract, and generalized words. To produce messages that communicate your intentions, use precise verbs, concrete nouns, and vivid adjectives.

Precise Verbs

The most direct way to improve lifeless writing is through effective use of verbs. Verbs not only indicate the action of the subject but also deliver the force of the sentence. Select verbs carefully so that the reader can visualize precisely what is happening.

Precise verbs make your writing forceful and intelligible.

General: Our salesperson will contact you next month.

Precise: Our salesperson will (*telephone, write, visit*) ...

General: The premier said that we should vote.

Precise: The premier (*urged, pleaded, demanded*) ...

General: We must consider this problem.

Precise: We must (*clarify, remedy, rectify*) ...

The power of a verb is diminished when it is needlessly converted into a noun. This happens when verbs such as *acquire, establish,* and *develop* are made into nouns (*acquisition, establishment,* and *development*). These nouns then receive the central emphasis in the sentence. In the following pairs of sentences, observe how forceful the original verbs are as compared with their noun forms.

Verb: The city *acquired* park lands recently.

Noun: *Acquisition* of park lands was made recently by the city.

Verb: Mr. Miller and Mrs. Dueck *discussed* credit-card billing.

Noun: Mr. Miller and Mrs. Dueck had a *discussion* concerning credit-card billing.

Verb: Both companies must *approve* the merger.

Noun: Both companies must grant *approval* of the merger.

Concrete Nouns

Nouns name persons, places, and things. Abstract nouns name concepts that are difficult to visualize, such as *automation, function, justice, institution, integrity, form, judgment,* and *environment*. Concrete nouns name objects that are more easily imagined, such as *desk, car,* and *light bulb*. Nouns describing a given object can range from the very abstract to the very concrete; for example, *object, motor vehicle, car, convertible, Mustang*. All of these words or phrases can be used to describe a Mustang convertible. However, a reader would have difficulty envisioning a Mustang convertible when given just the word *object*, or even *motor vehicle* or *car*.

Concrete nouns help readers visualize the meanings of words.

In business writing, help your reader "see" what you mean by using concrete language.

General	Concrete
a *change* in our budget	a *10 percent reduction* in our budget
that company's product	*Panasonic's Sensicolor* videotape
a person called	*Mrs. Tomei, the administrative assistant,* called
we *improved* the assembly line	we *installed 26 advanced Animate robots* on the assembly line

Vivid Adjectives

Including highly descriptive, dynamic adjectives is the easiest way to make writing more vivid and concrete. Be careful, though, not to overuse them or to lose objectivity in selecting them.

General: The report was on time.

Vivid: The *detailed 12-page* report was submitted on time.

General: Carlos needs a better truck.

Vivid: Carlos needs a *rugged, four-wheel-drive* truck.

General: We enjoyed the movie.

Vivid: We enjoyed the *entertaining* and *absorbing* movie.

Overkill: We enjoyed the *gutsy, exciting, captivating,* and *thoroughly marvellous* movie.

A thesaurus (on your computer or in a book) helps you select precise words and also increases your vocabulary.

A good writer combines precise verbs, concrete nouns, and vivid adjectives with other carefully selected words to give the reader specific facts rather than wordy generalizations. Notice how much more meaningful the concrete version is in each of the following sentence pairs:

General: One of the company's officers has proved unworthy of corporate trust.

Concrete: Don DeSoto, treasurer, embezzled $25,000 of Datacom's funds.

By describing facts with precise verbs, concrete nouns, and vivid adjectives, you can make sure your readers understand your message.

General: The computer is portable and handy.

Concrete: The 2-kilogram, notebook-sized MicroOffice "RoadRunner" portable computer uses removable, reusable cartridges.

General: The implementation of improved operations may change company productivity soon.

Concrete: By improving packaging, shipping, and distribution procedures, we expect to increase gross profits by 14 percent within three months.

General: A new management official was recently hired to improve the division.

Concrete: Appointed senior vice-president of marketing on August 27, Jane Bamford launched a comprehensive program to retrain sales representatives in her Market Services Division.

Clichés

Clichés are expressions that have become exhausted by overuse. These expressions not only lack freshness but also frequently lack clarity for some individuals who misunderstand their meaning. The following partial list contains representative clichés you should avoid in business writing.

Clichés are dull and sometimes ambiguous.

below the belt	keep your nose to the grindstone
better than new	last but not least
beyond the shadow of a doubt	make a bundle
easier said than done	pass with flying colours
exception to the rule	quick as a flash
fill the bill	shoot from the hip
first and foremost	stand your ground
hard facts	true to form

Can you think of any clichés to add to this list? How about, *it goes without saying*—(and it probably should)?

Buzz Words

Another category of overworked expressions is that of so-called buzz words. These expressions, often borrowed from industry or government, are words and phrases of fashion. They seem to be used more often to impress the reader than to express the user's meaning.

Buzz words are overworked expressions taken from industry or government.

commonality	parameter
configuration	productionwise (profitwise, budgetwise, and other *-wise* words)
dysfunction	prioritize
impact on	scenario
incremental	state of the art
interface	subsystem
interrelationships	systematized
logistical	unilateral
orientate	

Repetitious Words

Good communicators vary their words to avoid unintentional repetition. Observe how heavy and monotonous the following personnel announcement seems:

> Employees will be able to elect an additional six employees to serve with the four previously elected employees who currently constitute the employees' board of directors. To ensure representation, swing-shift employees will be electing one swing-shift employee as their sole representative.

The above announcement uses the word *employee* six times. In addition, the last sentence contains the similar words *representation* and *representative*. An easier-to-read version follows:

> Employees will be able to elect an additional six representatives to serve with the four previously elected members of the employees' board of directors. To ensure representation, swing-shift workers will elect their own board member.

In the second version, synonyms (*representatives, members, workers*) replaced *employee*. The last sentence was reworked by using a pronoun (*their*) and by substituting *board member* for the repetitious *representative*. Variety of expression can be achieved by searching for appropriate synonyms and by substituting pronouns.

Good writers are also alert to the overuse of the articles *a, an,* and particularly *the*. Often the word *the* can simply be omitted. Articles can also be eliminated by changing singular constructions to plurals. In the following revision, for example, *a change in the price of gas* becomes *changes in gas prices*:

Wordy: The deregulation of the natural gas industry has caused a change in the price of gas.

Improved: Deregulation of the natural gas industry caused changes in gas prices.

Redundant Words

Repetition of words to achieve emphasis or effective transition is an important writing technique we'll discuss in forthcoming chapters. The needless repetition, however, of words whose meanings are clearly implied by other words is a writing fault called *redundancy*. For example, in the expression *final outcome*, the word *final* is redundant and should be omitted, since *outcome* implies finality. Learn to avoid redundant expressions such as the following:

absolutely essential	*final* outcome
adequate *enough*	*grateful* thanks

advance warning	*mutual* cooperation
basic fundamentals	*necessary* prerequisite
big *in size*	*new* beginning
combined *together*	*past* history
consensus *of opinion*	reason *why*
continue *on*	red *in colour*
each *and every*	refer *back*
exactly identical	repeat *again*
few *in number*	*true* facts

Diversity Check—Language

Language represents one of the clearest differences between cultures. The difficulty of understanding someone from a different culture who does not speak English is obvious. Even the use of a translation does not entirely eliminate the problem, because the meaning of a particular message relies heavily on the context in which it is expressed. Creating your own message can be an even greater challenge. To use a Chinese dictionary, for example, you must have some understanding of the language and history of China.

Informal or technical language poses further difficulties for the language learner. For people who speak English as a second language, jargon, slang, clichés, and buzz words can create formidable barriers to understanding.

Idiomatic Expressions

Every language has its own *idiom*, that is, its own special way of combining words. In English, as in any language, it's important to use combinations of words that "sound right" to the typical speaker. Particularly important is the use of the right prepositions with certain words. Study the following examples:

acquainted *with* (not *on* or *about*)	guard *against* (not *from*)
agree *to* (not *with*) a proposal	in accordance *with* (not *to*)
agree *with* a person	independent *of* (not *from*)
angry *at* (not *with*) a thing	interest *in* (not *about*)
angry *with* a person	plan *to* (not *on*)
authority *on* (not *about* or *in*)	retroactive *to*

buy *from* (not *off of*)   sensitive *to*

capable *of*   try *to* (not *and*)

How to Increase Your Vocabulary in Five Steps

A direct correlation exists between vocabulary and success in employment. Studies show that managers and executives have larger vocabularies than the employees they direct. Often individuals are hired or promoted because they express their ideas persuasively and precisely. Here are the five steps that are most effective in helping adults increase their knowledge of words.[1]

- **Make a commitment**. Decide that you want to increase your vocabulary and that you are willing to work toward that goal.

- **Choose five good words important to your profession**. From your assigned homework reading in any class, select five good words each week. The words should be ones that are important in your profession and ones whose meanings you do not know. Record the words on cards or in a vocabulary journal, using this format: word, source, pronunciation, sentence in which you found the word, and dictionary definition.

- **Use a key image**. We can remember a new word by forming a mental picture or image of the word that relates to the definition. For example, the word *acrophobia* has two parts: *acro* means height and *phobia* means fear. Imagine the word *acrobat*, which starts with the same letters and could suggest a performer high in the air, a performer who conquered his or her fear of height. Form a mental picture of the acrobat. Make a sentence using this picture and the new word: *The acrobat performed skilfully on the high wire showing absolutely no acrophobia, a fear of heights*. Recall the picture when you want to recall the word.

- **Make concept cards**. If key imaging doesn't work, try recording the target word on a card. In the upper right-hand corner, record the topic or category into which the word could be classified. For example, the word *boilerplate* would be classified under the concept of *word processing*. On the back of the card, record the definition in your own words. Then show examples of the word, if possible, such as this one: "Examples—form-letter paragraphs used by insurance companies—one kind of boilerplate." Add any other personal associations or clues that will help you remember this word.

- **Practise your words**. Use the words in sentences and review your journal or cards regularly. Look for other occurrences of these words in your assignments

Students who follow these steps are much more successful in increasing their vocabularies than those who memorize word lists.

Summary

Using words skilfully requires that we think consciously about the words we choose; writers depend only on their words to convey meaning, and even speakers rely to an important degree on the vocabulary and expressions they use.

Choosing words that are familiar, concrete, plain, and forceful improves the chance that the reader will understand your message. Inflated, unnatural writing that is intended to impress readers can confuse them instead. Precise verbs and vivid adjectives help the reader understand your message. Avoiding jargon, slang, buzz words, clichés, and non-English expressions will clarify your messages.

The unconscious repetition of words and other forms of redundancy can create monotonous and boring messages that run the risk of being ignored.

APPLICATION AND PRACTICE—2

Discussion

1. Writers should always use familiar words. Discuss.

2. Because legal documents are written to be extremely precise, everyone should write like a lawyer. Discuss.

3. How can dull, lifeless writing be made forceful?

4. Because clichés are familiar and have stood the test of time, they help clarify writing. Discuss.

5. Why is idiom one of the hardest elements of language for non-English speakers to master?

Short Answers

6. Define *jargon* and provide three examples.

7. Define *slang* and provide three examples.

8. Why are verbs the most important words in sentences?

9. What happens when verbs are converted to nouns (for example, when *acquire* becomes *to make an acquisition*)?

10. Define *cliché* and provide at least one example (other than those shown in the chapter) that you have heard frequently.

11. What are articles, and what problem do they present to writers?

12. Define *redundant* and provide an example.

13. Define *idiom* and provide an example of an idiomatic expression.

Writing Improvement Exercises

Familiar Words.   Revise the following sentences using simpler language for unfamiliar terms. Use a dictionary if necessary.

Example: Please ascertain the extent of our fiscal liability.

Revision: Please find out how much we owe.

14. Profits are declining because our sales staff is insufficiently cognizant of our competitor's products.

15. He hypothesized that the vehicle was not operational because of a malfunctioning gasket.

16. It may be necessary to terminate the employment of Mr. Sims.

17. The contract stipulates that management must perpetuate the present profit-sharing plan.

Jargon, Slang.   Revise the following sentences using simpler language that would be clear to an average reader. Avoid jargon, non-English expressions, and slang.

Example: Because of a glitch in the program, the printout shows that the product is gratis.

Revision: Because of an error in the program, the printout shows that the product is being given away for free.

18. This contract contains a caveat stipulating that vendors must utilize bona fide parts.

19. Quality products had heretofore helped this organization perpetuate its central market position.

20. In regard to our advertising budget, Mr. Singh says that TV is going down the tubes because audiences are being fractionalized into special-interest groups.

21. This half-price promotional campaign sounds real gutsy, but I don't think we should touch it with a ten-foot pole.

Precise Verbs.   Rewrite these sentences, centring the action in the verbs.

Example: Mrs. Kinski gave an appraisal of the equipment.

Revision: Mrs. Kinski appraised the equipment.

22. The engineer made a description of the project.

23. In writing this proposal, we must make application to the new government department.

24. Streamlined procedures will produce the effect of reduction in labour costs.

25. The board of directors made a recommendation affirming abandonment of the pilot project.

26. An investigator made a determination of the fire damages.

27. The duty of the comptroller is verification of departmental budgets.

28. Please make a correction in my account to reflect my late payment.

Vivid Words.   Revise the following sentences to include vivid and concrete language. Add appropriate words.

Example: They said it was a long way off.

Revision: Management officials announced that the merger would not take place for two years.

29. Our new copier is fast.

30. Mr. Grant's record indicates that he is a good worker.

31. An employee from that company called about our new computer.

32. Please contact them soon.

33. They said that the movie they saw was very interesting.

Clichés, Buzz Words, Repetition.   Revise the following sentences to avoid clichés, buzz words, and unnecessary repetition.

Example: The prime minister said that it was the prime minister's job to spearhead the drive for energy conservation.

Revision: The prime minister said that it was her job to lead the drive for energy conservation.

34. The production manager arrived just in time to prevent the oil damage from damaging the floor.

35. New corporate taxes will impact on corporations in the course of events.

36. The contract will be considered a valid contract if the terms of said contract are configured to meet with the approval of all parties who will sign the contract.

37. Employees receive employee raises in orderly incremental-step raises.

38. Without rhyme or reason, Sales Manager Shimada refused to interface or have personal conferences with any sales reps face to face.

Redundant Words, Idiomatic Expressions.   Rewrite the following sentences to correct the use of redundant words and unidiomatic expressions.

Example: In accordance to your wishes, we have completely eliminated tipping.

Revision: In accordance with your wishes, we have eliminated tipping.

39. First and foremost, we plan on emphasizing an instructional training program.

40. If you will refer back to her file, you will see that the reason why Carmen Campis was chosen is that she has experience on many different areas.

41. It was the consensus of opinion of the committee that it should meet at 11 a.m. in the morning.

42. Although she was angry with the report, Lucy Williams collected together her facts to make a last and final effort.

43. One local resident asked for all the important essentials regarding small business loans.

Legalese, Bureaucratese, Jargon.   Find examples of legalese, bureaucratese, or jargon in newspapers, magazines, or other documents. Bring them to class for discussion.

GRAMMAR/MECHANICS CHECKUP—2

Pronouns

Review Sections 1.07 through 1.09 of the Grammar/Mechanics Handbook. Then study each of the following statements. In the space provided for each statement, write the word that completes the statement correctly and the number of the G/M principle illustrated. When you finish, compare your responses with those shown below. If your responses differ, study carefully the principles in parentheses.

Example: The Recreation and Benefits Committee will be submitting (its, their) report soon.

its   (1.09d)
_____

1. I was expecting Mr. Marks to call. Was it (he, him) who left the message?
   _____

2. Every one of the members of the men's bowling team had to move (his car, their cars) before the tournament could begin.
   _____

3. A serious disagreement between management and (he, him) caused his resignation.
   _____

4. Does anyone in the office know for (who, whom) this paper was ordered?
   _____

5. It looks as if (her's, hers) is the only report that contains the sales figures.
   _____

6. Mrs. Simard asked my friend and (I, me, myself) to help her complete the work.
   _____

7. My friend and (I, me, myself) were also asked to work on Saturday.
   _____

8. We sent both printers in for repair, but (yours, your's) should be returned shortly.
   _____

9. Give the budget figures to (whoever, whomever) asked for them.
   _____

10. Everyone except the broker and (I, me, myself) claimed a share of the commission.
    _____

11. No one knows that problem better than (he, him, himself).
    _____

12. Investment brochures and information were sent to (we, us) shareholders.
    _____

13. If any one of the women tourists has lost (their, her) scarf, please see the driver.
    _____

14. Neither the glamour nor the excitement of the position had lost (its, it's, their) appeal.
    _____

15. Any new subscriber may cancel (their, his or her) subscription within the first month.*
    _____

---

1. he (1.08b) 3. him (1.08c) 5. hers (1.08d) 7. I (1.08a) 9. whoever (1.08j) 11. he (1.08f) 13. her (1.09c) 15. his or her (1.09b)

---

*How could the last statement be reworded to avoid the awkward his or her construction? See 1.09b.

GRAMMAR/MECHANICS CHALLENGE—2

Document for Revision

The following memo has faults in grammar, spelling, punctuation, capitalization, word use, and number form. Drawing upon the guidelines provided in the Grammar/Mechanics Handbook, revise the memo.

Poor Memo

TO: Janet Williams   DATE: July 24, 199x

FROM: Roxanne Crosley, Manager, Payroll

SUBJECT: DEPARTMENTAL ERROR

Last month our central accounting department changed it's computer program for payroll processing. When this computer change was operationalized some of the stored information was not transferred to the new information database. As a consequence of this maneuver several errors occurred in employee payroll cheques (1) parking payments were not deducted (2) pension deductions were not made and (3) errors occurred in Federal income tax calculations.

Each and every one of the employees effected has been contacted; and this error has been elucidated. My staff and me has been working overtime to replace all the missing data; so that corrections can be made about the August 30th payroll run.

Had I made a verification of the information before the cheques were ran this slip-up would not have materialized. To prevent such an error in the future I decided to take the bull by the horns and implement a rigorous new verification system.

Note

1. Based on Michele L. Simpson, Sherrie L. Nist, and Kate Kirby, "Ideas in Practice: Vocabulary Strategies Designed for College Students," *Journal of Developmental Education* (November 1987), p. 20.

Developing Tone and Style

3

In this chapter, you will learn to do the following:

- Appreciate how writing tone and style affect good will.
- Recognize and develop reader benefits in your writing.
- Distinguish between formal and conversational language.
- Avoid outdated expressions.

- Improve your writing by condensing wordy phrases.
- Use positive language.
- Project confidence.
- Use gender-neutral terms.

In addition to using words skilfully, good communicators work to refine the tone and style of their messages. They know consciously or unconsciously how their words sound to listeners and readers. In this chapter, techniques for developing and improving tone and style will be featured. These techniques include using conversational and current language, writing concisely, including reader benefits, expressing ideas positively, showing confidence, and being sensitive to sexist terms.

Cultivating Good Will

Before we turn to specific techniques for improving tone and style, let's consider the concept of good will. Good will is an abstract quality that represents the favour, prestige, and reputation that a business enjoys. Some companies develop good will by making donations to local projects and charities or by offering special discounts to students and senior citizens. Others train their employees to greet all customers by name. Businesses know that good will is a valuable asset.

Good will reflects the favourable attitude of customers toward a business.

Developing good will is worthwhile not only for business organizations but for individuals as well. As individuals, we appreciate being treated with courtesy. We enjoy working and living in environments that are harmonious. We feel better and we make others feel better when our actions promote harmony and good will.

The techniques for developing good will that you will learn in this chapter and throughout the book are designed to help you communicate effectively. You will find, moreover, that many of these same techniques may be applied in your personal life.

In business messages, good will is achieved through appropriate tone and style. Tone in a business letter describes the mood of a message; it reflects the writer's attitude toward the reader. The tone of a letter may be constructive or destructive, casual or formal, patronizing or sincere, arrogant or helpful, objective or subjective, pompous or humble, subtle or blunt, demanding or conciliatory, old-fashioned or contemporary. Notice how harsh and patronizing the following sentence sounds:

> If you would take the time to read your operator's manual, you will see that your car should have received full servicing at 15,000 kilometres.

The writer's feelings toward the reader come through in the tone of this message. Here are techniques for helping you cultivate appropriate tone and style in your business communication.

Conversational Language

Business letters and memos replace conversation. Therefore, they are most effective when they convey an informal, conversational tone instead of a formal, artificial tone.

Do you go through a Dr. Jekyll–Mr. Hyde personality change when you begin writing?

A casual, conversational tone in letters is harder to achieve than it may appear. Many writers tend to become formal, unnatural, and distant when they compose their letters or memos. Perhaps this is a result of composition training in schools. Many students were rewarded when they used big words, complex sentences, and abstractions, even if their ideas were not altogether clear. After leaving school, some writers continue to use words that inflate ideas, making them sound important and intellectual. Instead of writing as they would speak in conversation, their sentences become long, complex, and confusing. Rather than using familiar pronouns such as *I, we,* and *you,* they depersonalize their writing by relying on third-person constructions such as *the undersigned, the writer,* and *the affected party.*

To develop a warm, friendly tone in your letters, imagine that you are sitting next to the reader. Talk to the reader with words that sound comfortable to you. Don't be afraid to use an occasional contraction such as *we're* or *I'll.* Avoid legal terminology, technical words, and formal constructions. Your writing will be easier to read and understand if it sounds like the following conversational examples:

Formal Language	Conversational Language	
All employees are herewith instructed to return the appropriately designated contracts to the undersigned.	Please return your contracts to me.	You can develop a conversational tone in your written messages by using familiar words, an occasional contraction, and first-person pronouns (*I, me*) instead of third-person expressions (*the writer*).
Pertaining to your order, we must verify the sizes that your organization requires prior to consignment of your order to our shipper.	We'll send your order as soon as we confirm the sizes you need.	
The writer wishes to inform the above-referenced individual that subsequent payments may henceforth be sent to the address cited below.	Your payments should now be sent to us in Lakewood.	
To facilitate ratification of this agreement, your negotiators urge that the membership respond in the affirmative.	We urge you to approve the agreement by voting yes.	
It may interest you to be informed that your account has been credited in the aforementioned amount, and a copy of your account showing the newly calculated balance is enclosed.	I am happy to send you a copy of your June bill showing your credit of $37.14.	

The preceding examples illustrate effective conversational style. Although friendly, the tone of these messages is businesslike and objective. Successful letter writers are able to make their business letters conversational without becoming chatty, friendly without becoming familiar, and warm without becoming intimate. A conversational style appropriate for business communication avoids slang and achieves the proper balance between objectivity and friendliness.

Business letters can be warm and friendly without becoming familiar and intimate.

Outdated Expressions

Some business writers continue to use antiquated phrases and expressions. In the 1800s, letter writers "begged to state" and "trusted to be favoured with" and assured their readers that they "remained their humble servants." Such language suggests powdered wigs, quill pens, and sealing wax.

Compare these two versions of a letter acknowledging an order. The first uses old-fashioned language that was appropriate a century ago. The second represents a modern, efficient style.

Dear Sirs,

Your esteemed favour of the 10th has been received and contents duly noted. Please be advised that your shipment is forthcoming. Trusting to be favoured by future orders and assuring you of my cooperation,

I remain,

The same message today might sound like this:

Ladies and Gentlemen:

Your order for 75 Datacom Desk Planners should reach you by July 1. Call me collect at (204) 757-7008 to place future orders. We appreciate your business.

Sincerely,

Replace outdated expressions such as those shown here with more modern phrasing.

Outdated Expressions	Replacements
as per your request	at your request
enclosed please find	enclosed
kindly advise	please write
pursuant to your request	at your request
the aforementioned	mentioned before

Concise Wording

In business, time is indeed money. Translated into writing, this means that concise messages save reading time and, thus, money. In addition, messages that are written directly and efficiently are easier to read and comprehend. Say what you have to say and then stop.

Developing a concise writing style requires conscious effort and time. Taking the time to make your writing concise means that you look for other, shorter ways to say what you intend. Examine every sentence that you write. Could the thought be conveyed in fewer words? In addition to eliminating repetitious words (Chapter 2), you should concentrate on shortening wordy phrases, eliminating expletives, deleting excessive prepositions, revising negatives, avoiding long lead-ins, and omitting needless adverbs.

Shorten Wordy Phrases

Eliminate wasted words by reducing a phrase to its essence. Consider the wordy expressions shown here and the more concise forms shown in parentheses.

at a later date (later)
at this point in time (now)
afford an opportunity (allow)
are of the opinion that
    (believe)
at the present time (now, at
    present)
despite the fact that (though)
due to the fact that (because,
    since)
during the time (while)
feel free to (please)
for the period of (for)

fully cognizant of (aware)
in addition to the above (also)
in spite of the fact that (even
    though)
in the event that (if)
in the amount of (for)
in the near future (soon)
in view of the fact that
    (because)
inasmuch as (since)
more or less (about)
until such time as (until)

Rewrite sentences with wordy expressions, omitting the wasted words.

Wordy: Inasmuch as you have had an excellent credit history previous to your illness, we are willing to extend your due date until a later date.

Concise: Since you had an excellent credit history before your illness, we are willing to extend your due date.

Wordy: In regard to your request for a parking permit, we would like to tell you that first of all we must see your motor vehicle registration.

Concise: We can issue a parking permit after we see your registration.

Eliminate Expletives

Expletives are sentence fillers such as *there* and occasionally *it*. Avoid expletives that lengthen sentences with excess words.

Wordy: There are three vice-presidents who report directly to the president.

Concise: Three vice-presidents report directly to the president.

Wordy: It was the federal government that protected the health of workers.

Concise: The federal government protected the health of workers.

An *expletive* is a word such as *there* or *it* that is used to fill in a sentence.

Delete Excessive Prepositions

Some wordy prepositional phrases may be replaced by single adverbs. For example, *in the normal course of events* becomes *normally* and *as a general rule* becomes *generally*.

Wordy: Datatech approached the merger *in a careful manner.*

Concise: Datatech approached the merger *carefully.*

Wordy: The merger will *in all probability* be effected.

Concise: The merger will *probably* be effected.

Revise Wordy Negatives

Shorten negative expressions by using the prefixes *un-* and *dis-* (for example, *unclear* for *not clear* and *dissatisfied* for *not satisfied*), or shorten negative constructions by using a positive construction (for example, *didn't have any excuse* becomes *had no excuse*).

Wordy: James was *not happy* with his bonus.

Concise: James was *unhappy* with his bonus.

Wordy: Dr. Francisco *did not agree* with the report.

Concise: Dr. Francisco *disagreed* with the report.

Avoid Long Lead-ins

Thomas Jefferson said, "The most valuable of all talents is that of never using two words when one will do."

Delete unnecessary introductory words. The main idea of the sentence often follows the word *that* or *because.*

Wordy: *I am sending you this announcement to let you all know that* the office will be closed Monday.

Concise: The office will be closed Monday.

Wordy: *You will be interested to learn that* you may now use the automatic teller at our Lynwood branch.

Concise: You may now use the automatic teller at our Lynwood branch.

Omit Needless Adverbs

Eliminating adverbs like *very, definitely, quite, completely, extremely, really, actually, somewhat,* and *rather* streamlines your writing and makes the tone more businesslike.

Wordy: We *actually* did not really give his plan a very fair trial.

Concise: We did not give his plan a fair trial.

Wordy: Professor Chiu offered an *extremely* fine course that students definitely appreciated.

Concise: Professor Chiu offered a fine course that students appreciated.

Reader Benefit

It is natural for individuals to be most concerned with matters that relate directly to themselves. If we weren't interested in attending to our own needs, we could not survive.

Most of us are also concerned with others. We are interested in their lives, and we care about their feelings. Individuals who are successful in the business world—and in their personal lives—often possess a trait called *empathy*. Empathy is the capacity to put yourself into another's position and experience that person's feelings.

Empathetic business writers care about readers and express that concern in their communication. They try to see the reader's viewpoint. Place yourself in the reader's position. How would you react? How would you feel? When you read a message, you're very likely thinking, consciously or unconsciously, "What's in it for me?" When you write a message, say to yourself, "What's in it for the reader?" In what aspect of your message would the reader be most interested? How will it benefit the reader? Once you've answered these questions, write your message so that it emphasizes the benefits to the reader.

Be especially alert to the overuse of first-person pronouns such as *I, my, we,* and *our.* These words indicate that the writer is most interested in only one narrow view—the writer's. On the other hand, you should not sacrifice fluency, brevity, and directness to avoid an occasional *I* or *me.*

Compare the following sets of statements. Notice how first-person pronouns are deemphasized and second-person pronouns (*you, your*) become more obvious when the focus shifts to the benefits and interests of the reader. Some authorities refer to this emphasis as the *you*-attitude.

> **Look at your message from the reader's position.**

> **Overemphasis of the pronouns *I* and *me* reflect the writer's interests instead of the reader's.**

Instead of	Try this
I am very pleased that I am able to offer my customers a new investment program.	You are the first of our customers to be offered our new investment program.
We are happy to announce the opening of our new bank branch in Newton to meet all banking needs.	You will now be able to use our new Newton branch for all your banking needs.
I have been an insurance agent for over 25 years, and I am confident that I can serve all the insurance needs of business executives.	You will benefit by dealing with an agent who has more than 25 years of experience in serving the insurance needs of successful executives like you.
All new employees are required to complete and return the attached parking application if they want to park in our lot.	You may begin enjoying company parking privileges as soon as you complete and return the attached card.
Before we can allow you to write cheques on your account, we request that you sign the enclosed signature card.	For your protection, please sign the enclosed signature card before you begin to write cheques on your account.

> **Develop the *you-attitude* by emphasizing reader benefits.**

Diversity Check—Tone and Style

Writing techniques and practices that are standard in Canadian business writing may not be appropriate in other cultural contexts. Consider the following when engaging in intercultural communication.

- **Concise wording.** Although highly valued in the Canadian context, concise wording may not be appropriate when communicating with contacts abroad. Businesspeople in some European countries flavour their writing with highly descriptive passages. For these individuals, a concise document may convey the wrong tone by coming across as overly abrupt. Similarly, an emphasis on reader benefit (the *you*-attitude) may be considered intrusive or impolite in some cultures.

- **Vocabulary.** Choosing words carefully is important when communicating with people in other cultures. You should also be aware of vocabulary differences among English-speaking cultures. A *wrench* is a *spanner* in Britain, and if you were to say *chesterfield* in the United States, you would be met with questioning looks. Avoid slang, buzz words, jargon, and clichés in intercultural communication just as you would in any other business writing.

- **Weights and measures.** The International System of Units (SI), the most recent version of the metric system, is expected to become the international standard of measurement. Imperial units continue to be used, however, particularly in the United States. In your business communications, the preferences of your recipients should determine the system you adopt. You should also be thoroughly familiar with the currencies used in the countries you are dealing with.

- **Other usage.** Wording of the address and salutation, along with date style, should follow standard practice in the country with which you are corresponding.

Positive Language

Readers learn more when you write positively.

The tone of a letter is considerably improved if you use positive rather than negative language. Moreover, positive language generally conveys more information than negative language does. Positive wording tells what *is* and what *can be done* rather than what *isn't* and what *can't be done*. For example, *Your order cannot be shipped by January 10*, is not nearly so informative as *Your order will be shipped January 20*.

Analyze what you have to say, and then present it in positive language. Here are examples of statements in which the negative tone can be revised to reflect a positive impression.

Negative: We are unable to send your shipment until we receive proof of your payment.

Positive: We are happy to have your business and look forward to sending your shipment as soon as we receive your payment.

Negative: We are sorry that we must reject your application for credit at this time.

Positive: At this time we can serve you on a cash basis only.

Negative: We cannot use this computer keyboard efficiently until we receive the proper instruction manual.

Positive: After we receive the proper instruction manual, we will be able to use this computer keyboard efficiently.

Note that in the following example the revised version not only uses positive language but also emphasizes the reader's benefit.

Negative: Although I've never had a paid position before, I have worked as an intern in a law office while completing my degree requirements.

Positive: My experience in a law office and my recent training in legal procedures and office automation can be assets to your organization.

Confidence

Your business letters should sound as if you have confidence in yourself, your organization, and your ideas. Expect your reader to be persuaded by your words. Listen to the tone of each of the following examples:

Lacks confidence: If you think that you may be able to be our speaker, we can arrange for you to stay at the Mission Inn.

Confident: When you speak to our Riverside group, we will arrange for you to stay at the Mission Inn.

Lacks confidence: Although some employees have complained about the proposed flexible work schedule, most employees will find that it gives them greater freedom.

Confident: Most employees are looking forward to the proposed flexible work schedule because they expect greater freedom in arranging their work hours.

Lacks confidence: Would you like to have our representative call?

Confident: Our representative will be in your area June 9 and will be able to visit you in your showroom.

Appear confident but not overconfident. Avoid expressions that sound presumptuous, such as *I am sure that*, *we know that you will*, and *you will agree*.

Gender-Neutral Terms

Notice the use of the masculine pronouns *he* and *his* in the following sentences:

> If a physician is needed, *he* will be called.
> Every homeowner must read *his* insurance policy carefully.

Sensitive writers today try to use gender-neutral terms, such as letter carrier instead of mailman.

These sentences illustrate an age-old grammatical rule called "common gender." When a speaker or writer did not know the gender (sex) of an individual, masculine pronouns (such as *he* and *his*) were used. Masculine pronouns were understood to indicate both men and women.

Today, however, writers and speakers strive for accurate descriptions. To refer automatically to a physician or a homeowner as *he* may be misleading and even offensive. Writers today avoid common-gender pronouns by choosing an alternative construction.

Instead of	Try this
Every lawyer has ten minutes for *his* summation.	All *lawyers* have ten minutes for *their* summations. (Use a plural noun and plural pronoun.)
	Lawyers have ten minutes for summations. (Omit *entirely*.)
	Every lawyer has ten minutes for *a* summation (Use an article instead of a pronoun.)
	Every lawyer has ten minutes for *his or her* summation. (Use both a masculine and a feminine pronoun.)

A stereotype is a standardized, usually oversimplified opinion.

The last alternative—including a masculine and a feminine pronoun—is wordy and awkward. Don't use it too frequently.

Another form of stereotyping is the use of a feminine pronoun to refer to workers in roles traditionally considered female. Notice the feminine pronoun in each of the following examples:

> Each nurse must complete *her* duties before lunch.
> A secretary must keep *her* desk organized.

To suggest that all nurses or secretaries are female by using of a feminine pronoun (*her* or *hers*) is just as misleading as suggesting that all carpenters or top executives are male.

Other words are considered sexist because they suggest stereotypes. For example, the nouns *fireman* and *mailman* suggest that only men hold these positions. Avoid misleading or offending your reader by using gender-neutral job titles such as these: *firefighter, letter carrier, salesperson, flight attendant, department head, committee chair, technician,* and *police officer.*

How to Overcome the Fear of Writing

The following techniques will help individuals who fear writing and find it hard to begin the writing process.

- **Don't try to be a novelist**. While creative writers are practising an art, business writers are practising a craft. Crafts are skills that can be learned by using the right tools, following instructions, seeing models, and practising. The first step in overcoming a fear of writing is developing a realistic level of expectation.

- **Start with small, easy tasks**. Begin by writing short memos and letters that respond to previous documents. If you have longer projects, such as reports, break these tasks into smaller, more manageable parts.

- **Write down major ideas**. Usually, you are responding to something—letters, memos, reports. In the margin of these documents, make notes of your thoughts. These notes need not be a formal outline, but they will give you a guide to information you want to include.

- **"Talk" your writing**. Imagine you are speaking with a friend or colleague. Would you say, "It has come to my attention that questions are being asked by many employees in regard to our parking policy?" Of course not. Probably you'd say something like, "Many employees are asking questions about our parking policy." If you're able to express your ideas orally, you will have no problems getting started in writing. Later, you'll rewrite.

- **Don't write backward**. Many writers fall into the trap of writing a message in the same order in which they thought it. They begin with background information and end with the most important idea. But readers need to learn the primary idea (action to be taken or the solution to a problem) first so that they know immediately why they are reading this message. Instead of writing backward, start out directly with the big idea.

- **Embrace the KIS formula**. Keep It Simple is good advice for both novice and experienced writers. Short sentences (17 words is average length), short paragraphs, and familiar words produce messages that are understandable. And that should be your goal—writing that readers can comprehend. Thinking that writing must be formal to be correct, some writers sabotage their writing by using long, impressive-sounding words.

- **Expect to revise**. Don't expect your first version to be perfect. Read it again to listen to its sound, to add punctuation, and to revise sentence structure. Professional writers revise many times. You should plan to reread and revise at least two or three times.

■ **Switch places**. Put yourself in the shoes of the receiver as you read your message. Will that person understand what you have written? Don't let an unclear phrase pass, hoping the reader will understand what you meant. Add a word or rephrase a statement to make it absolutely clear. Then ask yourself, "Does this message sound like me?" Remember that you are not present to smile and soften the effect of your words. Nor can you observe the face of the reader to assess comprehension.

By observing these techniques, anyone can overcome a fear of writing. And with supervised practice, a novice writer can make great progress.

Summary

Tone and style affect the way the reader understands your message. They contribute to the good will our messages produce by setting the mood. Tone and style often reflect the writer's attitude toward the reader. They can be an effective way to transmit reader benefit, a positive attitude, and confidence.

To create a positive tone, concentrate on writing as you would speak. Be concise and conversational. Try to emphasize reader benefit by seeing the reader's point of view—by empathizing with the reader. Avoid overuse of personal pronouns such as *I*, *me*, and *we*. Strive to use positive, confident language and avoid sexist terms.

APPLICATION AND PRACTICE—3

Discussion

1. The establishment of good will in business communication requires time, energy, and skill. Such effort produces extra costs for an organization. Justify this expenditure.

2. Explain why and how empathetic business writers try to see the reader's viewpoint.

3. If it's easier to state an idea negatively, why should a writer make an effort to state it positively?

4. Why is a conversational tone in business writing hard to achieve?

Short Answers

5. List two objectives that successful business messages accomplish.

6. Define *good will*.

7. List three ways to define or characterize tone in a business letter.

8. List seven ways to make writing more concise.

9. What is an *expletive*?

10. Give an original example of a long and wordy lead-in to a sentence.

11. Define *empathy*.

12. List five examples of sexist pronouns and nouns.

13. Supply shorter words for the expressions shown below:

in addition to the above
in view of the fact that
until such time as

14. Make the following negative constructions positive (and concise):

He didn't have time.
She doesn't say anything.
We don't have a reason.

Writing Improvement Exercises

Reader Benefits.   Revise the following sentences to emphasize benefits to the reader.

Example: We have just designed an amazing computer program that automatically computes income tax.

Revision: You will be amazed by our computer program that automatically computes your income tax.

15. Our extensive experience in investments enables us to find our customers the most profitable programs.

16. Our company policy demands that individuals who rent power equipment must demonstrate a proficiency in its use.

17. We are offering a new series of short-term loans that may be used for carrying accounts receivable and for stocking inventory.

18. For just $250 per person, we have arranged a three-day trip to Banff that includes deluxe accommodation, a complete ski-rental package, and selected meals.

Conversational Language.   Revise the following sentences to make the tone more conversational.

Example: As per your recent request, the undersigned is happy to inform you that we are sending you forthwith the brochures you requested.

Revision: I'm happy to send you the brochures you requested.

19. Pursuant to your letter of the 12th, please be advised that your shipment was sent June 9.

20. Kindly be informed that your vehicle has been determined to require corrective work.

21. As per your recent request, attached herewith please find our quotation for the computer equipment.

22. The undersigned respectfully reminds affected individuals that employees desirous of changing parking locations must so indicate before December 30.

Outdated Expressions.   Revise the following sentences to eliminate outdated expressions and to improve tone.

Example: This is to inform you that we are sending you under separate cover one dozen toner cartridges as per your request.

Revision: We're sending you one dozen toner cartridges.

23. We are in receipt of your letter of October 3, and, as per your request, we are sending to you two complimentary passes to Expo 2000.

24. Attached please find instructions for completing the above-referenced claim.

25. Please allow the writer to take the liberty of offering his congratulations on your recent promotion.

26. Thanking you in advance, we genuinely hope that you can accept this invitation to address our organization.

Wordy Phrases.   Revise the following sentences to eliminate wordy phrases. Be particularly alert to negative constructions, long lead-ins, imprecise words, and needless adverbs such as *very* and *quite*.

Example: This is to notify you that our accountant actually couldn't find anything wrong with your report.

Revision: Our accountant could find no fault with your report.

27. This memorandum is to inform you that all books and magazines must be taken back to the library by June 1.

28. This is to let you know that you should feel free to use your credit card for the purpose of purchasing household items for a period of 60 days.

29. You may be interested to learn that there are a number of references in medical literature citing support for higher-dose aspirin.

30. Filling out an application is not really necessary unless you are basically interested in that position.

Expletives.   Revise the following sentences to avoid wordy expressions using the expletives *there* and *it*.

Example: There are four major areas in accounting. They are public accounting, private accounting, government accounting, and auditing.

Revision: The four major areas in accounting are public accounting, private accounting, government accounting, and auditing.

31. The report shows that there are numerous employers looking for qualified job applicants.

32. As a result of our research, we learned that there is no single factor causing the decline of interest in our product.

33. There are specialized areas one can enter, such as tax accounting, teaching, management advisory services, and investment banking.

34. There is a great demand for legal secretaries because of the growing number of lawyers beginning new practices.

Prepositional Phrases. Wordy Phrases.   Revise the following sentences to eliminate wordy expressions. Be alert to prepositional phrases that could be reduced to an adverb or adjective, and watch for unnecessary expletives.

Example: Under ordinary circumstances, there are two technicians to repair appliances.

Revision: Ordinarily, two technicians repair appliances.

35. There are two sources of funding that we have available for your business.

36. At an early date you may be sure that Mr. Granovsky will see you in regard to providing supplies for your office.

37. In very few cases do we revoke the privileges of our credit cards.

38. During our spring sale there is a week of private previews that may be enjoyed by our preferred customers.

Positive Language.   Revise the following sentences to use positive language. Add information if needed.

39. We regret to inform you that your order did not reach us immediately, so we cannot ship your electrical conduits until August 1.

40. Parking is not permitted in any lot other than South Lot D.

41. We are sorry to inform you that you do not qualify for a charge account at this time.

42. Because your name was overlooked, you will not receive our introductory packet until we make our second mailing.

Expressing Confidence and Using Gender-Neutral Language.   Revise the following sentences to show confidence and to use gender-neutral expressions.

43. Every employee has the right to examine his personnel file under the most recent federal regulations.

44. When you can spare the time, please look at our catalogue of computer and office supplies.

45. Any applicant for the position of fireman must submit a medical report signed by his physician.

Outside Reading.   Bring in three to five examples of writing that demonstrate (or fail to demonstrate) concepts from this chapter: reader benefits, concise writing, gender-neutral expression, and so forth.

GRAMMAR/MECHANICS CHECKUP—3

Verbs

Review Sections 1.10 through 1.15 of the Grammar/Mechanics Handbook. Then study each of the following statements. Underline any verbs that are used incorrectly. In the space provided for each statement, write the correct form and the number of the G/M principle illustrated. If a sentence is correct, write C. When you finish, compare your responses with those provided below. If your responses differ, study carefully the principles in parentheses.

Example: Our inventory of raw materials <u>were</u> presented as collateral for a short-term loan.　　　　　　　　　　　　　　　　　　 ___was___ (1.10c)

1. Located across town is a research institute and our product-testing facility.　 _____

2. The deposits in every single bank in Canada is insured by the federal government.　 _____

3. The Bank of Montreal, along with the other large national banks, offer a variety of savings plans.　 _____

4. Locating a bank and selecting a savings/chequing plan often require considerable research and study.　 _____

5. Neither the plans that this bank offers nor the service just rendered by the teller are impressive.　 _____

6. The budget analyst wants to know if the Equipment Committee are ready to recommend a product.　 _____

7. Either of the products that the committee selects is acceptable to the budget analyst.　 _____

8. If Mr. Catalano had chose the Maximizer Plus savings plan, his money would have earned maximum interest.　 _____

9. Although the applications have laid there for two weeks, they may still be used.　 _____

10. Mrs. Gebhardt acts as if she was the manager.　 _____

11. One of the reasons that our Yukon sales branches have been so costly are high transportation and living costs.　 _____

In the space provided, write the letter of the sentence that illustrates consistency in subject, voice, and mood.

12. **(a)** If you will read the instructions, the answer can be found.
　　(b) If you will read the instructions, you will find the answer.　 _____

13. **(a)** All employees must fill out application forms; only then will you be insured.
　　(b) All employees must fill out application forms; only then will they be insured.

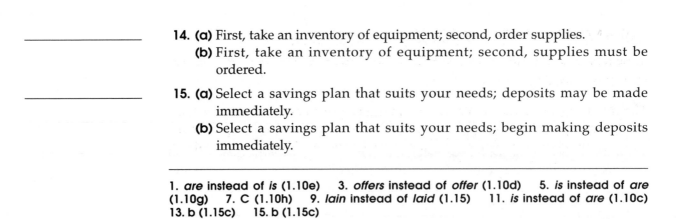

14. **(a)** First, take an inventory of equipment; second, order supplies.
   (b) First, take an inventory of equipment; second, supplies must be ordered.

15. **(a)** Select a savings plan that suits your needs; deposits may be made immediately.
   (b) Select a savings plan that suits your needs; begin making deposits immediately.

---

1. *are* instead of *is* (1.10e)   3. *offers* instead of *offer* (1.10d)   5. *is* instead of *are* (1.10g)   7. C (1.10h)   9. *lain* instead of *laid* (1.15)   11. *is* instead of *are* (1.10c) 13. b (1.15c)   15. b (1.15c)

GRAMMAR/MECHANICS CHALLENGE—3

Document for Revision

The following letter has faults in grammar and punctuation. It also contains outdated expressions, wordy phrases, long lead-ins, and other problems. Drawing upon the guidelines provided in the Grammar/Mechanics Handbook and what you learned in this chapter, revise the letter.

Poor Letter

Ms. Kay Bradley
Title Guaranty and Abstract Company
52 Waterloo Street
Saint John, NB E2L 3P4

Dear Kay:

Pursuant to our telephone conversation this morning, this is to advise that two (2) agent's packages will be delivered to you next week. Due to the fact that new forms had to be printed; we do not have them immediately available.

Although we cannot offer a 50/50 commission split, we are able to offer new agents a 60/40 commission split. There are two new agreement forms that show this commission ratio. When you get ready to sign up a new agent have her fill in both forms.

When you send me an executed agency agreement please make every effort to tell me what agency package was assigned to the agent. On the last form that you sent you overlooked this information. We need this data to distribute commissions in a expeditious manner.

If you have any questions, don't hesitate to call on me.

Sincerely,

4

The Process of Writing Effective Sentences, Paragraphs, and Messages

In this chapter, you will learn to do the following:

- Avoid three basic sentence faults.
- Vary the length and structure of sentences.
- Emphasize important ideas.
- Match sentence parts in achieving parallelism.

- Use active- and passive-voice verbs appropriately.
- Develop clear, unified, and coherent paragraphs.
- Organize the process of writing.

In this chapter, you will practise the techniques that help you achieve variety, emphasis, and unity in your writing. You will learn how to make effective use of parallelism and active- and passive-voice verbs. In addition, you will study how to compose unified and coherent paragraphs developed deductively and inductively. Finally, you will examine the entire process of writing. A logical place to start is with a review of sentence components.

Sentence Structure

Clauses give subjects and verbs; phrases do not.

The construction of effective sentences begins with an understanding of the role of phrases and clauses. A *phrase* is a group of related words without a subject and a verb. Study the phrases in the following example:

We will be making a decision about the case in two weeks.

      verb phrase   prepositional   prepositional
                       phrase   phrase

A group of related words including a subject and a verb is a *clause*.

Mr. Lee is our shipping manager, and he will call you.

           clause   clause

An *independent clause* makes sense and is complete in itself. A *dependent clause*, although it has a subject and a verb, depends for its meaning upon an independent clause.

If you are able to attend, the meeting is next Tuesday.

    dependent clause   independent clause

Effective sentences are built by combining dependent and independent clauses. Sentences can be simple, compound, complex, or compound-complex.

A *simple* sentence is a single independent clause.

Mr. Lee is our shipping manager.

A *compound* sentence contains two or more independent clauses that may be linked with a comma and coordinating word (*and, but, or, nor, for, so,* or *yet*) or with a semi-colon.

Mr. Lee is our shipping manager, and he will call you.

A *complex* sentence contains an independent clause and one or more dependent clauses.

If you are able to attend, the meeting is next Tuesday.

A *compound-complex* sentence contains at least two independent clauses and one or more dependent clauses.

Although Mr. Severin signed the contract, Mr. Lee is our shipping manager, and he will call you.

> Four types of sentences can be produced by combining phrases and clauses. They are: (1) simple, (2) compound, (3) complex, and (4) compund-complex.

Verbs

Effectively used verbs are a necessary part of effective sentences. Three types of verbs deserve special mention: linking, transitive, and intransitive verbs.

A *linking verb* joins the subject to a word or group of words that describe the subject. The forms of the verb *to be* (*is, are, was, were, being,* or *been*) can be linking verbs.

The outcome *was* uncertain even after the vote.

Other verbs, such as *appear, become, feel, grow, look, make,* and *seem,* can also serve as linking verbs.

The board members *seem* pleased.

A *transitive verb* expresses action that is directed toward the object of the verb.

Henri *will revise* his proposal.

When a sentence requires the passive voice, use a transitive verb.

An *intransitive verb* also expresses action, but in the absence of an object.

The stock market *plummeted*.

Active- and passive-voice verbs are discussed later in the chapter.

Three Basic Sentence Faults

Writers sometimes produce sentences with one or more of the following three glaring faults.

Three common sentence faults are (1) fragments, (2) run-on sentences, and (3) comma splices.

1. **Fragment**. A fragment is part of a sentence, usually a phrase or a dependent clause, punctuated as if it were an independent clause. Notice how the following fragments do not make sense by themselves.

   Persuading employees to support the United Way, to learn how to program a computer, or to prepare for an assignment in a new department. These activities all require human change. (The italicized fragment is a series of phrases.)

   Federal regulations in the financial field have been changed. *Which explains why financial institutions are now more competitive.* (The italicized fragment is a dependent clause.)

   Most attempts at change are likely to meet some resistance. *Change that brings about doubt and that may be seen as a threat to a worker's security and salary.* (The italicized fragment is an incomplete sentence.)

   Do not capitalize and punctuate a fragment as if it were complete. The fragment can be attached to an independent clause to make a complete sentence.

2. **Run-on sentence**. When one independent clause follows another without appropriate punctuation, a run-on sentence results.

   The Intel Corporation makes computer chips *it serves a large portion of the computer industry.* (The clause beginning with *it* should be capitalized to form a new sentence, and a period should follow *chips*.)

3. **Comma splice**. When two independent clauses are joined together inappropriately with a comma, a comma splice results.

   Comma splice: We are sorry that your order was delayed, your shipment will be sent out this afternoon.

   Comma splice: The titles of the jobs were quite similar, the duties of the jobs were substantially different.

Sentences with comma splices can be revised in several ways, as you see here:

Comma splice: The workshops for the managers start on Tuesday, the sessions for representatives begin Wednesday.

Revision: The workshops for managers start on Tuesday. The sessions for representatives begin Wednesday.

Revision: The workshops for managers start on Tuesday; the sessions for representatives begin Wednesday.

Revision: The workshops for managers start on Tuesday, and the sessions for representatives begin Wednesday.

Sentence Variety and Length

Good writers vary the length and structure of their sentences. Messages composed totally of sentences that sound the same are monotonous to read. Such messages may also divert the reader's attention from what is being said to how it is being said. Compare these two versions of the same paragraph:

Lacks variety: We congratulate you on the purchase of your new home. It will be a source of pride and enjoyment for many years. It will increase in value. It can provide a valuable hedge against inflation. We encourage you to protect that investment.

Shows variety: Congratulations on the purchase of your new home. We know that it will be a source of pride and enjoyment for many years. As it increases in value, it can provide a valuable hedge against inflation. We encourage you to protect that investment.

Sentences with varied structures are interesting to readers.

The first paragraph bores the reader because it relies solely on simple sentences of about the same length with the same subject-verb-object structure. The second paragraph is more interesting because it includes both short, emphatic sentences and longer sentences with dependent clauses. As a result of its varied sentence structures, the second paragraph is less choppy.

Generally, it's best to write short sentences, since they are more easily understood. The average sentence length is between 15 and 20 words. This doesn't mean that all sentences should be 15 or 20 words long, however. Effective paragraphs contain a mixture of sentences, some shorter and some longer.

Average sentences contain between 15 and 20 words.

Emphasis

Speakers can emphasize main ideas by saying them loudly, by repeating them slowly, or by using nonverbal cues such as pounding the table. Writers, however, must rely upon other means to tell their readers what ideas are most

Writers may emphasize their ideas by using mechanical or stylistic devices.

important. Emphasis in writing can be achieved primarily in two ways: mechanically or stylistically.

Emphasis through Mechanics

To emphasize an idea in print, a writer may use any of the following devices:

Underlining: <u>Underlining</u> draws the eye to a word.

Typeface: Using a different typeface, such as **boldface**, is like shouting a word.

Capitals: Notice how the words FREE GIFT stand out when typed in capital letters.

Dashes: Dashes—if used sparingly—can be effective in capturing attention.

Tabulation: Listing items vertically makes them stand out:

> 1. First item
> 2. Second item
> 3. Third item

Other means of achieving mechanical emphasis include the arrangement of space, colour, lines, boxes, columns, titles, headings, and subheadings to set off ideas.

Emphasis through Style

Although mechanical means are occasionally appropriate, more often a writer achieves emphasis stylistically. That is, the writer chooses words carefully and constructs sentences skilfully to emphasize main ideas and de-emphasize minor or negative ideas. Here are four suggestions for emphasizing ideas stylistically:

1. **Use vivid words**. Vivid words, as you recall from Chapter 2, are emphatic because they help the reader picture ideas clearly.

General:	*One business* uses *personal* selling techniques.
Vivid and emphatic:	*Avon* uses *face-to-face* selling techniques.
General:	*A customer* said that she wanted the contract returned *soon*.
Vivid and emphatic:	*Ms. Choquette* insisted that the contract be returned *July 1*.

2. **Label the main idea.** If an idea is significant, tell the reader.

Unlabelled:	Explore the possibility of leasing a site, but also hire a business consultant.
Labelled:	Explore the possibility of leasing a site; but most importantly, hire a business consultant.

3. **Place the important idea first or last in the sentence.** Ideas have less competition from surrounding words when they appear first or last in a sentence. Notice how the concept of productivity is emphasized in the first and second examples:

Emphatic: *Productivity* is more likely to be increased when profit-sharing plans are linked to individual performance than to group performance.

Emphatic: Profit-sharing plans that are linked to individual performance rather than to group performance are more effective in increasing *productivity.*

Unemphatic: Profit-sharing plans are more effective in increasing *productivity* when they are linked to individual performance rather than to group performance.

4. **Place the important idea in a simple sentence or in an independent clause.** Don't dilute the effect of the idea by making it share the spotlight with other words and clauses.

Emphatic: You are the first trainee that we have hired for this program. (Use a simple sentence for emphasis.)

Emphatic: Although we considered many candidates, you are the first trainee that we have hired for this program. (Independent clause contains main idea.)

Unemphatic: Although you are the first trainee that we have hired for this program, we had many candidates and expect to expand the program in the future. (Main idea is lost in a dependent clause.)

De-emphasis

To de-emphasize an idea, such as bad news, try one of the following stylistic devices:

1. **Use general words.** Just as vivid words emphasize, the use of general words can soften an unpleasant point when necessary.

Vivid: Our records indicate that *you were recently fired.*

General: Our records indicate that *your employment status has changed.*

2. **Bury the bad news in the middle of a sentence or in a dependent clause.** Instead of placing a negative point where it is conspicuous and perhaps painful to the reader, include it in a dependent clause.

Emphasizes bad news: We cannot issue you credit at this time, but we do have a plan that will allow you to fill your immediate needs on a cash basis.

De-emphasizes bad news: We have a plan that will allow you to fill your immediate needs on a cash basis, though we cannot issue you credit at this time.

The word *stylistic* refers to literary or artistic style as opposed to content.

Bad news can be made less painful by de-emphasizing its presentation.

Additional tips and strategies for announcing bad news will be provided in Chapter 8.

Unity

Unified sentences contain thoughts that are related to only one main idea. The following sentence lacks unity because the first clause has little or no relationship to the second clause:

Lacks unity: Our insurance plan is available in all provinces, and you may name anyone as a beneficiary for your coverage.

Three factors that destroy sentence unity are zigzag writing, mixed constructions, and misplaced modifiers. Let's consider each of these faults.

Zigzag Writing

Confusing writing may result when too many thoughts are included in one sentence or when one thought does not relate to another. To rectify a zigzag sentence, revise it so that the reader understands the relationship between the thoughts. If that is impossible, move the unrelated thoughts to a new sentence.

Zigzag sentence: I appreciate the time you spent with me last week, and I have purchased a personal computer that generates graphics.

Revision: I appreciate the time you spent with me last week. Because of your advice, I have purchased a personal computer that generates graphics.

Zigzag sentence: The stockholders of a corporation elect a board of directors, although the chief executive officer is appointed by the board and the CEO is not directly responsible to the stockholders.

Revision: The stockholders of a corporation elect a board of directors, who in turn appoint the chief executive officer. The CEO is not directly responsible to the stockholders.

Mixed Constructions

Writers who fuse two different grammatical constructions destroy sentence unity and meaning.

Mixed construction: The reason I am late is *because* my car battery is dead.

Revision: The reason I am late is *that* my car battery is dead. (The construction introduced by *the reason is* should be a noun clause beginning with *that*, not an adverbial clause beginning with *because*.)

Mixed construction: When the stock market index rose five points was our signal to sell.

| Revision: | When the stock market index rose five points, we were prepared to sell. *Or,* Our signal to sell was an increase of five points in the stock market index. |

Misplaced Modifiers

Sentence unity can also be destroyed by the separation of phrases or clauses from the words that they modify.

Keep phrases and clauses close to the words they describe.

Misplaced modifier:	We will be happy to send a park map for all motorists *reduced to a smaller scale.*
Revision:	We will be happy to send all motorists a park map *reduced to a smaller scale.*
Misplaced modifier:	Whether you travel for business or for pleasure, charge everything to your credit card *in Canada.*
Revision:	Whether you travel for business or for pleasure *in Canada,* charge everything to your credit card.

In each of the preceding sentences, the sentence made sense once the misplaced phrase was moved closer to the words it modified.

Another modifier fault results when an introductory verbal phrase is not followed immediately by a word that it can logically modify. This is called a *dangling modifier.* Notice in each of the following revisions of dangling modifiers that the sentence makes sense once we place the logical modifier after the introductory phrase.

Beware of introductory verbal phrases that are not immediately followed by the words they describe.

Dangling modifier:	To receive a degree, 120 credits are required. (This sentence reads as if *120 credits* are receiving a degree.)
Revision:	To receive a degree, a student must earn 120 credits.
Dangling modifier:	When filling out an employment application, the personnel manager expects each applicant to use ink. (The personnel manager is not filling out the application.)
Revision:	When filling out an employment application, each applicant is expected to use ink.

Parallelism

Parallelism is a writing technique that involves balanced writing. Sentences written so that their parts are balanced or parallel are easy to read and understand. To achieve parallel construction, use similar structures to express similar ideas. For example, the words *computing, coding, recording,* and *storing* are parallel because they all end in *-ing.* To express the list as *computing, coding, recording,* and **storage** is disturbing because the last item is not what the reader expects. Try to match nouns with nouns, verbs with verbs, phrases with phrases, and clauses with clauses. Avoid mixing active-voice verbs with passive-voice verbs. Keep the wording balanced in expressing similar ideas.

Balanced wording helps the reader anticipate your meaning.

Lacks parallelism: The market for industrial goods includes manufacturers, contractors, wholesalers, and *those concerned with the retail function.*

Revision: The market for industrial goods includes manufacturers, contractors, wholesalers, and *retailers.* (Parallel construction matches nouns.)

Lacks parallelism: Our primary goals are to increase productivity, reduce costs, and *the improvement of product quality.*

Revision: Our primary goals are to increase productivity, reduce costs, and *improve product quality.* (Parallel construction matches verbs.)

Lacks parallelism: We are scheduled to meet in Toronto on January 5, *we are meeting in Ottawa on the 15th of March,* and in Hamilton on June 3.

Revision: We are scheduled to meet in Toronto on January 5, *in Ottawa on March 15,* and in Hamilton on June 3. (Parallel construction matches phrases.)

Lacks parallelism: Ms. Horne audits all accounts lettered A through L; accounts lettered M through Z are audited by Mr. Faheem.

Revision: Ms. Horne audits all accounts lettered A through L; Mr. Faheem audits accounts lettered M through Z. (Parallel construction matches active-voice verbs in balanced clauses.)

> **All items in a list should be expressed in balanced constructions.**

In presenting lists of data, whether shown horizontally or tabulated vertically, be certain to express all the items in parallel form. Which item in the following tabulated list is not parallel?

Lacks parallelism: Three primary objectives of advertising are as follows:
1. Increase frequency of product use
2. Introduce complementary products
3. Enhancement of the corporate image

Active and Passive Voice

In sentences with active-voice verbs, the subject is the doer of the action. In passive-voice sentences, the subject is acted upon.

Active voice: Mr. Wong *completed* the tax return before the April 30 deadline. (The subject is the doer of the action.)

Passive voice: The tax return *was completed by* Mr. Wong before the April 30 deadline. (The subject, *tax return*, is acted upon.)

In the first sentence, the active voice emphasizes Mr. Wong. In the second sentence, the passive voice emphasizes the tax return. In sentences with passive-voice verbs, the doer of the action may be revealed or left unknown.

Most writers prefer active verbs because such verbs tell the reader clearly what the action is and who or what is performing that action. On the other hand, passive verbs can be employed to perform certain necessary functions. They are helpful in (1) emphasizing an action or the recipient of the action (*You have been selected to represent us*); (2) de-emphasizing negative news (*Your watch has not been repaired*); and (3) concealing the doer of an action (*A major error was made in the estimate*). In business writing, as well as in our personal relations, some situations demand tact and sensitivity. Instead of using a direct approach with active verbs, we may prefer the indirectness that passive verbs allow. Rather than making a blunt announcement with an active verb (*Mr. Sullivan made a major error in the estimate*), we can soften the sentence with a passive construction (*A major error has been made in the estimate*).

> Although active-voice verbs are preferred in business writing, passive-voice verbs perform useful functions.

How can you tell if a verb is active or passive? Identify the subject of the sentence and decide if the subject is doing the acting or if it is being acted upon. For example, in the sentence *An appointment was made for January 1*, the subject is *appointment*. The subject is being acted upon; therefore, the verb (*was made*) is passive. Another clue in identifying passive-voice verbs is this: they always have a *to be* helping verb, such as *is, are, was, were, being,* or *been.*

Paragraphs

We have thus far concentrated on the basic unit of writing, the sentence. The next unit of writing is the paragraph. A paragraph is a group of sentences with a controlling idea, usually stated first. Paragraphs package ideas into meaningful groups for readers. Often when you're writing the first draft of a message, the idea units are not immediately clear. In revising, though, you see that similar ideas should be placed together. You recognize ways to improve the sequencing of thoughts so that the reader follows your thoughts more easily. Here are suggestions for working with paragraph unity, coherence, length, and organization.

Paragraph Unity

Just as sentences require unity, so do paragraphs. A paragraph is unified when all its sentences concern just one topic or idea. Any sentence that treats a new topic should begin a new paragraph or be revised to relate to the paragraph topic.

Lacks unity: Supporters of the Edmonton expansion argue that it is necessary because of anticipated new business. Edmonton has plenty of big city amenities like theatre, art galleries, and festivals. We do 25 percent of our business in Edmonton and like our current location.

Revision: Supporters of the Edmonton expansion argue that it is necessary because of anticipated new business. However, the economic climate is such that any near-term increase in business is highly unlikely. Expansion in Edmonton should be considered only when the economy improves.

Paragraph Coherence

Three ways to create paragraph coherence are (1) repetition of key ideas, (2) use of pronouns, and (3) use of transitional expressions.

Coherence is a quality of good writing that does not happen accidentally. It is consciously achieved through effective organization and through skilful use of three devices.

1. **Repetition of key ideas or key words.** Repeating a word or key thought from a preceding sentence helps guide a reader from one thought to the next. This redundancy is necessary to build cohesiveness into writing.

   Quality control problems in production are often the result of poor-quality raw materials. Some companies have strong programs for ensuring the *quality* of *incoming production materials and supplies.*

The second sentence of the preceding paragraph repeats the key idea of *quality.* Moreover, the words *incoming production materials and supplies* refer to raw materials mentioned in the preceding sentence. Good writers find other words to describe the same idea, thus using repetition to clarify a topic for the reader.

2. **Use of pronouns.** Pronouns such as *this, that, they, these,* and *those* promote coherence by connecting the thoughts in one sentence to the thoughts in a previous sentence. To make sure that the pronoun reference is clear, consider following the pronoun with the word to which it refers, thus making the pronoun—*This* in the following example—into an adjective.

   Xerox has a four-point program to assist suppliers. *This program* includes written specifications for production materials and components.

   Be very careful in using pronouns. A pronoun without a clear antecedent can be most annoying. The reader doesn't know precisely to what the pronoun refers.

   Faulty: When company profits increased, employees were given a bonus, either a cash payment or company stock. *This* became a real incentive to employees.

   Improved: When company profits increased, employees were given a bonus, either a cash payment or company stock. *This profit-sharing plan* became a real incentive to employees.

3. **Use of transitional expressions.** One of the most effective ways to achieve paragraph coherence is through the use of transitional expressions. These expressions act as road signs: they indicate where the message is headed, and they help the reader anticipate what is coming. Here are transitional expressions grouped according to uses:

Time Association	Contrast	Illustration
before, after	although	for example
first, second	but	in this way
meanwhile	however	
next	instead	
until	nevertheless	
when, whenever	on the other hand	

Cause, Effect	Additional Idea
consequently	furthermore
for this reason	in addition
hence	likewise
therefore	moreover

As the following paragraph demonstrates, transitional expressions help the reader see how ideas and sentences are related, thus achieving paragraph coherence.

Although some people believe that business expansion during tough economic times is risky, several companies have successfully expanded in the last few years. For example, when TeleFax expanded into Calgary last year, the company increased its business by 15 percent. However, Telefax could not have achieved this positive result without careful planning and efficient execution.

Paragraph Length

Have you ever avoided reading a document because the paragraphs were forbiddingly long? If so, you're like most readers, who find short paragraphs more inviting than long ones. As a writer, you can make your messages more attractive by controlling paragraph length. In business letters, first and last paragraphs are often very short (one to four typed lines). Other paragraphs in letters and most paragraphs in reports should average about six lines, with ten lines being the maximum.

Paragraph Organization

Sentences within paragraphs are usually arranged either deductively (directly) or inductively (indirectly).

Deductive Method.   In the deductive arrangement a topic sentence appears first, followed by other information. A topic sentence serves to orient readers so that they know what this paragraph is going to be about. It may be a summarizing statement followed by explanation and amplification of the main idea.

Diversity Check—Planning Messages

In some cultures, business writers are much less straightforward than their Canadian counterparts in the use of the inductive method of paragraph organization. Instead of placing the topic sentence last, a Japanese business writer might bury it in the body of the message; two or three readings on the part of the recipient may be required before the main idea is located.

As the sender of a message to a receiver from another culture, consider the following:

1. **The culture of the recipient**. Before planning your message, think about the cultural characteristics of the people with whom you wish to communicate. Learn about their world view, social organization, and values.

2. **The purpose of your message**. Ask yourself what purpose you have in writing or speaking. Are you requesting, responding to, or providing information? Other cultures have expectations about the way each type of message is worded. In Japan, a request would probably require an introduction and expression of good will before the big idea is presented. A courteous and respectful tone is especially important when making requests.

3. **The complexity of your message**. Is your message organized as effectively as it could be? Will translation be a problem? Have you used words and sentences that are easy to understand?

4. **The appropriateness of the reader benefit**. What would be considered a benefit in Canada would not necessarily be viewed as such—or in quite the same way—in another culture. Some cultures, for example, may place considerably more value on personal prestige than on financial success.

5. **Your relationship with the receiver**. What expectations does your recipient have of your role in the business partnership? Consider the case of an Australian businessperson who was concluding a manufacturing deal with a business partner from Singapore. When the Australian went to Singapore to sign contracts, he found that the Singapore businessperson had planned several days of recreational activities for both of them to participate in together. It became clear to the Australian that a business transaction of this sort was not just a matter of signing a few papers. Indeed, it marked the beginning of a much closer relationship than the Australian had ever had with business partners in his own country.

This orienting sentence provides an introduction so that readers can better understand the sentences that follow. Without a topic sentence, readers must guess at why the paragraph is being written. Readers need the frame of reference provided by a topic sentence. Notice how the topic sentence in the following paragraph provides an overview:

> *Personnel administrators for large companies are changing their preferences for items included in résumés of prospective employees.* Recent surveys show that today's companies want to see evidence of achievement such as grade-point average, work experience, and campus activities. They are not interested in personal items such as birth date, marital status, health, and number of dependents. A new category that many personnel officers said they would like to see is a summary of qualifications.

Inductive Method.   The inductive (indirect) plan supplies examples and reasons first and then draws conclusions from them. Paragraphs or entire messages may be arranged inductively. This technique, discussed more fully in Chapters 8 and 9, is especially useful when bad news is being presented or when persuasion is necessary. Instead of bluntly announcing the primary idea in the first sentence of a paragraph, the author delays the big idea. The topic sentence comes at the end of the paragraph. If you were a student about to ask your parents for a new car, would you make the request immediately? Or would you first build a case by discussing many solid reasons why you deserve and need a new car, followed by the big idea? Successful business writers have learned that indirectness has value in certain instances. In the following paragraph, notice that the topic sentence comes last. It is a conclusion drawn from the previous sentences.

> Employees have rightfully complained recently of a lack of parking space in our company lots. As more employees are needed and hiring escalates, it's more difficult for us to provide guaranteed parking for everyone. *For this reason, we've purchased two company vans that will be used in a car-pooling plan.*

Most paragraphs and most business messages are organized deductively with primary ideas presented first. However, when tactfulness or persuasion is necessary, inductive organization is appropriate. You'll learn more about these strategies in forthcoming chapters.

The Process of Writing

Now that we've considered using words skilfully, developing effective sentences, and organizing unified paragraphs, let's look at the total process of writing. Experienced writers generally follow a series of five steps in producing messages and documents. These five steps, which we'll call the POWER plan, include Planning, Organizing, Writing, Editing, and Re-examining.

■ **Planning.** Every successful document begins with planning. Examine your message in relation to the communication cycle. What is your purpose, and what effect do you hope to achieve? Consider your audience, and anticipate reader reaction to the message. Decide on the medium for your message, considering noise and feedback. Decide what ideas to emphasize and which to de-emphasize or omit. This planning process should take place whether you are responding to another message or initiating communication. In its simplest form, planning occurs when the writer reads an incoming letter and underlines significant points or makes marginal notes regarding the response. In a more complex form, planning may involve research to solve a problem.

■ **Organizing.** The next step in the process of writing is organizing the message. Follow a deductive (direct) strategy, shown more fully in Chapter 5, for good news and for neutral messages. Use an inductive (indirect) strategy, presented in Chapter 8, for negative messages and persuasion. Novice writers often need help in organizing messages effectively. To give you practice in developing this skill, we will provide writing plans and organizational tips for a variety of business writing situations in forthcoming chapters. As you develop your skills, though, fewer organizational suggestions are provided. Learn to sketch a brief outline or list of points to be covered before you begin to write any message.

■ **Writing.** Once you have planned a document and organized its content, begin writing. Some writers compose a rough draft at a typewriter; others prefer pencil and paper. Increasingly, writers are learning the joys of word processing for ease in composition and revision. Your first version should be considered a rough draft only. If you have time and if the document is significant, put it aside for a day before revising it. Fresh insights may help you see the subject differently—perhaps more clearly. Apply the principles you have learned in writing effective sentences and paragraphs.

■ **Editing.** Read over your rough draft critically. Is the tone appropriate? Will the reader understand what you have said? Will this message achieve your purpose? Edit your message by crossing out awkward and unclear sections. Replace dull or meaningless words with precise, vivid ones. Look for ways to polish the content and structure of your message. Many experts consider the editing phase the most important step in the process of writing. After prudent editing, prepare the final copy.

■ **Re-examining.** The final step is a careful re-examination of the message. Proofread the final copy not only for meaning and expression but also for typographical errors, as well as spelling, grammar, capitalization, and other errors. Consider its appearance. Is it attractive and neat? Is it balanced on the page? Are names, addresses, and numbers expressed accurately?

As you start writing business documents in the next chapter, apply the POWER formula. Too often, inexperienced writers begin writing a document immediately, without preparing and without aiming toward a goal.

How to Measure Readability: The Fog Index

Everyone would agree that articles in *Maclean's* or *Time* are much easier to read than articles in scientific journals, such as *The Journal of Abnormal Psychology* or *Science*. Exactly why is that? It's because magazines for popular audiences concentrate on material with two common elements: short words and short sentences. To measure the readability of writing, Robert Gunning developed a formula, called the Fog Index, based on these two elements. Read the following paragraph, taken from *Innovation and Entrepreneurship*[1] by Peter F. Drucker, noted authority on management. How readable is this segment of Drucker's writing? When you finish, we'll apply the Fog Index to determine its readability. The underscored words will be explained as part of the analysis to follow.

1. "Planning" as the term is commonly understood is actually incompatible with an entrepreneurial society and economy.

2. Innovation does indeed need to be purposeful and

3. entrepreneurship has to be managed.

4. But innovation, almost by definition, has to be decentralized, *ad hoc*, autonomous, specific, and micro-economic.

5. It had better start small, tentative, flexible.

6. Indeed, the opportunities for innovation are found, on the whole, only way down and close to events.

7. They are not to be found in the massive aggregates with which the planner deals of necessity, but in the deviations therefrom—in the unexpected, in the incongruity, in the difference between "The glass is half full" and "The glass is half empty," in the weak link in a process.

To determine the readability of the above passage (or any of your choosing), select a section of contextual material (sentences) with 100 to 150 words. Then follow these steps:

1. Count the total number of words. Count hyphenated words, such as *micro-economic*, as two words. (Our sample has 119 words.)

2. Count the number of sentences. Independent clauses are considered separate sentences. Therefore, count compound sentences as two sentences. (Our sample has seven clauses that count as sentences.)

3. Divide the total number of words (119) by the number of clauses (7), resulting in the average sentence length (17 words).

4. Underscore the long words (25). A word is *long* if it has three or more syllables. However, do not count the following:

   a. Proper nouns (capitalized words)

b. Combinations of easy words (such as *understood*)

c. Verbs made three syllables by the addition of *ed* or *es*

5. Divide the number of long words (25) by the total number of words in the passage (119). This results in the percentage of long words (0.21 or 21 percent).

6. Add the average sentence length (17) and the percentage of long words (21 percent), dropping the decimal point. The result is 38.

7. Multiply the answer in Step 6 by 0.4. The result is 15.2. Therefore, the Fog Index for this passage is 15.2.

If you thought this passage was fairly difficult to read, you were right. Its readability score of 15.2 indicates a level between the third and fourth year of university. Level 12 indicates the last year of high school.

Although readability indexes are not exact scientific measures, they are helpful in providing a general sense of reading ease or difficulty. Many magazines are written at Grade 10 and 11 levels to appeal to their wide readership.

Most business writing is between Grade 8 and 12 levels. As a business writer, keep your sentences short, but not choppy. Strive to use short words, but don't necessarily sacrifice a long word if it is precise. Try to make your writing readable without being monotonous.

Recap of Fog Index Calculation

1. Count total words.

2. Count total sentences.

3. Find average sentence length. (Divide number of words by sentences.)

4. Count long words.

5. Find percentage of long words. (Divide total number of words by long ones.)

6. Add number of long words and the percentage from Step 5.

7. Multiply by 0.4.

If the answer falls between 8 and 12, the passage is within the range of most business writing.

Summary

The process of writing effective messages requires that you master several techniques for effective development of sentences and paragraphs. Writers must begin with an understanding of basic grammar to ensure that they avoid common sentence problems such as fragments, run-ons, and comma splices. You can create interesting sentences and emphasize your ideas through the effective use of stylistic and mechanical devices, including varied sentence structure and length. Avoid stylistic faults that detract from the coherence of your sentences.

When composing paragraphs, concentrate on unity. Strive for coherence through repetition of key words, use of pronouns, and use of transitional expressions. Try to vary the length of your paragraphs. In organizing paragraphs, choose carefully between the deductive and inductive method.

Writing is a process that can be done in five steps. The POWER plan for writing effectively shows the five-step process, beginning with the planning stage and ending with editing and the final product.

APPLICATION AND PRACTICE—4

Discussion

1. How are speakers and writers different in the manner in which they emphasize ideas?

2. Why is parallelism an important technique for writers to master?

3. Why are active-voice verbs preferred in business writing?

4. How does a writer achieve paragraph unity?

5. Differentiate between the deductive and inductive methods for organizing paragraphs.

Short Answers

6. Write definitions for these words:
   a. phrase
   b. clause

7. What is the difference between an independent and a dependent clause?

8. Write definitions for these sentence faults:
   a. fragment
   b. run-on sentence
   c. comma splice

9. Name the five steps in the POWER formula that describe the process of writing.

10. What is the average length of a sentence?

11. List five techniques for achieving emphasis through mechanics.

12. List four techniques for achieving emphasis through style.

13. List two stylistic techniques for de-emphasizing an idea.

14. Define *zigzag writing*.

Writing Improvement Exercises

Sentence Structure. Each of the following groups of words could be classified as a fragment, comma splice, or run-on sentence. In the space provided, name the fault. Be prepared to discuss how to remedy sentence faults.

Example: Since the trip originates in Toronto and makes one stop in Winnipeg.   <u> fragment </u>

15. We would like to inspect your car, please contact your authorized dealer immediately.   _____

16. If the necessary work has already been done or if you no longer own your Volkswagen.   _____

17. We would very much appreciate your completing the enclosed questionnaire return it in the postage-paid envelope.   _____

18. Because they know they can save money and time when they shop with us.   _____

19. Bills are mailed on the 16th of each month, they are payable by the 10th of the next month.   _____

20. We are happy to grant your request for a credit account with us we welcome you as a charge customer.   _____

21. Accounts that are payable by the 10th of each month and subject to a finance charge of 1 percent if unpaid.   _____

22. Your credit record, Mr. Deckman, is excellent, therefore, we are happy to welcome you as a charge customer.   _____

Emphasis. For each of the following sentences, circle a or b.

23. Which is more emphatic?

    a. It is a good idea that we advertise more.
    b. It is critical that we advertise heavily.

24. Which sentence places more emphasis on product loyalty?

   a. Product loyalty is the primary motivation for advertising.

   b. The primary motivation for advertising is loyalty to the product, although other purposes are served also.

25. Which sentence places more emphasis on the seminar?

   a. An executive training seminar that starts June 1 will include four candidates.

   b. Four candidates will be able to participate in an executive training seminar that we feel will provide a valuable learning experience.

26. Which sentence places more emphasis on the date?

   a. The deadline is December 30 for applications for overseas assignments.

   b. December 30 is the deadline for applications for overseas assignments.

27. Which is less emphatic?

   a. Ms. Curtis said that her financial status had worsened.

   b. Ms. Curtis said that she had lost her job and owed $2000.

28. Which sentence de-emphasizes the credit refusal?

   a. We are unable to grant you credit at this time, but we will reconsider your application later.

   b. Although we welcome your cash business, we are unable to offer you credit at this time; but we will be happy to reconsider your application later.

29. Which is more emphatic?

   a. Three departments are involved: (1) Legal, (2) Accounting, and (3) Distribution.

   b. Three departments are involved:
     1. Legal
     2. Accounting
     3. Distribution

Sentence Unity.   The following sentences lack unity. Rewrite, correcting the identified fault.

Example: (Dangling modifier) By advertising extensively, all the open jobs were filled quickly.

Revision: By advertising extensively, we were able to fill all the open jobs quickly.

30. (Dangling modifier) To open a money market account, a deposit of $3000 is required.

31. (Mixed construction) The reason why Mr. Brasseur is unable to travel extensively is because he has family responsibilities.

32. (Misplaced modifier) Identification passes must be worn at all times in offices and production facilities showing the employee's picture.

33. (Misplaced modifier) The editor-in-chief's rules were to be observed by all staff members, no matter how silly they seemed.

34. (Zigzag sentence) The business was started by two engineers, and these owners worked in a garage, which eventually grew into a million-dollar operation.

Parallelism.   Revise the following sentences so that their parts are balanced.

35. (Hint: Match verbs.) Some of our priorities include linking employee compensation to performance, keeping administrative costs down, the expansion of computer use, and the improvement of performance-review skills of supervisors.

36. (Hint: Match active voice of verbs.) Sally Strehlke, of the Vancouver office, will now supervise our Western Division; and the Eastern Division will be supervised by our Toronto office manager, James McFee.

37. (Hint: Match nouns.) Word processing is being used in the fields of health care, by lawyers, by secretaries in insurance firms, for scripts in the entertainment industry, in the banking field, and in many other places.

38. If you have decided to cancel our service, please cut your credit card in half, and the card pieces should be returned to us.

39. We need more laboratory space, additional personnel is required, and we also need much more capital.

40. The application for a grant asks for this information: funds required for employee salaries, how much we expect to spend on equipment, and what is the length of the project.

41. To lease an automobile is more expensive than buying one.

42. The teleconferencing service allows on-line users to send data, data can be received by users, they can discuss the data, and data are clarified.

Active-Voice Verbs.   Revise the following sentences so that verbs are in the active voice. Put the emphasis upon the doer of the action. Add subjects if necessary.

Example: The computers were started each morning at 7 a.m.

Revision: Juan started the computers each morning at 7 a.m.

43. Initial figures for the bid were submitted before the June 1 deadline.

44. Substantial sums of money were saved by customers who enroled early in our stock option plan.

45. A significant financial commitment has been made by us to ensure that our customers will be able to take advantage of our discount pricing.

46. Smaller-sized automated equipment was ordered so that each manager could have an individual computer.

Passive-Voice Verbs.   Revise the following sentences so that they are in the passive voice.

Example: Ms. Murdock did not turn in the accounting statement on time.

Revision: The accounting statement was not turned in on time.

47. Mr. Kelly made a computational error in the report.

48. We cannot ship your order for 50 motors until June 15.

49. The government first issued a warning regarding the use of this pesticide over 15 months ago.

50. The private laboratory rated products primarily on the basis of their performance.

Inductive/Deductive Organization.   Read the lettered statements below and answer the following questions. Be prepared to justify your responses.

51. If you were organizing the lettered ideas in a deductive strategy, with which statement would you logically begin?   _____

52. If you were organizing the lettered ideas in an inductive memo, with which statement would you conclude?   _____

   a. The Winnipeg Convention Centre has facilities to accommodate over 250 exhibitors and thousands of visitors.

   b. Winnipeg is a large metropolitan centre that will attract a sizable audience for the conference.

   c. The Winnipeg Convention Centre has excellent parking facilities and better-than-average transportation connections.

   d. The conference planning committee recommends that the next National Automation Conference be held in Winnipeg.

Readability.   From a magazine or textbook select a passage of 100 to 150 words. Determine its readability level by applying the Fog Index. Write a paragraph describing your findings. Do you think the level is appropriate for the intended audience? How could the author alter the readability of the passage?

CASE 4–1

Paragraph Unity

The following paragraph is poorly organized and lacks unity and coherence. On a separate sheet of paper, revise the paragraph following the suggestions provided in the text. Add or delete information as necessary. Pay particular attention to the use of transitions to connect thoughts coherently.

> We are pleased to welcome you to North Country Trust. Our family of banking customers is satisfied with North Country Trust. Group term life insurance is offered. This is one of the services we make available to our customers. This group term life insurance program has many benefits. It is low in cost. No medical examination is necessary to qualify for this program. The cost of living is steadily rising, and our premium rates remain reasonable. Take a look at the enclosed outline describing our group term life insurance.

CASE 4–2

Paragraph Organization

The following material is part of a letter of application. It lacks organization, emphasis, and coherence. Its unity could be improved by including only relevant information. Revise this paragraph to remedy its faults. (Do not rewrite the entire letter.)

> You will see that I have wide variety in the field of communications in course work, and I have some work experience. My résumé that is enclosed shows this. I had a course in media analysis, one in business writing, one in communications law, and television ethics. I was active in the Scouts, the Junior Chamber of Commerce, the Band Club, and my church. I worked with a newspaper for a while, television special events, and did a radio show. I have studied reporting, how to edit, and public relations.

CASE 4–3

Paragraph Organization

Select one of the topics below to write a well-organized, unified 100- to 150-word paragraph. Identify your topic sentence and method of organization.

1. Explain to an instructor why you feel a grade you received should be changed.

2. Explain to an employer why you feel you should work different hours or be given a different assignment.

GRAMMAR/MECHANICS CHECKUP—4

Adjectives and Adverbs

Review Sections 1.16 and 1.17 of the Grammar/Mechanics Handbook. Then study each of the following statements. Underscore any inappropriate forms. In the space provided for each statement, write the correct form and the number of the G/M principle illustrated. You may need to consult your dictionary for current practice regarding some compound adjectives. When you finish, compare your responses with those shown below. If your answers differ, study carefully the principles in parentheses.

Example: He was one of those individuals with a do-or-die attitude.   **do-or-die (1.17e)**

1. Most large corporations do not rely upon one source of long term financing only.   _____

2. Many subscribers considered the $25 per year charge to be a bargain.   _____

3. Other subscribers complained that $25 per year was exorbitant.   _____

4. The computer supplied the answer so quick that we were all amazed.   _____

5. He only had $1 in his pocket.   _____

6. If you expect double digit inflation to return, look for safe investments.   _____

7. Jeremy found a once in a lifetime opportunity.   _____

8. Although the house was four years old, it was in good condition.   _____

9. Of the two sample colours shown in the brochure, which do you think is best?   _____

10. Angela To is very well-known in her profession.   _____

11. Channel 12 presents up to the minute news broadcasts.   _____

12. Lower tax brackets would lessen the after tax yield of some bonds.   _____

13. The conclusion drawn from the statistics couldn't have been more clearer.   _____

14. The new investment fund has a better than fifty fifty chance of outperforming the older fund.   _____

15. If you feel badly about the transaction, contact your portfolio manager.   _____

---

1. **long-term (1.17e)**   3. **C (1.17e)**   5. **had only (1.17f)**   7. **once-in-a-lifetime (1.17e)**
9. **better (1.17a)**   11. **up-to-the-minute (1.17e)**   13. **have been clearer (1.17b)**   15. **bad (1.17c)**

GRAMMAR/MECHANICS CHALLENGE—4

Document for Revision

The following letter has faults in grammar, punctuation, spelling, number form, and lead-ins. It also contains flaws discussed in this chapter. Drawing upon the guidelines provided in the Grammar/Mechanics Handbook and what you learned in the chapter, revise the letter.

Poor Letter

November 4, 199x

Mr. John Chiang, Manager
Village Home Centre
Swift Current, SK
S1R 2L3

Dear Mr. Chiang:

This is to inform you that we will definitely credit your account for five hundred fifty dollars for the 2 no. 115 Electric Motors that arrived in damaged condition.

According to our records you received 9 electric motors. Pleas keep in mind that you are still eligible for the 10% discount on the 6 remaining motors. If you pay within 30 days. Remember too that the 10 percent discount is applicable on you reorder; should you wish us to replace the damaged motors.

We are happy to learn that the 9 batteries and 3 drills arrived in good condition. If your like our other customers you'll be particularly pleased with the results of the No. 118 drill. Nearly 100 customers have wrote to tell us of it's superiority over other drills on the market.

Please return the damaged electric motors to our Regina distribution centre, if you wish us to replace them, just complete the enclosed authorization.

Sincerely yours,

Note

1. Peter F. Drucker, *Innovation and Entrepreneurship: Practice and Principles* (New York: Harper & Row, 1985), p. 255.

UNIT 2

APPLYING THE DIRECT STRATEGY

5

Memorandums That Inform, Request, and Respond

In this chapter, you will learn to do the following:

- Distinguish between direct and indirect writing strategies.
- Recognize functions, characteristics, and kinds of memorandums.
- Write memorandums that make requests.

- Write memorandums that respond to other documents.
- Write memorandums that deliver information.

Memos deliver messages within organizations.

Memorandums (memos) are forms of internal communication; that is, they deliver information within an organization. In many organizations, more internal memos are written than letters addressed outside the company. One study revealed that executives rank memos first in frequency among 20 forms of written communication.[1] Another study indicated that the typical manager writes seven memos a week.[2]

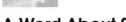

A Word About Strategies

Before we continue our discussion of memos, we need to consider plans or strategies. Business writing usually follows one of two strategies: the direct (deductive) plan or the indirect (inductive) plan. In Chapter 4, you learned to organize paragraphs inductively and deductively. Now we'll apply those same strategies to complete messages. How do you know which strategy to use? By analyzing your message and the anticipated reader reaction to that message, you can determine whether to use the direct or the indirect strategy. Most messages can be divided into three categories:

1. **Positive or neutral messages.** Expect the reader to be pleased or at least not displeased.

2. **Negative messages.** Expect the reader to be displeased.

3. **Persuasive messages.** Expect the reader to be initially uninterested.

For positive or neutral messages, the direct strategy is most effective. You will learn to apply the direct strategy in writing informational memos in this chapter. In Chapters 6 and 7, you will use the direct strategy for routine request letters and for routine replies. In Chapters 8 and 9, you will learn to use the indirect strategy for negative letters and for persuasive messages.

Most messages can be divided into three categories.

The anticipated reader reaction determines whether a message should be written directly or indirectly.

Functions of Memos

Memos are a vital means of communicating within an organization. They explain policies, procedures, and guidelines. They make announcements, request information, and follow up on conversations. They provide a record of decisions, telephone conversations, and meetings. They save time by relaying information to many people without the need for a meeting. Moreover, they ensure that all concerned individuals receive the same message, which would be unlikely if the message were transmitted orally.

When used judiciously, memos serve useful functions. When misused, however, they waste time, energy, and resources. Whether on paper or electronic, a memo should not be sent if a telephone call or personal comment would function as well. Memos should not be written as self-serving attention-getters. Some individuals churn out lengthy memos on the slightest pretense, such as the need for catered coffee service or assigned parking spaces. Moreover, copies of memos should be sent only to concerned individuals. The fact that the office has an excellent copy machine or that E-mail is available does not justify sending copies of memos to all employees.

Memos should be used for producing a permanent record, for gathering information, and for transmitting information when a personal meeting is impossible.

Memos can save time and provide a written record.

Kinds of Memos

Most memos can be classified into four groups: (1) memos that inform, (2) memos that request, (3) memos that respond, and (4) memos that persuade. In this chapter, we will be concerned with the first three groups because they use the direct strategy. The fourth group, persuasive memos, uses the indirect strategy, which will be presented in Chapters 8 and 9.

Characteristics of Memos

Well-considered memos have the following characteristics:

1. They begin with *To, From, Date,* and *Subject*.

2. They cover just one topic.

3. They are informal. 회사내의

4. They are concise.

Memos use an efficient standardized format, as shown in Figure 5.1. See page 395 for more information about formatting memos. You may prepare memos on preprinted forms, either handwriting or typing them, or using E-mail software. Use of the headings *To, From, Date,* and *Subject* has two benefits. First, headings force the sender to organize his or her thoughts in order to compose the subject of the message. Second, headings are invaluable aids for filing and retrieving memos.

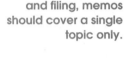

To facilitate action and filing, memos should cover a single topic only.

A memo normally covers only one topic. This facilitates action and filing. If an executive, for example, discusses both the faulty exhaust system on the company car and the approaching company banquet in the same memo, the reader may file the memo with other information relating to company cars and forget the details of the company banquet.

Memos may be written somewhat more informally than letters addressed outside the organization. Because you usually know and work with the reader, building good will and creating a favourable image are less important for memos than for messages sent outside the company.

Although informality is appropriate in memos, the degree of informality depends upon the relationship between the receiver and the sender. If a close working relationship exists, then a warm personal tone is fitting. It is important to remember that your messages should always be concerned with reader benefit and include positive language.

Like business letters, memos should sound like conversation. For example, *Please be informed that* is much more formal than *I'd like you to know that ....* Which would you be more likely to say in conversation?

The techniques that you learned in Chapters 2, 3, and 4 for writing concisely will help make your memos succinct. Memos are more likely to be read and acted upon if they are just long enough to say what is necessary.

Direct Strategy
중립의.

Memos that carry neutral or positive messages are most effective when written directly.

Figure 5.1   Sample Memorandum

DT DATATECH, INC.
INTERNAL MEMO

TO: Carlita Robertson

FROM: Edwina Jordan E.J.

DATE: February 6, 19xx

SUBJECT: FORMATTING COMPUTER MEMORANDUMS

Writers of memos usually place their initials here.

Here is the information you requested regarding appropriate formatting for memorandums keyed at computers and printed on plain paper.

1. Use 3-cm side margins.

2. Leave a top margin of 3 to 5 cm.

3. Type in all caps the headings TO, FROM, DATE, and SUBJECT.

4. Single-space within paragraphs but double-space between them.

We prefer to make a master memo document with all the format settings. Then we read that command file into any new memo. This method is fast and accurate.

If you'd like to discuss formatting computer memos further, please call me at Ext. 606.

Notice that memos do not end with a closing such as Sincerely.

Outline of Direct Strategy

■ Big idea first

■ Details or explanation

■ Closing thought

The direct strategy gets right down to business quickly; it uses the BIF approach: Big Idea First. If your memo has a new procedure to announce, summarize that announcement in the first sentence. Don't explain why the new procedure is being introduced or what employee reactions to the new procedure might be. Save explanations and details for later.

The direct strategy starts with the Big Idea First (BIF).

Providing the main idea first has several advantages:

■ It saves readers time. They don't have to skim the first part of the message quickly to find a key sentence telling what the message is about.

■ It enables readers to develop the proper mind-set. After they learn the main idea, the following explanations and details make sense. Readers comprehend more quickly because they anticipate what is coming.

■ It helps the writer organize the message logically. Once the writer has stated the main idea, the rest of the message is easier to write.

Remember, however, that the direct strategy is useful only if you expect that the reader will not be displeased by the content of the message. If the announcement of a new procedure might generate resistance, then persuasion is necessary and the indirect strategy (Chapter 9) would be more effective.

Developing a Memo-Writing Plan

Once you have decided upon the strategy for your message, proceed to a writing plan. In this book, you will be shown a number of writing plans appropriate for different messages. These plans provide a skeleton; they are the bones of a message. Writers provide the flesh. Simply plugging in phrases or someone else's words won't work. Good writers provide details and link together their ideas with transitions to create fluent and meaningful messages. However, a writing plan helps you get started and gives you ideas about what to include. At first, you will probably rely on these plans considerably. As you progress, they will become less important. Here is the writing plan for a memo that is not expected to create displeasure or resistance.

Writing Plan for Memos

A writing plan helps you organize a complete message.

■ **Subject line**—summarizes memo contents.

■ **First sentence**—states the main idea.

■ **Body**—provides background information and explains the main idea.

■ **Closing**—requests action or summarizes the message.

Writing the Subject Line

A subject line must be concise but meaningful.

Probably the most important part of a memo is the subject line, which summarizes the contents of the memo in concise language. It should be brief, but not so brief that it is senseless. The subject line *Revised Procedures* is probably meaningless to a reader. An improved subject line might read, *Revised Procedures for Scheduling Vacations.*

A subject line is like a newspaper headline. It should attract attention, create a clear picture, and present an accurate summary. It should be a phrase and should rarely occupy more than one line. Cramming comprehensive information into one dense line is a challenge that many writers enjoy because it tests their word and organizational skills.

Beginning with the Main Idea

Although an explanation occasionally must precede the main idea, the first sentence usually states the primary idea of the memo. An appropriate opening sentence for a memo that announces a new vacation procedure is as follows:

Here are new guidelines for employees taking two- or three-week vacations between June and September.

Don't open a memo by asking the reader to refer to another memo. Attach a copy of that document if necessary. Or provide a brief review of the relevant points. Asking the reader to dig out previous correspondence is inefficient and inconsiderate.

The first sentence may constitute the entire first paragraph. If more information is needed to present the main idea, write a unified paragraph using the techniques suggested in Chapter 4. In many memos, however, the first paragraph consists of a single sentence.

It's better to attach a copy of previous correspondence than to ask the reader to find it.

Explaining in the Body

In the body of the memo, explain the main idea. If you are asking for detailed information, arrange the questions in logical order. If you are providing information, group similar information together. When considerable data are involved, use a separate paragraph for each topic. Establish effective transitions between paragraphs.

The tone of memos is informal. Don't be self-conscious about using contractions (*won't*, *didn't*, *couldn't*), conversational language, and occasional personal pronouns (*I*, *me*, *we*). Make an effort, though, to de-emphasize first-person pronouns. Concentrate on developing the *you*-attitude.

Memos are most effective when they are concise. For this reason, lists often appear in memos. Lists boil down information into readable and understandable form. Tips on writing effective lists are provided later in this chapter.

Closing the Memo

End the memo with a request for action, a summary of the contents of the memo, or a closing thought. If action on the part of the reader is sought, spell out that action clearly. A vague request such as *Drop by to see this customer sometime* is ineffective because the reader may not understand exactly what is to be done. A better request might be: *Please make an appointment to see John Ayers before August 5.* Another way to close a memo is by summarizing its major points. This is particularly helpful if the memo is complicated.

If no action request is made and a closing summary is unnecessary, the writer may prefer to end the memo with a simple closing thought. Although it is unnecessary to conclude memos with good will statements such as those found in letters to customers, some closing statement is useful to prevent a feeling of abruptness. For example, a memo might end with *I'll appreciate your assistance* or *What do you think of this proposal?*

End a memo with a request for action, a summary, or a closing remark.

Memos That Inform

The memo format is useful to explain organization policies, procedures, and guidelines. As policy-making documents, memos that inform should be particularly clear and concise.

The memo shown in Figure 5.2 informs employees about a new storewide policy. It begins directly by telling the reader what the memo is about. The next paragraph explains why the new policy is needed; a list enumerates policy information and guidelines, making them easy to read and understand.

FIGURE 5.2   Memo with Enumerated List

DATE: December 2, 199x

TO: Pat Walker, Cecille Cabanne, Don Deonne, Gil Sweeney, and
                 Kathy Pedroza

FROM: E.W. Lauderman, Store Manager *EWL*

Summarizes contents of memo.

SUBJECT: STORE POLICY REGARDING OFF-PLANET DOLLS

Combines main idea with brief explanation.

Because we anticipate heavy customer interest in the popular Off-Planet dolls, I would like you to share the following information and newly developed GemMart policy with all your employees.

Explains why new policy is needed.

I've just learned that a GemMart buyer recently appeared in a taped television interview that will appear nationally this week. Apparently our buyer said that the Off-Planet dolls would be available in some GemMart stores. Since we expect our stores to be swamped with telephone calls from customers asking specifically about this series of dolls, we have decided that all employees in all of our area stores should have the same policy information to help them answer questions consistently. Please note the following points:

Lists items in parallel form for easy reading.

■ GemMart currently has no Off-Planet dolls.

■ We do not know if we will receive any in the future.

■ We will neither issue raincheques nor take any orders for these dolls.

Closes with directions and promise.

Please discuss this policy with your employees. I'll be sure to let you know immediately if we receive a shipment of Off-Planet dolls.

Memos That Request

Memos that make requests are most effective when they use the direct approach. The reader learns immediately what is being requested. However, if you have any reason to suspect that the reader may resist the request, then an indirect approach would probably be more successful.

Requests should be courteous and respectful, not demanding or dictatorial. The tone of the following request would be likely to antagonize its recipient:

> I want you to find out why the Davis account was not included in this report, and I want this information before you do anything else.

So that the intent of the memo is not misunderstood, requests should be considered carefully and written clearly. What may seem clear to the writer may not always be clear to a reader. Therefore, it's wise to have a fellow worker read a critical memo for clarity before it is sent out.

Whenever possible, the closing paragraph of a request memo should be *end dated*. An end date sets a deadline for the requested action and gives a reason for this action to be completed by the deadline. Such end dating prevents procrastination and allows the reader to plan a course of action to ensure completion by the date given. For example, a request that an employee order mailing labels might conclude with the following:

> Please submit your order by December 1 so that sufficient labels will be on hand for mailing the year-end reports January 15.

Many requests within organizations relate to the collection of information necessary for decision making. The memo shown in Figure 5.3 requests data about personal computers.

The tone of a request memo should encourage cooperation.

End dating includes a deadline and, if possible, a reason explaining the deadline.

Memos That Respond

Much office correspondence reacts or responds to other memos or documents. When responding to a document, follow these preparatory steps: (1) collect whatever information is necessary, (2) organize your thoughts, and (3) make a brief outline of the points you plan to cover. You may wish to make your outline or notes right on the document you are answering. Begin the memo with a clear statement of the big idea, which often is a summary of the contents of the memo. You will not want to follow the example of the following wordy and stilted opening, which begins with an outdated expression: *Pursuant to your request of January 20, I am herewith including the information you wanted.*

Lois Jones, manager of Legal Support Services, responded to Joseph Ferguson's request for computer information with the memo shown in Figure 5.4. Notice that the memo begins directly with a clear reference to Mr. Ferguson's request. It also answers his questions in the same order in which they were asked.

FIGURE 5.3   Survey Request Memo

TO: All Department Heads

DATE: February 20, 199x

FROM: Joseph Ferguson ᴊℱ
                 Vice-President, Operations

SUBJECT: SURVEY OF PERSONAL COMPUTER EQUIPMENT

Please answer the questions below regarding the kinds of personal
computers your department is now using.

States request
courteously.

Because many of our departments now find it necessary to exchange
word processing and spreadsheed information on diskette, we are trying
to make sure that all departments use the same software. Using the same
software packages will ensure that the diskettes we exchange are compatible. Your answers to the following questions will help us select the
proper software.

Lists questions for
ease in reading.

1. What kinds of personal computers does your department currently
   use?

2. What software programs are you now using?

3. What kinds of computer equipment will you be buying in the near
   future?

Provides end date
and reason.

I'll appreciate your answers by March 7 so that we can analyze your
responses before our budget requests are due March 18.

Electronic Memos

E-mail is an effective means of delivering messages quickly and efficiently. As
with other forms of communication, it is important to consider the recipient
when using E-mail. An E-mail to a vice-president in response to a request for
information will differ considerably in tone and style from an E-mail to a co-
worker confirming a lunch date.

Choose the proper
tone and style for an
E-mail message by
considering the
recipient.

An example of an effective E-mail message is given in Figure 5.5. The
sender, Mabel Lam, has used the BIF approach in providing the main idea first.
In the second, and concluding, sentence, she has provided a brief explanation
of the main idea. The subject line above, *Summer Vacation Dates*, presents an
accurate and concise summary of the memo's contents. An effective response to
Lam's memo is given in Figure 5.6.

FIGURE 5.4 Memo That Responds

TO: Joseph Ferguson   DATE: March 5, 19xx
             Vice-President, Operations

FROM: Lois R. Jones L R J
             Manager, Legal Support Services

SUBJECT: SURVEY OF COMPUTER EQUIPMENT IN LEGAL SUPPORT
             SERVICES

Here is the information you requested regarding personal computers in   **Identifies response**
Legal Support Services.   **immediately.**

1. Our staff members are now using three PCs, one Mac, and one Sun   **Lists numbered**
   system. All of the machines have a 3 1/2-inch drive. The PCs also   **answers in same**
   have a CD drive.   **order they were**
                                                                            asked.

2. Our software includes the WordPerfect Office and Lotus 1-2-3.

3. We are considering purchasing two more PCs soon, but we have not
   yet decided on a vendor.

Let me know if I may offer additional information.   **Closes with**
                                                                            reassuring remark.

Figure 5.5 E-mail Message That Requests

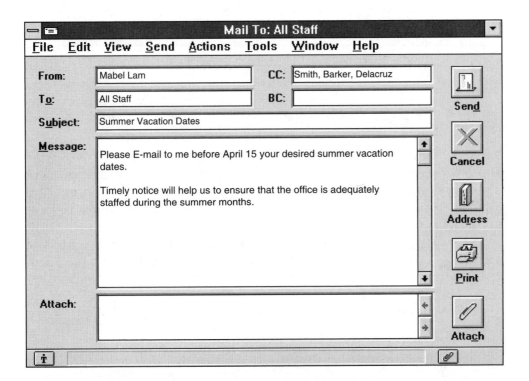

Figure 5.6   E-Mail Message That Responds

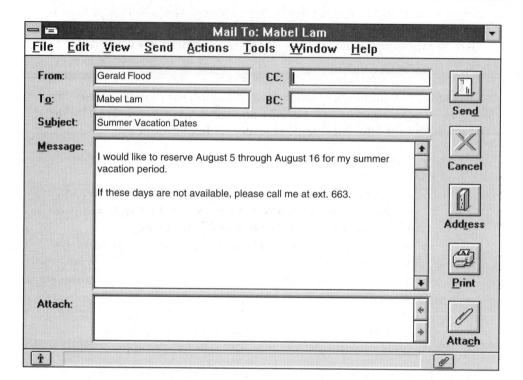

Here are some suggestions for the effective use of E-mail.[3]

1. **Use E-mail to respond to an E-mail message.** Receiving a paper response to an E-mail message can be confusing. An E-mail response to an E-mail message allows the recipient to file the response with the message.

2. **Make plans for the handling of your E-mail when you go on holiday.** E-mail functions like a telephone answering machine in that it saves and stores messages. If you share storage space with others, there is a danger that your messages will take up too much of the available space when you are away on vacation. Many E-mail programs allow you to stop receiving mail once a predetermined number is reached. You might also consider having a co-worker download your E-mail to a diskette or storage drive.

3. **When appropriate, send part of the original document with your reply.** This can be a useful reminder, especially if there is a long delay between the initiating message and your response.

4. **Be discreet.** E-mail is not private; it can be forwarded, printed, or read on screen. Be professional about what you say about others.

How to Write Winning Lists

A list is a group or series of related items, usually three or more. Business and professional writers have learned that presenting similar information in list form improves readability and emphasis. Because lists require fewer words than complete sentences, they are faster to read and easier to understand. Listed information stands out; therefore, it's swiftly located and quickly reviewed. Professional writers who strive for readability, comprehension, and emphasis frequently use lists.

How can you write good lists? Concentrate on two concepts: (a) the list itself, and (b) the paragraph or sentence that introduces it.

Items in List

Use lists only if the items that are related can be shown in the same form. If one item is a single word but the next item requires a paragraph of explanation, the items are not suitable for listing.

Items in a list must be balanced, or parallel, in construction. Use similar grammatical form.

Instead of	Try this
Her primary pastimes are sleeping, eating, and work.	Her primary pastimes are sleeping, eating, and working.
We are hiring the following: sales clerks, managers who will function as supervisors, and people to work in offices.	We are hiring the following: sales clerks, supervising managers, and office personnel.
Some of the most pressing problems are refunds that are missing, payments directed to the wrong place, and numerous lost documents.	These are the most pressing problems: missing refunds, misdirected payments, and lost documents.

A list of instructions demands the reader's attention if each item is a command starting with a verb. Notice in the next example that periods signal each item.

Here are instructions for using the copy machine:

- Insert the departmental metre in the slot.
- Load paper, curved upward, in the upper tray.
- Feed flat copies through the feed chute.

Some items are most efficiently shown with headings:

Date	City	Speaker
September 16	Fredericton	Dr. Roietta Fulgham
October 30	Saint John	Professor Iva Upchurch

Occasionally, listed items are longer, requiring more than one sentence. Strive for consistency in construction within the items. For example:

McDonald's was able to increase its productivity and profits with three effective techniques.

1. Unnecessary and redundant tasks in the workplace were identified and eliminated, resulting in simplification.

2. Functions not requiring face-to-face customer contact were centralized in an administrative centre.

3. Routine tasks, such as bill paying and simple customer service, were automated with a touch-tone voice-response system.

Items may be listed vertically or horizontally. Items shown vertically, obviously, stand out more—but they require more space. To use less space and to show less separation from the surrounding paragraph, arrange items horizontally. In horizontal lists, items are usually part of one sentence. Notice that each item is followed by a comma and that the word *and* precedes the last item in the series. If the items are too long for incorporation in one sentence, use a vertical list or rewrite the material without a list. Using letters or numbers for listed items gives them more importance and separation.

Many individuals backslide on their resolutions regarding fitness. To keep exercising, you should (a) make a written commitment to yourself, (b) set realistic goals for each day's workout, and (c) enlist the support of your spouse or a friend.

The health club has four sign-up months: January, May, August, and October.

Welcome to the following new members. They all signed up for aerobics classes beginning in January.

Jeffrey Moss	Chandell B. Handley
Monica Fernando	Marc Fillion

Introductory Words

The introductory words to a list must make sense with each item in the list. The introduction should be as complete as possible so that the same words do not have to be repeated in each item.

Instead of	Try this
Our goal	Our goal is to recruit sales reps who are
■ Is to recruit intensely competitive sales reps	■ Intensely competitive

- Is to use reps who are familiar with our products
- Recruit intelligent reps who learn quickly

- Familiar with our products
- Intelligent and learn quickly

Punctuating and Capitalizing Lists

Although some flexibility exists, most writers follow similar guidelines in punctuating and capitalizing words in lists. Study the examples above for illustration of the following suggestions.

1. Use a colon following the introduction to most lists. However, there are three exceptions.

   - Do not use a colon if the listed items follow verbs or prepositions (thus functioning as complements or objects to elements in the introduction).

   - Do not use a colon after the introduction if another sentence comes before the list.

   - You may choose to use a period (or a colon) after the introduction if both the introductory statement and the listed items are complete sentences, as shown in the McDonald's example above.

2. Omit punctuation after any item listed vertically. Use a period *only* if the item is a complete sentence.

3. Capitalize the initial letter of any item listed vertically.

Summary

Memos are used to transmit information within organizations. They may inform, request, or respond. They can save time by substituting for meetings and provide a written or electronic record of verbal exchanges. A memo should cover only one topic. Memos usually fall into three categories: positive or neutral messages, negative messages, and persuasive messages.

Choosing the organization for messages depends on the reader's anticipated reaction. The direct strategy, which is used when your message is positive or neutral, should always begin with the big idea.

A writing plan helps you organize your message. It includes a meaningful subject line, a first sentence that states the big idea, a body that provides information and explanation, and a closing that requests action and provides an end date.

The tone of your memos should encourage cooperation. When composing an E-mail message, you should strive for an appropriate tone, just as you would if producing a handwritten memo.

APPLICATION AND PRACTICE—5

Discussion

1. Explain the functions of memos within organizations.

2. Distinguish between the direct and indirect strategies.

3. How can memos waste time, money, and resources?

4. What are the differences between internal and external correspondence for an organization? *memo* *letter*

5. Name four classifications of memos and explain what strategy each should follow.

6. Suggest some advantages of E-mail memos over written memos.

Short Answers

7. List three categories into which most messages can be divided.

p.87.

8. Explain what reader reaction you might expect for each of the three categories of messages you listed above.

9. What are the four guide words that appear at the top of most pre-printed memo forms?

To, From, Date, Subject

10. The use of a standardized memo format benefits whom?

11. Why should a memo cover only one topic?

12. List three ways to close a memo.

p.91.

13. List and describe briefly the four parts of the writing plan for a memo.

① Subject. ② first sentence of body ③ Explain body ④ closing

14. What is end dating?

15. Most memos will use which strategy?

Writing Improvement Exercises

Memo Openers and Organizations.   Compare the sets of memo openers below. Circle the letter of the opener that illustrates the BIF plan. Be prepared to discuss the weaknesses and strengths of each opener shown.

16. a. For some time now we have been thinking about the possibility of developing an in-service training program for some of our employees.

   b. Employees interested in acquiring and improving computer skills are invited to an in-service training program beginning October 4.

17. a. I am asking our Customer Relations Department to conduct a study and make recommendations regarding the gradual but steady decline of customer chequing accounts.

   b. We have noticed recently a gradual but steady decline in the number of customer chequing accounts. We are disturbed by this trend, and for this reason I am asking our Customer Relations Department to conduct a study and make recommendations regarding this important problem.

Opening Paragraphs.   The following opening paragraphs to memos are wordy and indirect. After reading each paragraph, identify the big idea. Then, write an opening sentence that illustrates the BIF plan. Use a separate sheet if necessary.

18. Some of our staff members are interested in computer software that might reduce our work here in Accounting. Several staff members asked if they could attend a seminar February 11. This seminar previews accounting software that might be effective in our department. I am allowing the following employees to attend the seminar: Dave Neufeld, Tayreez Mushani, and Gail Switzer.

19. Your TechData Employees Association has secured for you discounts on auto repair, carpet purchases, travel arrangements, and many other services. These services are available to you if you have a Buying Power Card. All TechData employees are eligible for their own private Buying Power Cards.

Lists

20. Use the following information to compose a vertical list with an introductory statement.

Traditional employee suggestion programs often fail for a number of reasons. To make them more successful, participation must be increased. Try to get more people to participate. For one thing, invitations should be extended to managers, part-timers, temporary workers, and even representatives of suppliers. But the rules must be simple—so simple that anyone may suggest anything at any time. And when they do submit a suggestion, they should be rewarded immediately. It's easy to give a simple reward, such as a button or a coffee mug, to anyone as soon as a suggestion is made.

21. Use the following information to compose a horizontal list with an introductory statement.

Your lease is about to mature. When it does, you must make a decision. Three options are available to you. If you like, you may purchase the equipment at fair market value. Or the existing lease may be extended, again at fair market value. Finally, if neither of these options is appealing, the equipment could be sent back to the lessor.

CASE 5-1

Memo That Requests

Play the part of Patricia Isaac, president of Alloy Products. You must send a memo to Sylvie Marchand, assistant personnel director, asking her to write a report comparing group extended health insurance plans. The Board of Directors of Alloy Products has authorized this study in preparation for the eventual adoption of a plan for your employees. The board has several key factors to consider in the comparison: the cost to the company for each employee covered; kinds of illnesses and/or injuries covered; total annual health benefits allowed per employee; the costs to employees; and the coverage for hospital, outpatient, and home visits. You want Sylvie to make a thorough investigation of the plans offered by seven or eight companies in your area. You need the report by July 12. In her report, she should recommend the three plans that are most appropriate. The board will make the final selection.

To help you organize your memo according to the principles you have learned in this chapter, read the options suggested here. Circle appropriate responses.

1. From the point of view of the person receiving the memo, what is the big idea in this memo?

   a. The Board of Directors is considering a health plan for employees.
   b. Sylvie is to make a comparative study of group health plans.
   c. The Board of Directors has certain key factors to consider.
   d. Sylvie's report must be submitted by July 12.

2. An effective opening sentence for your memo might be

   a. At its last meeting the Board of Directors considered adopting an employee group health insurance plan.
   b. We are very interested in employee group health insurance plans.
   c. Please make a comparative study of employee group health insurance plans as a preliminary step in selecting a suitable program for our employees.
   d. I have been authorized by the Board of Directors to begin an investigation of employee group health insurance plans.

3. The body of your memo should include

   a. An explanation of what the Board of Directors has authorized.
   b. A description of the Board of Directors' meeting.
   c. An inquiry about the personnel file of Jack Hays, which you gave her last week.
   d. References to complaints from employees regarding the lack of health benefits.

4. An effective closing for this memo might be

   a. Thanks for your assistance in this matter, Sylvie.
   b. Please submit your comparison report to me by July 12.
   c. If I may be of assistance to you, please do not hesitate to call on me.
   d. I wonder, Sylvie, if you would be able to speak to a group of high-school students who asked us to supply a speaker on the topic of high-tech employment.

Use your memo for class discussion or use it as a writing assignment. If your instructor so directs, write the entire memo to Sylvie on a separate sheet. Begin with an appropriate subject line. You may wish to incorporate some of the sentences you selected here. Add other information and join your thoughts with logical transitions. Be sure that your list of key factors is concise and parallel.

CASE 5–2

Memo That Requests

Analyze the following poorly written memo. List at least five faults. Outline an appropriate plan for a memo that requests. Then, on a separate sheet, write an improved version of this memo, rectifying its faults.

TO: Susan Hsu   DATE: April 3, 199x
          Community Relations Coordinator

FROM: H.W. Rosenblum
          President

SUBJECT: SUMMER INTERNSHIP PROGRAM

As you know, Susan, we at TechData have not been altogether pleased with the quality of the new employees we attract each year. We do not feel that we are getting the crème de la crème of the college graduates on the market, so to speak.

Our Management Council has suggested that we make a consideration of the possibility of adding a summer internship program for the express purpose of attracting superior college students to our company.

A number of questions arise. Accordingly, this memo is to make a request that you do some research on this possibility. Here are some things I want you to find out about. How much would such a program cost? I would like this question and the others answered in a report that you submit to me by June 15. Has this kind of program been tried in other companies? Do you think colleges and universities would participate? And if so, which ones would participate? We need to know if such a plan is likely to improve our present situation. We're also wondering if the company would be obligated to offer permanent positions to these summer interns.

If you'd like to talk with me about this project, Susan, just give me a jingle.

CASE 5–3

Memo That Responds

Cynthia Chomsky, secretary of the Management Council of DataTech, wrote a first draft of the following memo. Then she attended a company workshop on improving communication techniques. She wrote comments to herself based on some of the things she learned. Revise the memo using her suggestions.

Long-winded memo . . . wastes everyone's time!

TO: Martin Reid, Craig Joseph, Jacquie Laurendeau

FROM: Cynthia Chomsky

DATE: February 3, 199x

this first ¶ is a real drag!

SUBJECT: Reminder   *← really vague . . . must improve*

I already know all this stuff . . . condense or leave out

As you know, the Management Council is very concerned about our employee hiring techniques. This has become a problem in our company. I heard many of you say at our last meeting in January that you felt we had to improve our selection of employees. I understand that some new employees are hired for positions for which they are unsuited, and we don't seem to learn about the problem until it's too late. We really need to improve the entire personnel selection process, beginning with the writing of job specifications to the interviewing process. One area where we have been particularly lax is the checking of applicants' references.

too much "I" – not enough "you"

(I) was asked at our last meeting in January to find speakers. (I) spent a lot of time finding individuals who I thought would bring us valuable information about improving our interviewing and other hiring techniques. (I) think you're all really going to benefit from the programs (I've) arranged. Please be reminded that the Management Council meets at 2:30 p.m. in Conference Room C.   *need this?*   *add end date*   *move to end*

If for some reason you cannot attend any of these meetings, you must call me. We also voted, if you will recall, to include outside guests at these last three sessions. So, if you would like to invite anyone, tell me his name so I can send him an invitation.──by when?   *sexist!*

arrange in list ... use headings?

Here are the three speakers I have arranged. The first is Norman J. Withers, from ABC Consultants. He will speak February 20 on the topic of "Job Specifications." Dr. Ann D. Seaman, University of Calgary, is the next speaker. She will speak on the topic of "The Interviewing Process," and her date is March 28. Last but not least is Erick Basil, from Smith & Burney, Inc. The title of his talk is "Reference Checking," set for April 30.   *cliché*   *check spelling of names*

shorten entire memo!

Case 5–4

Personal Writing Situation

Write the following memo from your own work or personal experience. Some employees have remarked to the boss that they are working more than other employees. Your boss has decided to study the matter by collecting memos from everyone. He asks you to write a memo describing your current duties and the skills required for your position. If some jobs are found to be overly demanding, your boss may redistribute job tasks or hire additional employees. Write a well-organized memo describing your duties, approximately how much time you spend on each task, and the skills needed for what you do. Provide enough details to make a clear record of your job. Use actual names and describe actual tasks. If you have no work experience, use experience from an organization or institution to which you belong. Report to the head of the organization, describing the duties of an officer or of a committee. Your boss or organization head appreciates brevity. Keep your memo under one page.

Additional Problems

1. Assume you are Stephanie Adams, new products manager for Visualize, Inc. Write a memo to Gail Mirreau, general counsel in the Legal Department, requesting information on nondisclosure agreements. Visualize is considering a proposal by Effects Management to work on the development of a computer game. Peter Seimens, a project director at Effects Management, has informed you that Visualize will be required to sign an agreement that swears you to secrecy on the project should the company agree to undertake it. This is your first experience with nondisclosure agreements, and you have many questions. Who in your company should sign the agreement? How many people will it cover? If all 200 staff in your organization are to be bound by the agreement, what steps can you take to ensure compliance? Should a staff member break the agreement, what will the legal ramifications be for Visualize? Your memo should be no more than one page.

2. You have been asked to draft a memo to the office staff about the company's Christmas party. Include information about where the party will be held, when it is, what the cost will be, a description of the food to be served, whether guests are allowed, and whom to make reservations with.

3. Assume you are Pamela Haas, marketing director, Can-Am Foods, Inc. Write a memo to V.A. McFee, vice-president, informing him about the following advertising program. You have just completed the planning stages of a promotion campaign for your pasta product, Creamettes. Together with Okanagan Growers, Inc., you have worked out an agreement to launch a joint campaign aimed at combining the use of Creamettes with Okanagan apples. The details for the planned campaign were formulated by your advertising agency, Kusyk and Kwan, over the past two months. The promotion will concentrate on light recipes for summer

consumption. Along with the recipes, discount coupons on Creamettes will be offered. The coupons and recipes will be published in appropriate magazines and in the Thursday food sections of 15 daily newspapers in the western provinces. The campaign will be concentrated in June, July, and August. You expect this campaign to cost $190,000 for advertising in newspapers and magazines, $90,000 for redeemed coupons (300,000 coupons at 30 cents each), and $37,000 to Kusyk and Kwan. Okanagan will provide one-fifth of these costs. Mr. McFee has no prior knowledge of this promotion; he'll need all the details you can provide.

4. As director of employee relations of Can-Am, write a memo to all employees informing them of new banking services soon to be available. You have arranged with the Bank of Montreal to install an automated banking machine (ABM) in your lobby. It will operate from 6 a.m. to 9 p.m., six days a week, beginning next week. Describe the advantages of ABMs. Tell employees that a representative from the Bank of Montreal will be present in the lobby for the next two weeks. This representative will be able to open accounts for employees who want to take advantage of the new banking services, including a range of combination chequing and savings accounts. RSP Saving Accounts, CDs (certificates of deposit), and time deposits are available. The company has also arranged with the Bank of Montreal to enable employees to deposit their paycheques directly into the bank. Describe the advantages of direct deposits. Encourage employees to visit the Bank of Montreal representative in the next two weeks.

5. As Sanford Henry, vice-president for personnel at Can-Am, write a memo to Kathleen Lam, director of information services. Tell her that you have attended a conference on ergonomic office environments. You learned of employee complaints in some organizations where automated information processing equipment has been introduced. Ask her if she is aware of any dissatisfaction among word processing specialists regarding muscular discomfort or eyestrain. Has she noticed increased absenteeism among word processors? Have operators expressed unhappiness with their jobs? Do we have a high turnover rate? Have any steps been taken to reduce job discomfort and dissatisfaction? You are very concerned about the health and happiness of employees. Ask Ms. Lam to give this matter her immediate consideration. You want a quick response. You don't expect her to conduct an elaborate investigation.

6. As Kathleen Lam, director of information services, respond to Mr. Henry's memo request described in No. 5 above. You don't know of any employee complaints about aching necks and shoulders. Only one employee, Edith Glover, the chief editor/proofreader, complained of eye trouble. You tried to solve that problem by rotating the task of editing among all word processing operators. You are concerned, too, about providing an ergonomically satisfactory work environment. You encourage employees who are performing eye-straining tasks to take ten-minute breaks every hour. You make sure that furniture is adjusted to the body size of users. You've checked on the absenteeism of your division compared with other divisions, and you find that yours is lower. You have also installed glare-resistant screens on your monitors to reduce eyestrain. You admit that you

have had a higher turnover rate than you would like, but employees seem to be leaving for better-paying word processing positions elsewhere. You are also experimenting with job-enrichment tasks to try to reduce any employee dissatisfaction in the Information Services Division. If Mr. Henry has any suggestions for you, you'll be glad to hear them. Encourage him to visit your division.

7. Again as Sanford Henry, vice-president for personnel, write a memo to all department managers of Can-Am Foods. The Board of Directors is concerned that the company might be infringing copyright laws by using pirated computer programs. They are also worried about the possibility of employees adding personal programs to their PCs, which may inject a computer virus into the company system. To address these concerns, the directors have mandated that employees "shall adopt, implement, and maintain a written policy that prohibits the personal copy or transmission of company-owned computer software." Managers must also "ensure that employee computers do not contain any programs that were illegally copied and loaded into the company system." Make this announcement to your department managers. Tell the managers that you want them to set up departmental committees to ensure that each department's system is free of unauthorized programs. Explain why this is a good policy.

8. You are Mike O'Dell, manager of accounting services for Can-Am Foods, responding to Mr. Henry's memo in No. 7. You could have called Mr. Henry, but you prefer to have this problem set out in writing. The problem is the difficulty you are experiencing in enforcing the new policy with several of your senior accountants. When these employees started, the company was in the process of computerizing. They chose to bring in a spreadsheet program that they all knew already. Now, most of the Accounting Department uses the most current version of ACCPAC. However, since these workers have always done an effective job with the older program, they were not required to update with the rest of the department. Also, you are aware of a personal program the department uses to organize the softball league and yearly office party. You are receiving complaints about the new policy because your employees see nothing wrong with using the programs they have. What suggestions does Mr. Henry have for dealing with this situation? Your committee members can find no other unauthorized programs in use; in fact, they believe that the directive from the board has been complied with by all other employees. You need help from a higher authority. Appeal to Mr. Henry for solutions. Perhaps he should visit your department.

GRAMMAR/MECHANICS CHECKUP—5

Prepositions and Conjunctions

Review Sections 1.18 and 1.19 of the Grammar/Mechanics Handbook. Then study each of the following statements. Write *a* or *b* to indicate the sentence that is expressed more effectively. Also record the number of the G/M principle illustrated. When you finish, compare your responses with those provided below. If your answers differ, study carefully the principles shown in parentheses.

Example: a. Raoul will graduate college this spring.
      b. Raoul will graduate from college this spring.

        <u>   b   </u> (1.18a)

1. a. DataTech enjoyed greater profits this year then it expected.
     b. DataTech enjoyed greater profits this year than it expected.

2. a. I hate it when we have to work overtime.
     b. I hate when we have to work overtime.

3. a. Dr. Simon has a great interest and appreciation for the study of robotics.
     b. Dr. Simon has a great interest in and appreciation for the study of robotics.

4. a. Gross profit is where you compute the difference between total sales and the cost of goods sold.
     b. Gross profit is computed by finding the difference between total sales and the cost of goods sold.

5. a. We advertise to increase the frequency of product use, to introduce complementary products, and to enhance our corporate image.
     b. We advertise to have our products used more often, when we have complementary products to introduce, and we are interested in making our corporation look better to the public.

6. a. What type computers do you prefer?
     b. What type of computers do you prefer?

7. a. Many of our new products are selling better then we anticipated.
     b. Many of our new products are selling better than we anticipated.

8. a. The sale of our Halifax branch office last year should improve this year's profits.
     b. The sale of our branch office in Halifax during last year should improve the profits for this year.

9. a. Do you know where the meeting is at?
     b. Do you know where the meeting is?

10. a. The cooling-off rule is a provincial government rule that protects consumers from making unwise purchases at home.
     b. The cooling-off rule is where the provincial government has made a rule that protects consumers from making unwise purchases at home.

11. **a.** Meetings can be more meaningful if the agenda is stuck to, the time frame is followed, and if someone keeps follow-up notes.

    b. Meetings can be more meaningful if you stick to the agenda, follow the time frame, and keep follow-up notes.

12. **a.** They printed the newsletter on yellow paper like we asked them to do.

    b. They printed the newsletter on yellow paper as we asked them to do.

13. **a.** A code of ethics is a set of rules spelling out appropriate standards of behaviour.

    b. A code of ethics is where a set of rules spells out appropriate standards of behaviour.

14. **a.** We need an individual with an understanding and serious interest in black-and-white photography.

    b. We need an individual with an understanding of and serious interest in black-and-white photography.

15. **a.** The most dangerous situation is when employees ignore the safety rules.

    b. The most dangerous situation occurs when employees ignore the safety rules.

---

1. b (1.19d) 3. b (1.18e) 5. a (1.19a) 7. b (1.19d) 9. b (1.18b) 11. b (1.19a)
13. a (1.19c) 15. b (1.19c)

GRAMMAR/MECHANICS CHALLENGE—5

Document for Revision

The following memo has faults in grammar, punctuation, spelling, number form, repetition, wordiness, and other areas. Study the guidelines in the Grammar/Mechanics Handbook to sharpen your skills. Then, correct the errors.

Poor Memo

To: Amy MacKenzie   Date: June 25, 199x

From: Ira White

Subject: Collecting Data for Annual Report

You have been assigned a special project, to collect information for next years annual report. You'll probably need to visit each department head personally to collect this information individually from them.

The Corporate Communications division which oversee the production of the annual report is of the opinion that you should concentrate on the following departmental data;

1. specific accomplishments of each department for the past year.

2. you must find out about goals of each department for the coming year.

3. in each department get names of interesting employees and events to be featured.

In view of the fact that this is a big assignment Maria Marquez has been assigned to offer assistance to you. Inasmuch as the annual report must be completed by September first; please submit your data in concise narrative form to me by August fifth.

Notes

1. Donna Stine and Donald Skarzenski, "Priorities for the Business Communication Classroom: A Survey of Business and Academe," *The Journal of Business Communication* 16 (1979), p. 17.

2. Martha H. Rader and Alan P. Wunsch, "A Survey of Communication Practices of Business School Graduates by Job Category and Undergraduate Major," *The Journal of Business Communication* 17 (1980), p. 39.

3. Adapted from Arlene Rinaldi, *The Net: User Guidelines and Netiquette* Rinaldi@ACC.FAU.EDU. Last updated: 27 April 95. URL = http://www.fau.edu/rinaldi/net/user.html

Letters That Make Routine Requests

In this chapter, you will learn to do the following:

- Analyze letter content and select an appropriate writing strategy.
- Write letters that request information concisely.
- Order merchandise clearly and efficiently.
- Write letters that make justified claims.

External Communication

Written communication outside an organization is conducted through electronic and nonelectronic letters. Executives, managers, and supervisors at all levels of management, as well as nonmanagement employees, are called upon daily to exchange information with customers and other organizations. Although information is also exchanged verbally, letters are necessary to provide a convenient, well-considered, and permanent communication record.

Content and Strategy

Like memos, letters are easiest to write when you have a strategy or plan to follow. The plan for letters, just as for memos, is determined by the content of the message and its anticipated effect on the receiver. Letters delivering bad news require an indirect approach (Chapter 8). Many letters, however, carry good or neutral news. Because such letters will not produce a negative effect on their readers, they follow the deductive or direct strategy.

The content of a message and its anticipated effect on the reader determine the strategy you choose.

Direct Strategy

- Big idea first
- Details or explanation
- Closing thought

The routine business of an organization often involves three kinds of letters: (1) information requests, (2) order requests, and (3) claim requests. These three kinds of letters will be presented in this chapter. Each follows the direct strategy, but each has its own writing plan. Therefore, you will find three different writing plans in this chapter.

Information Requests

The first kind of letter to be described in this chapter is the information request. Although the specific subject of each inquiry may differ, the similarity of purpose in routine requests enables writers to use the following writing plan.

Writing Plan for an Information Request

- **Opening**—asks the most important question first, or expresses a polite command.

- **Body**—explains the request logically and courteously, and asks other questions.

- **Closing**—requests specific action with end date, if appropriate, and shows appreciation.

Opening Directly

Readers find the openings and closings of letters most interesting.

The most emphatic positions in a letter are the first and last sentences. Readers tend to look at them first. The writer, then, should capitalize upon this tendency by putting the most significant statement first. The first sentence of an information request is usually a question or a polite command. It should not be an explanation or justification, unless resistance to the request is expected. When the information requested is likely to be forthcoming, immediately tell the reader what you want. This saves the reader's time and may ensure that the message is read. A busy executive who skims the mail, quickly reading subject lines and first sentences only, may grasp your request rapidly and act upon it. A request that follows a lengthy explanation, on the other hand, may never be found. The following inquiry about a computer program gets off to a slow start.

> I read about the E-mail tax filing program in the June 5 issue of the *Calgary Herald*. Because I have a personal computer and because I have a business preparing tax returns primarily for construction contractors, I am very interested in this program. Would you please send me information about it.

The same request with the big idea first, expressed as a polite command, is far more effective because the reader knows immediately what is being requested.

> Please send me information about your E-mail tax filing program that was advertised in the *Calgary Herald* on June 5.

When a request demands exact information, the first sentence of the inquiry letter will probably be a question. For example:

> Will the E-mail tax filing program advertised in the *Calgary Herald* run on my computer? I have a 486 DX2 66 with 8 mb of RAM.

Open with a question when you seek specific information.

If several questions must be asked, use one of two approaches: ask the most important question first, or introduce the questions with a summary statement. The following example poses the most important question first, followed by other questions.

> Will the *Canadian Business* seminar at the Holiday Inn in Quebec City July 30 offer postsecondary credit? Please answer these additional questions:
>
> 1. How much of the total expense for this seminar is tax deductible?
> 2. If I make a reservation and then must cancel, may I receive a refund?

If you want to ask many questions that are equally important, begin with a summarizing statement.

> Will you please answer the following questions about the *Canadian Business* seminar in Quebec City.

Notice that the summarizing statement sounds like a question, but it has no question mark. That's because it's really a command disguised as a question. Rather than bluntly demanding information (*Answer the following questions*), we often prefer to soften commands by posing them as questions. Such statements (also called rhetorical questions) should not be punctuated as questions because they do not demand answers.

A rhetorical question is one for which no answer is expected.

Details in the Body

The body of a letter that requests information should provide necessary details. For example, if you want information about the type of printer that is appropriate for your personal computer, you must explain what kind of computer you have and what your requirements are. Requesting general information without specifying your exact demands may produce a general response that requires a second inquiry.

The body of a request letter may carry an explanation or a list of questions.

If a summarizing statement opens the letter, the body of your request may consist of a list of specific questions. Compare the two following methods of requesting information. The first is ineffective and generalized.

> I am interested in the cash value of my insurance policy. I am also thinking of borrowing against this policy. How do I do this? Also, a friend told me that if I didn't pay the premium, it would be automatically paid from the cash value of the policy. Is this true?

This second request asks the same questions but enumerates them.

> **1.** What is the current cash value of my insurance policy?
>
> **2.** What is the current loan value of this policy?
>
> **3.** What is the procedure for borrowing against this policy?

4. If I do not pay the policy premium, is it automatically paid from the policy's cash value?

Would you rather read items enumerated in a list or items bunched in a paragraph?

The enumerated request is more effective for these reasons: (1) each question stands by itself and is numbered, (2) each request is phrased as a question that requires a specific answer, and (3) each item is structured in parallel form so that the reader may anticipate and grasp its meaning quickly.

The quality of the information obtained from a request letter depends upon the clarity of the inquiry. If you analyze your needs, organize your ideas, and frame your request logically, you are likely to receive a meaningful answer.

Closing with an Action Request

The ending of a request letter should tell the reader what you want done and when.

Use the last paragraph to ask for specific action, to set an end date, if appropriate, and to express appreciation.

As you learned in working with memos, a request for action is most effective when an end date and reason for that date are supplied. If it's appropriate, use this kind of end dating:

> Please have your accountant fill out the enclosed survey and return it to me by February 15. This will help us update your file before you come in for your tax preparation.

It's always appropriate to end a request letter with appreciation for the action taken. However, don't fall into a cliché trap, such as *Thanking you in advance, I remain ...* or the familiar *Thank you for any information you can send me.* Your appreciation will sound most sincere if you avoid mechanical, tired expressions. Here's a simple but sincere closing to a request for insurance information:

> I would appreciate this information by July 10, when I will be re-evaluating my entire insurance program.

Illustrating the Plan

Appendix 1, p. 388, shows letter formats and styles.

The letter shown in Figure 6.1 requests information about conference accommodations and illustrates the writing plan you have learned. The writer has many questions to ask and begins with the most important one. The letter also illustrates block style, the most popular letter style.

Electronic Letters

The writing plan for making information requests is the same for E-mail letters as it is for nonelectronic letters (Figure 6.2). When using E-mail, you should keep in mind that your communication may not reach its destination because of a technological problem. Depending on the importance or urgency of your communication, you may choose to attach a request for immediate confirmation of receipt. You should also keep the following guidelines in mind when composing your E-mail messages.

Electronic letters should have a "signature" that provides important information about the sender.

▪ **Include an electronic "signature" with your Internet E-mail.** As shown in Figure 6.2, this signature provides important information about the sender. Try to restrict your signature to four or five lines.

one that we are going to use

← left margin

FIGURE 6.1 Letter That Requests Information—Block Style, Mixed Punctuation

R. KAPPER INDUSTRIES

Letterhead

255 Cherry Street
Corner Brook, NF
A2L 3W5

August 20, 19xx

Dateline

Ms. Jane Mangrum, Manager
Vancouver Hilton Hotel
6333 North Scottsdale Road
Vancouver, BC
V0H 1W4

Inside address

Dear Ms. Mangrum:

Salutation

Can the Vancouver Hilton provide meeting rooms and accommodations for about 250 Geotech sales representatives from May 25 through May 29?

Body

It is my responsibility to locate a hotel that offers both resort and conference facilities appropriate for the spring sales meeting of my company. Please answer these additional questions regarding the Vancouver Hilton:

1. Does the hotel have a banquet room that can seat 250?

2. Do you have at least four smaller meeting rooms, each to accommodate a maximum of 75?

3. Do you provide public address systems, audiovisual equipment, and ice water in each meeting room?

4. Do you offer special room rates for conferees?

5. Do you provide transportation to and from the airport?

I will be most grateful for answers to these questions and for any other information you can provide regarding your resort facilities. May I please have your response by September 1 so that I can meet with our planning committee September 4.

comma

Sincerely yours,

Complimentary close

Marlene Frederick

Marlene Frederick
Corporate Travel Department

Author's name

Identification

mef

Reference initials

Figure 6.2   E-mail Letter That Requests Information

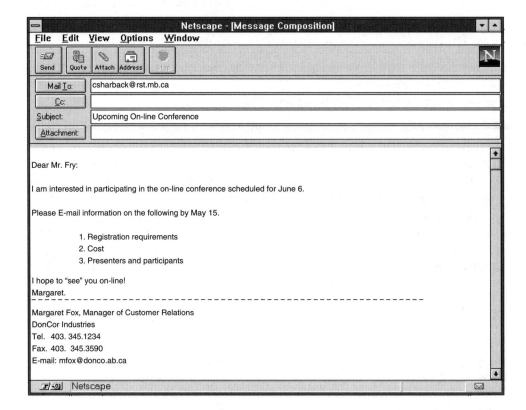

- **Don't assume an Internet audience will understand your cultural references.** Referring to a current hit television show or movie may not have meaning for international readers.

- **Avoid using words that rely on pronunciation for their meaning.** *Appropriate* can mean *seize* or *take hold of,* or it can mean *proper* or *suitable.*

- **Use acronyms with care.** Acronyms are often difficult for uninitiated readers to understand.

Order Requests

The second category of letter to be presented in this chapter is that of order requests. Orders for merchandise are usually made by telephone or by filling out an order form. On occasion, though, you may find it necessary to write a letter ordering merchandise. For example, if you had a merchandise catalogue but couldn't find its order forms, or if you were responding to an advertisement in a magazine, you'd have to write a letter to place an order.

Order requests use the direct strategy, beginning with the big idea.

Ordering merchandise may occasionally require a letter.

Writing Plan for an Order Request

- **Opening**—authorizes purchase and suggests method of shipping.

- **Body**—lists items vertically; provides quantity, order number, description, and unit price; and shows total price of order.

- **Closing**—requests shipment by a specific date, tells method of payment, and expresses appreciation.

Authorizing Purchase in the Opening

The first sentence of an order letter should authorize the purchase and shipment of merchandise. It should specify that the letter is an order and not a request for information. It should not be an explanation or an ambiguous expression of interest, such as *I was fascinated by your advertisement describing your digital camera;* nor should an order letter begin, *I certainly liked my friend's solar calculator and would like to have one for myself.* These two examples give no indication that the letter is intended to place an order. They leave the reader wondering about the intent and purpose of the writer.

A more effective opening begins with specific order language, such as *Please send me.* The opening should also tell how the order is to be shipped, unless you have no preference, and may include the source of the information for the order. This opening sentence leaves no doubt about the intent of the letter:

Please send by courier the following items listed in your 1997 price list.

Let the reader know immediately that your letter is an order and not a request for information.

Listing Items in the Body

If you are ordering more than one item, list them vertically rather than describing them in a paragraph. Include as much of the following information as possible: quantity, order number, complete description, unit price, and total price. Here's an example of a vertical order list for several items:

2	No. 9A57313 ionization smoke alarms @ $24.99	$49.98
2	No. 9A5709 Diehard 9-volt batteries @ 2.39	4.78
1	No. 9A58031 Zytel fire extinguisher @ 51.99	51.99
1	No. 9A58051 heavy-duty mounting bracket @ 3.99	3.99
	Subtotal	$110.74
	GST and PST	14.20
	Estimated shipping costs	4.50
	Total	129.44

Closing with Specifics

In closing an order letter, tell how you plan to pay for the shipment. Since shipping costs may be unknown, some individuals prefer to provide a credit-card number so that the order can be shipped immediately. Organizations may have credit agreements that allow the manufacturer to ship goods without prior payment.

End an order letter by stating how you plan to pay for the merchandise and when you expect to receive it.

In addition to including payment information, the closing of an order letter should indicate when the goods should be sent (end dating) and may express appreciation. Observe how the following closing achieves this goal:

> We would appreciate your sending these items before May 5. Please bill us at our usual terms of 2/10, n/30.

The term *2/10, n/30* means that a 2-percent discount will be given if the invoice is paid within 10 days; the total bill (net) is due in 30 days.

Order Letters That Succeed and Fail

The ineffective order letter shown in Figure 6.3 is faulty for many reasons. Its opening is too general, failing to show that the letter authorizes the purchase of goods. The first sentence is also 46 words long, making its meaning difficult to comprehend. Most sentences should average 15 to 20 words. In addition, this letter does not describe sufficiently the items being ordered, and it fails to mention a method of payment.

An improved version of this order letter (Figure 6.4) begins with specific order language, itemizes and describes the goods clearly, includes shipping and payment information, and closes with an end date.

This letter illustrates modified block style, second only to block (page 117) style in popularity. Notice that in modified block style, the date and closing lines begin approximately at the centre of the page. Notice, too, that this letter uses a company name in its closing. When included in the closing lines, company names are typed in capital letters and are double-spaced below the complimentary close.

FIGURE 6.3   Poor Order Letter

Uses outdated salutation.	Dear Sirs:
Fails to use order language.	My company has never been able to find a way to print our business cheques using our own computer system, but I notice in your catalogue that just arrived in the mail that you have cheque forms that are compatible with a number of computers.
Lacks sufficient description of goods.	I would be interested in 500 multipurpose cheques at the price listed in the catalogue. I am also interested in your multipurpose microcomputer forms for invoices. These are listed at 500 for $36.79.
Omits method of payment and end date.	May I have these items at your convenience.
	Sincerely,

middle

FIGURE 6.3   Improved Order Letter—Modified Block Style,
Mixed Punctuation

sender

❖ DUXLER SHEET METAL FABRICATION, INC. ❖
102 INSTER INDUSTRIAL PARK
WINNIPEG, MB R3L 2E7

January 24, 199x

Quill Corporation
P.O. Box 4700
Halifax, NS
B4L 2E2

Ladies and Gentlemen:

SUBJECT: ORDER FOR COMPUTER CHEQUE FORMS AND INVOICES

Please courier the following items shown in your April sale catalogue:

500 No. 202-82411-1 cheques for the Turbo-PC	$61.14
500 No. 292-85011 invoice forms for the Turbo-PC	36.79
Subtotal	97.93
GST	6.85
Total	$104.78

I would appreciate your prompt handling of this order so that we may
have these forms by February 10. The enclosed cheque for $109.53
includes shipping costs of $4.75. If there are additional charges, please
bill my company.

> This order letter
> includes all the
> elements necessary
> for a successful
> transaction.

Sincerely,

DUXLER SHEET METAL FABRICATION, INC.

Melba Herrick

Melba Herrick
Vice-President

jf
Enclosure

Simple Claim Requests

The third category of letters to be presented in this chapter is that of simple claim requests. A claim is a demand for something that is due or is believed to be due. A simple claim is one to which the writer believes the reader will agree—or *should* agree. For example, a purchaser has a legitimate claim for warrantied products that fail, for goods that are promised but not delivered, for damaged products, or for poor service. When the writer feels that the claim is justified and that persuasion is not required, a claim request should follow the direct strategy.

The direct strategy is best for simple claims that require no persuasion.

Writing Plan for a Simple Claim

▪ **Opening**—describes clearly the desired action.

▪ **Body**—explains the nature of the claim, tells why the claim is justified, and provides details regarding action requested.

▪ **Closing**—ends pleasantly with good-will statement, and includes end dating, if appropriate.

Opening with Action

Start with a clear statement of the action you want taken.

In a simple claim request, tell the reader immediately what action you would like taken. Such directness may appear to be blunt, but actually it's businesslike and efficient. Don't begin a claim letter with an attempt to establish good will or an explanation, such as this one:

> We've used Pentack tools for years and have always appreciated the quality product that you produce and the prompt service that we have received when we placed our orders.

Save the explanation for the body and the good will for the closing. Tell the reader what you want in the opening sentence:

> Please send us two 1-cm socket sets to replace the two 0.75-cm sets sent with our order shipped October 23.

With this direct opening, the reader knows what you want and can read the remainder of the letter in the proper context.

Justifying in the Body

Explain the reasons that justify your claim without becoming angry or emotional.

Here's where you explain why you feel your claim is justified. Provide the necessary details so that the problem can be rectified without misunderstanding. Avoid the tendency to fix blame. Instead of saying *You failed to send the items we ordered*, describe the situation objectively. Omit negative or angry words that offend the reader and may prevent compliance with your claim.

An objective explanation of the reason for replacing merchandise could read as follows:

How to Approach the Salutation Dilemma

Letters usually begin with a salutation, a greeting to the reader. This greeting is included to personalize a letter. If the name of the individual receiving the letter is known, the salutation is *Dear Kevin* or *Dear Mr. Diegues* or *Dear Mrs. Hayden*. But what should be used when no name is known? The salutation dilemma perplexes many writers today. In the past, we used *Dear Sirs* or *Gentlemen* to address an organization and *Dear Sir* for anonymous individuals. With increasing diversity in the workplace and a new sensitivity to the power of language, writers are avoiding the masculine salutations of the past.

What are the alternatives? Whenever possible, use the name of the individual to whom you're writing. Just how much of the name should you use in the salutation? Generally, include only a courtesy title and the last name: *Dear Ms. Jones*. Include the entire name only if gender is uncertain and you cannot decide on the title: *Dear Leslie Jones*.

When no name is available and you are addressing organizations with men and women in management, it is acceptable to use *Ladies and Gentlemen*.

One way to sidestep the salutation dilemma altogether is to use the simplified letter style exemplified in Figure 6.6. In this letter style, the salutation is omitted.

On October 10 we placed a telephone order requesting, among other things, two 1-cm socket sets. However, when the order arrived yesterday, we noted that two 0.75-cm socket sets had been sent. Because we cannot use that size, we are returning the 0.75-cm sets by courier.

This unemotional presentation of the facts is more effective in achieving the writer's goal than an angry complaint.

After you have presented the circumstances of your claim objectively, you may wish to suggest alternatives to solving the problem; for example, *If it is impossible to send 1-cm socket sets, please credit my account*. When goods are being returned, you should inquire about the proper procedure. Some companies will allow returns only with prior authorization.

Closing Pleasantly

End the claim letter pleasantly with an effort toward maintaining good will. If appropriate, include a date by which you want the claim satisfied.

We realize that mistakes in ordering and shipping sometimes occur. Because we've been impressed by your prompt delivery in the past, we hope that you will be able to send the 1-cm socket sets to us by November 1.

Effective and Ineffective Claim Letters

The claim letter shown in Figure 6.5 is unlikely to achieve its goal. In demanding that a tire warranty be honoured, the writer fails to provide sufficient information. The account of what happened to the tire is incoherent, and the reader is not made fully aware of what action the writer wants. In addition, the tone of the letter is angry and harsh.

An improved version of the letter takes a different tone and approach. In the first sentence, this improved letter (Figure 6.6) forthrightly asks for a refund under the tire warranty. The letter includes an unemotional, logical explanation of the problem. Its rational tone and sensible expression are more appealing to the reader, who needs to understand the problem before the organization can resolve it.

FIGURE 6.5   Angry, Ineffective Claim Letter

Gentlemen:

Begins with emotional, illogical, unclear demand.

What good is a warranty if it's not honoured? I don't agree with your dealer that the damage to my tire was caused by "road hazards." This tire was defective, and I am entitled to a refund.

Provides inadequate explanation of what happened.

My company purchased a GasSaver tire September 5, and it had been driven only 14,000 kilometres when a big bubble developed in its side. The gas station attendant said that its tread had separated from its body. But the dealer where my company bought it (Harbour Tire Company) refused to give us a refund. The dealer said that the damage was caused by "road hazards." They also said that they never make refunds, only replacements.

Ends with threat instead of an attempt to establish goodwill.

My company has always purchased GasSaver tires, but you can be sure that this is our last. Unless we get the refund to which we are rightfully entitled, I intend to spread the word about how we were treated.

Yours truly,

The improved letter shown in Figure 6.6 illustrates the simplified letter style. As with block style, all lines begin at the left margin. Notice, however, that the salutation is replaced by a subject line in capitals. The complimentary close is omitted, and the writer's name and identification appear on one line in capital letters. Some writers prefer this streamlined style because it eliminates the problem of choosing an appropriate salutation for the receiver.

The claim letter shown in Figure 6.7 seeks permission to return a microcomputer to the manufacturer for repair. Normally, repairs are made locally,

FIGURE 6.6   Simple Claim Letter—Simplified Style

R. KAPPER INDUSTRIES

255 Cherry Street
Corner Brook, NF
A2L 3W5

March 4, 199x

Goodday Tire Manufacturers
770 Broad Street
Fredericton, NB
E1W 4Y5

WARRANTY REFUND ON GASSAVER TIRE

Please honour the warranty and issue a refund for one GasSaver radial
tire that was purchased for my company car at Harbour Tire Company on
September 5.

This whitewall tire cost $109.13 and carried a warranty for 50,000 km.
It had only 14,000 km of wear when trouble developed. On a business
trip to St. John's recently, I noticed that the tire made a strange sound.
When I stopped the car and inspected the tire, it had an ugly bulge
protruding from its rim. A service station attendant said that the tread
had separated from the tire body. I was forced to purchase a replacement
tire at considerably more than the price we paid for the GasSaver tire.

When I returned the GasSaver tire to Harbour, they would not honour the
warranty. They said the tire was damaged by "road hazards" and that
refunds could not be made.

My company generally purchases GasSaver tires, and we have been
pleased with their quality and durability. Enclosed are copies of the sales
invoice and the tire warranty for the tire in question. Also enclosed is a
receipt showing that the defective tire was returned to Harbour Tire
Company.

I am confident that you will honour my request for a refund of the
purchase price of $109.13 prorated for 14,000 km of wear.

Ron Kapper

RON KAPPER, PRESIDENT

eha

Enclosures

Simplified style uses
subject line but no
salutation.

Provides rational,
coherent,
explanation.

Ends courteously
with specific request
for action.

Simplified style omits
complimentary
close.

but this computer defies diagnosis. The letter writer does not angrily blame the local dealer for ineptness or criticize the manufacturer for producing a faulty product. Instead, the letter cleverly invites the manufacturer to help solve a "mystery." Notice that the letter opens by asking for instructions on how to return the computer rather than by asking for permission to return the computer. The request for shipping instructions suggests the writer's confidence that the manufacturer will want to do the right thing and repair the malfunctioning computer. This personal letter is shown with the return address typed above the date. Use this style when typing on paper without a preprinted letterhead.

FIGURE 6.7 Simple Claim Letter—Modified Block Style, Mixed Punctuation

Return address is typed above address.	23956 Hamlin Street Ottawa, ON K3W 2H5 August 14, 199x

CompuCap, Inc.
2308 Borregas Avenue
Toronto, ON
M5W 3L3

Ladies and Gentlemen:

SUBJECT: RETURN OF MALFUNCTIONING COMPUCAP 2-X

Opens confidently requesting instructions for return of computer.

Please tell me how I may return my malfunctioning CompuCap 2-X microcomputer to you for repair.

Describes malfunction coherently.

I am sure you will be able to solve a problem that puzzles my local dealer. After about 45 minutes of normal activity, the screen on my 2-X computer suddenly becomes filled with a jumble of meaningless letters, numbers, and symbols. Computers For You, the dealer from whom I purchased my 2-X, seems to be unable to locate or correct the malfunction.

Closes pleasantly with assurance that manufacturer will want to do the right thing.

Although I am expected to have my computer serviced locally, my dealer has been unable to repair it. I am confident that you can solve the mystery and that you will repair my 2-X quickly.

Sincerely yours,

Carole Eustace

(Mrs.) Carole Eustice

Summary

Letters deliver messages outside an organization and are generally of three types: information letters, requests, and responses. As with memos, the organization that you choose for a letter depends on the effect you expect your message will have on the reader.

A letter of request opens directly with a question. Continue in the body of your message with either an explanation or additional questions enumerated in a list. Close your letter by telling the reader what you want done and provide an end date for the action.

When ordering merchandise, begin by authorizing purchase and shipment of the goods you are ordering. Show the reader immediately that you are ordering. List the items you want in the body and close by stating how you plan to pay and when you expect to receive the goods.

A simple claim letter usually calls for direct organization, especially if no persuasion is required. Start with a clear statement of the action you want taken, explain the reasons that justify your claim without expressing anger, and close pleasantly with an effort to maintain good will.

APPLICATION AND PRACTICE—6

Discussion

1. How are letters like memos? How are they different?

2. Why should routine letters, such as inquiries and orders, follow the direct strategy?

3. Which is more effective in claim letters—anger or objectivity? Defend your position.

4. Why should the writer of a claim letter offer alternatives for solving the problem?

5. The quality of the information obtained from a request depends upon the clarity of the inquiry. Discuss.

6. What should a sender consider including in an E-mail request?

Short Answers

7. List three reasons for exchanging business information in letter form rather than in oral form.

8. When a request seeks exact information, the first sentence of the inquiry letter will probably be what?

9. Consider the situations below. Which strategy would be most effective? Write *Direct* or *Indirect* to indicate your choice.

   _____ **a.** You need information about skiing equipment advertised in a magazine.

   _____ **b.** You want to convince your boss to change your assigned work schedule.

   _____ **c.** You want a replacement for a defective CD player, still under warranty, that you ordered by mail.

   _____ **d.** You want to find out how much it costs to rent a houseboat in the Lake of the Woods region for you and your family.

   _____ **e.** As credit manager of a department store, you must tell a customer that he has been denied credit.

   _____ **f.** You wish to order merchandise from a catalogue.

10. What are the two most emphatic positions in a letter? *opening / closing position*

11. What is the most popular letter style? *Block style.*

12. List two ways that you could begin an inquiry letter that asks many questions.

13. What is an enumerated request?

14. What three elements are appropriate in the closing of a request for information?

15. The first sentence of an order letter should include what information?

16. The closing of an order letter should include what information?

Writing Improvement Exercises

Routine Request Openers.   Revise the following openers from routine request letters so that they are more direct.

17. I am interested in your rental rates for a three-bedroom cabin on Lac St. Jean in August.

18. The Hi-Sound stereo set that I ordered from you has arrived, and it seems to have a problem in the amplifier. I'm wondering if you can tell me where I may take it for repair.

19. Your spring sale catalogue shows a number of items in which I am interested. I would like the following items.

Order Request Letter. Analyze the following poorly written order letter and respond to the questions following it.

Gentlemen:

I need an electronic organizer called The Communicator shown in your fall catalogue. Its catalogue number is 3G5301C and it costs $599.95. This includes the carrying case and port connector for my PC, but I would like to add some other features, including an extra battery (No. 3G54012) and adapter cord (No. 3G54014). Each of these items costs $36.99. I'll need a SCSI adapter as well (No. 3G5455) at $86.99. I'll pay for this with MasterCard; I need everything by September 1.

20. What does the opening lack?

21. Write an appropriate opening for this order letter.

22. How would you group the order information so that it is orderly and logical? Name five headings you could use.

23. Write an appropriate closing for this order request.

Letter Format. Read about letter formats and parts in Appendix 1 (page 000). Then answer the following questions.

24. If you are typing a letter for yourself on plain paper, what items appear above the date?

25. How is simplified letter style different from block style, and why do some writers prefer simplified style?

26. In what two places could an attention line be typed?

27. If you write a letter to Data General Corporation, what salutation would be appropriate?

28. When letters are addressed to individuals, should their names always contain a courtesy title, such as Mr., Ms., Miss, or Mrs.?

CASE 6–1

Information Request

Assume that you are Mrs. Stephanie Jones. Based on an ad that you saw in a magazine, you wish to write to Mary Shimano, Manager, Garden Court Rentals, Inn-by-the-Sea, Box 45, Qualicum, British Columbia V7K 3B3. You want information about renting a two-bedroom condominium with an ocean view. You'd like to be there from July 17 through July 25, which is the time of the Qualicum Beach Festival. You'll need accommodations for three (you, your husband, and your daughter). You're interested in having kitchen utensils, dishes, and bedding. Both you and your husband are interested in nearby golf courses, and your daughter wants to know how close the beach is. You'll need to know what time you can arrive July 17 and how much the rental fee is. You'd like this information by April 1 so that you can complete your summer plans.

Before writing the letter, answer the following questions:

1. What should you include in the opening of an information request?

2. What should the body of your letter contain?

3. How should you close the letter?

4. What is the most important question Mrs. Jones has to ask?

5. How can the other questions be handled effectively?

On a separate sheet, write the letter. Use modified block style, and write on plain paper. Be sure to include your return address above the date. (See Appendix 1, page 394.)

CASE 6-2

Claim Request

Play the role of Raj Bellary. On June 24, your company had the basement walls of its office building insulated with Modac II, an acrylic coating. This sealant was applied to reduce heat loss in the basement so that you could store company files in this area. The contractor, Peter Muscarelli, promised that this product would effectively seal the walls and reduce heat loss, as well as prevent peeling, chalking, and colour fading for many years. He said that if you had any trouble, he might have to give it a second coat. After several cold days in September, you realized that the walls of the basement were not insulated completely, making it necessary for you to remove the files stored there. Write a claim letter to Mr. Muscarelli asking that he correct the situation. Let him know that you want the basement effectively sealed by October 30 because cold winter temperatures usually begin in November.

To help you organize your letter according to the principles you studied in this chapter, read the following suggestions and circle the most appropriate responses. Be prepared to discuss each of the possible responses that follow.

1. To open this letter directly, you might

   a. Remind Mr. Muscarelli that he recommended Modac II and that it just wasn't doing the job.
   b. Describe your disappointment in the ineffectiveness of Modac II and angrily demand that Mr. Muscarelli repeat this job and do it right this time.
   c. Ask Mr. Muscarelli to apply a second coat of Modac II to the basement walls of your company to prevent heat loss.
   d. Review chronologically the beginning of this project and your initial dealings with Mr. Muscarelli.

2. The body of this letter would probably

   a. Review the sealing process and your understanding of how you expected Modac II to insulate your walls.
   b. Threaten to sue if Mr. Muscarelli doesn't rectify this matter immediately.
   c. Explain that the June 24 coat was ineffective and that Mr. Muscarelli promised to apply a second coat if necessary.
   d. Blame Mr. Muscarelli for doing a poor job and specify clearly what he must do to satisfy your claim.

3. The closing of this letter should

   a. Explain when and why you want the second coat applied, and express appreciation for Mr. Muscarelli's efforts to keep your basement warm.
   b. Summarize all your dealings with Mr. Muscarelli and reiterate your dissatisfaction with Modac II and with his workmanship as well.

c. Tell Mr. Muscarelli that you need this storage space badly and that you'd like to use it as soon as possible.

d. Thank Mr. Muscarelli for his past work and express confidence that he will do the right thing for your company.

Use this letter for class discussion, or write the entire letter on a separate sheet to Mr. Peter Muscarelli, 5807 Thompson Drive, Thompson, Manitoba R5L 2E6. Add any information that you feel is necessary. Assume that you are writing this letter on letterhead stationery. Use block style. (See Appendix 1, page 391.)

CASE 6–3

Order Request

Analyze the following ineffective request for merchandise. List at least five faults. Outline a writing plan (opening, body, closing) for an order request. Then, on a separate sheet, rewrite this request. Use modified block style, and place your return address above the date. Send the letter to Cameratone, Inc., 140 Northern Boulevard, Swift Current, Saskatchewan S3R 2T5. Add any necessary information.

Dear Sir:

I saw a number of items in your summer/fall catalogue that would fit my Lentax M3 camera. I am particularly interested in your Super Zoom 55-200-mm lens. Its number is SP39971, and it costs $139.95. To go with this lens I will need a polarizing filter. Its number is EKF29032 and costs $22.95 and should fit a 52-mm lens. Also include a 05CC magenta filter for a 52-mm lens. That number is SF29036 and it costs $9.95. Please send also a Hikemaster camera case for $24.95. Its number is SF28355.

I am interested in having these items charged to my credit card. I'd sure like to get them quickly because my vacation starts soon.

Sincerely,

CASE 6–4

Personal Order

Write a letter ordering items advertised in a magazine, newspaper, or catalogue. Assume that no order form is available. Attach the advertisement to your letter. Be sure to use an appropriate letter style for a personal business letter.

CASE 6–5

Personal Routine Claim

Write a routine claim letter for a product or service you have purchased. Assume that the product or service required a claim to the dealer or manufacturer because the product was defective or the service was not what you expected. Use a situation where you can reasonably expect the manufacturer to honour your claim.

Additional Problems

1. Assume that you are Marc Vannault, manager of a health spa and also an ardent backpacker. You are organizing a group of hikers for a wilderness trip to the Yukon. One item that must be provided is freeze-dried food for the three-week trip. You are unhappy with the taste and quality of backpacking food products currently available. You expect to have a group of hikers who are older, affluent, and natural-food enthusiasts. Some are concerned about products containing preservatives, sugar, and additives. Others are on diets restricting cholesterol and salt. You heard that Rocky Mountain High, Box 51, Canmore, Alberta T0L 2P2, offers a new line of freeze-dried products. You want to know what they offer and if they have sufficient variety to serve all the needs of your group. You need to know where their products can be purchased and the range of cost. You'd also like to try a few of their items before placing a large order. You are interested in how they produce the food products and what kind of ingredients they use. If you have any items left over, you wonder how long they can be kept and still be usable. Write an inquiry letter to Rocky Mountain High.

2. Play the role of Lisa Chan, assistant vice-president, Bank of Nova Scotia. You have been given the responsibility of developing an employee suggestion program for the bank, which employs over 15,000 workers in Ontario. You have done some research and have collected helpful ideas, but now you'd like to gather reactions from an organization with firsthand experience. A friend suggested that you write to Bill Antayac, Director, Employee Development Division, Stel-Can Steel Inc., P.O. Box 25438, Hamilton, Ontario L2N 1L4. Stel-Can implemented a suggestion program three years ago, and Mr. Antayac has indicated that he would be happy to share details of how successful the company's employee suggestion program has been. You are interested in the way the program works. You need to know how employees are encouraged to participate, how they submit their suggestions, who evaluates them, and what kind of awards are made. You wonder if suggestions should go to supervisors or local administrators first, or if they should go directly to an evaluation committee. You are concerned about legal problems. Also, should you have minimum and maximum awards? You wonder if you must respond to every suggestion. What if an employee protests the decisions of the evaluation committee? You have many questions, but you realize that you can't burden Mr.

Antayac with all of them. However, he was reported to be quite enthusiastic about employee suggestion programs. Write an inquiry letter to him.

3. You are Greg Fontecilla, manager, Datatronics, Inc. You want to order some items from an office supply catalogue, but your catalogue is not the most recent one and you have lost the order form. You're in a hurry. Rather than write for a new catalogue, you decide to take a chance and order items from the old catalogue (fall 1996), realizing that prices may be somewhat different. You want three Panasonic electric pencil sharpeners, Item 22-A, at $39.95 each. You want one steel desktop organizer, 150 cm long, Item No. 23-K. Its price is $137.50. Order two Roll-a-Flex files for 5- by 10-cm cards at $18.50 each. This is Item 23-G. The next item is No. 29-H, file folders, box of 100, letter size, at $8.29. You need ten boxes. You would like to be invoiced for this purchase, and you prefer courier delivery. Even though the current prices may be somewhat higher, you decide to list the prices shown in your catalogue so that you have an idea of what the total order will cost. Write a letter to Blackfield's Discount Office Furniture, 2890 Post Road, Yorkton, Saskatchewan S5L 2R3.

4. Assume that you are Monique Giraud, president, Sure Tech Security. Six months ago Visual Services, Inc., produced a promotional video for your firm, which manufactures security control systems. The video was a great success when you featured it at a recent sales convention. You plan to run the video at an upcoming event but have just discovered that the single copy you were provided with is missing. Your contract states that there is a $10 fee for each replacement copy. You are reluctant to pay this fee because you recently found out that it is standard practice among video producers to provide clients with multiple copies at no extra charge. In addition, according to the contract, you were entitled to *two* copies at the outset. Visual Services provided only one. You would like two copies of the video and feel that all fees should be waived. Write to Dave Windton, Business Manager, Visual Services, Inc., 359 Western Road, Vancouver, British Columbia V8N 1L3.

5. Assume that you are Sandra Fenwick, president of Fenwick Consulting Services. Since your consulting firm is doing very well, you decided to splurge and purchase a fine executive desk for your own office. You ordered an expensive desk described as "Canadian white oak embellished with hand-inlaid walnut cross-banding." Although you would not ordinarily purchase large, expensive items by mail, you were impressed by the description of this desk and by the money-back guarantee promised in the catalogue. When the desk arrived, you knew that you had made a mistake. The wood finish was rough, the grain looked uneven, and many of the drawers would not pull out easily. The advertisement had promised "full suspension, silent ball-bearing drawer slides." You are disappointed with the desk and decide to send it back, taking advantage of the money-back guarantee. You want your money refunded. You're not sure whether they will refund the freight charges, but it's worth a try. Supply any details needed. Write a letter to Nova Scotia Wood Products, P.O. Box 488, Sydney, Nova Scotia B1W 4E6.

6. Assume that you are Paul Friedman, purchase manager, Datatronics, Inc., 2569 Church Street, Merritt, British Columbia V5N 2E9. You purchased for your company two Ever-Cool window air conditioners, Model D-2, Serial Nos. 38920 and 38921. One of the units, Serial No. 38920, is not working properly. It worked when it first arrived, but after two weeks it is malfunctioning. The compressor comes on and off from time to time, but the room does not cool down or remain cool. Perhaps the thermostat is the problem. The control knob is also defective. You would not normally mention such a small matter, but since the entire unit needs repair, it seems worth mentioning the control knob, too. No service representative is convenient to you in the Merritt area. You have a six-month warranty. How can this unit be repaired? It's very warm in Merritt at this time of the year, and employees are complaining about the lack of air conditioning. Write a claim letter and send a copy of your sales invoice and warranty to Ever-Cool Manufacturing Company, 951 Lawrence Drive, Toronto, Ontario M2W 4R6.

GRAMMAR/MECHANICS CHECKUP—6

Commas, 1

Review Sections 2.01 through 2.04 of the Grammar/Mechanics Handbook. Then study each of the following statements and insert necessary commas. In the space provided for each statement, write the number of commas that you add; write *0* if no commas are needed. Also record the number of the G/M principle illustrated. When you finish, compare your responses with those shown below. If your answers differ, study carefully the principles shown in parentheses.

Example:　In this class students learn to write business letters, memos, and reports clearly and concisely.　　　　　　　　　　　　　　　　<u>　2　(2.01)　</u>

1. We do not as a rule allow employees to take time off for dental appointments.　　　　　　<u>　　　　　</u>

2. You may be sure Mrs. Schwartz that your car will be ready by 4 p.m.　　　　　　<u>　　　　　</u>

3. Anyone who is reliable conscientious and honest should be very successful.　　　　　　<u>　　　　　</u>

4. A conference on sales motivation is scheduled for May 5 at the Montreal Marriott Hotel beginning at 2 p.m.　　　　　　<u>　　　　　</u>

5. As a matter of fact I just called your office this morning.　　　　　　<u>　　　　　</u>

6. We are relocating our distribution centre from Windsor Ontario to Winnipeg Manitoba.　　　　　　<u>　　　　　</u>

7. In the meantime please continue to address your orders to your regional office.　　　　　　<u>　　　　　</u>

8. The last meeting recorded in the minutes is shown on February 4 1990 in Charlottetown.　　　　　　<u>　　　　　</u>

9. Mr. Silver Mrs. Feldberg and Ms. Esfahan have been selected as our representatives.　　　　　　<u>　　　　　</u>

10. The package mailed to Ms. Leslie Holmes 3430 Larkspur Lane Regina Saskatchewan S5L 2E2 arrived three weeks after it was mailed.　　　　　　<u>　　　　　</u>

11. The manager feels needless to say that the support of all employees is critical.　　　　　　<u>　　　　　</u>

12. Eric was assigned three jobs: checking supplies replacing inventories and distributing delivered goods.　　　　　　<u>　　　　　</u>

13. We will work diligently to retain your business Mr. Fuhai.　　　　　　<u>　　　　　</u>

14. The vice-president feels however that all sales representatives need training.　　　　　　<u>　　　　　</u>

15. The name selected for a product should be right for that product and should emphasize its major attributes.　　　　　　<u>　　　　　</u>

---

1. (2) not, rule, (2.03)　3. (2) reliable, conscientious, (2.01)　5. (1) fact, (2.03)　7. (1) meantime, (2.03)　9. (2) Silver, Feldberg, (2.01)　11. (2) feels, say, (2.03)　13. (1) business, (2.02)　15. (0)

GRAMMAR/MECHANICS CHALLENGE—6

Document for Revision

The following letter contains faults in grammar, punctuation, spelling, and number form, in addition to problems discussed in this chapter. Drawing upon the guidelines provided in the Grammar/Mechanics Handbook and what you learned in the chapter, revise the letter. Then, correct the errors.

Poor Letter

March 3, 199x

Ms. Susan Petishen, Manager
Customer Service Department
Steel Cabinets, Inc.
Calgary, AB
T2L 4F3

Dear Ms. Petishen:

Please rush a shipment of twenty-three No. 36-440 verticle file cabinets to us, to replace those damaged in transit recently.

We appreciate you filling our order for 100 of these file cabinets as shown on the accompanying Invoice. Twenty-three of them however were damaged in transit and cannot be sold in there present condition. Because of the fact that 2 transit companies handled the shipment of the file cabinets we cannot determine whom is responsable for the damage

These verticle files were featured in our newspaper add and we expect to sell a good many in our presale which is scheduled to begin 3/15. Therefore we would appreciate you rushing these cabinets by Red Dog Freight before 3/12. Moreover please let us know what should be done with the damaged cabinets.

Sincerely,

Letters That Respond Positively

In this chapter, you will learn to do the following:

- Apply the direct strategy in letters that respond positively.
- Write clear and efficient letters and memos that deliver information.
- Promote good will in acknowledging order requests.
- Grant claims efficiently and effectively.

Letters that respond positively bring good news to the reader. They answer requests for information and action, they acknowledge orders, and they agree to claims. These letters deliver positive news that the reader expects and wants. Therefore, they follow the direct strategy with the big idea first.

Deliver good news early in a response letter.

Responding to Information Requests

Applying the direct strategy to replies for information results in the following writing plan:

Writing Plan for an Information Response

- **Subject line**—identifies previous correspondence.
- **Opening**—delivers the most important information first.
- **Body**—arranges information in a logical sequence, explains and clarifies, provides additional information, and builds good will.
- **Closing**—ends pleasantly.

Subject-Line Efficiency

Use the subject line to refer to previous correspondence.

Although it's not mandatory, a subject line is useful in responding to requests. It allows the writer to identify quickly and efficiently the previous correspondence, and it reminds the reader of the request. By putting identifying information in a subject line, the writer reserves the first sentence (the most important location in a letter) for the big idea. Here's an effective subject line that responds to a request for interest information:

> SUBJECT: YOUR JULY 2 LETTER ABOUT INTEREST RATES ON
>   SAVINGS

Opening Strength

Reveal immediately what the reader expects to learn.

As the most emphatic position in the letter, the first sentence should carry the most important information. A response to an inquiry about the current interest rate on a customer's savings plan would reveal the rate immediately:

> The current interest rate on our Golden Passbook savings account is 3 percent.

Compare the preceding direct opening with the following indirect opening:

> We have received your letter of July 17 requesting information regarding interest rates on our savings programs.

If you are responding to a number of questions, use one of two approaches. The most direct approach is to answer the most important question in the first sentence. Other answers may be supplied in the body of the letter. For example, the following response to a complex request with many questions begins directly:

> Yes, the *Canadian Accounting* seminar at the Holiday Inn in Toronto July 30 will offer postsecondary credits from York University.

A less direct approach starts with a summary statement that shows the reader you are complying with the request:

> Here is the information you requested about the *Canadian Accounting* seminar at the Holiday Inn in Toronto on July 30.

Then, answers to the questions are contained in the body of the letter.

Either of these two approaches is superior to the familiar openings *Thank you for your letter of ...* or *I have received your letter asking for ...* These openings are indirect, overworked, and obvious. Stating that you received the customer's letter is superfluous, because you are answering it.

Logic in the Body

Give explanations and additional information in the body of a letter that responds to an information request, if necessary. If you are answering a number of questions or providing considerable data, arrange your information logically. It may be possible to enumerate information, as shown in this response to the inquiry about the *Canadian Accounting* seminar:

1. The seminar is authorized to offer three credits from York University.

2. Because the seminar helps participants maintain or improve professional skills, the total cost (fees, travel, meals, lodging) is tax deductible.

3. Reservations cancelled less than five working days prior to the seminar are subject to a $25 service charge.

If your responses require more explanation, devote an entire paragraph to each.

In answering request letters, you have an opportunity to build good will toward yourself and for your organization by offering additional advice or data. Don't confine your response to the questions presented. If you recognize that other facts would be helpful, present them. For example, if a special rate applies for a seminar participant who registers early, include that information. If a customer asks many questions about a printer for a computer but neglects to ask its price, you might include pricing data. If a student inquires about a course of study at your college, you could include answers to the particular questions as well as information about career possibilities in the field.

> Provide extra information if you think it would be helpful.

Personalized Closing

To avoid abruptness, include a pleasant closing remark that shows your willingness to help the reader. Tailor your remarks to fit *this* letter and *this* reader. Since everyone appreciates being recognized as an individual, avoid form-letter closings such as *If we may be of any further assistance, do not hesitate to call upon us.*

> Readers appreciate personalized remarks instead of all-purpose form-letter language.

Your interest in our bank's savings programs is appreciated. You can stop in to discuss them with our customer service representative, Judy Gustafson, any time between 9 a.m. and 4 p.m. Monday to Friday.

Just call me at 899-3032 if you need additional information about the *Canadian Business* seminar July 30 in Toronto.

Good luck in your survey of computer software programs. I hope that my answers contribute to the accuracy and completeness of your results.

Good and Bad Responses to Information Requests

The letter shown in Figure 7.1 is a reply to a bank that has requested information from an insurance company about a customer's policy that is about to be assigned to the bank. Since the insurance company does business with the bank and is able to supply the information, the response should be direct. However, the approach in this letter is indirect.

This letter suffers from a number of weaknesses. It begins poorly with *Dear Sir*, a salutation that is dated, impersonal, and perhaps offensive to some readers. It's always better to address the reader by name. This should be easy to do because the inquiry letter was probably signed. Beyond the salutation, the first paragraph is indirect and wordy. Much of this information could be handled efficiently in a subject line. The body of this letter presents in narrative form information that would be easier to read if it were enumerated. The letter makes no effort to develop good will, and the closing is meaningless.

> A poor letter demonstrates what to avoid in responding to an information request.

Ineffective writing

FIGURE 7.1   Poor Information Response Letter

Dear Sir:

Wastes the reader's time by stating the obvious.

I have before me your bank's request dated November 5 in which you ask about the insurance policy of Patrick Beckett. His policy number is 230-38-6958M. This request has been referred to my attention, and I am happy to supply herewith the information you request.

Presents information in disorganized manner.

Mr. Beckett's policy has an approximate cash value of $15,500 as of September 1 of this year. According to our records, no liens exist against this policy at this time. On June 1 and again on January 1 of each year the policy has premium due dates.

We do not know of any contingent beneficiaries that would preclude assignment of this policy to your bank.

Closes with overworked, meaningless expression.

If we may be of further assistance, please do not hesitate to call upon us.

Sincerely,

A well-organized response begins directly and enumerates answers to questions asked.

An improved version of this letter, shown in Figure 7.2, opens with a personal salutation and a time-saving subject line. Although the first sentence does not begin directly with an answer to one of the questions posed in the inquiry, it does offer a summary statement introducing the responses. The body of the letter enumerates logically and in parallel form the information requested. It uses familiar language instead of jargon. This improved letter also includes unsolicited information that may be helpful to the reader. The cordial closing is individualized so that the reader knows it was written just for this letter.

The poorly expressed letter shown in Figure 7.3 responds to a telephone call requesting information about the location of two electronic calculators. The first sentence of this ineffective letter uses dated language (*pursuant to*), a wordy expression (*this is to advise you about*), and needless repetition (*two [2]*). In addition, the first sentence does not deliver the information requested. The second paragraph opens with *The writer*, a formal expression, instead of the more conversational *I*. Moreover, the tone of the body of the letter is rather harsh and negative, and the closing sounds insincere. The information conveyed in the preceding message could be more effectively delivered by using the direct strategy and by improving the tone of the letter. Notice how the letter shown in Figure 7.4 achieves its objective.

FIGURE 7.2   Information Response Letter—Simplified Style

CanShield Assurance
930 Taylor Avenue
Regina, Saskatchewan
S4A 2Y4

February 12, 199x

Ms. Irene McKenzie
Customer Services Division
Toronto-Dominion Bank
230 Bay Street
Toronto, Ontario
M5R 3T5

YOUR NOVEMBER 5 REQUEST FOR INFORMATION REGARDING POLICY
NO. 230-38-6958M

Here is the information you requested about the insurance policy of
Patrick Beckett.

   1. The September 1 cash value of this policy was about $15,500.

   2. No liens exist against this policy.

   3. Six-month premiums are due on January 1 and June 1.

   4. We have no knowledge of possible beneficiaries that would prevent
      assignment of this policy to your bank.

Although you did not ask, you may be interested to know that it is our
practice to notify the assigned bank if policy premiums are not paid. We
would also notify the assigned bank automatically if a premium loan is
made against the policy.

I am pleased to be able to help you obtain information about Mr. Beckett's
insurance policy.

Keith Bell

KEITH BELL,
EXECUTIVE VICE-PRESIDENT
obm

*Begins directly and
provides answers in
logical listing.*

*Uses familiar
language.*

*Offers helpful extra
information.*

Ineffective writing

FIGURE 7.3   Poor Information Response Letter

Dear Mr. Meyers:

Opens directly
and uses legalese.

Pursuant to our telephone conversation of yesterday morning, this is
to advise you about the two (2) electronic calculators in which you are
interested.

Sounds harsh and
needlessly formal.

The writer has been in contact with Mary Kopec, our office manager, and
she has no record of these machines. These machines are not now on our
premises nor have they been on our premises for almost two years. She
is convinced that someone from your organization (she knows not who)
picked these machines up some time ago.

Uses tired,
insincere-sounding
closing.

It is my hope that this answers your question. If I may be of further
assistance, please let me know.

Sincerely,

FIGURE 7.4   Improved Information Response Letter

Dear Mr. Meyers:

Gives requested
information
immediately.

Apparently the two electronic calculators about which you called yesterday are not on our premises.

Explains courteously
and informally.

I checked with Mary Kopec, our office manager, and she feels that these
two machines were picked up by your organization nearly two years ago.
It is possible, however, that the machines were transferred to our
Newbury Park facility without Mary's knowledge. I suggest that you call
Barbara Merton, our Newbury Park office manager, at (306) 882-8902 to
make further inquiries.

Suggests way to
obtain additional
information.

Ends cordially.

I'll be happy to help if I can.

Sincerely,

Responding to Order Requests

Many companies acknowledge orders by sending a printed postcard that merely informs the customer that the order has been received. Other companies take advantage of this opportunity to build good will and to promote new products and services. A personalized letter responding to an order is good business, particularly for new accounts, large accounts, and customers who haven't placed orders recently. An individualized letter is also necessary if the order involves irregularities, such as delivery delays, back-ordered items, or missing items.

Letters that respond to orders should deliver the news immediately; therefore, the direct strategy is most effective. Here's a writing plan that will achieve the results you want in acknowledging orders.

Letters that follow up orders create excellent opportunities to improve the company image and to sell products.

Writing Plan for an Order Response

- **Opening**—tells when and how shipment will be sent.

- **Body**—explains details of shipment if necessary, discusses any irregularities in the order, includes resale information, and promotes other products and services if appropriate.

- **Closing**—builds good will and uses friendly, personalized closing.

Give Delivery Information in the Opening

Customers want to know when and how their orders will be sent. Since that news is most important, put it in the first sentence. It is unnecessary to say that you have received an order. An inefficient opener such as *We have received your order dated June 20* wastes words and the reader's time by providing information that could be inferred from more effective openers. Even a seemingly courteous opening like *Thank you for your recent order* does not really tell readers what they want to know. Instead of stating that an order has been received, imply it in a first sentence that provides delivery details. Here's an example:

The first sentence should tell when and how an order wil be sent.

> We are sending your cheques and invoice forms by Z Express air freight service, and these forms should arrive by February 8.

This opening sentence provides delivery information, and it is certainly superior to the two perfunctory openers shown above. However, it could still be improved. Notice that it emphasizes "we" instead of "you." Because this letter is primarily a good-will effort, its effect can be enhanced by presenting its message from the viewpoint of the reader. Notice how the following version suggests reader benefits and emphasizes the *you*-attitude.

A perfunctory opening is routine, superficial, mechanical.

> Your cheques and invoice forms for your IBM-PC were sent by Z Express air freight service. They should reach you by February 8—two days ahead of your deadline.

Put Details in the Body

You should include details relating to an order in the body of a letter that acknowledges the order. You should also discuss any irregularities about the order. If, for example, part of the order will be sent from a different location or prices have changed or items must be back-ordered, present this information.

The body of an order response is also the appropriate place to include resale information. *Resale* refers to reselling or reassuring customers that their choices were good ones. You can use resale in an order letter by describing the product favourably. You might mention its features or attributes, its popularity among customers, and its successful use in certain applications. Perhaps your competitive price recommends it. Resale information confirms the discrimination and good judgment of your customers and encourages repeat business. After an opening statement describing delivery information, resale information such as the following is appropriate:

> The multipurpose cheques you have ordered allow you to produce several different cheque formats, including accounts payable and payroll. Customers tell us that these computerized cheques are the answer to their cheque-writing problems.

Order acknowledgment letters are also suitable vehicles for sales-promotion material. An organization often has other products or services that it wishes to highlight and promote. For example, a computer supply company might include the following sales feature:

> Another good buy from Quill is our popular 3 1/2-inch disk available in our "mini" bulk pack of 25 disks at only $1.69 each. And we will send you a free desk storage tray for your disks.

Use sales-promotion material in moderation; too much can be a burden to read and therefore irritating.

Show Appreciation in the Closing

The closing should be pleasant, forward-looking, and appreciative. Above all, it should be personalized. That is, it should relate to one particular letter. Don't use all-purpose form-letter closings such as *We appreciate your interest in our company* or *Thank you for your order* or *We look forward to your continued business*.

Notice that the following personalized closings refer to the customers' current orders.

> You may be certain that your cheques and invoice forms will reach you before your February 10 deadline. We genuinely appreciate your business and look forward to serving you again.

> You have our appreciation for this order and our assurance that your future orders will be processed as efficiently and as promptly as this one.

> You can rely on the quality and durability of your Super-Grip 4-ply tires. Your satisfaction with our products and our service is our primary concern. We hope it will be our privilege to serve you again.

When a sales clerk tells you how good you look in the new suit you just purchased, the clerk is practicing "resale."

Resale emphasizes a product already sold; promotion emphasizes additional products to be sold.

The best closings are personalized; that is, they related to one particular letter.

Skilful and Faulty Letters That Respond to Orders

The letter shown in Figure 7.5 reflects a wordy and inefficient style that some businesspeople still use. This letter has many faults. Can you find them all?

You're right if you said that this order letter starts out poorly with an impersonal salutation. It continues to progress slowly in the first sentence with obvious information that could be implied. It also gives the reader no hint of when the books will arrive. The second paragraph of the letter is unnecessarily negative. Instead of capitalizing on the popularity of the books ordered, the writer uses negative language (*sorry to report, we will be forced*), implying that the shipment might be delayed. The letter contains a number of outdated and wordy expressions (*pursuant to your request, every effort will be made, attached please find*). The writer does not use resale or sales promotion to encourage repeat orders. Finally, the closing is wordy and overly formal.

FIGURE 7.5 Faulty Order Acknowledgment Letter

Ineffective writing

Dear Customer:

We are in receipt of your Purchase Order No. 2980 under date of March 15.

I'm sorry to report that the books you have ordered are selling so quickly that we cannot keep them in stock. Therefore, we will be forced to send them from our Winnipeg distribution centre. Pursuant to your request, every effort will be made to ship them as quickly as possible.

Attached please find a list of our contemporary issues.

May I take the liberty to say that we thank you for allowing us to serve your book needs.

Sincerely,

Here's a good example of what should not appear in a letter that responds to an order.

The improved version of this letter (Figure 7.6) is written in a confident style that promotes good feelings between the writer and the customer. Notice that the letter contains a personal salutation, and the first sentence reveals immediately when the books should arrive. The body of the letter confirms the wise selection of the reader by mentioning the successful sales of the books ordered. To promote future sales, this letter includes sales-promotion information. It closes with sincere appreciation that ties in directly with the content of the letter. Notice throughout the letter the emphasis upon the *you*-attitude and benefits to the reader.

FIGURE 7.6   Letter That Responds to Order—Block Style,
Mixed Punctuation

CHARTWELL'S BOOKS
5390 Tompkins Hill Road
St. John, NB
E4R 5T9
(506) 445-2378

March 20, 199x

Ms. Judy Dresser
231 Main Street
Fredericton NB
E2L 1R5

Dear Ms. Dresser:

SUBJECT: YOUR MARCH 15 PURCHASE ORDER NO. 2980 FOR BOOKS

Opens with information the reader wants most to learn.

Includes resale by reassuring reader of wise selections and also promotes future business.

Ties in appreciation for order with content of letter.

The books requested in your Purchase Order No. 2980 will be shipped from our Toronto distribution centre and should reach you by April 1.

The volumes you have ordered are among our best-selling editions and will certainly generate good sales for you at your spring book fair.

For your interest we are enclosing with this letter a list of contemporary issues recently released. If you place an order from this list or from our general catalogue, you will be eligible for special terms that we are offering for a limited time. For each $10 worth of books ordered at full list price, we will issue a $4 credit toward the purchase of additional books—as long as all the books are ordered at the same time.

We are happy to be able to help supply the books for your fair. Please take advantage of our special terms in placing your next order soon.

Sincerely,

Charles Bailey

Charles Bailey
Marketing Division

wuh

Responding to Claims

A claim is usually bad news to the organization receiving it. A claim means that something went wrong—goods were not delivered, a product failed to perform, a shipment was late, service was poor, or billing was incorrect. Large organizations have customer service departments that handle most claims. Smaller organizations respond individually to customer claims.

An individual who writes letters responding to claims has three goals: (1) to rectify the problem, if one exists, (2) to regain the confidence of the customer, and (3) to promote future business.

The writer has three important aims when responding to customer claims.

When a claim is received, you must first gather information to determine what happened and how you will respond. Some organizations automatically comply with customer claims—even when the claim may be unjustified— merely to maintain good public relations.

Once you have gathered information, you must decide whether to say yes or no to the claim. If you respond positively, your letter will represent good news to the reader. Use the direct strategy in revealing the good news. If your response is negative, arrange the message indirectly (Chapter 8). Here's a writing plan that responds favourably to a claim.

Writing Plan for Granting a Claim

- **Subject line** (optional)—identifies the previous correspondence.

- **Opening**—grants the request or announces the adjustment immediately, and includes resale or sales promotion, if appropriate.

- **Body**—provides details about how you are complying with the request, tries to regain the customer's confidence, and includes resale or sales promotion, if appropriate.

- **Closing**—ends positively with a forward-looking thought, expresses confidence in future business relations, and avoids apologizing or referring to unpleasantness.

Subject Line Provides Efficient Reference

A subject line refers to the reader's correspondence. Although it is optional, a subject line enables you to reserve the first sentence for announcing the most important information. Here are examples of subject lines that effectively identify previous correspondence.

A subject line enables you to save the first sentence for the big idea.

SUBJECT: YOUR JUNE 3 INQUIRY REGARDING INVOICE 3569

SUBJECT: REQUEST FOR EXTENSION OF WEAREVER TIRE WARRANTY

SUBJECT: YOUR DECEMBER 7 LETTER ABOUT YOUR SNO-FLAKE ICE CRUSHER

Opening Reveals Good News

Since you have decided to comply with the reader's claim, reveal the good news immediately.

Readers want to learn the good news immediately.

We agree with you that the warranty on your Data-Tec programmable calculator Model AI 25C should be extended for six months.

You may take your Sno-Flake ice crusher to Don's Appliances at 310 First Street, Saskatoon, where it will be repaired at no cost to you.

The enclosed cheque for $325 demonstrates our desire to satisfy our customers and earn their confidence.

In announcing that you will grant a claim, do so without a grudging tone—even if you have reservations about whether the claim is legitimate. Once you decide to comply with the customer's request, do so happily. Avoid half-hearted or reluctant responses like the following:

Although the Sno-Flake ice crusher works well when it is used properly, we have decided to allow you to take yours to Don's Appliances for repair at our expense.

Apologies are usually counterproductive in that they needlessly stir up unpleasant emotions.

Don't begin your letter with an apology such as *We are sorry that you are having trouble with your Sno-Flake ice crusher*. This negative approach reminds the reader of the problem and may rekindle the heated emotions or unhappy feelings experienced when the claim was written. Also, such an opening is indirect. It doesn't tell the reader the good news first.

Body Explains Compliance with Claim

Most businesses comply with claims because they want to promote customer goodwill.

In responding to claims, most organizations sincerely want to correct a problem. They want to do more than just make the customer happy. They want to stand behind their products and services.

In the body of the letter, then, explain how you are complying with the claim. In all but the most routine claims, you should also seek to regain the confidence of the customer. You might reasonably expect that a customer who has experienced difficulty with a product, with delivery, with billing, or with service has lost trust in your organization. Rebuilding that trust is important for future business. How to rebuild lost confidence depends upon the situation and the claim. If procedures need to be revised, explain what changes will be made. If a product has defective parts, tell how the product is being improved. If service is faulty, describe genuine efforts to improve it. Sincere and logical explanations can reduce hard feelings.

Sometimes the problem is not with the product but with the way it's being used. In other instances, customers misunderstand warranties or inadvertently cause delivery and billing problems by supplying incorrect information. Again, rational and sincere explanations will do much to regain the confidence of unhappy customers.

In your explanation, avoid using negative words that convey the wrong impression. Words like *trouble, regret, misunderstanding, fault, defective, error, inconvenience,* and *unfortunately* carry connotations of blame and wrongdoing.

Try to use as few negative words as possible. Keep your message positive and upbeat.

Because negative words suggest blame and fault, avoid them in letters that attempt to build customer goodwill.

In regaining the confidence of the reader, it may be appropriate to include resale information. If a customer is unhappy with a product, explain its features and applications in an effort to resell it. Depending on the situation, new product information could also be promoted.

Closing Shows Confidence

End positively with confidence that the problem has been resolved and that continued business relations will result. Don't apologize excessively or call the customer's attention to unpleasantness associated with the claim. You might mention the product in a favourable light, suggest a new product, express your appreciation for the customer's business, or look forward to future business. It's often appropriate to refer to the desire to be of service and to satisfy customers.

End your letter by looking ahead positively, not apologizing.

Do the following closings achieve the objectives suggested here?

Your Sno-Flake ice crusher will help you remain cool and refreshed this summer. For your additional summer enjoyment, consider our Smokey Joe tabletop gas grill shown in the enclosed summer catalogue. We genuinely value your business and look forward to your future orders.

We hope that this refund cheque convinces you of our sincere desire to satisfy our customers. Our goal is to earn your confidence and continue to justify that confidence with quality products and customer service.

You were most helpful in telling us about this situation and giving us an opportunity to correct it. We sincerely appreciate your cooperation.

In all your future dealings with us, you will find us striving our hardest to merit your confidence by serving you with efficiency and sincere concern.

Good and Bad Examples

The letter in Figure 7.7 is a response to an angry letter from Van Vieng of Sound, Inc., who did not receive a shipment of electronic equipment from Electronic Warehouse. Ms. Vieng wants her shipment sent immediately. When Glenda Emerson of Electronic Warehouse investigated, she found that the order was sent to the address shown on Sound, Inc., stationery. The claim letter Ms. Emerson just received was written on Sound, Inc., stationery with a different address. Ms. Vieng seems to be unaware of the discrepancy.

A confused address causes a shipping mix-up that necessitates a claim.

This response gets off to a bad start by failing to address Ms. Vieng personally. Then, instead of telling Ms. Vieng when she might expect this shipment, the opening sentence contains an apology. This serves only to remind her of the unpleasant emotions she felt when she wrote her original letter.

The tone of the letter does not promote good will. In a subtle way, it blames Sound, Inc., for the shipping problem as it grudgingly agrees to send the second shipment. The closing apologizes again—and insincerely at that—while at the same time sharply reminding Ms. Vieng of the address difficulty.

Ineffective writing

FIGURE 7.7 Poor Response to a Customer's Claim

Gentlemen:

Starts negatively with effusive apology.

We deeply regret the inconvenience you suffered in relation to your recent order for speakers, receivers, headphones, and other electronic equipment.

Blames customer for problem situation.

Our investigators looked into this problem and determined that the shipment in question was indeed shipped immediately after we received the order. According to the shipper's records, it was delivered to the warehouse address given on your stationery: 3590 University Drive, Saskatoon, Saskatchewan S5W 1E6. No one at that address would accept delivery, so the shipment was returned to us. I see from your current stationery that your company has a new address. With the proper address, we probably could have delivered this shipment.

Uses grudging and reluctant tone.

Although we feel that it is entirely appropriate to charge you shipping and restocking fees, as is our standard practice on returned goods, in this instance we will waive those fees.

Fails to promote future business.

Once again, please accept our apologies for the delay in filling this order. We hope this second shipment finally catches up with you at your current address.

Sincerely,

An effective claim response neither blames the customer nor begrudges compliance with the claim.

The claim from Ms. Vieng does represent a problem for Electronic Warehouse. Ms. Emerson must decide if a second shipment is justified. If so, who should pay the shipping and restocking fee? In this instance, Ms. Emerson decides to promote good will by sending a second shipment and by having her company absorb the extra costs. Once this decision has been made, good news should be announced immediately and positively.

Figure 7.8 shows an improved version of the response to Ms. Vieng. In this letter, Ms. Emerson explains what happened to the first shipment. She graciously accepts blame for the incident. In reality, the customer is probably equally guilty for not providing the proper shipping address.

Notice in Ms. Emerson's improved letter how effectively she achieves two of the three goals of an adjustment letter. She corrects the problem suffered by the customer and successfully regains her confidence. She treats the third goal—promoting future business—tactfully in the closing, without the use of resale or sales promotion.

FIGURE 7.8   Effective Response to Claim—Modified Block Style, Mixed Punctuation

Electronic Warehouse

930 Taylor Avenue
Regina, Saskatchewan
S4A 2Y4

February 21, 199x

Ms. Van Vieng
Sounds, Inc.
2293 Eighth Avenue
Saskatoon, Saskatchewan
S5W 2F8

Dear Ms. Vieng:

SUBJECT: YOUR FEBRUARY 18 LETTER REGARDING YOUR JANUARY
20 PURCHASE ORDER

You should receive by February 25 a second shipment of the speakers, receivers, headphones, and other electronic equipment that you ordered January 20.

Announces good news immediately.

The first shipment of this order was delivered January 28 to 3590 University Drive, Saskatoon, Saskatchewan S5W 1E6. When no one at that address would accept the shipment, it was returned to us. Now that I have your letter, I see that the order should have been sent to 2293 Eighth Ave., Saskatoon, Saskatchewan S5W 2F8. When an order is undeliverable, we usually try to verify the shipping address by telephoning the customer. Somehow the return of this shipment was not caught by our normally painstaking shipping clerks. You can be sure that I will investigate shipping and return procedures with our clerks immediately to see if we can improve existing methods.

Regains confidence of customer by explaining what happened and by suggesting plans for improvement.

As you know, our volume business allows us to sell wholesale electronics equipment at the lowest possible prices. However, we do not want to be so large that we lose touch with our customers. Over the years it is our customers' respect that has made us successful, and we hope that the prompt delivery of this shipment will earn yours.

Closes confidently with genuine appeal for customer's respect.

Sincerely,

Glenda Emerson

Glenda Emerson
Distribution Manager

c David Cole
Shipping Department

Some claims involve minimal loss of customer confidence. In the letter shown in Figure 7.9, Mrs. Eustice (see her request letter, Figure 6.6, in Chapter 6) is generally happy with her computer but asks a favour of the company. She wants the company to repair her computer. In responding to her request, the company could merely have sent Mrs. Eustice instructions for packing and shipping the computer. Instead, it took this opportunity to maintain and promote customer good will with a friendly letter explaining the company's service policy. Notice that the letter avoids mentioning negatives, such as the malfunctioning computer. In the closing, rather than dwelling on the loss of her computer while it's being repaired, the letter uses this opportunity to confirm the customer's satisfaction with her computer by referring to her dependence on it. The letter ends with a forward-looking promise of the computer's speedy return.

In this chapter, you learned to write letters that respond favourably to information requests, orders, and claims. These messages employ the deductive strategy; that is, they begin directly with the main idea. In the next chapter, you will learn to use the inductive strategy in conveying negative news.

FIGURE 7.9   Simple but Effective Response

Dear Mrs. Eustice:

Announces good news in first sentence.	We are indeed intrigued by your CompuCap 2-X computer mystery and authorize you to send your 2-X to our Diagnostic Department for inspection.
Explains company procedures and provides details on how company is complying with customer request.	Normally, we try to have our computers repaired locally to minimize transportation costs and to reduce stress to internal parts. However, your mystery case may require our special attention. We are enclosing a return authorization slip with instructions on how to pack your computer for shipping.
Ends confidently and promises quick return of computer.	Most 2-X users find that they can't get along without their computers for even a day. We will do our best to have your 2-X on its way back to you within four working days of its receipt here in Sunnyvale. We hope that this speedy service indicates to you our sincere interest in satisfying our customer.

Sincerely,

Summary

Responding to requests for information, agreeing to claims, and acknowledging orders usually suggest positive messages. They should follow the direct strategy because they bring good news to the reader. A subject line referring to previous correspondence is an effective way to begin. Reveal the information the reader expects in the first line. Provide any extra information you think may be helpful in the body, and close with a specific ending that shows your willingness to help the reader. Readers appreciate personalized closings.

Following up on orders by acknowledging them with a letter is an excellent way to improve your company image and to sell products. Begin by telling when and how the order will be sent. Include details important to the reader in the body and add resale and promotion information if appropriate. Try to personalize the closing by relating it to the particular order.

When responding to a claim, you are trying to rectify a wrong, regain the confidence of the customer, and promote future business. A subject line identifies previous correspondence and allows you to save the first sentence for the big idea. Provide good news immediately in the first sentence and do not remind the reader of the problem by apologizing. The body explains why you are complying with the reader's claim and avoids negative words that suggest fault or blame. The closing looks ahead positively to future business.

APPLICATION AND PRACTICE—7

Discussion

witch

1. Why is it advisable to use a subject line in responding to requests?

2. Since brevity is valued in business writing, is it ever advisable to respond with more information than requested? Discuss.

3. Why is it a good business practice to send a personalized acknowledgment of an order?

4. Distinguish between resale and sales promotion.

5. Discuss the policy of granting all customer claims, regardless of merit.

Short Answers

6. What is the most important position in a letter?

opening

7. Name two ways to open a letter that responds to multiple questions.

8. Name three instances when it is particularly appropriate to send a personalized order acknowledgment.

9. What do customers want to know first about their orders?

10. Give an example of resale.

11. List five situations when claim letters might be written by customers.

12. What are three goals that the writer strives to achieve in responding to customer claims?

13. Name at least five negative words that carry impressions of blame and wrongdoing.

14. What should be included in the subject line of a response to a claim?

15. What's wrong with a salutation like *Dear Sirs*?

Writing Improvement Exercises

Subject Lines.   Write effective subject lines for the following messages that appeared in this chapter.

16. Information response letter addressed to Mr. Meyers, page 144.

17. Simple but effective response addressed to Mrs. Eustice, page 154.

Letter Openers.   Indicate whether the following letter openers are direct or indirect. Be prepared to explain your choices.

	Direct	Indirect
18. Thank you for your letter of December 2 in which you inquired if we have No. 19 bolts in stock.		✓
19. We have an ample supply of No. 19 bolts in stock.	✓	⊘
20. This will acknowledge receipt of your letter of December 2.		✓
21. Yes, the Omni Cruise Club is planning a 15-day Mediterranean cruise beginning October 1.	✓	
22. I am pleased to have the opportunity to respond to your kind letter of July 9.		✓
23. Your letter of July 9 has been referred to me because Mr. Halvorson is away from the office.		✓
24. We sincerely appreciate your recent order for plywood wallboard panels.	⊘	✓
25. The plywood wallboard panels that you requested were shipped today by Coastal Express and should reach you by August 12.	✓	

Opening Paragraph

26. Revise the following opening paragraph of an information response.

Thank you for your letter of March 3 inquiring about the RefreshAire electronic air cleaner. I am pleased to have this opportunity to provide you with information. You asked how the RefreshAire works and specifically if it would remove pollen from the air. Yes, the RefreshAire removes pollen from the air—and smoke and dust as well. It then recirculates clean air. We think it makes offices, conference rooms, and cafeterias cleaner and healthier for everyone.

Closing Paragraph

27. The following concluding paragraph to a claim letter response suffers from faults in strategy, tone, and emphasis. Revise and improve.

According to your instructions, we are sending a replacement shipment of air conditioners by InterMountain Express. It should reach you by June 5. Once again, please accept our sincere apologies for the inconvenience and lost sales you have suffered as a result of this unfortunate incident.

CASE 7–1

Favourable Response to Claim

You are Peter Sawatsky, manager of WoodDoors, Inc., a firm that manufactures quality precut and custom-built doors and frames. You have received a letter dated March 21 from Isabelle Savoie, 382 Dufresne Road, Laval, Quebec H3P 3A6. Ms. Savoie is an interior designer, and she complains that the oak French doors she ordered for a client recently were made to the wrong dimensions.

Although they were the wrong size, she kept the doors and had them installed because her clients were without outside doors. However, her carpenter charged an extra $286.50 to install them. She claims that you should reimburse her for this amount, since your company was responsible for the error. You check her order and find that she is right. Instead of measuring a total of 3.23 m, the doors were made to measure 3.15 m. At the time her doors were being constructed, you had two new craftspeople in the factory; they may have misread or mismeasured her order. Normally, your Quality Control Department carefully monitors custom jobs. You don't know how this job was missed. You resolve, however, to review personally the plant's custom product procedures.

Ms. Savoie is a successful interior designer and has provided WoodDoors with a number of orders. You value her business and decide to send her a cheque for the amount of her claim. You want to remind her that WoodDoors has earned a reputation as the manufacturer of the finest wood doors and frames on the market. Your doors feature prime woods, and the craftsmanship is meticulous. The design of your doors has won awards, and the engineering is ingenious. You have a new line of greenhouse windows that are available in three sizes. You are thinking of including a brochure describing these windows.

Before you write your letter, answer the following questions.

1. What is the good news that should be revealed in the first sentence of this letter?

2. What item requires resale? How can you do that?

3. What can you say to regain the trust of this customer?

4. Should you include sales promotional items in this letter? How and where?

5. Should you apologize for the inconvenience your error caused?

   NO.

6. How can you close this letter?

Review the writing plan for granting a claim. Use this letter for class discussion or write a response to Ms. Savoie on a separate sheet. Use block style.

CASE 7-2

Response to Information Request

Analyze the following poorly written message from an insurance company to one of its policyholders, Mrs. Helen Dumont, executive vice-president, Satellite Cable of Canada, 3980 East Fourth Street, Calgary, Alberta T1L 2O3. List at least five faults. Outline a writing plan for a response to an information request. Then, on a separate sheet, rewrite the message correcting the faults. Use block style.

Dear Helen:

SUBJECT: ACCIDENT LOSSES

Per your request by telephone on July 11, I have been thinking about your need for ways to make a reduction in your company's losses due to employee accidents. In response to your request, as I promised, I came up with some recommendations for things that I have found from our experience to be helpful in reducing company losses resulting from employee accidents.

One of the things you must do is ask your managers to complete an accident report whenever an accident occurs. It is also important that all employees be instructed in safe practices and safety requirements in their departments. In addition, we have found that a manager or supervisor must follow up any reported accident with an investigation. This investigation is necessary so that you can take corrective action in preventing a recurrence of the same kind of accident. Another recommendation regards the worksite. Someone should inspect to be sure that employees are following safe procedures. Are they wearing required protective clothing? Are they using safety equipment as required? Most important, of course, is that all employees be first instructed in the safe practices and safety requirements of their departments.

We have found, Helen, that no loss-prevention program will be successful if the supervisors and management of the organization do not give their 100 percent cooperation. If you think that your managers and supervisors might have trouble implementing the suggestions made above, a seminar in loss prevention might be arranged for you. If I may be of further assistance, please do not hesitate to call on me.

CASE 7–3

Order Response

Analyze the following poorly written message to Lou Venezia, McPherson Hardware, 4821 Shafter Avenue, London, Ontario N7W 1H6. List at least five major faults. Outline a writing plan (subject line, opening, body, closing) for an order response. Then, on a separate sheet, rewrite the message rectifying its faults. Use block style.

Gentlemen:

We have your kind order under date of November 28. Permit me to say that most of the order will be shipped soon.

Only the Brown & Drecker heavy-duty contour sanders will be delayed. We've had quite a run on these sanders, and we just can't keep them in stock. Therefore, they will be sent separately from Buffalo, New York, and will probably arrive sometime around December 16. All the other items (the lightweight drill sets, sabre saw blade assortments, and steel router tables) are being sent today by East-Can Express and will, in all probability, reach you by December 5.

We also have some new items that your hardware store might like. One item is especially interesting. It's a rotary/orbital-action sander that does the job with less fatigue. Attached please find a brochure describing some of our newer items.

If we can be of further service, do not hesitate to call on us.

Sincerely,

CASE 7–4

Response to Request for Information

A friend in a distant city is considering moving to your area for more education and training in your field. This individual wants to know about your program of study. Write a letter describing a program in your field (or any field you wish to describe). What courses must be taken? Toward what degree, certificate, or employment position does this program lead? Why did you choose it? Would you recommend this program to your friend? How long does it take? Add any information you feel would be helpful.

CASE 7–5

Favourable Response to Claim

Assume that you are a manager in the business where you now work (or one about which you have some knowledge). Imagine that a customer, colleague, or employee has made a legitimate claim against your organization. Write a letter granting the claim. Make the letter as realistic and factual as possible.

Additional Problems

1. As Rochelle Cornell, owner of Rocky Mountain High, producer of freeze-dried backpacking foods, answer the inquiry of Marc Vannault (described in Chapter 6, page 134, Additional Problem No. 1). You are eager to have Mr. Vannault sample your new all-natural line of products containing no preservatives, sugar, or additives. You want him to know that you started this company two years ago after you found yourself making custom meals for discerning backpackers who rejected typical camping fare. Some of your menu items are excellent for people on restricted diets. Some dinners are cholesterol- and salt-free, but he'll have to look at your list to see for himself. You will send him your complete list of dinner items and the suggested retail prices. You will also send him a sample "Saturday Night on the Trail," a four-course meal that comes with fruit candies and elegant appetizers. All your food products are made from choice ingredients in sanitary kitchens that you personally supervise. They are flash frozen in a new vacuum process that you patented. Although your dried foods are meant to last for years, you don't recommend that they be kept beyond 18 months because they may deteriorate. This could happen if a package were punctured or if the products became overheated. Your products are currently available at Pacific Camper, 2035 Spruce Avenue, Whitehorse, Yukon Y3R 4E4. Large orders may be placed directly with you. You offer a 5 percent discount on direct orders. Write a response to Marc Vannault, 3175 First Street, Edmonton, Alberta T8L 4A3.

2. Play the role of Bill Antayac, director, Employee Development Division, Stel-Can Steel Inc. (described in Chapter 6, page 134, Additional Problem No. 2). You are eager to respond to the request of Lisa Chan, assistant vice-president, Bank of Nova Scotia, 743 Bay Street, Toronto, Ontario M5W 4E6. Send her a copy of an article you wrote for *Personnel Today* describing the employee suggestion program you implemented at Stel-Can. In answer to her specific questions, you encourage employees to participate by publicizing the suggestion plan. You post notices on bulletin boards in all departments, you insert announcements into pay envelopes, and you place articles describing employees who have won awards for their suggestions in the company newsletter and local newspapers. As your article states, suggestions are first screened by department managers. The best ones are then sent to an evaluation committee. You base your awards on the savings that result for the company. Employees receive a percentage of the actual savings. Your largest award was made to an engineer who suggested a

way to discard less waste steel, saving Stel-Can $9.7 million! You have found that an individual response to every suggestion is excellent for employee morale. You cover such problems as legal considerations and employee protests in your article. You have one important piece of advice for Ms. Chan. She should enlist the support of top management immediately before working on the details of a program. You think that your results-oriented suggestion program has forged a stronger partnership between employees and management. Write a response to Ms. Chan.

3. Respond to the order placed by Greg Fontecilla, manager, Datatronics, Inc., 2003 Maple Street, Swift Current, Saskatchewan S2L 2Z3 (described in Chapter 6, page 135, Additional Problem No. 3). Yes, all of the prices listed in your old catalogue have increased. That's the bad news. The good news is that you have nearly everything he ordered in stock. The only item not immediately available is the desktop organizer, Item No. 23-K. That has to be shipped from the manufacturer in Toronto. You've been having trouble with that supplier lately, perhaps because of heavy demand. However, you think that the organizer will be shipped no later than three weeks from the current date. You're pleased to have Datatronics's order. They might be interested in your new line of office supply products at discount prices. Send him a new catalogue and call his attention to the low price on continuous-form computer paper. It's just $39.95 for a box containing 2700 sheets of 9-by-11-inch, 20-pound printout paper. All the items he ordered, except the organizer, are on their way via Can-Fed Express and should arrive in three days.

4. Play the role of Dave Windton, business manager, Visual Services. You are responding to a letter from Monique Giraud (described in Chapter 6, page 135, Additional Problem No. 4). You are pleased to inform her that SureTech Security will receive two gratis copies of the promotional video within five business days. In addition, you will make a concerted effort to determine the reasons for the shortfall in copies provided. You hope that she will be intrigued by the enclosed brochure. In keeping with your company's reputation for being on the cutting edge of video production, it features recently acquired hardware and software that will enable Visual Services to produce Hollywood-quality morphing animations. Write this response to Monique Giraud, President, SureTech Security, 132 Broadway Avenue, Vancouver, British Columbia V6L 1T2.

5. Assume that you are Mike Volkhov, sales manager, Nova Scotia Wood Products. It is your job to reply to customer claims, and today you must respond to Sandra Fenwick, president, Fenwick Consulting Services, 2248 26th Avenue West, Halifax, Nova Scotia B3R 1W5 (described in Chapter 6, page 135, Additional Problem No. 5). You are disappointed that she is returning the executive desk (Invoice No. 3499), but your policy is to comply with customer wishes. If she doesn't want to keep the desk, you will certainly return the purchase price plus shipping charges. On occasion, desks are damaged in shipping, and this may explain the marred finish and the sticking drawers. You want her to give Nova Scotia Wood Products another chance. After all, your office furniture and other wood products are made from the finest hand-selected woods by master artisans.

Since she is apparently furnishing her office, send her another catalogue and invite her to look at the traditional conference desk on page 10-E. This is available with a matching credenza, file cabinets, and accessories. She might be interested in your furniture-leasing plan, which can produce substantial savings. You promise that you will personally examine any furniture she may order in the future. Write her a letter granting her claim.

6. Assume the role of Marilyn Thatcher, customer service representative, Ever-Cool Manufacturing Company. You are responding to the claim of Paul Friedman, purchase manager, Datatronics, Inc., 2569 Church Street, Merritt, British Columbia V5N 2E9 described in Chapter 6, page 136, Additional Problem No. 6). Tell Mr. Friedman that the Ever-Cool air conditioner can be taken to A-Z Appliance Repairs, 2320 Davis Avenue, Kamloops, British Columbia V6P 1R5 for warrantied repair. Rarely do these heavy-duty room air conditioners need service. You are happy to honour the warranty. If Datatronics would like faster service, Ever-Cool has an agreement with Merritt Mobile Service. For a nominal fee ($30), Merritt will come to his office and, if possible, make the repair on the spot. This is sometimes more convenient than removing a heavy, mounted room air conditioner. He can make an appointment with Merritt Mobile Service by calling (800) 574-8900. Write to Datatronics.

GRAMMAR/MECHANICS CHECKUP—7

Commas, 2

Review Sections 2.05 through 2.09 of the Grammar/Mechanics Handbook. Then study each of the following statements and insert necessary commas. In the space provided for each statement, write the number of commas that you add; write *0* if no commas are needed. Also record the number of the G/M principle illustrated. When you finish, compare your responses with those shown below. If your answers differ, study carefully the principles shown in parentheses.

___1___ _(2.06a)_

Example: When businesses encounter financial problems‸ they often reduce their administrative staffs.

1. As stated in the warranty this printer is guaranteed for one year.

2. Today's profits come from products currently on the market and tomorrow's profits come from products currently on the drawing boards.

3. Companies introduce new products in one part of the country and then watch how the product sells in that area.

4. One large automobile manufacturer which must remain nameless recognizes that buyer perception is behind the success of any new product.

5. The imaginative promising agency opened its offices April 22 in Lethbridge.

6. The sales associate who earns the highest number of recognition points this year will be honoured with a bonus vacation trip.

    _____

7. André Michaud our sales manager in the Quebec City area will make a promotion presentation at the June meeting.

    _____

8. Our new product has many attributes that should make it appealing to buyers but it also has one significant drawback.

    _____

9. Although they have different technical characteristics and vary considerably in price and quality two or more of a firm's products may be perceived by shoppers as almost the same.

    _____

10. To motivate prospective buyers we are offering a cash rebate of $2.

    _____

Review of Commas 1 and 2

11. When you receive the application please fill it out and return it before Monday January 3.

    _____

12. On the other hand we are very interested in hiring hard-working conscientious individuals.

    _____

13. In March we expect to open a new branch in Nanaimo which is an area of considerable growth.

    _____

14. As we discussed on the telephone the ceremony is scheduled for Thursday June 9 at 3 p.m.

    _____

15. Dr. Adams teaches the morning classes and Mrs. Wildey is responsible for evening sections.

    _____

---

1. (1) warranty, (2.06a)   3. (0)   5. (1) imaginative, (2.08)   7. (2) Michaud, area, (2.09)
9. (1) quality, (2.06a)   11. (2) application, Monday, (2.06, 2.04)   13. (1) Nanaimo,
(2.06c)   15. (1) classes, (2.05)

GRAMMAR/MECHANICS CHALLENGE—7

Document for Revision

The following letter contains faults in grammar, punctuation, spelling, and number form, in addition to problems discussed in this chapter. Drawing upon the guidelines provided in the Grammar/Mechanics Handbook and what you learned in the chapter, revise the letter.

Poor Letter

May 30, 199x

Mr. Benjamin Katz
Medical Supplies Inc.
P.O. Box 489
North York, ON
M3J 3K1

Dear Mr. Katz:

You will be recieving shortly the rubbermaid service and utility carts you ordered along with 5 recycling stack bins. Unfortunately, the heavy duty can crusher is not available but it will be sent from the factory in albany New York and should reach you by May 31st.

You may place any future orders, by using our toll free telephone number (1-800-499-9091), or our toll free fax number (1-800-499-8525). If you need help with any items ask for one of the following sales representatives, Bill Small, Susan Freed, or Rick Woo. When the items you order are in our currant catalogue it will be shipped the same day you place you're order. For products to be custom imprinted please provide a typed or printed copy with your order.

Remember we are the only catalogue sales company that guarantees your full satisfaction. If you are not pleased we'll arrange for a prompt refund, credit or replacement. We'll also refund or credit all shipping costs associated with the returned items. We want your business.

Yours truly,

UNIT 3

APPLYING THE INDIRECT STRATEGY

8

Letters and Memos That Carry Negative News

In this chapter, you will learn to do the following:

- Identify the need for indirectness in delivering bad news.
- Recognize six components in an effective indirect strategy.
- Apply skilful writing techniques in refusing requests.

- Retain good will while refusing claims.
- Demonstrate tact in refusing credit requests.

Analyzing the Message

If your message delivers bad news, use the indirect method.

As you have learned, the first step in writing a business letter or memo is analyzing your message and the effect you expect to have on the reader. If you think the message will antagonize, disappoint, upset, hurt, or anger the recipient, an indirect strategy may be more effective than the direct method you have been using up to now. Examples of letters that deliver disappointing news are those that deny requests, refuse claims, reveal price increases, decline invitations, announce shipping delays, turn down job applicants, discontinue services, or deny credit.

Recipients of good news like to learn the news quickly. That is why the direct strategy is most effective. Directness, however, is not usually effective for bad news. Coldly delivering bad news at the beginning of a letter may upset the reader. He or she is in a poor frame of mind to receive the remainder of the letter. Or, worse yet, the bad news may cause the reader to stop reading completely. Reasons for the refusal and explanations that follow may never be seen. The principal goal of the indirect strategy is this: we want the reader to read our reasons and explanations before we reveal the bad news.

The indirect method allows the writer to explain before announcing the bad news.

The indirect strategy, which we will discuss shortly, is generally better for negative news—but not always. Some readers may prefer frankness and directness. If you know the reader well, the direct strategy may be appropriate even for negative messages. For example, assume that David Li, a good customer with whom you are friendly, must be told that his company's order can't be filled immediately. You know that David is a no-nonsense, up-front person who values candour. For him, the direct strategy may be appropriate. Further, if you have been unsuccessful in getting your message across by writing one or more messages using the indirect strategy, you may decide that bluntness is needed. The direct approach, for example, might be appropriate in responding to Sally Kelly. She has been told twice, in memos using an indirect strategy, that she does not qualify for a promotion because she lacks post-secondary training in her profession. She applied for the promotion a third time and still had not enroled in the necessary courses. This time her superior wrote a direct memo that spelled out the denial immediately and then explained the reasons for the denial.

Typically, though, we try to soften the effects of bad news by delaying it until after we have explained reasons justifying it. Delaying the bad news is just one part of an overall strategy that has proved effective in delivering messages with negative news. The indirect strategy includes six elements, which we will consider now.

Indirect Strategy

- Buffer
- Transition
- Explanation
- Bad news
- Alternative(s)
- Good-will closing

Six components in the indirect strategy help shape a message that brings negative news.

Applying the Indirect Strategy

The indirect strategy gives you a general outline for presenting negative news. Before implementing it, however, you need to analyze each step and study illustrations that show how these steps are used in writing letters and memos. After you have examined the steps, you'll learn how to put them together in writing letters for common business situations that involve delivering negative news. By developing skill in using this strategy in the most common situations, you should be able to adapt it to similar business problems.

We'll discuss the indirect strategy in the order shown, but the thinking process actually follows a slightly different order. Skilful writers first decide whether their message will be likely to elicit a positive or negative reaction from the reader. If a request must be denied or a claim refused, they analyze their reasons for refusing. If they don't have good reasons, they can't write convincing letters. Thus, the explanation shapes the rest of the letter and determines the content and tone. Although the letter begins with a buffer, the thinking process begins with the reasons for delivering the bad news.

Developing a Good Buffer

A buffer is a device that reduces surprise. In denying a request or delivering other bad news, we can reduce the shock a reader may suffer by opening with a buffer paragraph. This opening should put the reader in a receptive frame of mind. Remember, our objective is to induce the recipient to read the entire letter. We want the reader to understand our reasons and explanations before we disclose the bad news.

An effective buffer is neutral, upbeat, and relevant.

An effective buffer generally possesses three characteristics: (1) it is *neutral*, (2) it is *upbeat*, and (3) it is *relevant*. A buffer is neutral when it does not signal the bad news that is to follow or falsely suggest that good news will be forthcoming. A buffer is upbeat if it emphasizes something positive for the reader. The positive element could be resale material that relates to a product, a compliment or praise for the reader, or a statement that builds good will. A buffer is relevant if it refers to the situation at hand. A buffer statement that describes the unusually good weather may be neutral and upbeat, but it has no relation to the bad news.

Here are a number of buffer statements for negative letters. The first is the opening statement for a letter delivering the news that a candidate will not receive a job offer after an interview. The buffer refers to the interview positively but does not suggest that the candidate will be hired.

> I enjoyed talking with you last week about your background and the Business Administration program at Western.

A letter denying a request for credit for merchandise that a customer wishes to return employs a resale buffer:

Try not to forecast bad news nor falsely imply good news.

> Your choice of the Ambassador Executive attaché case is a good one because this product combines contemporary styling with quality workmanship.

A letter refusing an invitation to speak at an awards banquet begins with a compliment to the reader:

> You have done an excellent job of organizing the program for the October 5 awards banquet of Ducks Unlimited.

A letter denying an adjustment to a customer's account opens with a sympathetic statement about the customer's past payment record:

> We genuinely appreciate the prompt payments you have always made in response to our monthly invoices.

Building a Smooth Transition

Reference to a key word or idea builds a transition between the buffer and the following explanation.

After the opening buffer statement, use a transition that guides the reader to the explanation that follows. Avoid problem words such as *but, unfortunately,* and *however,* because they imply that bad news is to come. That expectation may reduce the attention paid to the rest of your message.

Experienced writers try to position a key word or idea in the buffer or transition that leads the reader naturally to the reasons for the refusal. In this next example, a business must refuse a request for campaign contributions for a city council candidate. Notice how the key words *candidate* and *contribution* form a link between the buffer and the explanation for refusing the request.

Your efforts to build a campaign fund for city council candidate Jackie Ohlson are commendable. This candidate deserves the support of civic-minded businesses and individuals who are able to make contributions.

Buffer

Transition

If elected, your candidate will help administer funds to municipal departments and offices. As you may know, a significant portion of our business involves providing supplies for city offices. City council members who have accepted campaign contributions from vendors supplying city accounts may be accused of conflict of interest. Rather than place your candidate in this awkward position, our lawyer advises us to avoid making financial contributions to the campaigns of city council candidates. Although we are unable to provide financial support, many of our employees will be contributing their time and efforts to work personally for the election of your candidate.

Explanation

Alternative

We hope that the participation of our staff will contribute to a successful campaign for Jackie Ohlson.

Good-will closing

Presenting the Explanation Before the Bad News

In the preceding example, key words in the buffer and transition lead the reader smoothly to the explanation. As you know, the explanation is the most important part of a negative letter. Without sound reasons for denying a request or refusing a claim, the letter will fail, no matter how cleverly it is written. The explanation is, after all, the principal reason for using the indirect method. We want to be able to explain before refusing.

The success of a negative letter depends on how well the explanation is presented.

In the explanation, as in the transition, don't let problem words (*but, however, unfortunately*) signal the refusal. Your explanation should show that you have analyzed the situation carefully. Tell clearly why a refusal is necessary. An item is no longer under warranty or was never warrantied in the first place, or a customer demands a refund for an item that cannot be resold, or a product fails because it was misused. In some instances, such as the denial of credit or the refusal to allow damaged goods to be returned, the explanation can emphasize reader benefits. The reader, along with other customers, benefits from lower prices if a business is able to avoid unnecessary credit costs and unfair returns.

Strive to project an unemotional, objective, and helpful tone. Don't lecture or patronize (*If you will read the operating instructions carefully ...*), avoid sounding presumptuous (*I'm sure the salesman who demonstrated this unit explained that ...*), and don't hide behind company policy (*Our company policy prevents us from granting your request*). Explain specifically why the company policy is necessary. If you have more than one reason for refusing, begin with the strongest reason. Present the bad news, and then continue with additional reasons for refusing.

Breaking the Bad News

You can soften the blow of bad news by using some of these seven techniques.

In Chapter 4, you learned stylistic techniques for de-emphasizing ideas. Now we will expand those techniques and apply them as you learn to announce bad news.

1. **Avoid the spotlight**. Don't put the bad news in a conspicuous position. The most emphatic positions in a letter are the first sentence and the last sentence. Other conspicuous places are at the beginning and at the end of sentences and paragraphs. The reader's attention is drawn to these positions and often stays there. Strategically, these are not good locations for mentioning bad news. To give the least emphasis to an idea, place it in the middle of a sentence or in the middle of a paragraph halfway through your letter.

2. **Use long sentences**. Short sentences emphasize content. Since we want to de-emphasize bad news, avoid short, simple sentences (*We cannot ship your goods*). Longer sentences diffuse the bad news and also give you a chance to explain the bad news or offer alternatives (see point 7).

3. **Put the bad news in a subordinate clause**. Grammatical attention in a sentence is always focused on the independent clause. To de-emphasize an idea, put it in a less conspicuous spot, such as a subordinate clause; for example, *Although your credit application cannot be approved at this time, we welcome your cash business*. The bad news is subordinated in the dependent clause (*Although your credit application ...*), where the reader is less likely to dwell on it.

Be selective in applying these techniques whenever you break bad news.

4. **Use the passive voice**. The active voice, recommended for most business writing, is direct and identifies the subject of a sentence (*I cannot allow you to examine our personnel files*). To be less direct and to avoid drawing unnecessary attention to the writer, use the passive voice (*Examination of our personnel files cannot be permitted because ...*). The passive voice focuses attention on actions rather than personalities; it helps you be impersonal and tactful.

5. **Be clear but not overly graphic**. Bad news is best received when it is clear but not painfully vivid. For example, the following refusal is unnecessarily harsh because it provides too many details:

> We cannot pay for your freelance services in cash, as you request. Such payment is clearly illegal and violates federal law. All freelance services that we authorize must be supported by cheque payments to individuals whose social insurance numbers are included in the record of the payment.

This refusal would be more tactful if it were less direct and less graphic:

> Federal law requires that payments to freelancers be made by cheque and be supported by social insurance numbers.

6. **Imply the refusal**. In certain instances, a refusal does not have to be stated directly. In the preceding example, the tactful revision does not actually say

We cannot pay you in cash. Instead, the refusal is implied. Recall the letter refusing campaign funds:

> Rather than place your candidate in this awkward position, our lawyer advises us to avoid making financial contributions to the campaigns of city council candidates.

Instead of hammering home the bad news (*Therefore, we cannot contribute to this campaign*), the author gave consideration to the feelings of the reader by implying the refusal.

Here's another example of an implied refusal. Instead of refusing an invitation to speak at a college job symposium, a business executive writes:

> Although my appointment schedule is completely booked during the week of your employment symposium, I wish you success with this beneficial event.

Implying a refusal is not quite as devastating as communicating an explicit, detailed denial. Such subtleness saves the feelings of both the writer and the reader. Be very careful, however, in using this technique. It is imperative that the reader understand the refusal. Don't be so vague that additional correspondence is required to clarify the refusal.

What is the danger of an implied refusal?

7. **Offer an alternative**. If appropriate, suggest some recourse to the reader. You might offer a compromise, a substitute, or an alternative offer:

> For security reasons, visitors are not allowed inside Building J. It is possible, however, to tour our assembly facility in the fall during our Open House.

> My schedule prevents me from speaking to your group, but I have asked my colleague, Dr. Gail R. Duffy, to consider addressing your conference.

Closing with Good Will

After explaining the bad news clearly and tactfully, shift to an idea that renews good feelings between the writer and the reader. In our letter refusing to pay a freelancer in cash, the closing regains the reader's confidence:

Provide a courteous, pleasant, and forward-looking closing that doesn't refer directly to the bad news.

> We hope that we may use your services as a freelancer again in the future.

If an alternative is presented, make it easy to accept:

> Dr. Duffy is an excellent speaker, and I'm sure your group would enjoy her presentation. I am including Dr. Duffy's address so that you may write her directly.

When writing to customers, encourage continued business relations. Resale or sales promotional material may be appropriate:

> I am enclosing a sample of a new imported fragrance and a coupon to save you $15 on your initial purchase. We look forward to serving you soon.

For the most effective closings, avoid these traps:

- **Don't refer to the bad news.** Focus on positive, friendly remarks. Don't needlessly remind the reader about the difficulty.

- **Don't apologize.** You have valid reasons for refusing, and you've explained these reasons clearly. An apology at the end of your message undermines your explanation.

- **Don't conclude with clichés.** Remarks such as *If we may be of further service* or *Thank you for understanding our position* sound particularly insincere and ironic in messages delivering negative news.

- **Don't invite further correspondence.** Expressions such as *If you have any further questions* or *If you would like to discuss this further* suggest that the matter is still open for discussion. Don't encourage an exchange of mail or telephone calls. Your decision is fair and final.

> Irony is the use of words to express something other than, and especially opposite of, the literal meaning.

Refusing Requests

When you must refuse a request and you feel that the refusal is likely to antagonize, upset, hurt, or anger the reader, use an indirect approach, as illustrated in the following writing plan:

Writing Plan for Refusing a Request or Claim

- **Buffer**—identifies previous correspondence incidentally or in a subject line and begins with neutral statement on which both the reader and the writer can agree.

- **Transition**—plants key idea or word that leads naturally to the explanation.

- **Explanation**—presents valid reasons for refusal, avoids problem words that forecast bad news, and includes resale or sales-promotion material if appropriate.

- **Bad news**—softens the impact by de-emphasizing the refusal.

- **Alternative**—suggests a compromise, alternative, or substitute if possible.

- **Closing**—renews good feelings with a positive statement, avoids referring to the bad news, and doesn't apologize.

Expert and Faulty Letters That Refuse Requests

The letter shown in Figure 8.1 begins fairly well. The opening sentence is neutral, although it contains unnecessary information that could be implied. The letter then deteriorates quickly with a blunt refusal of a magazine writer's request for information about employee salaries. It creates a harsh tone with such negative words as *sorry, must refuse, violate,* and *liable.* Since the refusal precedes the explanation, the reader probably will not be in a receptive frame of mind to accept the reasons for refusing. Notice, too, that the bad news is emphasized by appearing in a short sentence at the beginning of a paragraph. It stands out here and hurts the reader by its conspicuousness. The refusal explanation is overly graphic, containing references to possible litigation. Instead of offering constructive alternatives, this letter reveals only tiny bits of the desired data. Finally, the insincere closing does not build good will.

FIGURE 8.1 Blunt Refusal of Request

Dear Mrs. Marcus:

I have your letter of October 21 in which you request information about the salaries and commissions of our top young salespeople.

I am sorry to inform you that we cannot reveal data of this kind. I must, therefore, refuse your request. To release this information would violate our private employee contracts. Such disclosure could make us liable for damages, should any employee seek legal recourse. I might say, however, that our salespeople are probably receiving the highest combined salary and commissions of any salespeople in this field.

This refusal makes a poor impression because it sounds harsh, negative, and insincere.

If it were possible for us to help you with your fascinating research, we would certainly be happy to do so.

Sincerely yours,

In Figure 8.2, the same request is refused more skilfully. Its opening reflects genuine interest in the request but does not indicate compliance. The second sentence acts as a transition by introducing the words *salespeople* and *salaries,* repeated in the following paragraph. Reasons for refusing this request are objectively presented in an explanation that precedes the refusal. Notice that the refusal (*Although specific salaries and commission rates cannot be released ...*) is a subordinate clause in a long sentence in the middle of a paragraph. To further soften the impact, the letter offers an alternative. The sincere closing refers to the alternative, avoids mention of the refusal, and looks to the future.

It's always easier to write refusals when alternatives can be offered to soften the bad news. But often no alternatives are possible. The refusal letter in Figure 8.3 involves a delicate situation in which an Information Technology manager has been asked by her colleagues to violate a contract. Several other managers have privately asked her to make copies of a licensed software program for them. Some of them want a free copy of the program for their personal computers. Others want the program at not cost for their entire department. Making copies is forbidden by the terms of the software licensing agreement, and the

When you must refuse and you have no alternatives to suggest, the explanation and reasoning must be particularly logical.

FIGURE 8.2   Skilful Request Refusal—Modified Block Style, Mixed Punctuation

CANON ELECTRONICS INTERNATIONAL

205 BLOOR STREET
TORONTO, ONTARIO
M4A 1W5
(416) 593-1098

January 15, 199x

Mrs. Sylvia Marcus
887 Queen Street
Peterborough, Ontario
K6N 1Y5

Dear Mrs. Marcus:

Buffer shows genuine interest, and transition sets up explanation.

The article you are now researching for *Business Management Weekly* sounds fascinating, and we are flattered that you wish to include our organization. We do have many outstanding young salespeople, both male and female, who are commanding top salaries.

Explanation gives good reasons for refusing request.

Each of our salespeople operates under an individual salary contract. During salary negotiations several years ago, an agreement was reached in which both sales staff members and management agreed to keep the terms of these individual contracts confidential. Although specific salaries and commission rates cannot be released, we can provide you with a ranked list of our top salespeople for the past five years. Three of the current top salespeople are under the age of thirty-five.

Closing is pleasant and forward looking.

Enclosed is a fact sheet regarding our top salespeople. We wish you every success with your article, and we hope to see our organization represented in it.

Cordially,

Lloyd Kenniston

Lloyd Kenniston
Executive Vice-President

je
Enclosure: Sales Fact Sheet

FIGURE 8.3 Tactful Memo Refusing Request and Offering No Alternatives

TO: All Production Managers   July 8, 199x

FROM: Barbara Stordevent, Manager, Information Technology BS

SUBJECT: PERSONAL AND DEPARTMENTAL COPYING OF LICENSED
           SOFTWARE

A number of computer users have expressed interest in the licensed word processing program WordWrite, which we recently acquired for the microcomputers used by our office technologists.

Opens with relevant but neutral buffer.

This program, like many licensed programs, requires that each purchased copy be used only on a single machine. The licensing agreement not only forbids that the program be copied for home use but also forbids making copies for additional computers in other departments. With all of our software programs, we honour both the letter and the spirit of our license agreements. Without these agreements, software companies would have a hard time continuing in business.

Transition picks up key word *licensed*.

Explanation neither preaches nor patronizes.

When we purchased the WordWrite program, we agreed to limit its use to those machines covered by the agreement. Although this program cannot be copied at no cost, our licensing agreement does allow us to purchase additional copies. Should you require the program, we can extend the license to include the computers in your department. You can request an extended license through Richard Molini in Purchasing.

De-emphasized refusal diverts attention to reader benefits.

Please drop by to see our new desktop publishing system.

Closes with an off-the-subject but friendly remark.

---

manager refuses to do this. Rather than saying no to each manager who asks her, she writes a memo using the indirect strategy (Figure 8.3).

The opening tactfully avoids suggesting that any manager has actually asked to copy the software program. These professionals may prefer not to have their private requests made known. A transition takes the reader to the logical reasons against copying. Notice that the tone is objective, neither preaching nor condemning. The refusal is softened by being linked with a positive statement. To divert attention from the refusal, the memo ends with a friendly remark.

Refusing Claims

All businesses offering products or services will receive occasional customer claims for adjustments. Claims may also arise from employees. Most of these claims are valid, and the customer or employee receives a positive response. Even unwarranted claims are sometimes granted because businesses genuinely desire to create a good public image and to maintain friendly relations with employees.

Some claims, however, cannot be approved because the customer or employee is mistaken, misinformed, unreasonable, or possibly even dishonest. Letters responding to these claims deliver bad news. The indirect strategy announces bad news with the least negative effect. It also allows the writer to explain why the claim must be refused before the reader realizes the bad news and begins resisting.

Effective Letters That Refuse Claims

The letter in Figure 8.4 is in response to a customer who wants a cash refund for a vacuum cleaner that he has used for three months. He claims that the vacuum doesn't do a good job of cleaning his thick carpeting. The machine, which was returned to catalogue sales, shows heavy use and cannot be resold. It has a warranty covering repair of defective parts, but apparently the customer is not claiming that anything needs to be repaired. He writes a letter demanding a refund of the full purchase price. The customer is understandably upset; he has invested in a vacuum that appears to be a poor choice for his needs. However, the store cannot accept the returned vacuum because it could not be sold as new merchandise.

Even when the customer is wrong, the indirect strategy is useful to minimize customer discontent.

The letter in Figure 8.4 opens with a neutral remark to which both the reader and the writer can agree. It includes the clause *for which it is designed*, skilfully leading to an explanation of the design and merit of the vacuum being returned. The explanation capitalizes on resale information while at the same time describing a more appropriate model for the customer's thick carpeting. The gentle explanation does not blame the customer for making a poor choice; the tone is objective and constructive. Regarding the customer's request for a cash refund, the writer explains that the returned vacuum is used and cannot be resold. Without actually saying *We will not give you your money back*, the writer implies this refusal by presenting convincing reasons explaining why such a refund is impossible. Two alternatives further de-emphasize the bad news. A friendly invitation concludes the letter.

Refusing Credit

Banks, other financial institutions, and businesses often deny credit by using impersonal form letters. These letters may list a number of possible reasons for the credit rejection, such as insufficient credit references, irregular employment, delinquent credit obligations, insufficient income, inadequate collateral, temporary residence, or inability to verify income.

Form letters announcing credit refusals are efficient for the sender but many displease the receiver.

Form letters are convenient for the writer, but they often antagonize the reader because they are unclear, inappropriate, or insensitive. Even when individuals are poor credit risks (and they probably know this), they may be hurt by tactless and blunt form letters. Form-letter refusals or poorly written letters

FIGURE 8.4   Tactful Claims Refusal—Block Style, Open Punctuation

Home Shopper Services

1200 Granville Street
Vancouver, BC
V0N 1E4
(604) 783-8823

June 11, 199x

Mr. Jim Vandermark
123 Main Street
Victoria, BC
V1L 2W4

Dear Mr. Vandermark:

SUBJECT: YOUR JUNE 5 LETTER ABOUT YOUR DOVER CANISTER
                   VACUUM

You have every right to expect a newly purchased vacuum cleaner to do
a good job of cleaning the type of carpeting for which it is designed.

Your Dover 2-peak HP canister vac was designed as a powerful tool for
cleaning plush carpeting, area rugs, wood and vinyl floors, and draperies.
This model has deep-cleaning suction and quiet operation at an economy
price. As our catalogue states, this canister model does not contain the
beater-bar construction of the more powerful but more expensive models.
To properly clean thick carpets like yours, the best model is the 4.2-peak
HP Dover Power-Mate beater-bar unit.

Since your present canister vacuum has been used for three months and
is no longer new, it cannot be resold as a new unit. As you know, we sell
only new merchandise through our catalogue service. However, a considerable market for used units exists. If you believe the 2-peak HP canister
model is inadequate for your present carpeting, you might consider selling it or keeping it for lighter cleaning. Then, examine in our fall catalogue the beater-bar models recommended for thick carpets like yours.
Most of these have adjustable height settings, allowing you to select the
proper level for your carpet.

We are sending you an advance copy of the fall catalogue showing our
full line of fine Dover vacuums. If you would like a personal demonstration of the Power-Mate model, we would be happy to show you how it
operates on thick carpeting at the display centre in our retail store.

Sincerely,

Melanie Tang

Melanie Tang
Service Consultant

tra

**Subject line identi-
fies customer's letter.**

**Buffer opens with
remark to which
everyone can agree.**

**Reasoning subtly
suggests that reader
purchased wrong
model.**

**Implied refusal
avoids saying "No"
directly.**

**Alternatives soften
the bad news.**

**Sincere and friendly
closing mixes sales
promotion with
invitation.**

not only hurt the feelings of the reader but also ignore an opportunity to build future business. An individual or business that is a poor credit risk today may become a good credit risk and a potential customer in the future.

An effective plan for writing a credit refusal follows the principles of the indirect strategy.

Writing Plan for a Credit Refusal

Credit refusals use five-part strategy to break the bad news.

- **Buffer**—expresses appreciation for order or for credit application and includes resale information if appropriate.

- **Transition**—moves from buffer to explanation logically and repeats key idea or word if possible.

- **Explanation**—shows concern for the welfare of the reader, explains objectively why credit must be refused, and doesn't preach or hide behind company policy.

- **Bad news**—implies refusal or states it briefly, offers alternatives, and suggests possible extension of credit in the future.

- **Closing**—projects an optimistic look to the future and includes resale or sales-promotion material.

Tactful and Tactless Credit Refusals

Credit refusals can be separated into two groups: refusals to businesses and refusals to individuals. Although the same general strategy applies to both, some variations exist.

Use similar techniques for refusing credit to individuals and to businesses.

In Figure 8.5, the credit refusal to a business has several major faults. First, it offends the reader with insensitive, negative language (*we regret, unsatisfactory, your firm is considered a poor credit risk*). Second, the letter does not try to convert this order into a cash transaction. Third, it does not attempt to promote good will or build future business. Notice that the letter begins with the overused and mechanical *Thank you for your order.* Although this beginning is a little better than stating the bad news directly, it shows that the writer made no effort to individualize this letter. Throughout the letter the tone is destructive rather than constructive. The last paragraph places unnecessary emphasis on the profit motive.

The letter shown in Figure 8.6 treats the same credit refusal in a totally different manner. It strives to retain the business represented by Mr. Sargema's order, providing a plan for reducing the order so that a cash purchase might be possible. The tone of the letter is cordial, and the alternative is constructive. The implied refusal shows concern for the reader but does not patronize.

When refusing credit to individuals, apply the same indirect strategy you learned in refusing credit for businesses. Be extremely careful, though, to avoid making the refusal sound like a personal attack on the individual's reputation. Instead, base the refusal on objective factors, such as the individual's income, expenses, and ability to repay.

FIGURE 8.5 Credit Refusal That Hurts Business

Ineffective writing

Dear Mr. Sargema:

Thank you for your order of February 14 for 36 of our Unifax cordless phone systems.

Opening expresses appreciation mechanically.

Although we would like to do business with you, we regret to report that our credit investigation of your firm proved unsatisfactory. Because of excessive current credit obligations, your firm is considered a poor credit risk.

Bad news is blurted out before explanation.

Explanation is factual but tactless.

We hope that you will understand that, as a small business producing a quality product with a small profit margin, we have to be extremely careful to avoid credit losses.

Closing offends reader by implying a credit loss.

Sincerely,

Adapting the Indirect Strategy

In this chapter, you learned how to use the indirect strategy for refusing requests, refusing claims, and denying credit. The same general principles of indirectness are appropriate whenever bad news must be delivered. For example, a company announcement reducing health coverage for employees would certainly represent bad news to the employees. The indirect strategy would be best for such an announcement. News that a supplier is out of a needed item, that a certain item is no longer manufactured, or that the price of an item has risen—all these messages will be irritating to a customer. The indirect strategy is again most effective.

Application of the principles of indirectness is often successful in solving personal problems.

We have applied this strategy only to written business messages. However, the strategy is also appropriate in oral communication and in interpersonal relations. If you must tell a friend that you can't fulfil a promise, a good explanation preceding the refusal may help you retain the friendship. If you must tell your brother that you dented the fender of his car, the indirect strategy described in this chapter will help you announce the bad news. Now that you've learned this strategy, you'll be able to adapt it to many situations beyond the letter and memo writing plans illustrated here.

FIGURE 8.6   Effective Letter That Refuses Credit to a Business—Modified Block Style, Mixed Punctuation

UNIFAX COMMUNICATION SYSTEMS

349 McKinnon Drive
Saskatoon, SK
S4W 8T7

February 19, 199x

Mr. Greg Sargema
Federated Bound Suppliers
320 Ring Road
Regina, Saskatchewan
S3T 2R5

Dear Mr. Sargema:

Opens confidently with resale.

You've come to the right place for cordless telephone systems. The Nomad 400 model that you have ordered offers outstanding features, including two-way paging, pulse dialing, and intercom capabilities.

Moves from product discussion to credit investigation by means of effective transition.

Implies refusal without stating it directly.

Because we'd like to see this product distributed by your full-service dealership, we investigated your credit application. We found that you have current and long-term credit obligations that are nearly twice as great as your firm's total assets. This financial picture suggests that it would be unwise for your firm to incur further credit obligations at this time. When your firm's financial situation improves, however, we would sincerely like to serve you on a credit basis.

Suggests alternative plan for cash purchase.

Emphasizes reader benefits.

In the meantime, consider this plan. Order one dozen of the Nomad 400 units today. By paying for this reduced order with cash, you would receive a 2 percent cash discount. After you have sold these fast-moving units, place another cash order through our toll-free order number. We promise to deliver your items immediately so that your inventory is never depleted. In this way, you can obtain the units you want now, you can enjoy cash discounts, and you can replace your inventory almost instantaneously.

Looks forward optimistically to future business.

We're proud of our quality products and our competitive prices. If we can do business with you now or in the future, please call us at (800) 896-3320.

Yours truly,

Margaret Gormann

Margaret Gormann, Manager
Marketing Unit One

meg

How to Avoid 15 Dangerous Word Traps

Certain words are treacherous because they sound and look very much like other words. Test your knowledge of the following confusing words by circling the best choice for each sentence. Check your responses on page 197.

1. New employees must (adapt, adept, adopt) our policies.

2. He liked movies but was (adverse, averse) to standing in long lines.

3. Higher admission prices will certainly (affect, effect) our attendance.

4. The (biannual, biennial) meetings are normally held in March and October.

5. Despite the investment of much (capital, capitol), the venture failed.

6. We received (complementary, complimentary) passes to the vampire movie.

7. The speakers included three (eminent, imminent) chief executive officers.

8. From Ann's remarks, I (imply, infer) that she is uninterested in this job.

9. Some of the company's (personal, personnel) must be transferred.

10. Before we can (precede, proceed), we must investigate your credit.

11. Her (principal, principle) means of income is her monthly salary.

12. We would rather promote from within (than, then) advertise publicly.

13. Please (disperse, disburse) your personnel throughout the sales region.

14. Employees are concerned about (their, they're, there) insurance benefits.

15. We must decide (weather, whether) to increase vision-care benefits.

Summary

The first step in writing any business message is analyzing the effect it will have on your reader. If you determine that the effect will be negative, then the indirect strategy may be more effective than the direct method.

The indirect strategy allows the writer to explain before announcing the bad news. It consists of six components: buffer, transition, explanation, bad news, alternatives, and good-will closing. These components help the writer shape the message that brings negative news.

An effective buffer is neutral, upbeat, and relevant and doesn't forecast the bad news. The transition moves the reader from buffer to explanation by using a key word or idea. The explanation should be clear, unemotional, and objective. The bad news should be clear but not emphasized. Soften the blow of your message by using the following techniques: don't put the bad news in a conspicuous position; use a long sentence and try to put the bad news in a subordinate clause; use the passive voice and, in some cases, imply the refusal; and try to offer an alternative. The closing should be courteous, pleasant, and forward-looking, and should not refer directly to the bad news or invite further correspondence.

Employ the indirect strategy when refusing requests and claims. Even when the customer is wrong, the indirect strategy helps minimize customer discontent.

Credit refusals use a five-part strategy to break the bad news: the buffer; the transition; the explanation, which shows concern for the welfare of the reader; the bad news; and the closing, which looks positively to the future.

APPLICATION AND PRACTICE—8

Discussion

1. Discuss at least five situations in which the indirect strategy would be appropriate for delivering a negative message.

2. The indirect strategy appears to be an effort to manipulate the reader. Discuss.

3. The organization and development of a message delivering negative news begins with the explanation. Discuss.

4. Analyze the effectiveness of the following opening statements for negative news letters:

   a. Unfortunately, we would like to approve your credit application, but we cannot.

   b. I enjoyed talking with you last week when you came in to be interviewed for the position of assistant to the registrar.

   c. The weather recently has been pleasant for this time of year, hasn't it?

5. Analyze the effectiveness of the following closing statements for negative letters:

   a. Once again, please let me say that we would like to grant your request but we cannot allow outsiders to use our confidential company files even for such worthy research as you describe.

   b. If you have any further questions about this matter, please remember that I am available to serve you.

   c. Although we regret very much any inconvenience our shipping error has caused you, we trust that you will understand our position in this matter.

Short Answers

6. The indirect strategy should be used when you expect what kind of reader reaction?

7. List in proper sequence the six elements involved in organizing a negative message according to the indirect strategy.

8. What are three characteristics of a good buffer?

9. How can a writer develop a transition between the opening of a letter and an explanation that follows?

10. List seven ways to de-emphasize bad news. Be prepared to discuss each.

11. List four ways in which you should not close a negative message.

12. Name three problem words.

13. Name four emphatic positions in a letter.

Writing Improvement Exercises

Subordinate Clauses.   You can soften the effect of bad news by placing it in a subordinate clause that begins with *although, since,* or *because.* The emphasis in a sentence is upon the independent clause. Instead of saying *We cannot serve you on a credit basis,* try *Since we cannot serve you on a credit basis, we invite you to take advantage of our cash discounts and sales prices.*

Revise the following refusals so that the bad news appears in a subordinate clause.

14. We no longer manufacture the Model SF-7. However, we now make a substitute, the Model SF-9, which we would like to send you.

15. We hope to have our plant remodelling completed by October. We cannot schedule tours of the bottling plant until after we finish remodelling.

16. Island Airways cannot accept responsibility for expenses incurred indirectly from flight delays. However, we do recognize that this delay inconvenienced you.

Passive-Voice Verbs.   Passive-voice verbs may be preferable in breaking bad news because they enable you to emphasize actions rather than personalities. Compare these two refusals:

Active Voice: I cannot authorize you to take three weeks of vacation in July.

Passive Voice: Three weeks of vacation in July cannot be authorized.

Revise the following refusals so that they use passive-voice instead of active-voice verbs.

17. We cannot refund cash for the items you purchased on credit.

18. I have already filled my schedule on the date you wish me to speak.

19. We do not lend money to clients until we have verified their credit rating.

Implied Refusals.   Bad news can be de-emphasized by implying a refusal instead of stating it directly. Compare these refusals:

Direct Refusal: We cannot send you a price list nor can we sell our lawn mowers directly to customers. We sell only through dealers, and your dealer is HomeCo, Inc.

Implied Refusal: Our lawn mowers are sold only through dealers, and your dealer is HomeCo, Inc.

Revise the following refusals so that they are implied.

20. We cannot open a credit account for you because your application states that you have no regular employment. This allows us to serve you only as a cash customer.

21. I find it impossible to contribute to the fund-raising campaign this year. At present, all the funds of my organization are needed to lease new equipment and offices for our new branch in Richmond.

22. Your order was not accompanied by payment, so we are not shipping your fresh fruit baskets. We have it ready, though, and will rush it to its destination as soon as you call us with your credit-card number.

CASE 8–1

Favour Refusal

Imagine that you are Ron Levin, manager of Datatech Computers. You have received a letter from Professor Lydia Keuser, at nearby Assiniboine College, who wants to bring her class of 30 office technology students to your showroom to see the latest microcomputer hardware and software. You are eager to have 30 potential customers visit your showroom, where you carry a comprehensive line of microcomputers, compatible printers, and state-of-the-art software. But you can't possibly accommodate 30 people at once. Your workstations are arranged for demonstrations to only one or two viewers at a time. You must refuse Professor Keuser's request. However, since you hate to pass up this opportunity, suggest to her that you could bring a computer to her classroom for a demonstration, or she could divide her class into smaller groups for demos at the showroom.

Consider the refusal letter to Professor Keuser. Analyze the following options in relation to the indirect strategy. Circle the letters representing the most appropriate possibilities for the refusal letter.

1. To open this letter appropriately, you might

   a. Point out immediately that your showroom is too small to accommodate her entire class at once.

   b. Express appreciation that Professor Keuser and her office technology class are interested in the microcomputers and software offered by Datatech Computers.

   c. Explain that Datatech Computers carries only professional programs and that your stock does not include computer games, in which some college students may be interested.

   d. Suggest that she divide her class into thirds and let you demonstrate your comprehensive line at three different times.

2. A logical transition for this letter might be for you to

   a. Use sales promotion by describing the outstanding features of your best-selling computer and one of your software programs.

    b. Warn Professor Keuser that 30 students gathered around one screen would create an impossible viewing situation.

    c. Mention that you normally demonstrate your comprehensive line of microcomputers, printers, and software programs to individual customers.

    d. Inquire regarding the level of computer expertise represented by the students in this class.

3. In explaining why you cannot accommodate the class, you might say that

    a. Demonstrating to this large a student group would interfere with sales to genuine customers in your showroom.

    b. Customers usually come in individually or in pairs; hence you are prepared for demonstrations to small groups only.

    c. You never demonstrate to large groups because individuals complain that they can't see what's on the screen or hear what's being said.

    d. You would prefer not to demonstrate to students because many will not understand the complexities of computers; moreover, they are unlikely to make purchases in the near future.

4. Which of the following sentences softens the refusal most effectively?

    a. Although your class cannot be accommodated in our showroom, we might be able to arrange a demonstration in your classroom.

    b. We cannot accommodate your class in our showroom because your class is too large.

    c. Although we might be able to arrange a demonstration in your classroom, we cannot accommodate your class in our showroom.

    d. We sincerely regret that we cannot allow your class to come to Datatech Computers for a demonstration.

Use this problem for discussion. At the option of your instructor, write the entire letter (individually or as a class project) to Professor Lydia Keuser, Assiniboine College, 210 Park Avenue, Brandon, Manitoba R4H 1E5. You may wish to incorporate some of the sentences you selected here, but consider this no more than an outline. Complete your letter with explanations, examples, appropriate connecting thoughts, and a good-will closing. Use modified block style with indented paragraphs.

CASE 8–2

Request Refusal

Analyze the following poorly written message, and list at least five faults. Outline a writing plan for refusing a request. Then, on a separate sheet, rewrite the message, rectifying the faults.

TO: Anita Ho, Records Manager   DATE: June 20, 199x

FROM: Connie Clark, President

SUBJECT: CONFERENCE

Please be informed that I have taken under advisement your request to be allowed to attend the conference of the Association of Records Managers and Administrators, Inc., in Montreal. Unfortunately, this conference is six days long and comes in September, a very critical time for us.

Ineffective writing

I'm sorry to have to deny your request, because it looks like a worthwhile conference. It would afford an opportunity for records management personnel, like you, to learn more about current procedures and technologies. You've been doing an outstanding job of transferring our paper files to the new database.

But to have you gone for a period of six days in September, when, as you know, we complete our budget requests for the following fiscal year is out of the question. We need you at our budget-planning meetings, particularly since you have proposed the purchase of computer equipment that will make better use of the database. Another reason that you can't go in September, in spite of the fact that I would like to see you go, is that Cathy Watson, in your department, has been granted a leave for the months of August through October. Your absence, together with hers, would put us in a real bind.

For these reasons, I cannot allow you to leave in September. However, if there is a suitable conference at some other time in the year when your absence would be less critical, I would be happy to let you go. I'm sorry about this matter, Anita. This is certainly little thanks for the excellent progress you are making in the massive task of converting our filing system.

CASE 8–3

Credit Refusal

Analyze the following poorly written message, and list at least five faults. Outline a writing plan for refusing credit. Then, on a separate sheet, rewrite the message, rectifying its faults. Address the letter to Ms. Abina Sennar, 876 First Street, Thunder Bay, Ontario P2W 3R7. Use modified block style with indented paragraphs.

Dear Ms. Sennar:

Thank you very much for your April 23 order for computer paper, copy paper, and other supplies. We are delighted by your interest in our products and our company. Unfortunately, we cannot fill your order because of your poor credit rating.

Ineffective writing

Your application for credit indicates that your dealership now has a current assets ratio of only 1 to 1. Most financial authorities recommend that businesses of your size maintain a 2-to-1 ratio of current assets to liabilities. Our company policy prohibits us from issuing credit to any organization that does not meet this minimum requirement. We hope you will understand our desire to avoid any credit losses.

Since your dealership appears to be experiencing good sales, we're sure you will want to practise sound financing and avoid increasing your liabilities with additional credit purchases. For this reason, we invite you to let us fill your order on a cash basis.

At the present time we have in stock all the items that you requested. We can't send them, though, unless you have cash. If you would like these items rushed to you, call me personally at (705) 883-2980. If I can be of further service, don't hesitate to call on me.

Sincerely,

Pamela Wright

Pamela Wright
Credit Manager

CASE 8–4

Claim Refusal

For class discussion analyze the following poorly written message. Discuss at least five faults, and suggest a writing plan for refusing a claim. Then, at the option of your instructor, on a separate sheet rewrite the message, rectifying its faults. Address the letter to Mr. Ahmed Sharjah, 422 Bond Avenue, Red Deer, Alberta T5A 6U7. Use modified block style with indented paragraphs.

Dear Mr. Sharjah:

Ineffective writing   We have your letter of May 23 demanding repair or replacement for your newly purchased BeautyTest mattress. You say that you enjoy sleeping on it; but in the morning when you get up, you claim that the mattress has body impressions that remain all day.

Unfortunately, we can neither repair nor replace your mattress because those impressions are perfectly normal. If you will read your warranty carefully, you will find this statement: "Slight body impressions will appear with use and are not indicative of structural failure. The body-conforming coils and comfort-cushioning materials are beginning to work for you and impressions are caused by the natural settling of these materials."

When you purchased your mattress, I'm sure your salesperson told you that the BeautyTest mattress has a unique, scientifically designed system of individually pocketed coils that provide separate support for each person occupying the bed. This unusual construction, with those hundreds of independently operating coils, reacts to every body contour, providing luxurious comfort. At the same time, this system provides firm support. It is this unique design that's causing the body impressions that you see when you get up in the morning.

Although we never repair or replace a mattress when it merely shows slight impressions, we will send our representative out to inspect your mattress, if it would make you feel better. Please call for an appointment at (403) 322-9800. Remember, on a BeautyTest mattress you get the best night's rest possible.

Cordially,

Additional Problems

1. As the sales manager of Wholesale Copier Exchange, you are faced with a difficult decision. The daughter of one of your best friends operates Eastland Auto. For the past ten months, as a favour, you have allowed her to lease from you a full-featured Toshiba copier at a low rate of $200 per month. Now she wants to purchase the Toshiba, and she wants you to apply the lease payments against the purchase price. That means that she wants to deduct $2000 from the basic purchase price of $7695. Your quoted purchase price is already very low. You have been able to build business by selling a high volume of units while keeping your margin of profit quite low. Although you do have a limited leasing business, none of your leasing agreements includes an option to apply the lease payments toward the purchase of a unit. Other companies may permit such an arrangement, but their purchase prices are probably much higher than yours. Even at $7695, you will be earning a very slim profit. To allow a $2000 discount would certainly mean a loss for you; and even for the daughter of a friend, you don't want to absorb such a loss. Eastland seems to like the performance it has received from this Toshiba, Model DC-3E. You have slightly cheaper models, but they have fewer features. If Eastland wants to give up the reduction and enlargement capability as well as the automatic paper selection device, you might be able to bring the purchase price down $1500. Regardless of what Toshiba model Eastland purchases, you guarantee 6-hour emergency service and a 1-million-copy or 8-year warranty. Write a letter to Rachel Ramberg, Eastland Auto, 480 Bower Boulevard, Ottawa, Ontario K6L 1Y3, retaining her friendship and business but refusing her request.

2. Assume that you are plant operations manager for United Distributors Association. You have received a letter from Mr. Donald T. Webster, president of the Cabbagetown Community Association. Mr. Webster writes at the suggestion of Victor Cortez, whom you know well as the supervisor of your shipping fleet and one of your most valued employees. Mr. Cortez is the coordinator of the association's food-bank drive and has been instrumental in collecting food for the local food bank. He has suggested to Mr. Webster that United Distributors might allow the community association to borrow a small truck over a weekend to pick up articles left at the Community Centre, as well as at drop-off points in suburban Scarborough and Mississauga, and deliver them to the Toronto Harvest Food Bank. You support the goals of the community association and would like to encourage this worthwhile endeavour. However, company trucks cannot be lent to outside organizations or individuals, even for worthy causes. Your liability insurance limits equipment coverage to specific deliveries, routes, and licensed drivers. You cannot allow any company truck to be borrowed officially (or unofficially), even by a trusted company employee for an admirable project. Write a refusal letter that recognizes the worth of this charitable project and acknowledges the high regard you hold for Mr. Cortez. Address the letter to Mr. Donald T. Webster, Cabbagetown Community Association, 401 Parliament Street, Toronto, Ontario M5N 2E8, and send a copy to Victor Cortez in the company mail.

3. As Lentax consumer affairs representative, you must refuse the claim of Gabriella Marconi, a professional photographer who purchased a Lentax macrofocusing teleconverter lens two years ago. Ms. Marconi wants the lens replaced, claiming that it no longer works properly, although it worked well for two years. Your service department has examined the returned teleconverter and determined that either it was improperly attached to another lens or it was dropped, causing a lack of synchronization with Ms. Marconi's aperture-priority camera. Lentax products are built to the highest standards and should provide years of satisfaction. The Lentax Limited 5-Year Warranty clearly states the following: "Malfunctions resulting from misuse, tampering, unauthorized repairs, modifications, or accident are not covered by this warranty." Refuse the request for replacement. Tell her, however, that since she purchased this lens from an authorized dealer, she may receive a 25 percent discount on repairs. Write to Ms. Gabriella Marconi, 120 Carlisle Street, Edmonton, Alberta T3L 2T5.

4. As Richard Green, owner of Greenscapes, Inc., you must refuse the following request. Mr. and Mrs. John Nabor have asked that you replace the landscaping in the home they recently purchased in Portage la Prairie. You had landscaped that home nearly a year ago for the former owner, Mrs. Kumar, installing a sod lawn and many shrubs, trees, and flowers. It looked beautiful when you finished, but six months later, Mrs. Kumar sold the property and moved to Winnipeg. Four months elapsed before the new owners moved in. The newly installed landscaping suffered from four months of neglect and a hot, dry summer. You guarantee all your work and normally would replace any plants that do not survive. Under these circumstances, however, you do not feel justified in making any refund because your guarantee necessarily presumes proper maintenance on the part of the property owner. Moreover, your guarantee is made only to the individual who contracted with you, not to subsequent owners. You would like to retain the good will of the new owners, since this is an affluent neighbourhood and you hope to attract additional work here. On the other hand, you can't afford to replace the materials invested in this job. You believe that the lawn could probably be rejuvenated with deep watering and fertilizer. You would be happy to inspect the property and offer suggestions to the Nabors. In reality, you wonder if the Nabors might not have a claim against the former owner or the escrow agency that had change of the home after her departure for failing to maintain the property. Clearly, however, the claim is not against you. Write to Mr. and Mrs. John Nabor, 471 Highgate Drive, Portage la Prairie, Manitoba R3L 2T2.

5. As manager of the Sports Connection, you must refuse the application of Geri Meyers for an extended membership in your athletic club. This is strictly a business decision. You liked Geri very much when she applied, and she seems genuinely interested in fitness and a healthful lifestyle. However, your "extended membership" plan qualifies the member for all your testing, exercise, aerobics, and recreation programs. This multiservice program is necessarily expensive and requires a solid credit rating. To your disappointment, however, you learn that Geri's credit rating is decidedly negative. She is reported to be delinquent in payments to four businesses,

including Holiday Health Spa, your principal competitor. You do have other programs, including your "Drop In and Work Out" plan that offers use of available facilities on a cash basis. This plan enables a member to reserve space on the racquetball and handball courts; the member can also sign up for exercise and aerobics classes, space permitting. Since Geri is in considerable debt, you would feel guilty allowing her to plunge in more deeply. Refuse her credit application, but encourage her cash business. Write to Geri Meyers, Apartment 4, 235 Hillcrest Avenue, Sudbury, Ontario P2N 3E4.

GRAMMAR/MECHANICS CHECKUP—8

Commas, 3

Review Sections 2.10 through 2.15 of the Grammar/Mechanics Handbook. Then study each of the following statements and insert necessary commas. In the space provided for each statement, write the number of commas that you add; write *0* if no commas are needed. Also record the number of the G/M principles(s) illustrated. When you finish, compare your responses with those shown below. If your answers differ, study carefully the principles shown in parentheses.

Example: It was Ms. Jeffreys ⋏not Mr. Simpson ⋏who was assigned the Madison account.

2 (2.12)

1. "The choice of a good name" said President Gordon "cannot be overestimated." _____

2. Lois A. Wagner Ph.D. and Durva S. Peshawar M.B.A. were hired as consultants. _____

3. Their August 15 order was shipped on Monday wasn't it? _____

4. Brand names are important in advertising specialty goods such as refrigerators and television sets. _____

5. The bigger the investment the greater the profit. _____

Review Commas 1, 2, and 3

6. As you requested your order for ribbons file folders and envelopes will be sent immediately. _____

7. We think however that you should re-examine your networking system and that you should consider electronic mail. _____

8. Within the next eight-week period we hope to hire Van Vo who is currently working in private industry. _____

9. Our convention will attract more participants if it is held in a resort location such as Banff Jasper or Whistler. _____

10. If everyone who applied for the position were interviewed we would be overwhelmed. _____

11. Our chief goal is to provide quality products backed by prompt efficient service.

12. In the past ten years we have employed over 30 qualified individuals many of whom have selected banking as their career.

13. Your shipment has been charged to your new account which we were pleased to open on the basis of your admirable credit.

14. Steven Sims who spoke to our class last week is the author of a book entitled *Writing Winning Résumés*.

15. Anne Hartung uses market research extensively and keeps a close watch on her own operations her competition and the market in order to identify the latest trends.

---

1. (2) name, "Gordon, (2.14a)   3. (1) Monday, (2.14b)   5. (1) investment, (2.12)   7. (2)* think, however, (2.03)   9. (2) Banff, Jasper, (2.01)   11. (1) prompt, (2.08, 2.15)   13. (1) account, (2.06c, 2.15)   15. (2) operations, competition, (2.01)

---

*No comma precedes *and* because the words following are not an independent clause.

Word Trap Answers*

1. **adopt**, *v.*: borrow, to accept as one's own. [**adept**, *adj.* = skilled; **adapt**, *v.* = to make fit, adjust, or modify]

2. **averse**, *adj.*: unwilling, disinclined. [**adverse**, *adj.* = unfavourable, hostile]

3. **affect**, *v.*: influence, impress. [**effect**, *n.* = result, outcome; **effect**, *v.* = to produce (a change)]

4. **biannual**, *adj.*: occurring twice a year. [**biennial**, *adj.* = occurring once every two years]

5. **capital**, *n.*: assets, cash. [**Capitol**, *n.* = building where U.S. Congress meets; **capitol**, *n.* = building where U.S. state legislatures meet. Note also: **capital**, *n.* or *adj.* = city where government is based]

6. **complimentary**, *adj.*: free. [**complementary**, *adj.* = acting to complete or fill out]

7. **eminent**, *adj.*: famous, distinguished. [**imminent**, *adj.* = impending]

8. **infer**, *v.*: conclude, deduce. [**imply**, *v.* = suggest indirectly, hint]

9. **personnel**, *n.*: employees, staff. [**personal**, *adj.* = private]

10. **proceed**, *v.*: continue, move forward. [**precede**, *v.* = preface, come before]

11. **principal**, *adj.*: chief, main. [**principle**, *n.* = rule, belief, guideline]

12. **than**, *conj.*: function word used in making a comparison. [**then**, *adv.* = next, at that time]

13. **disperse**, *v.*: distribute, give, disseminate. [**disburse**, *v.* = pay, apportion]

14. **their**, *possessive pron.*: of or belonging to them. [**they're**, *pro. + v.* = they are; **there**, *adv.* = at that place or at that point]

15. **whether**, *conj.*: function word introducing alternatives. [**weather**, *n.* = atmospheric conditions]

*From page 183.

GRAMMAR/MECHANICS CHALLENGE—8

Document for Revision

The following memo contains faults in grammar, punctuation, spelling, and number form, in addition to problems discussed in this chapter. Drawing upon the guidelines provided in the Grammar/Mechanics Handbook and what you learned in the chapter, revise the memo.

Poor Memo

TO: Jason Su   February 22, 199x

FROM: Roger Franco

SUBJECT: REQUEST TO ATTEND CONFERENCE IN THE MONTH OF MAY

The Management Counsel and me are extremely pleased with the leadership you have provided in setting up live video transmission to our regional offices. As a result of your professinal commitment, I can understand your desire to attend the Tellecommunications Expo in Vancouver in the Spring.

Unfortunately, the last two weeks in May has been set aside for budget planning. Just between you an I we've only just scratched the surface of our teleconferencing projects for the next 5 years. As a result of the fact that you are the specialist, and we rely heavily on your expertise, we need you hear for those planning sessions.

If your able to attend a simular event in the Summer, and if your work loads permit, we'll try to send you then. Your a valueable player, Jason and I'm greatful your on our MIS team.

Letters and Memos That Persuade

9

In this chapter, you will learn to do the following:

- Use the indirect strategy to persuade.
- Write convincing claim and favour request letters.
- Present new ideas in persuasive memos.

- Analyze techniques used in sales letters.
- Compose carefully planned sales letters.
- Compose formal and informal proposals.

The ability to persuade is a key factor in the success you achieve in your business messages. Persuasive individuals are those who present convincing arguments that influence or win over others. Because their ideas generally prevail, these individuals become decision-makers—managers and executives. This chapter will examine the techniques for presenting ideas persuasively.

Being able to use persuasion skilfully is a primary factor in personal and business success.

Persuasive Requests

Persuasion is necessary when resistance is anticipated or when ideas require preparation before they can be presented effectively. For example, if Karima Bhanji purchased a new car and the transmission repeatedly required servicing, she might be forced to write to the dealership where she bought it asking that the company install a new transmission in her car. Karima's claim letter should be persuasive; she must convince the dealership that replacement, not repair, is needed.

Routine claim letters, such as those you wrote in Chapter 6, are straightforward and direct. Persuasive requests, on the other hand, are generally more effective when they are indirect. Reasons and explanations should precede the big idea. To overcome possible resistance, the writer must lay a logical founda-

Use persuasion when you must change attitudes or produce action.

tion before the big news is delivered. A writing plan for a persuasive request requires deliberate development.

Writing Plan for a Persuasive Request

- **Opening**—obtains the reader's attention and interest.
- **Persuasion**—explains logically and concisely the purpose of your request and proves that your request has merit.
- **Closing**—asks for a particular action and shows courtesy and respect.

Claim Request

The most important parts of a claim letter are the sections describing the desired action and the proof that such action is reasonable.

The organization of an effective persuasive claim centres on the closing and the persuasion. First, decide what action you want taken to satisfy the claim. Then decide how you can prove the worth of your claim. Plan carefully the line of reasoning you will follow in convincing the reader to take the action you request. If the claim is addressed to a business, it is generally effective to appeal to the organization's pride in its products and services. Refer to its reputation for integrity and your confidence in it. Show the validity of your claim and why the company will be doing the right thing in granting it. Most organizations are sincere in their efforts to produce quality products that gain consumer respect.

Anger and emotional threats against an organization do little to achieve the goal of claim letters. Claims are generally referred to a customer service department. The claims adjuster answering the claim probably bears no responsibility for the design, production, delivery, or servicing of the product. An abusive letter may serve only to offend the claims adjuster, thus making it difficult for the claim to be evaluated rationally.

Claim letters should avoid negative and emotional words and should not attempt to attribute blame.

The most effective claim captures the attention of the reader immediately in the opening and sets up the persuasion that follows. In the body of the claim, you should present convincing reasons to justify the claim. Try to argue without overusing negative words, without fixing blame for the problem, and without becoming emotional. To create the desired effect, arrange the reasons in a logical, orderly manner with appropriate transitions to guide the reader through the persuasion.

Following the persuasion, spell out clearly the desired action in the closing. Remember, the most successful claims are respectful and courteous.

Observe how the claim letter shown in Figure 9.1 illustrates the preceding suggestions. The opening statements secure the reader's attention and at the same time set up the description of events and persuasive arguments that follow. Notice the absence of hostility and harsh words, although the writer probably experienced angry feelings over these events. Notice, too, that the closing rounds out the letter by tying in a reference to the opening statement.

Favour Request

Asking for a favour implies that you want someone to do something for nothing—or for very little. Common examples are requests for the donation of time,

FIGURE 9.1 Claim Request—Block Style, Open Punctuation

⊞ *AMS LIMITÉE*

Local
National
International

495, rue de la Morenie
Sherbrooke, Québec G3Y 4E6
(819) 883-3918

January 23, 199x

D. Gerard, Inc.
3350, avenue Montmorency
Montréal, Québec
G2L 2E9

Ladies and Gentlemen:

SUBJECT: BUTONE MODEL 150 HOT-WATER HEATING SYSTEM

Your Butone hot-water heating system appealed to my company for two reasons. First, it promised high-efficiency heat with a 36 percent savings in our heating costs. Second, your firm has been in the heating business for 40 years, and such a record must indicate a reputation of concern for your customers.

> Gains attention with favourable comments about the company.

We think that we were right about your heating system, and we hope that your regard for your reputation will move you to take action on our behalf.

Last September we purchased a Butone Model 150 and had it installed in our eight-room office building by your dealer, Chauffage Saint-Laurent. For two weeks it heated our offices comfortably. One morning, though, we arrived and found our rooms cold. We called Chauffage Saint-Laurent, and their technician came out to inspect our system. He reported that the automatic ignition device had failed. He replaced it, and the system worked well for two days. Then, on the third day after this repair, a fire developed in the combustion area of the heating unit, destroying the circulating pump and its motor. Technicians from Chauffage Saint-Laurent returned immediately and replaced the entire heating unit.

> Explains events in orderly, logical fashion.

We assumed that this replacement was covered by the system's five-year warranty. That's why we were surprised two days ago to receive a bill from Chauffage Saint-Laurent for $255.92 covering installation of the new unit. In a telephone conversation, James Wilkins of Chauffage Saint-Laurent said that the warranty covers only replacement of the unit. The cost of installation is extra.

Argues convincingly
that charge is
unjustified.

We feel that this charge is unjustified. The fire that destroyed the unit resulted from either a defective unit or faulty servicing by Chauffage Saint-Laurent. Since we feel responsibility for neither of these conditions, we believe that we should bear no charges. Our insurance carrier shares this view.

Closes with action
requests that ties in
with opening.

Please pay the attached bill or instruct Chauffage Saint-Laurent to cancel it. This would indicate to us that we were right both about your product and about your reputation.

Sincerely,

Pamela Dougherty

Pamela Dougherty
Office Manager

rpw

Attachment

---

money, energy, name, resources, talent, skills, or expertise. On occasion, everyone needs to ask a favour. Small favours, such as asking a co-worker to lock up the office for you on Friday, can be straightforward and direct, since you anticipate little resistance. Larger favours require careful planning and an indirect strategy. Consider the appeal to a busy executive who is asked to serve on a committee to help children with disabilities; or the appeal to a florist who is asked to donate table arrangements for a charity fund-raiser; or a request made to an eminent author to speak before a local library group. In each instance, persuasion is necessary to overcome natural resistance.

When you anticipate
resistance to a
favour request, use
persuasive
techniques.

The letter shown in Figure 9.2 illustrates a poorly conceived favour request. An organization without funds hopes to entice a well-known authority to speak before its regional conference. Such a request surely requires indirectness and persuasion, but the following ineffective letter begins with a direct appeal. The reader is given an opportunity to refuse the request before the writer has a chance to present reasons for accepting. The second paragraph also provides an easy opportunity to refuse the request. Moreover, this letter contains little to convince Dr. Abramsky that she has anything to gain by speaking to this group. Finally, the closing suggests no specific action to help her accept, should she be so inclined.

A favour request is
doomed to failure if
the writer fails to
consider its effect on
the reader.

Notice, now, how the letter to Dr. Abramsky in Figure 9.3 applies the indirect strategy to achieve its goal. The opening catches her interest and makes her want to read more regarding the reaction to her article. By showing how Dr. Abramsky's interests are related to the organization's, the writer lays a groundwork of persuasion before presenting the request. The request is then followed by reasoning that shows Dr. Abramsky how she will benefit from accepting this invitation. This successful letter concludes with an action closing.

FIGURE 9.2   Weak Favour Request

Dear Dr. Abramsky:

Would you be willing to speak to the Canadian Personnel Managers Association's regional conference in Vancouver on March 23?

Although we understand that your research, teaching, and consulting must keep you extremely busy, we hope that your schedule will allow you to be the featured speaker at our conference. We are particularly interested in the article you recently published in the *Canadian Business Review*. A number of our members indicated that your topic, "Cost/Benefit Analysis for Human Resources," is something we should learn more about. Perhaps you could select a topic that would be somewhat more practical and not so theoretical, since most of our members are personnel managers or personnel specialists.

We have no funds to pay you, but we would like to invite you and your spouse to be our guests at the banquet following the day's sessions.

We hope that you will be able to speak before our group.

Sincerely,

Persuasive Memo

Within an organization, the indirect strategy is appropriate when persuasion is needed in presenting new ideas to management or to colleagues, in requesting action from employees, and in securing compliance with altered procedures.

Whenever resistance is anticipated, a sound foundation of reasoning should precede the big idea so that it will not be rejected prematurely. New ideas can be expected to generate resistance, whether they are moving downward as directives from management, moving upward as suggestions to management, or moving laterally among colleagues. It is natural to resist change.

Prepare for resistance by anticipating objections, offering counterarguments, and emphasizing benefits. Don't assume that the advantages of a new plan are obvious and therefore may go unmentioned. Use concrete examples and familiar illustrations in presenting arguments.

In the memo shown in Figure 9.4, Randy MacArthur, communications supervisor, argues for the purchase of an expensive new piece of equipment, an optical character reader (OCR). He expects his manager to resist this purchase because the manager knows little about OCRs, and because the budget is already overextended. Randy's memo follows the writing plan for a persuasive

FIGURE 9.3 Favour Request That Succeeds—Modified Block Style, Mixed Punctuation

C A N A D I A N   P E R S O N N E L   M A N A G E R S   A S S O C I A T I O N
196 West 20th Street
Vancouver, BC V0L 3T4
(604) 543-8922

January 4, 199x

Professor Karen J. Abramsky
Caribou College
Kamloops, BC
V1L 2R4

Dear Dr. Abramsky:

Grabs attention of reader by appealing to her interests.

Cost/benefit analysis as applied to human resources is a unique concept. Your recent article on that topic in the *Canadian Business Review* ignited a lively discussion at the last meeting of the Vancouver chapter of the Canadian Personnel Managers Association.

Persuades reader that her expertise is valued.

Many of the managers in our group are experiencing the changes you describe. Functions in the personnel area are now being expanded to include a wide range of salary, welfare, benefit, and training programs. These new programs can be very expensive. Our members are fascinated by your cost/benefit analysis that sets up a formal comparison of the costs to design, develop, and implement a program idea against the costs the idea saves or avoids. We'd like to know more about how this is done.

Softens negative aspects of request with reader's benefits.

The members of our association have asked me to invite you to be the featured speaker March 23 when we hold our annual West Coast regional conference in Vancouver. About 150 personnel management specialists will attend the all-day conference at the Plaza Hotel. We would like you to speak at 2 p.m. on the topic of "Applying Cost/Benefit Analysis in Personnel Today." Although we cannot offer you an honorarium, we can offer you an opportunity to help personnel managers apply your theories in solving some of their most perplexing problems. You will also be able to meet managers who might be able to supply you with data for future research into personnel functions. In addition, the conference includes two other sessions and a banquet, to which you and a guest are invited.

Ends confidently with special action to be taken.

Please call me at (604) 543-8922 to allow me to add your name to the program as the featured speaker before the Canadian Personnel Managers Association, March 23 at 2 p.m.

Respectfully yours,

Joanne North

Joanne North
Executive Assistant

FIGURE 9.4 Persuasive Memo That Requests New Equipment

TO: George Romanoff,   DATE: May 2, 199x
             Director of Operations

FROM: Randy MacArthur RM
             Communications Supervisor, Central Services

SUBJECT: REDUCING OVERTIME AND IMPROVING TURNAROUND TIME

Last month we paid nearly $7500 in overtime to word processing special-
ists who were forced to work 50- and 60-hour weeks to keep up with the
heavy demand for printed documents. Despite this overtime, the average
turnaround time for documents submitted to Central Services is now eight
working days.

> Captures attention of reader with a problem that can be solved.

Many of the documents submitted to us are already in print and must be
entered into our word processing system by our operators. For example,
some of the engineers in Systems Design bring us rough-draft proposals
that they have produced on their microcomputers, which are not compatible with ours. As a result we are forced to re-enter the material.

> Explains background and rationale before making proposal.

I estimate that we could eliminate at least 60 percent of our overtime and
also reduce the turnaround time on documents by five days if we were to
use an optical character reader (OCR) to read printed documents into our
word processing system. OCRs look like photocopiers, but they read
printed images and convert them into electronic images.

> Points out concrete examples of savings to be realized.

OCRs are not perfect, of course. The medium-priced unit can now read
only selected typefaces, and it is most accurate when reading from white
paper only. However, most of the documents on which we would use the
OCR are printed in standard typefaces and on white paper.

> Anticipates objections and answers them.

Despite these limitations, I believe that 55 to 60 percent of the printed
documents coming to us could be read by an OCR. By eliminating this
tedious re-entering, we could save at least $4500 in overtime each month.
We could also reduce turnaround time in Central Services by as much as
60 percent. Moreover, by eliminating the re-entering of printed documents, fewer errors will be introduced; and, most importantly, our
specialists will be much happier employees.

> Summarizes advantages of purchasing new equipment.

For these reasons, I recommend that we purchase the TECH Turbofont
Model 303 optical character reader. It can read print from six typestyles
with 95 percent accuracy. Its purchase price of $12,300 will be recovered
from the savings due to reduced overtime within three months.

> Delays mention of price until after convincing arguments have been presented.

Enclosed is a specification sheet describing this model. Please give me
authorization to submit a purchase order for this OCR by June 1 so that
Central Services may improve turnaround time before we are asked to
begin work on the fiscal reports in July.

> Ends with explicit request and provides end dating.

request. It begins by describing a costly problem in which Randy knows the reader is interested. To convince the manager of the need for an OCR, Randy must first explain the operation of an OCR and how it could benefit the organization.

Instead of using generalities, Randy cites specific examples of how the OCR would function in their company and the amount of savings it would produce. Randy also anticipates the limitations of the OCR and discusses their effect on the proposal. In the closing, Randy asks for a specific action and provides support documentation to speed his request. He also includes end dating, which prompts the manager to act by a certain date.

Sales Letters

Recognizing and applying the techniques of sales writing can be helpful even if you never write an actual sales letter.

Direct-mail selling is a rapidly growing industry. The professionals who specialize in direct-mail marketing have made a science of analyzing a market, studying the product, preparing a comprehensive presentation that appeals to the needs of the target audience, and motivating the reader to act. This carefully orchestrated presentation typically culminates in a sales letter accompanied by a brochure, a sales list, illustrations of the product, testimonials, and so forth. We are interested in the strategy, organization, and appeals used in sales letters because understanding the techniques of sales writing will help you be more effective in any communication that requires persuasion and promotion. In a sense, every letter that we write is a form of sales letter. We sell our ideas, ourselves, and our organizations.

The following writing plan for a sales letter attempts to overcome anticipated reader resistance by creating a desire for the product and by motivating the reader to act.

Writing Plan for a Sales Letter

- **Opening**—captures the attention of the reader.
- **Body**—emphasizes a central selling point, appeals to the needs of the reader, creates a desire for the product, and introduces price strategically.
- **Closing**—stimulates the reader to act.

Analyzing the Product and the Reader

Both the product and the reader require careful analysis before a successful sales letter can be written.

Before implementing the writing plan, it's wise to study the product and the target audience so that you can emphasize features with reader appeal.

To sell a product effectively, learn as much as possible about its construction, including its design, raw materials, and manufacturing process. Study its performance, including ease of use, efficiency, durability, and applications. Consider warranties, service, price, and special appeals. Be knowledgeable not only about your product but also about the competitor's product so you can emphasize your product's strengths against the competitor's weaknesses.

By using selected mailing lists, sales-letter writers are able to make certain assumptions about the readers. Readers may be expected to share certain characteristics, such as interests, abilities, needs, income, and so forth. The sales letter, then, can be adapted to appeal directly to this selected group. In working with a less selected audience, the letter writer can make only general assumptions and must use a diffuse approach, hoping to find some appeal that motivates the reader.

Capturing the Reader's Attention

Gaining the attention of the reader is essential in unsolicited or uninvited sales letters. Attention-getting devices are less important in solicited sales letters, because readers have requested information.

> Attention-getting devices are especially important in unsolicited sales letters.

Provocative messages or unusual typographical arrangements can be used to attract attention in unsolicited sales letters. These messages may be found within the body of a letter, or in place of the inside address.

Offer:	Your free calculator is just the beginning!
Product feature:	Your vacations—this year and in the future—can be more rewarding thanks to an exciting new book from Equinox.
Inside-address opening:	We Wonder, Mrs. Crain, If You Would Like to Find Out How to Grow Rich With Mutual Funds
Startling statement:	Extinction is forever. That's why we need your help in preserving many of the world's endangered species.
Story:	On a beautiful late spring afternoon, 25 years ago, two young men graduated from the same college. They were alike, these two young men ... Recently, these men returned to their college for their 25th reunion. They were still alike ... But there was a difference. One of the men was manager of a small department of a manufacturing company. The other was its president.

Other effective openings include a bargain, a proverb, a solution to a problem, a quotation from a famous person, an anecdote, or a question.

Appealing to the Reader

Persuasive appeals fall into two broad groups: emotional appeals and rational appeals. Emotional appeals are those associated with the senses; they include how we feel, see, taste, smell, and hear. Strategies that arouse anger, fear, pride, love, and satisfaction are emotional. Rational strategies are those associated with reason and intellect; they appeal to the mind. In general, use rational appeals when a product is expensive, long-lasting, or important to health and security. Use emotional appeals when a product is inexpensive, short-lived, and nonessential.

> Emotional appeals relate to the senses; rational appeals relate to reasoning and intellect.

Banks selling chequing and savings services frequently use rational appeals. They emphasize saving money in chequing fees, earning interest on accounts, and receiving free personalized cheques. A travel agency selling a student tour to Mexico uses an emotional strategy by describing the "sun, fun, rockin' and partying" to be enjoyed. Many successful selling campaigns combine appeals, emphasizing perhaps a rational appeal while also including an emotional appeal in a subordinated position.

Emphasizing Central Selling Points

In your sales letters develop one or two central selling points and stress them.

Although a product may have a number of features, you should concentrate on just one or two of those features. Don't bewilder the reader with too much information. Analyze the reader's needs and fit your appeal directly to the reader. The letter selling a student tour to Mexico emphasized two points:

1. **We see to it that you have a great time.** Let's face it. By the end of term, you've earned your vacation. The books and jobs and stress can all be shelved for a while.

2. **We keep our trips cheap.** Mazatlan 1A is again the lowest-priced adventure trip offered in Canada.

The writer analyzed the student audience and elected to concentrate on two appeals: (1) an emotional appeal to the senses (having a good time), and (2) a rational appeal to saving money (paying a low price).

Creating a Desire for the Product

In convincing readers to purchase a product or service, you may use a number of techniques:

- **Reader benefit**. Discuss product features from the reader's point of view. Show how the reader will benefit from the product.

  You will be able to extend your swimming season by using our new solar pool cover.

- **Concrete language**. Use concrete words instead of general or abstract language.

  Our Mexican tour provides more than just a party. Maybe you've never set eyes on a giant 60-foot saguaro cactus ... or parasailed 1000 feet above the Pacific Ocean ... or watched a majestic golden sunset from your own private island.

- **Objective language**. Avoid language that sounds unreasonable. Overstatements using words like *fantastic, without fail, foolproof, amazing, astounding,* and so forth do not sound true. Overblown language and preposterous claims may cause readers to reject the entire sales message.

- **Product confidence**. Build confidence in your product or service by assuring customer satisfaction. You can do this by offering a free trial, a money-back guarantee, a free sample, or by providing a guarantee or warranty. Another way to build confidence is to associate your product with respected references or authorities.

Our concept of economical group travel has been accepted and sponsored by five city recreation departments. In addition, our program has been featured in *Maclean's*, *The Toronto Star*, *The Globe and Mail*, and *Le Devoir*.

- **Testimonials**. The statements of satisfied customers are effective in creating a desire for the product or service.

A student returning from Mazatlan's cruise last year said, "I've just been to paradise."

Introducing Price Strategically

If product price is a significant sales feature, use it early in your sales letter. Otherwise, don't mention price until after you have created the reader's desire for the product. Some sales letters include no mention of price; instead, an enclosed order form shows the price. Other techniques for de-emphasizing price include the following:

Introduce price early if it is a sales feature; otherwise, delay mentioning it.

1. **Show the price in small units**. Instead of stating the total cost of a year's subscription, state the magazine's price per issue. Describe insurance premiums by their cost per day.

2. **Show how the reader is saving money by purchasing the product**. In selling solar heating units, for example, explain how much the reader will save on heating bills.

3. **Compare your prices with competitors'**. Describe the savings to be realized when your product is purchased.

4. **Make your price a bargain**. A special introductory offer is one-third off the regular price, or the price includes a special discount if the reader acts immediately.

5. **Associate the price with reader benefits**. For example, "For as little as $3 a month, you'll enjoy emergency road and towing protection, accident insurance, emergency trip-interruption protection, and nine other benefits."

Price can be de-emphasized by using one of these five techniques.

Stimulating Action

The closing of a sales letter has one very important goal: stimulating the reader to act. A number of techniques help motivate action:

You can encourage the reader to act by applying one or more of these methods.

- **Make the action clear**. Use specific language to tell exactly what needs to be done.

Fill out the enclosed postage-paid card.
Call this toll-free number.
Send the enclosed reservation card along with your cheque.

- **Make the action easy**.

   Just use the enclosed pencil to indicate the amount of your gift. Drop the postage-paid card in the mail, and we'll handle the details.

- **Offer an inducement**. Encourage the reader to act while low prices remain in effect. Offer a gift or a rebate for action.

   Now is a great time to join the Can-West Travel Club. By joining now, you'll receive a handsome black-and-gold-tone electronic calculator and a quartz pen-watch.

- **Limit the offer**. Set a specific date by which the reader must act in order to receive a gift, a rebate, benefits, low prices, or a special offer.

   Act quickly, because I'm authorized to make this special price on solar greenhouses available only until May 1.

- **Make payment easy**. Encourage the reader to send a credit-card number or to return a coupon or card and be billed later.

Examining Sales Letters

The letter shown in Figure 9.5 illustrates many of the sales techniques suggested here. It attracts the reader's attention by showing how much money can be saved on a chequing account. This central selling feature is then developed throughout the letter, although other selling points are also mentioned. The bank's services are described with emphasis on reader benefits. Finally, the reader is motivated to respond with a special incentive that requires immediate action.

The sales letter shown in Figure 9.6 fails to achieve its purpose for a number of reasons: it lacks a central selling point, it fails to develop reader benefits, and its language is vague. The chocolates being sold obviously require an emotional appeal with a vivid description of the pleasures to be experienced from the purchase of this product. However, this letter stresses the money-back guarantee for a sampler offer that is only partially explained. The letter also fails to develop confidence in the product and doesn't tell the reader how to respond to the sampler offer.

An improved version of this sales letter, shown in Figure 9.7, illustrates considerable planning on the part of the writer. This letter is organized around the action to be taken (returning a card to receive a special sampler offer). It also concentrates on a central selling point (the blend by European experts), but it mentions other product features as well. The concrete language helps the reader envision the taste, look, and smell of fine chocolates. The description of the raw materials (the milk and cocoa) and the production process builds confidence in the product, as does the money-back guarantee. The effective closing tells the reader how to respond easily and painlessly. An added stimulus to immediate action is the reference to a limited product supply in the last sentence.

FIGURE 9.5 Effective Letter Selling Chequing Account Mixed Service—
Modified Block Style, Mixed Punctuation

TORONTO-DOMINION BANK

**320 BAY STREET, TORONTO, ON
M4W 3T3**

Marg Taylor
AVP & Manager
Personal Financial Centre

April 3, 199x

Mr. Chen Xian
405 Cuthbert Street
Toronto, ON
M4S 2O6

Dear Mr. Xian:

Why pay $50, $100, or even $150 a year in chequing account service
charges when TD Bank has the right price for chequing—FREE!

At Toronto-Dominion we want your business. That's why we're offering
"Totally Free Chequing." Compare the cost of your present chequing
account. We know you'll like the difference. We also have six other
personalized chequing plans, one of which is certain to be right for you.

In addition to the best price on chequing accounts, we provide a variety of
investment opportunities and two hassle-free credit-line programs. Once
you qualify, you can use your credit line at any time without applying for
a new loan each time you need money. With one of our credit-line
programs, you can write a cheque for just about anything, including a
vacation, home improvements, major purchases, unexpected bills, or
investment opportunities.

If you have not banked with Toronto-Dominion, you'll find that we have
over 50 convenient locations in your area alone.

Check out the details of our services described in the enclosed pamphlets.
Then check us out by stopping in to open your free chequing account at
one of our many convenient locations. You can also open your account by
simply filling out the enclosed postage-paid card and returning it to us.

If you open your TD chequing account before June 15, we'll give you 200
free cheques and we'll buy back any unused cheques you have from your
present chequing account. Act now to start saving money. We look
forward to serving you.

Sincerely yours,

Marg Taylor

Marg Taylor
Accounts Vice-President

mt:egh
Enclosures

Ineffective writing

FIGURE 9.6   Poor Sales Letter

Dear Sir:

Lacklustre opening doesn't motivate reader to continue.

We have a chocolate offer you can't refuse. If you enjoy good chocolate, read on.

We all remember when Europe produced the only really good chocolate. Since European integration and new tax policies, most of us genuine chocolate lovers have done without buying the more expensive imported chocolate.

Fails to develop a central selling point.

Describes product in general language references.

Well, now we're able to change all that. We'd like to send you a sampler of our chocolate that we think compares favourably with the finest chocolates produced in Europe. Our sampler contains an assortment of ten unique chocolates. Our factory-to-you distribution plan eliminates handling delays, so you get your chocolates when they are fresh.

Try them out. If you don't agree that these chocolates are among the finest you've ever had the pleasure of tasting, we'll be happy to refund your money. You will, of course, have to return whatever chocolates are left in your sampler to receive your refund.

Reader doesn't know how to respond.

Our sampler awaits your trial. Give these chocolates a chance. One taste of our dark chocolate will convince you that these are the finest chocolates this side of Belgium.

Sincerely,

Proposals

Proposals use persuasion to indicate the desirability of a course of action.

Proposals can be formal or informal depending on the audience.

A proposal is an offer or a bid to sell a product, provide a service, explore a topic, or solve a problem. Like persuasive letters and memos, proposals are designed to persuade the reader of the desirability of a particular course of action. In order to be approved, however, a proposal must contain far more supporting detail than either a letter or memo.

Proposals fall into two general categories. Informal proposals are written for an internal audience by employees seeking to persuade colleagues or superiors that a particular course of action is appropriate in response to a specific problem. Formal proposals are written for an external audience, usually in response to a request for proposal (RFP), and seek to persuade the reader that the writer is the most qualified candidate for a particular project. Both types of

FIGURE 9.7 Sales Letter That Appeals to the Senses—Modified Block Style,
Mixed Punctuation

The New World Company
355 Winfield Road, Kelowna, BC
V1L 2H4

July 11, 199x

Mr. M. Sebastian Landon
106 Fraser Street
Vancouver, BC
VOL 2E2

Dear Mr. Landon:

You can enjoy some of the finest chocolates produced anywhere—chocolates not available in any store—by simply returning the mailing label on this letter.

Attracts attention with special offer.

I've taken the liberty of reserving in your name one of our Sterling Sampler boxes of ten fine chocolates, including two dark chocolate, two bittersweet, four white chocolate, and two semi-sweet. Try them out. Put them to your own test. Unless you're 100 percent satisfied, return the partially empty box for a full refund—and no questions will be asked!

Plants references to desired action early in letter.

Makes reader feel special with personalized reference.

We can make this remarkable offer because we have complete confidence in these unique chocolates. Our peerless chocolates are made from the finest Canadian milk and South American cocoa. Through a special process, these ingredients are blended to perfection in our own manufacturing plant by European experts.

Builds confidence in product with guarantee.

Emphasizes central selling point: the blend by European experts.

Our custom-made chocolates are created with great care by craftsmen who learned their trade the Old World way. When your sampler box arrives, break the seal and open it. Choose a chocolate. Unwrap it. Smell it. Taste it and experience the complex flavour of expertly produced chocolate.

Concrete language appeals to senses of smell, touch, and sight.

The chocolates that will fill your sampler box now reside in our temperature- and humidity-controlled warehouse. Once we hear from you, we'll remove them and ship them to you immediately. They'll arrive in peak condition, rather than spending four to six months in distribution, as mass-produced chocolates do.

Continues to build product interest with additional sensory appeals.

De-emphasizes price and encourages immediate response.

Send no money now. Just return your mailing label in the postage-paid reply envelope. We'll send your Sterling Sampler of our fine chocolates and bill you only $9.95, a saving of $3.50 on the regular price. To avoid disappointment, return your mailing label today. Remember that there's a limit to the amount of top-quality chocolate we can produce; this offer can't be extended indefinitely.

Cordially yours,

Kendall J. Masters

Kendall J. Masters, President

Enclosures

---

proposals emphasize reader benefit and are driven largely by rational appeals relating to productivity, efficiency, and cost.

Formal and informal proposals typically include the following elements:

- **Introduction**—description of the problem or proposal.

- **Proposed Solution**—steps or procedures to solve problem.

- **Staffing**—those who will solve the problem and their qualifications.

- **Schedule**—timetable of procedures.

- **Cost**—budget of expected expenditures.

- **Authorization**—request for approval to begin project.

Let's consider an example of an informal proposal. Bianca Perez, sales manager, is concerned about declining sales at Telnon Manufacturing. In the *introduction* to her proposal to senior management, she articulates both the problem and her proposal:

Telnon has experienced a 15 percent decline in sales over the last two years. To reverse this trend, we need to implement a reorganization of the sales territories.

Providing rationale for a proposal helps persuade the reader of the need for change.

Bianca provides a rationale for her proposal by citing the dramatic improvement in performance that occurred in the Field Service Department in the aftermath of its reorganization three years ago. What worked for field service should work for sales, given the strong similarities between the two departments.

In the next stage of her proposal, the *proposed solution*, Bianca outlines the steps necessary to achieve the proposed reorganization. These steps are closely modelled on the field service experience. Bianca draws upon the field service reorganization further when preparing the *staffing, schedule,* and *cost* sections of her proposal. She concludes her proposal with a request to begin reorganization of the Sales Department (*authorization*).

Formal proposals generally contain more detail than informal proposals. Figure 9.8 shows portions of a proposal by Computer Assistance, Inc., to upgrade a firm's PC-based accounting system.

FIGURE 9.8   Proposal—Letter Style

COMPUTER ASSISTANCE, INC.
239 Cowchild Trail
Calgary, AB
T3H 1W4

                                                   May 15, 199x

Ms. Nedra K. Lowe, CPA
Lowe & Associates
549 Stony Plain Road
Edmonton, Alberta
T6L 1R4

Dear Ms. Lowe:

As you requested, we have prepared a proposal for assisting Lowe & Associates in upgrading its PC-based accounting system.

Introduction
We understand that Lowe & Associates wishes to upgrade its hardware and software to make each of its locations compatible with a networked accounting system. This compatibility will allow its four regional offices and head office to exchange information electronically and to consolidate their general ledger and accounts payable functions. The upgrade will enable the head office in Edmonton to combine information generated by the regional offices on a monthly basis for reporting purposes.

Our organization was formed in 1985 to assist businesses like yours in selecting and implementing PC-based accounting systems. Since then we have successfully installed a multitude of stand-alone and networked systems serving customers from accounting firms to restaurants to wholesale distributors.

Proposal
We suggest dividing the project into three phases: (1) software selection, (2) system design and setup, and (3) training.

1. **Software Selection.** The two current industry standards are MAS90 and ACCTRO Plus. Both of these software packages provide customizable financial statements, and they support departmentalization and company consolidation. Our user applications experts will demonstrate the features of each program and help you to choose the one that best meets your needs.

2. **System Design and Setup.** The tasks to be performed in this phase include the following:

   - Analyze existing computer and peripheral equipment in each office to determine usability in the new system
   - Determine hardware upgrades necessary to support the new network system
   - Establish file transfer protocols required to exchange information between different offices.
   - Initiate purchase and configuring of Intranet server equipment capable of delivering fast and reliable access to accounting data.

3. **Training.** The tasks to be performed in this phase include the following:
   User software training
   Technical support training

   -
   -
   -

Since they are legally binding, proposals to an external audience must be accurate.

Staffing

Beverly Husak, our manager of software development, and her team of support workers will assist in the software selection, design the network, and provide training and follow-up support. Ms. Husak has over ten years' experience designing network systems. The installation of the system will be supervised by our chief technician, Jose DaSilva, who has installed dozens of systems over the past five years.

Schedule

Some proposals include a detailed daily, weekly, or monthly schedule of activities.

We expect to complete a substantial portion of the project within four to five weeks after starting. Implementation follow-up will occur in the weeks immediately following the initial phase. Technical and accounting support is available as needed after the installation. We will require a meeting with the management staff involved in this project to clarify the specific installation and training requirements as described in this proposal prior to beginning the actual installation.

Cost

Our fees are based on the number of hours spent on the job by our staff multiplied by their respective billing rates. Our current rates are as follows:

Technicians and support workers	$60/hr
Software manager	110/hr
President	200/hr

See Appendix 1 for a detailed listing of the project costs for consulting, software, installation, and training.

Authorization

If this information correctly anticipates your needs and meets your expectations, please sign the enclosed duplicate copy and return it to us. In addition, include a retainer for the amount of $5000 as authorization for us to begin the project.

Sincerely,

Linda Wilkinson

Linda Wilkinson
President

psf

Enclosures

Summary

The ability to persuade skilfully is key to personal and business success. Persuasion is necessary when you must change attitudes or produce action. When requesting, you must clearly state the desired action and the proof that such action is reasonable. Avoid negative and emotional words and do not attempt to attribute blame. Generally, a writing plan for a persuasive request includes an opening that gets the reader's attention, a body that explains your purpose logically and tries to prove the value of your request, and a courteous closing that asks for action.

When writing sales letters, you should consider carefully both the product and the reader. Attention-getting devices are especially important in sales-letter openings. The body appeals to the reader's emotions through vivid description and to the reader's intellect through rational appeals. Limit a sales letter to one or two central selling points so that these can be emphasized. Price should be introduced early if it is a selling feature or delayed if it isn't. Encourage action in the closing by making the action clear and easy; you may wish to offer an inducement, limit the offer to a specific date, and simplify payment.

Proposals appeal to the reader's intellect by offering to solve problems relating to productivity, efficiency, and cost. While informal proposals are written for an internal audience, formal proposals are usually written in response to a request for proposal (RFP) from an outside source. Both types of proposals include the same elements, but formal proposals are expected to contain considerably more detail.

APPLICATION AND PRACTICE—9

Discussion

1. Why is the ability to persuade a significant trait in both business and personal relations?

2. The organization of a successful persuasive claim centres upon the reasons and the closing. Why?

3. Should favour requests be written directly or indirectly? Discuss.

4. Some individuals will never write an actual sales letter. Why is it important for them to learn the techniques for doing so?

5. Why is it important to use rational appeals in a proposal?

Short Answers

6. In the indirect strategy, what should precede the big idea?

7. List at least four examples of favour requests.

8. The most effective sales letters are sent to what kind of audience?

9. List at least five ways to gain a reader's attention in the opening of a sales letter.

10. In selling a product, when are rational appeals most effective? When are emotional appeals most effective?

11. Name five writing techniques that stimulate desire for a product.

12. List six elements typically found in proposals.

13. What is the main difference between a formal proposal and an informal one?

Writing Improvement Exercises

Strategies.   For each of the following situations, check the appropriate writing strategy.

	Direct Strategy	Indirect Strategy
14. An appeal for a contribution to Children's World, a charity	_____	_____
15. An announcement that in the future all dental, extended health, and life insurance benefits for employees will be reduced	_____	_____
16. A request to another company for personnel information regarding a job applicant	_____	_____
17. A letter to a painting contractor demanding payment for replacing ceramic floor tiles damaged by sloppy painters	_____	_____
18. A request for information about an oak desk and computer workstation	_____	_____
19. A letter to a grocery store asking for permission to display posters advertising a school fund-raising car wash	_____	_____
20. A request for a refund of the cost of a computer program that does not perform the functions it was expected to do	_____	_____

CASE 9-1

Persuasive Request Letter

Analyze the following poorly written persuasive claim, and list at least five faults. Outline an appropriate writing plan for a persuasive claim. After class discussion, your instructor may ask you to rewrite this message, rectifying its faults. Address your letter to International Copy Services, 444 Fourth Street West, Calgary, Alberta T7L 2E3. Assume that you are writing on your company's letterhead. Use block style.

Ineffective writing

Gentlemen:

Our Regal compact system copier SP-270F has caused us nothing but trouble since it was installed. It was purchased in September, and repairs have been needed no less than five times since September. This means that we have been without our copier at times when we desperately needed it. Therefore, we want you to replace this copier that won't work and bring us a new unit—or you can refund the amount that it cost when it was purchased.

Just after it was installed, the automatic document feeder jammed. Your technician, after our telephone call, came out to promptly fix it. But we still lost almost a day of copier use. It wasn't long before another repair was needed. In October the document feeder jammed again, and our copies were looking light in appearance. On October 12 your technician made a replacement of parts in the document assembly; the toner apparatus was also cleaned by him. This worked fine for five days. Next the collator jammed. We tried different paper, as recommended by your technician, but it still doesn't work well. In just four months of ownership, that copier has required five repair calls. That means that we have been without a copier a lot of the time. And we are very angry about the time and energy required to have it serviced.

We selected the Regal SP-270F copier because it promised automatic document feeding, that two-sided copies could be made at once and it had automatic collation and fast speed.

Attached please find a copy of our service record with this SP-270F copier. We believed your advertisement that said that Regal made "tough copiers for tough customers." Now I'm getting tough. Call me at 469-2900 immediately because I want action by February 1.

Angrily,

CASE 9-2

Persuasive Request Memo

Imagine that you are Dan McMasters, president of Jelly Belly, Inc. The sales of your company's jelly beans have skyrocketed since Kevin King, star of a popular TV show, featured Jelly Bellies on his show. The big problem now is that you can't keep track of your inventories. You need to know how long your jelly beans have been on the shelves of your retailers so that you can replace the candy with fresh inventories when needed. Initially, you kept track of inventories by hand; then you moved to keypunched cards. However, sales are now so great that you can no longer keep adequate records. Your company cannot expand until you solve these inventory control and distribution problems. You believe that a computer-controlled system could be the answer.

However, Jane Braverton, manager of your Marketing Division, considers herself a people-oriented person, not a machine-oriented person. She's not keen on computers. Jane has been with the company since its inception. She's an excellent manager, and you want to keep her. You must convince her that automating inventory and distribution is essential if the business is to compete today and to grow in the future.

You want her to meet with you and Margaret Lau to begin the process of selecting and implementing a computer hardware and software package to help solve your problems. Since her division is greatly affected, you must have her cooperation. You will give her release time to learn about computer systems. You will work with her, and you will also hire consultants to help. You expect her department to run more efficiently after the system is installed. The overall workload for Jane and her staff should decrease.

Write a memo to Jane discussing your concerns. To get you started, answer these questions.

1. What is the big idea in this message?

2. What action do you want Jane to take?

3. What strategy should your memo follow?

4. What are some benefits that Jane will experience as a result of automating her division?

5. What objections do you expect Jane to have to your proposal?

6. What counterarguments can you offer to offset her anticipated objections?

CASE 9-3

Personal Persuasive Request

In your own work or organization experience, identify a situation where persuasion is necessary. Should a procedure be altered to improve performance? Would a new or different piece of equipment help you perform your work more efficiently? Do you want to work other hours or perform other tasks? Do you deserve a promotion?

Once you have identified a situation requiring persuasion, write a memo to your boss or organization head. Use actual names and facts. Employ the concepts and techniques in this chapter to help you convince your boss that your idea should prevail. Include concrete examples, anticipate objections, emphasize reader benefits, and end with a specific action to be taken.

CASE 9-4

Sales Letter Analysis

Select a one-page sales letter that you or a friend has received. (If you are unable to find one, your instructor may be able to help.) Read the letter carefully. Then answer the following questions.

1. At what audience is the letter aimed?

2. Is the appeal emotional or rational? Is the appeal effective? Explain.

3. What techniques capture the reader's attention?

4. Is the opening effective? Explain.

5. Is a central selling point emphasized? Explain.

6. Does the letter emphasize reader benefits? Explain.

7. List examples of concrete language.

8. How is confidence in the product or service developed?

9. How is price introduced?

10. What action is to be taken, and how is the reader motivated to take that action?

After class discussion, your instructor may ask you to write an improved version of this letter. Implement suggestions from this chapter.

CASE 9–5

Personal Sales Letter

Identify a situation in your own job or a previous job in which a sales letter is needed. Using suggestions from this chapter, write an appropriate sales letter. Promote a product or service. Use actual names, information, and examples. Make your sales letter as realistic as possible.

Additional Problems

1. Assume you are office manager for Mid Canada Services Inc. You have noticed lately that employees are selling things while in the office; one person is a cosmetics representative, another shows catalogues of shoes, and one is a part-time Tupperware distributor. You have observed that employees can get very involved in these transactions—on Mid Canada's time. What policy should the office adopt toward such practices? Should you allow this selling? If so, when? Write a persuasive memo to the staff describing your position. Remember that you need their cooperation; you don't want to sound like a dictator.

2. You are the business manager for Rodolfo's, a producer of gourmet ice-cream. Rodolfo's has 12 ice-cream parlours in the Edmonton area and a reputation for excellent ice cream. Your firm was approached by an independent ice-cream vendor who wanted to use Rodolfo's name and recipes for ice cream to be distributed through grocery stores and drug stores. As business manager, you worked with a law firm, Lancomb, Pereigni, and Associates, to draw up contracts regarding the use of Rodolfo's name and quality standards for the product. When you received the bill from Louis Lancomb, you couldn't believe it. The bill itemized 38 hours of attorney preparation, at $450 per hour, and 55 hours of paralegal assistance, at $100 per hour. The bill also showed $415 for telephone calls, which might be accurate, because Mr. Lancomb had to converse with the owners of Rodolfo's, who were living in Manila at the time. Write a persuasive letter to Mr. Lancomb. You doubt that an experienced attorney would require 38 hours to draw up the contracts in question. Perhaps some error was made in calculating the total hours. Moreover, you have checked with other businesses and found that excellent legal advice can be obtained for $300 per hour. Rodolfo's would like to continue using the services of Lancomb, Pereigni, and Associates for future legal business. Such future business is unlikely if an adjustment is not made on this bill. Write a persuasive request to Louis Lancomb, Barrister and Solicitor, Lancomb, Pereigni, and Associates, 234 Whyte Avenue, Edmonton, Alberta T7N 1L5.

3. As a full-time student, you are acutely aware of the importance of work experience. There are part-time positions available at The Selby Company that would give you practical experience in your area of interest. Write to Jerry Cohen, personnel manager, The Selby Company, asking him to hire you as a work-experience student. You could work 12 to 15 hours per week for one term but would have to arrange the work hours around your class

schedule. Describe your desire to function in a specific capacity, but express your willingness to serve wherever the company can accommodate you. Of course, you expect no remuneration, but you will be receiving up to three units of credit if Selby can take you for one semester. Write a persuasive letter to Jerry Cohen, Personnel Manager, The Selby Company, 190 Royal Road, Prince George, British Columbia V9N 2E6.

4. As employee relations manager of Blue Cross in Ontario, one of your tasks is to promote Project H.E.L.P. (Higher Education Learning Program), an on-the-job learning opportunity. Project H.E.L.P. is a combined effort of major corporations and the Association of Canadian Community Colleges. You must find 12 employees who will volunteer as instructors for 50 or more students. The students will spend four hours a week at the St. Catharines Blue Cross facility earning an average of five credits a term. This term the students will be serving in the Medical Review Claims, Word Processing, Corporate Media Services, Library, and Administrative Support departments. Your task is to write a memo to the employees in these departments to encourage them to volunteer. They will be expected to supervise and instruct the students. Employees will receive two hours of release time per week to work with the students. The program has been very successful so far. School officials, students, and employees alike express satisfaction with the experience and the outcomes. Write a persuasive memo with convincing appeals that will bring you 12 volunteers to work with Project H.E.L.P.

5. As corresponding secretary of your school graduation committee, you have been instructed to invite Laura T. Saranza, personnel director, RWR Corporation, to speak at your graduation banquet. RWR is a large employer in your city, and some graduates from your program are hired by RWR each year. The committee members are interested in the changes that technology is creating in employment at RWR. They're also eager for advice on the kinds of entry-level jobs available at RWR and the skills required for these positions. You know Ms. Saranza is busy, so you want to think of some way to make this invitation appealing. Because RWR encourages its executives to participate in community affairs, you might appeal to her organization's excellent record of civic involvement. Provide details of the event in your invitation. Write a favour request to Laura T. Saranza, Personnel Director, RWR Corporation, 12 Delwood Place, Dartmouth, Nova Scotia B2V 1S4.

6. You are Richard Delorme, owner of your own management consulting firm, RDG Management Consultants. Several months ago you did a study for Ali Ghazal of Infogroup Corporation regarding employee morale. The study found that morale was down significantly and recommended a comprehensive approach to addressing the problem. Mr. Ghazal is now contacting you because you were at the top of Infogroup's list for designing the response recommended in the report. Since this is a big job and Infogroup is a Crown corporation, Mr. Ghazal says that they must tender the job. They are interested in a proposal that indicates RDG's ability to provide a comprehensive solution.

You begin by considering the work plan. The approach you had in mind when you wrote the report was based on your experience with Comperion Inc., where you were asked to do the same type of thing. You know you can use your experience with Comperion because when you began work there, they were in the same situation that Infogroup is in now. You know that the entire comprehensive plan you put into effect at Comperion improved morale by 18 percent because of the follow-up study you did. You also know that in many ways, your experience with Comperion will be useful for Infogroup.

You remember that at the time you were writing the report for Infogroup, you were thinking of things like company-sponsored events such as golf tournaments. You just weren't sure how often they should be or whether they should be only sporting events. You think of other things for your work plan, including: a company magazine, training sessions that include people from various departments and levels in the organization, a company suggestion system, interdisciplinary work improvement teams, flex time for employee attendance, and other inducements that will help employees feel appreciated. The only problem is detailing the specifics for each one and the timing. You want the work plan to indicate clearly to Infogroup that you understand the importance of the job and the work that is required.

You are also concerned about putting together a staff to help. You know that you can contract help from Brian Johannsen, who has plenty of experience in this area, as well as Heather Middleton, who is an excellent communicator with experience in sensitivity training. You may need to bring on other experts to fully convince Infogroup of your ability to do the job. You also know that Mr. Ghazal has several good people in his human resource department.

Write a proposal for Ali Ghazal of Infogroup Corporation that indicates the nature of the problem, your proposed solution, staffing requirements, costs, and a schedule for developing and implementing the solution. Add any details that you might need to complete this problem. Send your proposal to Mr. Ali Ghazal, Manager of Human Resources, Infogroup Corporation, 1427 Nelson Road, Ottawa, ON L2R 3H4.

GRAMMAR/MECHANICS CHECKUP—9

Semicolon and Colon Use

Review Sections 2.16 through 2.19 of the Grammar/Mechanics Handbook. Then study each of the following statements. Insert any necessary punctuation. Use the delete sign (�) to omit unnecessary punctuation. In the space provided for each statement, indicate the number of changes you made and record the number of the G/M principle(s) illustrated. (When you replace one punctuation mark with another, count it as one change.) If you make no changes, write *0*. This exercise concentrates on semicolon and colon use, but you will also be responsible for correct comma use. When you finish, compare your responses with those that follow. If your responses differ, study carefully the specific principles shown in parentheses.

Example: The job of Mr. Wellworth is to make sure that his company has   **2   (2.16a)**
                enough cash to meet its obligations, moreover, he is responsible for
                locating credit when needed.

1. Short-term financing refers to a period of under one year long-term financ-   _____
   ing on the other hand refers to a period of ten years or more.

2. Cash resulting from product sales does not come in until December there-   _____
   fore our cash flow becomes critical in October and November.

3. We must negotiate short-term financing during the following months   _____
   September October and November.

4. Some of the large corporations that have important foreign sales are: _____
   MacMillan Bloedel, Northern Electric, Hydro-Québec, and Spar Aerospace.

5. Although some firms rarely, if ever, need to borrow short-term money;   _____
   many businesses find that they require significant credit to pay for current
   production and sales costs.

6. A supermarket probably requires no short-term credit, a greeting card   _____
   manufacturer however typically would need considerable short-term
   credit.

7. We offer three basic types of credit open-book accounts promissory notes   _____
   and trade acceptances.

8. Speakers at the conference on credit include the following businesspeople   _____
   Sheridan Black financial manager Lytton Industries Miriam Minkoff comptroller Royal Bank and Mark Kendall legal counsel Bank of Montreal.

9. The prime interest rate is set by the Bank of Canada and the Bank's director   _____
   accomplishes this by varying the amount of cash the chartered banks must
   deposit with it.

10. Most banks are in business to lend money to commercial customers for   _____
    example retailers service companies manufacturers and construction firms.

11. Avionics, Inc. which is a small electronics firm with a solid credit rating   _____
    recently applied for a loan but Maple Leaf Trust refused the loan applica-
    tion because the trust company was short of cash.

12. When Avionics, Inc., was refused by Maple Leaf Trust its financial   _____
    managers submitted applications to: Fidelity Trust, Farmers Credit Union,
    and CIBC.

13. The cost of financing capital investments at the present time is very high   _____
    therefore Avionics' managers may elect to postpone certain expansion
    projects.

14. If interest rates reach as high as 18 percent the cost of borrowing becomes   _____
    prohibitive and many businesses are forced to reconsider or abandon
    projects that require financing.

15. Several investors decided to pool their resources then they could find   _____
    attractive investments.

1. (3) year; financing, hand, (2.03, 2.16b) 3. (3) months: September, October, (2.10, 2.17a) 5. (1) money, (2.06a, 2.16b) 7. (3) credit: accounts, notes, (2.01, 2.17a) 9. (1) Canada, (2.05) 11. (3) Inc., rating, loan; (2.06c, 2.16c) 13. (2) high; therefore, (2.16) 15. (1) resources; (2.16b)

GRAMMAR/MECHANICS CHALLENGE—9

Document for Revision

The following letter contains faults in grammar, punctuation, spelling, and number form. It also exhibits wordiness, repetition, and problems discussed in this chapter. Drawing upon the guidelines provided in the Grammar/Mechanics Handbook and what you learned in the chapter, revise the letter.

Poor Letter

October 23, 199x

Ms. Christie Young
3625, rue St-Urbain
Montréal, PQ
H3A 1A3

Dear Ms. Young:

Enclosed are copies of this years Sportour ski brochure. This year, in addition to our charter program (which include all our charter trips to the Rockies and Europe and the United States we are introducing a new program in conjunction with Western Airlines.

The combination of these 2 programs, offer our customers the most complete ski package we have every created. Value, flexability and variety are all amalgamated in this years program.

Due to the fact that many dates and destinations are all ready beginning to fillup please select your trip and complete and fill out the reservation form included in the brochure. Send your deposit of two hundred dollars and forward to the Sportours Main Office as soon as possible.

We invite you to ski with us this comming season, and look forward to serving you, as a special incentive we're taking fifty dollars off the complete package price against the first 25 people who send in there reservations.

Sincerely,

Special Messages

In this chapter, you will learn to do the following:

- Recognize opportunities for writing good-will messages.
- Appreciate how special messages can build good will.

- Write letters of appreciation, congratulations, and sympathy.
- Write letters of recommendation and introduction.

This chapter includes a diverse group of special messages that require you to adapt the strategies and writing techniques you have learned in previous chapters. Some of the messages convey personal good will, and others carry business information of a special nature. None of them has a specific writing plan. You will find, as you progress in your development of the craft of writing, that you are less dependent on writing plans to guide you. Although you will not be provided with detailed writing plans, we will point out similarities between situations and make suggestions regarding appropriate strategies. This chapter will be helpful not only for its opportunities to adapt strategies but also for the models provided.

Letters that convey social approval satisfy deep human needs for both the sender and the receiver.

Good-Will Letters

Good-will letters carry good wishes, warm feelings, and sincere thoughts to friends, customers, and employees. These are letters that do not *have* to be written—and often are not written for a number of reasons. Because these letters are not urgent and because words do not come readily to mind, it's easy for writers to procrastinate. Writers may feel an urge to express thanks or congratulations or sympathy, but they put it off until the moment passes. Then it's too late. Yet, there's hardly an individual who doesn't appreciate receiving sincere thanks or words of congratulations. It is human nature to desire social approval: we want to be accepted, remembered, consoled, appreciated, and valued. Although busy or unsure business writers may avoid writing good-will letters, these messages are worth the effort because they gratify both senders and receivers and because they fulfil important human needs.

Greeting cards and commercial thank-you notes provide ready-made words, but they fail to express personal thoughts. When you receive a card, what do you read first—the printed words of the card maker or the handwritten remarks of the sender? The personal sentiments of the sender are always more expressive and more meaningful to the reader than is the printed message.

Good-will messages are most effective when they are immediate, spontaneous, sincere, and personal. They should follow a direct strategy.

1. Identify the situation.

2. Include specific detail and personal thoughts.

3. Close with a forward-looking thought or a concluding remark.

Letters of Appreciation

Extend thanks and show appreciation when someone has done you a favour or whenever an action merits praise. Letters of appreciation may be written to customers for their business, to hosts and hostesses for their hospitality, to colleagues for jobs well done, and to individuals for kindnesses performed. (See Figures 10.1, 10.2, and 10.3.)

FIGURE 10.1   Appreciation for a Customer's Business

Dear Mrs. Panko:

Staffing your organization with temporary office workers for the past six years has been our pleasure, and we appreciate your business.

Holidays are excellent opportunities for good-will greetings.

As we begin the new year, I want you to know that you may continue to count on us for temporaries who are as productive as your permanent employees. As a regular user of our services, you know how valuable it is to maintain a cost-effective staff, calling on us to help you fill in with temporaries during peak periods and for special projects.

Thank you for allowing us to send you our qualified temporaries and for the confidence you have shown in our agency for these past six years. We look forward to at least six more years of mutually profitable dealings.

Sincerely,

FIGURE 10.2   Letter of Appreciation for a Favour

Dear Ms. Blankenship:

Your guided tour of the Communications Services Centre at Warner Labs was the highlight of the term for our class.

This thank-you letter goes to the employee but a photocopy goes to her supervisor.

Your description of the Centre's operations and equipment enabled our business communications class to better understand some of the technical applications in this profession. We appreciated seeing how authors originate letters and reports using your Dextran central dictation system. Equally interesting was the flow of these documents through the entire production cycle. Your careful preparation for our group and your painstaking organization of the tour schedule allowed our class to see numerous operations in a short time. Many students commented on your enthusiastic and knowledgeable presentation.

Give the reader the spotlight by concentrating on his or her accomplishments.

Our trip to Warner was entertaining and instructive. We enjoyed the modern interior design, the indoor plants and trees, the colourful artwork and furniture, and the comfortable employee lounges. Most importantly, though, we appreciated your tour because it helped bridge the gap between classroom information and real-world applications in our profession.

Sincerely,

pc* Mrs. Carmen Sevelas
       Manager, Communication Services

_____

* The abbreviation pc means "photocopy" and replaces the carbon copy notation (cc).

Letters of Congratulations

Letters of congratulations deliver recognition for special events such as a promotion, appointment, award, graduation, or significant honour, and also mark personal events such as an engagement, marriage, anniversary, or birth. These messages contain warmth, approval, and praise. Avoid mechanical phrases like *Congratulations on your promotion. You certainly deserve it.* Try to include personal references and specific details that make your thoughts different from the bland and generalized expressions in greeting cards. Often brief and conversational in tone, congratulatory letters may be handwritten or typed. If a news clipping announced the good news, it's a nice touch to attach the article to your congratulatory letter.

Personalized references and details about the individual distinguish good congratulatory messages from commercial cards.

Successful administrators build positive employee relations by writing personal letters of appreciation and congratulations (see Figure 10.4).

FIGURE 10.3   Letter of Appreciation for Hospitality

Dear Professor and Mrs. Shelton:

Thanks for inviting our business club to your home for dinner last Saturday.

The warm reception you gave us made the evening very special. Your gracious hospitality, the delicious dinner served in a lovely setting, and the lively discussion following dinner all helped to create an enjoyable evening that I will long remember.

We appreciate the opportunity you provided for us students to become better acquainted with each other and with you.

Sincerely,

Thank-you letters generally refer to the fine food, warm hospitality, and good company provided.

FIGURE 10.4   Letter Congratulating Employee on Promotion

Dear Marie-Claire:

I am delighted to hear of your promotion to the position of supervisor of Reprographics. It seems only yesterday that you were an inexperienced part-time assistant who came to my office with excellent skills, bubbling enthusiasm, and a desire to succeed.

We missed you when you left our department, but we take great pride in your accomplishments and wish you every success in your new position.

Sincerely,

Letters of Sympathy

Grief is easier to bear when we know others care. Whatever the misfortune, show your concern with sympathetic words. Depending upon the situation, express the loss that you feel, console the reader, and extend your willingness to help in any way possible. If you are writing a letter of condolence following a death, recognize virtues in the loved one and assure the reader that he or she is not alone in this unhappy moment. If you need ideas for writing a message of sympathy, examine the model here. Inspiration can also be gleaned from the thoughts expressed in commercially prepared cards. Study the cards, adapt some of the ideas, and then write your own message.

Probably the hardest of all letters to write are those of sympathy; here are suggestions on what to include.

Figure 10.5 shows a letter written by a manager to a division secretary who lost her husband.

FIGURE 10.5 Letter of Sympathy

Dear Jane,

We were deeply saddened to learn of your loss. Although words are seldom adequate to express sympathy, I share your grief and understand the profound loss that you are experiencing. Sergio's kindness, patience, and charm were appreciated by all of us here. He will be missed. If there is any way that we may ease your sorrow, you know that we are here.

Sincerely,

Special Information Letters

Another group of special letters employing the direct strategy includes messages that introduce individuals, ask for recommendations, and offer recommendations.

Letter of Introduction

On occasion, a letter of introduction, such as the one in Figure 10.6, is helpful to expedite social or business activities or to reduce red tape, especially when an individual is far from home. Such letters establish a person's character or status and are supported by the writer's character or status. They may be written for friends, employees, or business acquaintances. In a letter of introduction, (1) identify your relationship, (2) explain why you are writing, (3) request help, and (4) express appreciation.

> A letter of introduction should do four things: (1) identify the writer's relationship with the subject, (2) explain the reason for writing, (3) ask for assistance, and (4) convey thanks.

Letter Requesting Recommendation

When individuals apply for employment, for admission to special programs, or for acceptance into some social organizations, recommendations may be requested. For example, if Ron Twersky were applying for a job, he might be asked to supply the names of individuals who could provide information about his work experience, skills, and character. These individuals might then be sent forms to fill out regarding Ron. Some organizations might request that they write letters in support of Ron's application.

Before listing individuals as references, always ask their permission. This is not only courteous but also prudent. By offering an opportunity to accept or refuse, applicants can find individuals who will write favourable recommendations. A word of encouragement to applicants: don't hesitate to request

FIGURE 10.6   Letter of Introduction

Dear Sheldon:

Ms. Natalie Kienzler, the daughter of one of my closest friends, will soon be moving to Regina. Natalie just graduated from Keewatin Community College in The Pas, Manitoba, and she seeks employment in a law firm.

As an attorney in Regina, you may have some suggestions for her when she arrives and begins her job search. I've given her your telephone number and encouraged her to call you.

I appreciate any assistance you can extend to Natalie.

Cordially,

When you ask for a letter of recommendation, provide a "brag sheet."

recommendations from instructors. Part of their duty involves helping students find employment. You can help by providing information about yourself: a résumé, data sheet, or "brag sheet." Indicate what characteristics or facts you think are important. Also mention the name, number, and year of the course you took with the instructor.

Figure 10.7 shows a letter asking for permission to list an instructor as a reference.

Letter of Recommendation

As you progress in your career, you may be asked to write letters of recommendation. Such letters typically fall into two categories: general recommendations and employment recommendations.

General recommendations may be written to nominate individuals for awards, to support applications for memberships in societies, or to admit individuals to special programs. Employment recommendations are written to support applications for employment.

Write letters of recommendation only for individuals you can truthfully support.

Writers of recommendations, of course, must be truthful. Even though recommendations are expected to show an applicant in a positive way, they should not be false or deceptive. If you are asked to write a recommendation, do so only for individuals about whom you can speak positively. If you have doubts about an individual's personal or professional qualifications or if you feel that you do not know the applicant well enough to write convincingly, refuse to complete a recommendation. Encourage the applicant to find a reference who can write knowledgeably and enthusiastically.

Once you accept an invitation to write a recommendation, ask the applicant to supply you with personal and professional data. Request a data sheet or a résumé, and ask what information the applicant wants emphasized.

FIGURE 10.7   Letter Request to a Potential Reference

Dear Professor Earle:

I am now completing my course work at George Brown College, and I plan
to begin looking for employment in merchandising.

Your course, Retail Merchandising 146, 1994, was my introduction to the
profession, and your instruction provided an excellent background in this
career area. Because you know this profession well and because you also
know my work as a student, may I use your name as a reference when I
apply for employment? I am enclosing a fact sheet that lists information
that may be helpful to you when you write about me.

*Never list an
individual as a
reference unless you
ask permission first.*

I am grateful to you both for the foundation you provided in merchandising and for any help you can provide in my job search. I have enclosed a
postage-paid card on which you can indicate your willingness to serve as
a reference.

                                   Sincerely,

In a general letter of recommendation, consider the following suggestions:

1. Identify the reason for writing.
2. Suggest the confidentiality of the recommendation.
3. Establish your relationship with the applicant.
4. Describe the applicant's professional and personal qualities.
5. Describe the applicant's relations with others.
6. Include specific details and examples that illustrate the applicant's personality and performance.
7. Compare the applicant with others in his or her profession.
8. Offer an overall rating of the applicant.
9. Summarize the significant attributes of the applicant.
10. Draw a conclusion regarding the recommendation.

*To write a complete
letter of
recommendation,
include these ten
topics.*

The letter in Figure 10.8 was written to recommend an employee for an
award. This letter uses all of the preceding suggestions except one: it does not
mention confidentiality. In this instance, the writer did not consider her
comments to be private or personal; she would not object if her letter were
shown to others or published.

FIGURE 10.8   General Letter of Recommendation

TO: Awards Selection Committee   DATE: April 12, 199x

FROM: Cindy Skelton, Manager *CS*
                   Communication Services

SUBJECT: RECOMMENDATION OF TANI PUROHIT

Identifies reason for writing.

It is with great pleasure that I recommend Tani Purohit for the Employee of the Year award.

Establishes relationship with applicant.

Tani has been employed by Eastern Assurance in Communication Services for nearly five years. For the past three years, I have been able to observe her performance carefully when she worked first as Senior Correspondence Writer and later as Lead Correspondence Writer in my division.

Describes candidate's skills and professional accomplishments with specific details.

Tani's language skills and keyboarding ability enable her to turn out documents rapidly and accurately. Because of her superior skills in quickly understanding technical material, she is in great demand. Tani also demonstrates genuine interest in and aptitude for the many kinds of technical writing assignments she has been asked to complete. She is so knowledgeable that I asked her to serve on the selection committee when Eastern recently hired a junior technical writer. While serving on this committee, Tani suggested a new method for efficiently testing the technical writing skills of employment candidates. Using Tani's plan, the committee was able to assess abilities at an earlier stage, thus making the selection process more efficient.

Describes personal attributes.

In addition to her writing, keyboarding, and problem-solving skills, Tani interacts well with her superiors and with her fellow workers. Her positive attitude, flexible expectations, and cheerful outlook make her a very pleasant person with whom to work.

Compares candidate with others in her field and offers an overall rating.

I rank Tani among the top 2 percent of employees I've supervised. Her skills are outstanding, her work excellent, and her attitude exemplary. Few employees have ever deserved to be named Employee of the Year more than Tani Purohit.

Letters of recommendation regarding employment are similar to general letters of recommendation. They not only cover the ten topics described earlier but also may include information relating to length of employment, job duties, and career potential.

Writers of letters of recommendation, particularly those letters that affect employment and future careers, should be aware of access-to-information and privacy-rights legislation in Canada. Written to protect individuals' rights of access to their records, these laws and subsequent court interpretations may allow files that were once considered confidential to be opened. Job applicants may now be able to read letters written about themselves, unless they choose to waive their rights or the documents fall under a provision in an act that precludes access. It is also important to remember that human-rights legislation in Canada protects job applicants against discrimination on the grounds of race, colour, ancestry, place of origin, political belief, religion, marital status, physical or mental disability, age, sex, and conviction for a criminal charge that is unrelated to the employment sought. (See the Employment and Immigration Canada publication *How to Find a Job* [1991].)

Despite the restrictions that writers may feel, letters of recommendation are still useful in the employment process. Because such letters describe a candidate's experience and qualifications, they help personnel officers match capable candidates with positions appropriate to their abilities.

> Letters of recommendation are most helpful when they illustrate a candidate's abilities and experience.

Letters of recommendation must be specific to be helpful. The letter shown in Figure 10.9 is ineffective because it presents little more than generalities. It describes the candidate as "responsible, creative, industrious, and cooperative." Such abstract words create a positive attitude toward the candidate, but they do not help a personnel officer place this candidate in a position suited to his skills and talents. The fourth sentence may actually result in Mr. Yuen's losing a chance at the job for which he applied.

An improved version of this recommendation for Christopher Yuen, shown in Figure 10.10, gives specific information. The letter illustrates the candidate's sense of responsibility by describing his willingness to work overtime when necessary. The writer also uses actual examples to show how the candidate is creative, industrious, and cooperative. In addition to using specific incidents and details, notice how this effective letter illustrates the suggestions given earlier regarding appropriate content in a letter of recommendation.

FIGURE 10.9   Letter of Recommendation That Lacks Specifics

> Ineffective writing

Dear Mr. Weld:

I am happy to recommend Mr. Christopher Yuen. In his work for us, he was an able technician. He was responsible, creative, industrious, and cooperative. Once in a while he was late, but we understood why.

If I may be of further service, please call on me.

Sincerely,

FIGURE 10.10   Effective Employment Letter of Recommendation—
Modified Block Style, Mixed Punctuation

➤ZANTROL, INC.

341, boul. Saint-Jacques
Québec, Québec
G2R 3T2
(418) 593-4391

June 4, 199x

M. René Duhamel
Human Resources Manager
LaSalle Limitée
345, boul. Saint-Laurent
Montréal, Québec
H3R 4H9

Dear M. Duhamel:

Establishes reason for writing and confidentiality of message.

Mr. Christopher Yuen, whom your organization is considering for a systems programmer position, asked me to submit confidential information on his behalf.

Reveals relationship of writer to applicant.

I supervised Mr. Yuen for the past two years when he worked as a part-time microcomputer technician in the Computer Users Centre of our executive headquarters. In helping employees learn to operate microcomputers and solve their problems, he demonstrated computer expertise and creativity.

Includes specific examples of applicant's work to illustrate work habits and capabilities.

Attempts to present a fair picture of the applicant's qualities but de-emphasizes negative traits.

His knowledge of computers and computer systems enabled him to work with our systems engineer in developing a local area network to link computers and share resources. Our programmers, systems engineers, and users considered Mr. Yuen to be helpful, reliable, knowledgeable, and responsible. Although he sometimes had difficulty getting to our offices on time because of his classes at McGill, he was always willing to work overtime when we needed him to complete a project.

Compares applicant with others in his field, offers an overall rating, and summarizes significant attributes.

Mr. Yuen accepted direction easily but could also work independently when necessary. For example, when I asked him to organize our software storage, he did a good job without supervision. Of all the microcomputer technicians we have employed, I consider Mr. Yuen to be among the top third. In his work for us, he demonstrated computer proficiency and a cooperative attitude. We admired his perseverance and the work ethic he demonstrated by maintaining a job while attending classes.

It is a pleasure to recommend Mr. Yuen, and I feel certain that he will be successful as a systems programmer.

Sincerely,

Jacques Dufresne

Jacques Dufresne
Operations Manager

rtt

When you leave a job, ask for a letter of recommendation. Even if you are not immediately applying for other employment, solicit a recommendation from your supervisor so that you will have references available when you need them. Too often, supervisors change jobs or businesses relocate, leaving former employees without contacts. An undirected letter of recommendation, as shown in Figure 10.11, begins with a general salutation.

FIGURE 10.11   Undirected Letter of Recommendation

To Prospective Employers:

Tanya Ivanovich was employed as a sales representative on our staff from June 1993 through June 1995. When she completed her bachelor's degree in 1995, she left our company to seek full-time employment in the Victoria area.

Ms. Ivanovich developed superior selling skills in the two years she sold our products. Twice she received bonuses for sales exceeding her assigned goal. She exercised initiative in organizing her territory and in using her computer to maintain a database of customers. Ms. Ivanovich was particularly effective in selling our line of makeup during holiday periods and over the summer.

She was reliable, honest, and hardworking, rarely missing a sales meeting or a report deadline. Of all the sales representatives we have employed, I would rank Ms. Ivanovich among the top 15 percent. We would be happy to hire her again, were she to apply.

Sincerely,

Draws conclusion regarding applicant's potential.

Ask for an undirected letter of recommendation when you leave a job.

Form and Guide Letters

Form letters are prewritten printed messages used to deliver repetitious and routine information. To save the expense of composing, transcribing, and printing individual letters, many organizations prepare standardized form letters for recurring situations. Form letters contain blanks for such variables as names and addresses, dates, balances, and other specific data. Form letters are efficient for sales messages, human resources policy announcements, procedural explanations for customers and suppliers, order acknowledgments, and other repetitive information.

Guide letters are individually typed, but they are composed of prewritten sentences and paragraphs.

Guide letters use prewritten sentences and paragraphs but, unlike form letters, are individually typed. Although somewhat more personalized, guide letters serve the same functions as form letters. Insurance companies, for example, send thousands of guide letters to policyholders to answer routine questions regarding their coverage. Rather than compose individual responses, company representatives select appropriate paragraphs from a book of ready-made answers and instruct a transcriptionist to use these paragraphs to prepare a letter.

When used properly, form and guide letters are efficient and cost-effective.

Form and guide letters unquestionably save time and money. Well-written repetitive messages used appropriately are expedient and accepted by readers. Poorly written or misused letters, on the other hand, are doubly offensive. Readers' feelings are hurt because they are treated mechanically, and they are also confused because a letter did not apply to them or did not answer their questions.

Word processing equipment makes the preparation and processing of form and guide letters simple. If you decide to use this means of delivering messages, follow these guidelines:

- Be certain that your form and guide letters are appropriate to the situation for which they will be used.
- Compose your letters so that they are responsive and yet require insertion of a minimum number of variables.
- Test your form and guide letters over a long period to see if they are effective.
- Revise your letters based on reader reactions.

The guide letter in Figure 10.12 shows how repetitive messages can be tailored to individual circumstances by inserting variable data in the places provided. Word processing equipment merges a shell document with variable data to produce personalized letters quickly and economically.

FIGURE 10.12   Repetitive Letter with Variables

(Name) _____

(Address) _____

_____

Dear _____ :

We appreciate your interest in the Canadian Studies program we offer to Japanese students. The enclosed pamphlet describes the program in detail and shows pictures of students who have participated in the past.

In brief, our organization, Connections International, supplies transportation, tours, and cultural/social programs for Japanese students coming to Canada to study the English or French language and Canadian culture.

Our next group is scheduled to arrive _____, and the tentative cost is per student per week. This covers transportation, travel, and entertainment as outlined in the enclosed pamphlet. A deposit of _____ at least three weeks in advance of departure is required. This payment is necessary in order to set the program in operation, retain the proper vehicles, and make necessary hotel and lodging reservations. It will be deducted from the total payment for the group.

Thank you very much for considering the cultural immersion programs of Connections International. We look forward to providing warm and rewarding experiences for your students.

                          Sincerely,

_____

Summary

Good-will letters are optional messages that convey good wishes to customers, friends, and employees. They can satisfy human needs for both the sender and the receiver. Generally, good-will messages are immediate, spontaneous, sincere, and personal. They follow the direct strategy and include identification of the situation, specific details and personal thoughts, and a forward-looking closing. Letters of appreciation are written to acknowledge a favour or praise an action. Congratulation letters deliver recognition for appointments, awards, or other significant honours. They may be sent to supervisors or other members of a company to inform them of achievements made by employees. Thank-you letters generally refer to special treatment or assistance offered by someone else and mention the assistance specifically. Letters of sympathy, probably the hardest of all letters to write, should include an expression of the loss you feel, some consolation for the reader, and an offer to help in any way. All these letters contain personalized references and details about the individual.

Special information letters, including introduction and recommendation letters, also use the direct strategy. Letters of introduction should do four things: identify the writer's relationship with the subject, explain the reason for writing, ask for assistance, and convey thanks. When writing to ask for a letter of recommendation, it is useful to provide a "brag sheet" or information package that reminds the reader of who you are and of some of your accomplishments.

Write a letter of recommendation only when you can support the applicant on whose behalf you are writing. Identify the reason for writing; establish your relationship with the applicant; describe, using specific details, the applicant's professional and personal qualities and relationship with others; compare the applicant with others in his or her profession; offer an overall rating of the applicant; include significant attributes of the applicant; and draw a conclusion regarding the recommendation.

Form and guide letters are individually typed but are composed of prewritten sentences and paragraphs. When used properly, form and guide letters are efficient and cost-effective.

APPLICATION AND PRACTICE—10

Discussion

1. Why do we frequently put off writing good-will letters?

2. Why write a letter of sympathy or congratulations when a greeting card will accomplish the same end?

3. Under what circumstances would a letter of introduction be appropriate?

4. Why should an applicant ask permission before listing an individual's name as a reference?

5. As a means of screening candidates, are letters of recommendation a valid source of information?

Short Answers

6. In good-will messages the writer typically covers what three areas?

7. Name three instances when letters of appreciation are appropriate.

8. Why should a copy of a letter of appreciation be sent to an employee's supervisor?

9. What four kinds of information or topics can you include in a letter of sympathy?

10. Name three instances when letters of recommendation, other than for employment, might be written.

11. What is a brag sheet?

12. List ten suggestions regarding information to be included in a letter of recommendation.

13. In addition to the ten items listed in your response to number 12, letters of recommendation for employment should include what extra information?

14. How can the writer of a letter of recommendation avoid generalities?

15. Most good-will letters would follow which strategy—direct or indirect?

CASE 10-1

Employment Recommendation

Assume that you are Ross Neil, manager of Builder's City. Alan B. Khory, one of your favourite department managers, has now completed his postsecondary education and will be leaving the store. Mr. Khory asks you to write a recommendation for him to enter a management trainee program for a large retailer. You know that he is a quiet, unassertive individual; nonetheless he has been an excellent hardware manager for you these past three years.

You ask Mr. Khory to refresh your memory about his performance at Builder's City. He reminds you that he started as a clerk and became department manager at the Brandon store within six months, while at the same time working toward a college diploma. His department has five employees. Within his department he tried to streamline operations. He reduced crowded displays so that the store wasn't so cluttered. He tried to increase inventory turnover so that fewer duplicate items were stored in the retail display area. He solved some problems that increased sales and, of course, increased profits. When the new computerized inventory system was introduced, he was very interested in it; his department was operational long before some others.

You feel that Mr. Khory has been one of your most enterprising and responsible department managers. You hate to lose him, but you can understand his desire to achieve his long-term goal in administrative management. In your letter, you want to show that he has those traits that are necessary to be a good manager. Your opinion is that he will be an excellent management trainee. Instead of *saying* that Mr. Khory is able to solve problems and possesses initiative, you want to *show how he demonstrates* these qualities. You also want to present a fair picture. You feel that you should mention that Mr. Khory is quiet, though he gets along well both with customers and with those employees that he supervises. He was, after all, responsible for training all new employees hired for the hardware department. He was also responsible for planning a work schedule that kept the employees happy and provided adequate sales coverage.

Before you begin writing this letter of recommendation, outline a plan. The information presented here is unorganized and poorly expressed. Improve it.

Add any realistic data necessary to create a good letter. Conclude your letter with a statement regarding the potential success of Mr. Khory. Use block style. Address your letter to Ms. Gena Bennett, Human Resources Director, Federated Stores, Inc., 390 Portage Ave., Winnipeg, Manitoba R3H 2E3.

CASE 10–2

Letter of Appreciation

You are genuinely appreciative of the care shown by Robert Chu, R.N., for your bedridden mother over the past two years. You decide to send him a small gift and the following note.

Dear Robert:

Thanks for everything you have done for Mother. We really appreciate your visits over the past two years. You helped us through some very difficult times. Thanks again for your help.

Most sincerely,

Then you reconsider. You decide to write a longer letter that expresses your gratitude and also lets his employer know what an outstanding employee he is. Here are some facts you should include in your letter. Nurse Chu not only took care of your mother's medical needs but also taught you how to care for your mother. He was enthusiastic and always cheerful; everyone felt better when he visited. He made suggestions and even gave you demonstrations of professional techniques for easing your mother's discomfort. The entire family appreciated Mr. Chu's compassion and concern for your mother. He visited for two years. During that time, your mother's condition improved, and now it has stabilized. You feel that he is an extraordinary nurse and an excellent representative of his employer, HomeCare, Inc.

Write the letter to Robert Chu, R.N., HomeCare, Inc., 210 Eglinton Avenue E., Scarborough, Ontario M2W 3E6. Use a modified block style. Add any necessary information. Be sure that his employer, Dr. Chandler H. Alexander, President, HomeCare, Inc., is informed of your praise.

CASE 10–3

Letter of Sympathy

Assume that the spouse of a colleague or friend has died. Write a letter of sympathy. Include enough detail to make your letter significantly different from greeting card messages.

CASE 10-4

Letter of Appreciation

Write a letter of appreciation to your boss (supervisor, manager, vice-president, president, or chief executive officer) and his or her spouse. Assume that you and other members of your immediate staff were entertained at an elegant dinner during the winter holiday season. Include specific details that make your letter personal, sincere, and concrete.

CASE 10-5

Request for Recommendation

Write to an instructor or a previous employer asking for permission to use that individual as a reference.

CASE 10-6

Letter of Recommendation

Assume that you are the manager of a department where you now work (or previously worked). Write a letter of recommendation for an employee of your choice. Assume that this individual is leaving the company and wants to take a letter of recommendation. Use as much factual information as possible, but fill in from your imagination if necessary. If you are not working at present, interview a fellow student. Assume that you are the student's instructor; write a letter of recommendation for the student.

Additional Problems

1. As correspondence secretary of your school graduation committee, write to Laura T. Saranza, thanking her for the informative and entertaining talk she presented at the graduation banquet (see Chapter 9, page 225, Additional Problem No. 5). Provide details. Send to the RWR employee newsletter a copy of your letter and a photograph of Ms. Saranza delivering her speech to the graduates.

2. Bill Sondberg, a part-time worker in your department for the past three years, has just completed the requirements for a bachelor's degree in Accounting. Although he will probably be leaving, you are very happy for him. Write a letter of congratulations.

3. The mother of one of your co-workers died after a lengthy illness. Death was inevitable, but your friend was devastated. Write a letter of condolence.

4. One of your instructors has been nominated for a teaching award. Selected students have been asked to write letters in support of the nomination. Write a letter recommending an instructor of your choice to Professor Sheila Watkins, Teaching Award Committee, Department of Business Administration.

5. As office manager of the law firm of Ernst, Katz, and Ernst, you have been asked to write a letter describing the service of Cho Misaki, who is moving to another city. Cho has been a fine legal secretary, and you are happy to accommodate her. Since she has not asked you to address the letter to a specific individual, write an undirected letter of recommendation.

6. After finishing the course of instruction at your school, you have taken a job in your profession. One of your instructors was especially helpful to you when you were a student. This instructor also wrote an effective letter that was instrumental in helping you obtain your job. Write a letter thanking your instructor.

7. Write a form or guide letter to selected students at your school. These students have filled out applications to graduate, but a computer search of their records indicates that they are missing one or more requirements. Leave a blank space to fill in the missing requirement(s). Tell these students that a mistake may have been made; perhaps their records have an error or are not up to date. Regardless, the students must come in for a conference with a records officer. Since time is limited, the conferences have already been scheduled. Leave a blank space for the date of the conference to be filled in for each student.

GRAMMAR/MECHANICS CHECKUP—10

Possessives

Review Sections 2.20 through 2.22 of the Grammar/Mechanics Handbook. Then study each of the following statements. Underscore any inappropriate form. In the space provided for each statement, write a correction and record the number of the G/M principle illustrated. If a sentence is correct, write C. When you finish, compare your responses with those provided below. If your answers differ, study carefully the principles shown in parentheses.

Example: In just two <u>years</u> time, the accountants and managers devised an entirely new system.   years' (2.20b)

1. Two supervisors said that Mr. Wilsons work was excellent.   _____

2. In less than a years time, the offices of both lawyers were moved.   _____

3. None of the employees in our Electronics Department had taken more than two weeks vacation.   _____

4. All the secretaries agreed that Ms. Lanhams suggestions were practicable.   _____

_____ **5.** After you obtain your head supervisors approval, send the application to Human Resources.

_____ **6.** We tried to sit at our favourite waitress station, but all her tables were filled.

_____ **7.** Despite Aldo grumbling, his wife selected two bonds and three stocks for her investments.

_____ **8.** The apartment owner requires two months rent in advance from all applicants.

_____ **9.** Four companies buildings were damaged in the fire.

_____ **10.** In one months time, we hope to be able to complete all the address files.

_____ **11.** Only one womans car had its engine running.

_____ **12.** One assistants desk will have to be moved to make way for the computer.

_____ **13.** Several sellers permits were issued for two years.

_____ **14.** Marks salary was somewhat higher than Alain.

_____ **15.** Lisas job in accounts receivable ends in two months.

1. Mr. Wilson's (2.20a, 2.21) 3. weeks' (2.20b) 5. supervisor's (2.20a) 7. Aldo's (2.22) 9. companies' (2.20b) 11. woman's (2.20a) 13. sellers' (2.20b) 15. Lisa's (2.20a)

GRAMMAR/MECHANICS CHALLENGE—10

Document for Revision

The following letter contains faults in grammar, punctuation, spelling, and number form. It also exhibits wordiness and problems discussed in this chapter. Drawing upon the guidelines provided in the Grammar/Mechanics Handbook and what you learned in the chapter, revise the letter.

Poor Letter

June 16, 199x

Ms. Nathalie Boudreau
Human Resources Department
Great Western Insurance Company
1010 Overlook Drive
Victoria, BC
V1L 2T3

Dear Ms. Boudreau:

This is to inform you that Mr. Darrell Dix who you are considering for a systems' programmer position, ask me to submit confidential information, on his behalf.

I had responsibility for supervision of Mr. Dix for the passed two years, when he worked as a part time computer technician in our computer users centre. In assisting our employees who use computers solve their computing problems; his computer expertise and creativity were demonstrated.

Mr. Dix excepted direction easily, but could also work independent when necessary. For example when I ask him to bring about the organization of our software storage; he did a good job with no supervision whatsoever.

Of all the technicians we have employed Mr. Dix ranks among the top 1/3. Its a pleasure to recommend him; and I feel certain that he well be successful as a systems programer.

Sincerely,

UNIT 4

EXPANDING COMMUNICATION SKILLS

11

Informal Reports

In this chapter, you will learn to do the following:

- Distinguish between informational and analytical reports.
- Plan and gather information for reports
- Organize report information deductively or inductively.

- Present data objectively to gain credibility.
- Write informational and analytical reports.

Reports play a significant role in delivering information within and among organizations. You can learn to write good reports by examining basic techniques and by analyzing appropriate models. In this chapter, we'll concentrate on informal reports. These reports tend to be short (usually under ten pages), they use memo or letter format, and they are personal in tone.

There are two general categories of reports: informational and analytical. In many instances, the boundaries of the categories overlap; distinctions are not always obvious. Individual situations, goals, and needs will dictate the type of report you produce. Still, there are general categories of reports that help beginning writers get started.

Informal reports are relatively short (under ten pages), written in memo or letter format, and are either informational or analytical.

Informational Reports

Informational reports present information in an organized and objective manner. They do not analyze.

Reports that collect and organize information are informative or investigative. They may record routine activities, such as daily, weekly, and monthly reports of sales or profits. They may investigate options, performance, or equipment. They may present information on routine operations, compliance with regulations, and company policies and procedures. Although they provide information, they do not analyze. In an informational report, your main goal is to present the information you collect in an organized and objective manner so that your readers can make effective business decisions.

Analytical Reports

Analytical reports are similar to informational reports in that they present information. However, they offer analysis in addition to data. They attempt to solve problems by evaluating options and offering recommendations.

Persuasion and logic are key aspects of analytical reports. For example, you may be asked to write a feasibility report that compares several possible locations for a new video rental outlet. After analyzing and discussing alternatives, you conclude that one site is preferable to others. Your report will provide readers with step-by-step insights into how you arrived at that conclusion.

Analytical reports use persuasion and logic to present problems and offer solutions.

Report Formats

How should a report look? The following four formats are frequently used.

1. **Letter format.** Letter format is appropriate for informal reports prepared by one organization for another. These reports are much like letters except that they are more carefully organized, using headings and lists where appropriate.

2. **Memo format.** Memo format is appropriate for informal reports written for circulation within an organization. They follow the conventions of memos (Chapter 5), with the addition of headings.

3. **Report format.** Report format is used for longer and somewhat more formal reports. Printed on plain paper (instead of letterhead or memo forms), these reports begin with a title followed by carefully displayed headings and subheadings.

4. **Prepared forms.** Prepared forms are useful in reporting routine activities, such as police arrest reports or merchandise inventories. Standardized headings save time for the writer and make similar information easy to locate.

Informal reports may appear in four formats: memo form, letter form, report form, or on prepared forms.

How to Design a Professional-Looking Report

Today, reports are produced using either word processing or desktop publishing software. These tools help you to design your reports in an attractive way. Through the use of templates and your own creative ability, you can enhance the presentation of your reports. You must be careful though. Software programs provide many choices for changing fonts, margins, even letter spacing. They also allow you to include lines, clip art, icons and other devices that may improve the look of your report but may take away from the impact it has on its audience. The following are some suggestions for avoiding common traps:

1. **Analyze your audience**. Reports designed for a conservative business audience should be conservative in design. For those readers who wish to browse, the contents should be made easy to read through effective headings and bulleted lists. For those who need to read in greater detail, readable fonts and plenty of white space on each page will help. Sales brochures and promotional letters are too flashy. Their main function is to attract attention. In most business reports, oversized type and fancy boarders appear out of place.

2. **Choose an appropriate type size**. For most business applications, 10–12 point type is recommended. Anything below 10 point is small—especially for detailed reports, which the audience will be reading closely. Anything above 12 point is too big and looks amateurish.

3. **Use a consistent font**. Word processing software can provide an endless choice of fonts. When beginning to design business reports, stay with a consistent family of fonts. The most common is Times Roman. For emphasis, you may use bold and italic selections. Just remember to be consistent. If you choose Times Roman 12 point for the body of the report, maintain that choice throughout. If you need to emphasize a word, do it either by using bold or italic. Whatever you choose, be consistent throughout the report.

4. **Don't justify right margins**. Unjustified right margins allow for ease of reading and provide more white space on each page.

5. **Design readable headlines**. Don't use all caps because this type of setting is much more difficult to read than either downstyle (lowercase) or up-and-down style (upper- and lowercase). You may consider a different font and type size to emphasize the heading. If so, choose one that is sans serif (without cross strokes or embellishment); Helvetica, Ariel, or any of a number of others are considered sans serif fonts.

6. **Strive for an attractive page layout**. Especially for title pages, it is important to consider the balance between print and white space and how effective the page is in drawing reader attention to the main idea. For the body of the document, you may wish to frame your page with information and graphics contained in headers and footers. Remember that the average reader scans a page from left to right and top to bottom in a Z pattern.

7. **Use graphics or clip art to improve your message only**. It is easy to include fancy clip art or other graphics in documents. This doesn't always improve your chances of getting the message across. Use these tools only when they serve a purpose. Use clip art or icons to visually reinforce what's in the text. This is especially useful when reinforcing recurring themes. Always use clip art or icons that are connected to your message. For example, if you are presenting several new ideas, you might consider a lightbulb to introduce each new idea.

8. **Produce clean, uncluttered documents**. Try not to fall into the trap of using all the capabilities a software program offers. Too many fonts, font sizes, and images will overwhelm readers.

9. **Develop your expertise**. Learn the graphics and layout features of your current word processing software. Both Microsoft Word and WordPerfect provide a broad range of capability to produce professional quality reports. They handle graphics well and allow you to create your own for insertion into documents.

Planning Informal Reports

Writing reports that will engage the reader requires preparation. As with letters and memos, developing a plan is the first step. You must consider your audience, the problem to be studied, the purpose of your report, and possible solutions.

Analyzing the Audience

Begin the process of planning by considering your readers. Ask yourself questions like these:

1. Who are my primary readers?

2. What do they already know and what do they need to know about the subject area?

3. What do they expect from the report?

4. Can my primary readers suggest guidelines regarding the subject and scope of the report or objectives that might form part of the purpose?

5. What positions do my primary readers hold in the organization and how will they respond to the information and conclusions in the report?

Report writers must take into account primary readers as well as more distant readers.

The expected audience for your report will influence your writing style, research methods, vocabulary, areas of emphasis, and presentation strategy. If your audience is the person who requested the report, you will be able to determine their expectations by speaking directly to him or her. If your readers are more distant, you will have to obtain this information through indirect means. In some cases, your audience will consist of more than one set of readers. For example, a report written for your supervisor may be circulated among members of upper management.

Defining the Problem

Once you have a clear understanding of your audience, your next step is to clearly define the problem your report will address. Often, the people who solicit reports express the problem in imprecise, overly general terms. A good way for you to clarify the problem is to develop a problem statement.

To illustrate this process, let's consider an example. Mike Tanaka is asked by Françoise Boyer, his supervisor, to investigate the problem of transportation as it affects sales representatives at Devcorp. Currently, some sales reps visit customers using company-leased cars; others drive their own cars and submit their travel expenses to the company. Devcorp's lease agreement will expire in three months' time, and Françoise wants to make a change. Mike's task is to investigate the "choices" and report his findings to Françoise.

Identify the problem to be solved in a clear statement.

To arrive at a problem statement, Mike must define in more precise terms "the problem of transportation as it affects sales representatives at Devcorp." He discusses the issue with Françoise and other relevant personnel. Their input allows him to develop this problem statement:

> The leases on all company cars will be expiring in three months. Devcorp must decide whether to renew them or develop a new policy regarding transportation for sales reps. The current system is both expensive and difficult to administer.

Determining the Purpose

A purpose statement defines the focus of the report.

Although Mike has defined the problem, the purpose of his report is still unclear. Is he writing the report to inform, to analyze, to offer recommendations, or to persuade? What does his audience expect? A comparative cost analysis of buying cars versus leasing cars? A nonevaluative report on alternatives to leasing? Information on travel procedures followed by Devcorp's main competitors?

Again, Mike turns to Françoise for clarification. From the information she gives him, he develops the following purpose statement:

> To recommend a transportation plan for sales representatives that is more cost-effective and easier to administer than the current plan.

Proposing Alternatives or Solutions

Before he begins the information-gathering process, Mike needs to come up with possible alternatives to Devcorp's current transportation plan for sales reps. These alternatives will serve as a guideline when he begins his research.

Under Devcorp's current plan, we learned earlier, some sales reps use company-leased cars while others use their own cars and have all their travel expenses covered by the company. Mike wonders if both costs and paperwork could be reduced if a uniform plan (that is, a plan applying to *all* sales reps) were introduced. Using this hypothesis as his starting point, he proposes these alternatives:

1. Buy cars for all sales reps.

2. Lease cars for all sales reps.

3. Have all sales reps use their own cars.

Next, Mike formulates for each alternative questions that will be critical to his research endeavour.

1. Buy cars for all sales reps.
   a. What are the capital costs?
   b. How much would it cost to insure, operate, and maintain company-owned vehicles?
   c. Would reps prefer to use company-owned cars?

2. Lease cars for all sales reps.
   a. What are the capital costs?
   b. How much does it cost to insure, operate, and maintain leased cars?
   c. Would reps prefer to use leased cars?

3. Have all sales reps use their own cars.
   a. What would it cost to cover the travel expenses of all sales reps?
   b. What are the administrative costs?
   c. Would reps prefer to be compensated for using their own cars?

Mike has developed the problem into three alternatives (1, 2, and 3) and three methods of choosing the best alternative (A, B, and C).

Divide your research problems in a consistent manner. Mike chooses to divide by alternative because of the wording of the original problem question and purpose statement. He then divides each alternative into consistent, testable criteria or factors (A. Capital Costs, B. Other Costs, and C. Employee Preference). The criteria will let Mike build objective evidence in support of his recommendation.

> Major report problems should be broken into testable criteria or factors.

Other types of problems for which this method of defining, analyzing, and refining works well include tests of effectiveness, and discovering methods to achieve a goal.

Determining Effectiveness

What if Mike recommended solution 1? In the future, Françoise may be interested in a report analyzing whether that choice was effective. For that report, Mike cannot divide the new research problem into possible alternatives. He will have to consider the ways in which solution 1 can be judged as effective or ineffective. The divisions for this problem might include the following:

> Other problems should be broken into testable criteria based on the nature of the problem.

How effective has the purchase of company cars been compared to other options over the last two years?

1. What have the long-term costs been compared to the expectations?
   a. What have the capital costs been compared to projections for alternatives 2 and 3?
   b. What have the other costs been compared to projections for alternatives 2 and 3?
   c. What unanticipated costs and benefits occurred?

2. What are employees' feelings about the program?
   a. How do the sales reps feel about the program?
   b. How has their opinion changed over the course of the program?

3. What are management's feelings about the program?

a. How do Françoise and the district manager feel about the program?

b. How has their opinion changed over the course of the program?

In this example, Mike has divided the research question into subquestions designed to assess whether the original decision was effective (1, 2, and 3). He then chooses criteria (A, B, and C) that will allow him to answer the research questions.

Assessing the Problem

Another problem situation occurs when research must be done to determine the best method of achieving an undetermined goal. What if Françoise had come to Mike and indicated that productivity in the sales department was down? She suspected that the sales force was not getting to customers fast enough and wondered if the problem was their transportation system. Mike would have begun this report by considering the elements that influence this situation:

Is there a problem with the current method of transportation used by the sales force?

1. Does the current transportation system affect reps' rates of customer response?

   a. Do sales people with company cars respond faster than those who use their own?

   b. Does filling out expense claims for mileage affect the speed of return calls?

2. What are the costs of the current system?

   a. How much paperwork is done to maintain the current transportation system?

   b. What are the dollar costs of current flows of paperwork?

   c. Who processes the transportation paperwork?

3. Is there a problem with morale among the sales staff regarding transportation?

   a. What do they think about the current methods of transportation?

   b. How do they think current transportation methods affect their rates of response?

In this example, Mike has divided the research question into areas of possible problems. This will give him a good idea of what contributes to the existing problem and to what degree each contributes.

Report problems should be divided into consistent, exclusive, and complete subproblems.

Whenever you are dividing a problem, make sure that your divisions are consistent (don't mix issues), exclusive (don't overlap categories), and complete (don't skip significant issues). Choose divisions that make sense for a problem and that represent what your audience is most interested in.

By this stage in the planning process, you will have developed a useful outline. If you don't know much about your topic area or are unsure whether your outline is complete, try talking to someone else in your organization.

Think of people who have experience in your topic area. Ask them to help in your efforts to brainstorm. Other people's opinions about the topic will help to ensure that your outline is complete.

You also have a clear and accurate purpose statement that indicates exactly what you intend to do. For informal reports this statement may be only one sentence; that sentence usually becomes part of the introduction.

Once planning is complete, the next step in the report-writing process is gathering information.

Gathering Information

Effective reports are founded on accurate information. Your first question should always be "What kinds of information do I need?" This question can be answered by using the outline you have developed to this point. Thus, Mike would begin the research phase of his report by considering the research questions he formulated in the planning phase.

Mike needs pricing, insurance, and maintenance-cost information relating to new, used, and leased cars. For information about the purchase price of new cars, Mike could survey costs at several local car dealerships. To determine insurance costs, he could consult various insurance providers. For information on operation and maintenance costs, he might examine consumer publications or speak with car manufacturers. Mike also needs to determine the attitudes of the sales reps toward each of his proposed alternatives. An obvious means of obtaining this information is to personally consult with each sales rep.

Writers of informal business reports often obtain their facts from company records, the Internet, observation, interviews, and research.

The facts for reports are often gained from company records, electronic resources, observation, interviews, and research.

Company Records Many business-related reports begin with examinations of company records and files. From those records you can observe past performance and methods used to solve previous problems. You can collect pertinent facts that will help determine a course of action.

Electronic Resources If your organization is on-line, you are linked to vast information resources. You can search databases, read documents, find specific industry publications, participate in conferences, and exchange information with colleagues working in your area of interest. You have at your fingertips access to information from a dizzying array of educational, research, government, and business facilities. Given this vastness, however, conducting searches on the Internet can be a time-consuming process. Random search methods can be useful when you need ideas to help you complete your outline. Considerably less time-consuming are keyword searches, which you can use once your outline is complete (except for the research results). To return to our Devcorp scenario, Mike could determine prices for new cars by using Ford, GM, or Chrysler as key search words and then visiting their respective home pages on the World Wide Web. In addition, he may have done a general search of the Web looking for information useful to other aspects of his research. This random activity, however, will significantly increase the amount of time Mike spends searching. Mike must evaluate whether the information he gets by using his on-line service is better than information he could get by using other sources. (In this case, Mike could also have telephoned a local car dealership to find out pricing information for new cars.)

Observation   Another logical source of information for many problems lies in personal observation and experience. For example, Mike might consider observing an administrator while he or she completes a travel-expense report. His observations would give him an idea of the amount of paperwork that alternative number 3 (having all sales reps use their own cars) would involve.

Interviews   Talking with individuals directly concerned with the problem produces excellent firsthand information. Interviews also allow for one-on-one communication, thus giving you an opportunity to explain your questions, if necessary, and thereby get the most accurate information possible. As noted, Mike will be interviewing the sales reps to determine their transportation preferences.

Research   The library can be an unlimited source of current and historical data. For short, informal reports, the most usable information will probably be found in periodicals. The *Canadian Business and Current Affairs Index* (available on CD-ROM) is the best source for Canadian business magazines and short publications. More detailed suggestions about library research will be found in Chapter 12.

Incorporating Research

Once Mike has completed his research, he can incorporate the results into his working outline. The first of his proposed alternatives might look something like this:

1. Buy cars for all sales reps.
   a. What are the capital costs?
      New—20 mid-sized cars @ $20,700 each
      Used—20 mid-sized cars @ $10,950 each
   b. How much would it cost to insure, operate, and maintain company-owned vehicles?
      New (per year)

Insurance:	20 x $950
Operation:	20 x $1000
Maintenance:	warranty

      Used (per year)

Insurance:	20 x $850
Operation:	20 x $1000
Maintenance:	20 x $1200

   c. Would reps prefer to use company-owned cars?
      25% responded in the affirmative

Notice how Mike has divided company-owned vehicles into *new* and *used*. These categories became evident to him only after his research into costs had begun.

Determining Organization

Like letters and memos, reports may be organized inductively (indirectly) or deductively (directly). Placement of the big idea (recommendations or conclusions) is delayed in the inductive approach. Figures 11.1 and 11.2 show the same material for a report organized two different ways.

FIGURE 11.1 Inductive Organization

Inductive Organization

Problem/ Introduction	Inadequate student parking on campus during prime class times.
Facts	10,000 permits sold for 3000 parking spaces; some parking lots unusable in bad weather; large numbers of visitors without permits fill parking spaces; no land for new lots
Discussion/Solutions	Survey Results

1. Carpool? — 80 percent of students dislike carpooling.
2. Try shuttles from distant parking lots? — 75 percent of students interested in this service.
3. Enforce current regulations more strictly? — 88% of students support this solution.
4. Charge premium for parking in prime locations or during prime times? — 93 percent of students opposed.
5. Build double-deck parking structures? — 85 percent of students in favour.

The difference between inductive and deductive strategy is the placement of conclusions and recommendations.

Breakdown of direct and indirect costs for items 2 through 5 attached

Recommendations
  Short-term   Begin shuttle program.
  Long-term   Solicit funds for hiring more parking attendants and building new multistorey structures.

FIGURE 11.2 Deductive Organization

	Deductive Organization
Problem/Introduction	Inadequate student parking on campus during prime class times.
Recommendations	
Short-term	Begin shuttle program
Long-term	Solicit funds for hiring more parking attendants and building new multistorey structures.
Facts:	10,000 permits sold for 3000 parking spaces; some parking lots unusable in bad weather; large numbers of visitors without permits fill parking spaces; no land for new lots.
Discussion/Solutions	Survey Results
1. Carpool	80 percent of students dislike carpooling.
2. Try shuttles from distant parking lots?	75 percent of students interested in this service.
3. Enforce current regulations more strictly?	88 percent of students support this solution.
4. Charge premium for parking in prime locations or during prime times?	93 percent of students opposed.
5. Build double-deck parking structures?	85 percent of students in favour.

In Figures 11.1 and 11.2, you see only the skeleton of facts representing a complex problem. However, you can see the effects of organization. The inductive approach brings the reader through the entire process of analyzing a problem. It mirrors our method of thinking: problem, facts, analysis, recommendation. As you learned earlier, this strategy is successful when persuasion is necessary. It's also useful when the reader lacks knowledge and must be informed. However, busy executives or readers already familiar with the problem may want to get to the point more quickly.

The deductive approach is more direct; recommendations and conclusions are presented first so that readers have a frame of reference for reading the following discussion and analysis. Business reports are commonly organized deductively. Analyze your audience and purpose to determine the best overall strategy.

Informational Reports

Because information reports don't draw conclusions or make recommendations, there is no need to choose between inductive or deductive organization. There are a number of ways to organize an informational report.

1. **Chronological method.** Information may be organized by sequence of events. For example, a report on an eight-week training course could be divided in eight sections, each one representing one week. A report detailing a month-long sales trip might describe customers visited in week 1, week 2, and so on. Progress reports are usually organized chronologically. Be careful of overusing chronological organization. These reports can be boring, repetitious, and lacking in emphasis.

2. **Topical method.** The organization of information by topic is common in business reports. Topics can be divided into such categories as geographic location and product types. For example, a report describing a company's plans for expansion might be organized by territory (e.g., West Coast, Prairie, and Atlantic regions) or by product types (e.g., personal products, consumer electronics, and household goods).

3. **Most important to least important (or vice versa).** Some writers begin their reports by stating their most important findings before proceeding to relate those of less significance. Other writers reverse this progress by deferring their main points to the end of the report.

4. **Convention.** Some companies prefer their reports to follow a standard company organizational style. This type of organization is usually reserved for recurring informational reports.

Informational reports present information chronologically, topically, by order of importance, or by using a company's standard organizational style.

Analytical Reports

Writers of analytical reports must first decide whether to use the inductive approach or the deductive approach. Then they must find a way to organize their research findings.

Let's consider Mike's report to Françoise. At the conclusion of the planning process, Mike chose three alternatives or solutions he wanted to test (buy new cars, lease cars, have sales reps use their own cars) and the criteria by which he would test each one (primary costs, secondary costs, and employee preference). Having completed his research, he must now decide whether to organize the results by alternative solution or by criteria:

Analytical reports use either the inductive or deductive approach.

Organized by Alternative	Organized by Criteria

Buy Cars
  Primary Costs
  Secondary Costs
  Employee Preference
	Primary Costs
	  Buy Cars
	  Lease Cars
	  Use Own Cars

Lease Cars
  Primary Costs
  Secondary Costs
  Employee Preference
	Secondary Costs
	  Buy Cars
	  Lease Cars
	  Use Own Cars

Use Own Cars	Employee Preference
Primary Costs	Buy Cars
Secondary Costs	Lease Cars
Employee Preference	Use Own Cars

Choosing to organize by alternative would allow Mike to retain his working outline. However, he opts for organization by criteria because it will allow Françoise to see at a glance how the alternatives compare on the basis of each criterion.

Writing the Report

Once the information is gathered and organized, the next step is to produce the first draft of the report. Before discussing the different requirements for informational reports and analytical reports, we will review some guidelines that apply to *all* reports.

Being Objective

Reports are convincing only when the facts are believable and the writer is credible. You can build credibility in a number of ways.

Reports are more believable if the author is impartial, separates fact from opinion, uses moderate language, and cites sources.

1. **Present a balanced view**. Discuss positives and negatives for all the positions you present. Show through logical reasoning why, in spite of the negatives, one position is superior. Remain impartial, letting the facts prove your point.

2. **Separate fact from opinion**. Facts are verifiable and often quantifiable; opinions are beliefs held with confidence, but without substantiation. When making a claim or presenting an important statement in a report, ask yourself, "Is this a verifiable fact?" Suppose a supervisor wrote, *Our department works harder and gets less credit than any other department in the company.* This opinion is difficult to prove, and it damages the credibility of the writer. A more convincing statement might be, *Our productivity has increased 6 percent over the past year, which I believe shows the extra effort all employees are making.* The first part of this sentence (*Our productivity has increased 6 percent over the past year*) is a verifiable fact; that the productivity increase *shows the extra effort all employees are making* is an opinion, which the writer indicates through the prefatory words *I believe.*

3. **Be sensitive and moderate in your choice of language**. Don't exaggerate. Instead of saying *most people think*, it might be more accurate to say *some people think.* Obviously, avoid using labels and slanted expressions and try to remove bias from your writing. If readers suspect that a writer is biased in one part of an argument, they may discount the entire argument.

4. **Cite sources**. Tell your readers where the information came from. For example, *In a telephone interview on October 15, Thomas Boswell, director of transportation, said ...* Or, *The Victoria* Times Colonist *(August 10, p. 40)*

reports that ... Always use quotation marks to enclose exact words you are citing. You can also use endnotes or footnotes to document your sources. By referring to respected sources, you lend authority and credibility to your statements. Your words become more believable and your argument becomes more convincing.

Using Effective Headings

Good headings are helpful to both the reader and the writer. For the reader, they serve as an outline of the text, highlighting major ideas and categories. They also act as guides for locating facts and in pointing the way through the text. Moreover, headings provide resting points for the mind and for the eye, breaking up large chunks of text into manageable and inviting segments. For the writer, headings force organization of the data into meaningful blocks.

Functional heads (such as *Problem, Summary,* and *Recommendations*) help the writer outline a report. But talking heads (such as *Students Perplexed by Shortage of Parking* or *Short-Term Parking Solutions*) provide more information to the reader. Many of the examples in this chapter use functional heads for the purpose of instruction. It's sometimes possible to make headings both functional and descriptive, such as *Recommendations: Shuttle and New Structures.* Whether your heads are talking or functional, keep them brief and clear.

Most informal reports are simple, requiring only one level of heading. Longer, more formal reports demand subdividing the topic into levels of headings (see page 293 in Chapter 12).

Here are general tips on displaying headings effectively:

Functional headings show the outline of a report; talking heads provide more information.

- **Strive for parallel construction**. Use balanced expressions such as *Visible Costs and Hidden Costs* rather than *Visible Costs and Costs That Don't Show.*

- **Don't enclose headings in quotation marks**.

- **Don't use headings as antecedents for pronouns**. For example, if the heading reads *Laser Printers*, don't begin the next sentence with *These are often used with desktop publishing software.* If there is no alternative, repeat the noun. *Laser printers are often used with desktop publishing software.*

Informational Reports

Some informational reports are highly standardized, such as police reports, hospital admittance reports, and monthly sales reports. Essentially, these are fill-in reports using prepared forms for recurring information. Other informational reports are more personalized (as illustrated in Figure 11.3). They often include these sections:

- **Introduction/Background**. In this section, do the following: (1) explain why you are writing; (2) describe what methods and sources were used to gather information and why they are credible; (3) provide any special background information that may be necessary; (4) give the purpose of the report; (5) offer a preview of your findings.

Informational reports usually contain three parts: introduction, findings, and summary.

- **Findings**. This section may also be called any of *Observations, Facts, or Results.* Important points to consider in this section are organization and display. As discussed earlier, findings may be organized using one of three methods: (1) chronological, (2) topical, or (3) most important to least important (or vice versa). The topical and chronological methods are illustrated in Figures 11.3 and 11.4, respectively.

To display the findings effectively, you can number the paragraphs, underline or boldface key words, or indent the paragraphs. Be sure that words used as headings are parallel. If the findings require elaboration, include this discussion with each segment of the findings or set aside a separate section entitled *Discussion*.

■ **Summary.** This section provides an objective summary of the findings. Although the summary traditionally appears at the end of the report, it may be placed at the beginning if the writer wishes to give it special emphasis (see Figure 11.4).

Because summarizing can be a difficult skill to master, here are some suggestions to improve your abilities:

1. **Make the main points clear and understandable** and indicate their importance relative to each other.

2. **Use transitional expressions** such as *however, therefore, according to,* and *as a result* to link sentences.

3. **Omit details and examples** unless the main point cannot be understood without them.

4. **Write the summary from scratch.** Don't reuse sentences that appear in the report.

5. **Don't introduce new information.** The summary is a short version of the original. It is not an opportunity to provide additional data or analysis.

6. **Use terms that the reader will understand.** Avoid jargon and provide sufficient information to allow the reader to understand the main points.

> A summary condenses the report's primary ideas, omits details, avoids new information, and is written in terms that can be understood easily.

Analytical Reports

In addition to the sections contained in informational reports, analytical reports include conclusions and recommendations. As noted, they may be organized inductively or deductively. Under the latter approach, conclusions and recommendations are presented first.

The introduction in an analytical report may contain the same elements as those described in relation to the informational report (see page 265). Generally, background information is presented in a separate section whose purpose is to introduce the problem or place the problem in context. The amount of detail provided in this section depends on the knowledge of the reader.

The value of an analytical report lies in the quality of its conclusions. When drawing conclusions, you can maintain objectivity by ensuring that each conclusion is solidly based on your research findings. Do not introduce new information into your conclusions; address the problem as it was originally defined to you.

> Conclusions must be based on findings as presented in the report. Recommendations are suggestions for action.

Recommendations are suggestions for specific actions that can be taken in response to the conclusions drawn in the report. Recommendations frequently include a method and schedule for implementing the actions, as well as

FIGURE 11.3   Informational Report—Letter Format

SERVICES JAGER, INC.

392, rue Sainte-Catherine
Montréal, Québec
H4J 2E8

August 4, 199x

Ms. Karen Dumoulin, Promotions Manager
Disques Cargo, Inc.
703, boul. Saint-Laurent
Montréal, Québec
H2S 3J4

Dear Ms. Dumoulin

SUBJECT: AVAILABILITY OF NAMES FOR NEW RECORDING SERIES

Here is the report you requested regarding the availability of names for
use in a new recording series within the Cargo Records label.

Introduction

The following information is based on trademark searches of the U.S.
Patent and Trademark Office, the Copyright office, several other sources
of patent information in the Canadian music industry, and the services of
our attorneys. My staff conducted a full search of the five names you
submitted. Of this group we find that two names are possible for your use.

> The findings may
> also be entitled
> *Observations, Facts,
> Results,* or *Discussion.*

Discussion of Findings

1. **Gold Label.** Our research disclosed one recording company using the
   "Gold Label" name, and this causes us some concern. However, our
   outside counsel advises us that the name "Gold Label" is available for
   Cargo's use in light of the trademark registrations for "Gold Note"
   currently owned by your affiliated companies.

2. **The Master Series.** Several registrations containing the word "Master"
   appear in the Patent and Trademark Office. Since many registrations
   exist, no one can assert exclusive rights to that word. Therefore,
   Cargo's use of the name "The Master Series" is not precluded.

3. **Heavenly Voices.** Our search of copyright records disclosed that
   approximately seven songs were recorded in 1990 on the "Heavenly
   Voices" record label, with an address in Los Angeles, California.

Repeated attempts to reach this business have been unsuccessful.

4. **Celestial Sounds.** A record label using this name produced 12 titles in 1987. Apparently the recording company is now defunct, but the trademark registration, No. 1,909,233, persists.

5. **Cherubim.** This name has at least one currently operating outstanding trademark, Trademark Registration No. 2,109,900 for "Cherubim Music."

<u>Summary</u>

Of the five names discussed here, the first two appear to be open to you: "Gold Label" and "The Master Series." The names "Heavenly Voices" and "Celestial Sounds" require additional research. Since "Cherubim" is trade-marked, it is unavailable for your consideration.

Should you have any other names you would like us to check, please call me at 978-8990. It's always a pleasure to serve you.

Sincerely,

Robert Jager

Robert Jager
President

era

---

mention of the personnel who will be involved. Some report writers qualify their recommendations by discussing limitations and potential risks.

To return to the Devcorp example, suppose that Mike draws the following conclusions in his report:

A new transportation plan whereby all sales representatives would be reimbursed for using their own cars would be (1) more cost-effective and (2) easier to administer than the current plan.

Having arrived at this conclusion, Mike might offer these recommendations:

(1) That leases on all company cars used by sales reps not be renewed upon expiry.
(2) That travel-expense accounts be set up for sales reps who currently use company-leased cars.

Analytical reports that have been organized inductively and deductively are shown in Figures 11.5 and 11.6, respectively.

FIGURE 11.4 Informational Report—Memo Style

MEMORANDUM

TO: Jeanne Dostourian, President   DATE: April 20, 199x

FROM: Gail Desler, Development Officer G.A.

SUBJECT: CONSTRUCTION PROGRESS OF MISSISSAUGA BRANCH
           OFFICE

Summary

Construction of Dostourian Realty's Mississauga branch office has
entered Phase 3. Although we are one week behind the contractor's original schedule, the building should be ready for occupancy August 15.

Past Progress

Phase 1 involved development of the architect's plans; this process
was completed February 5. Phase 2 involved submission of the plans for
municipal building code approval. The plans were then given to four
contractors for estimates. The lowest bidder was Holst Brothers
Contractors. This firm began construction on March 25.

Present Status

Phase 3 includes initial construction procedures. The following steps
have been completed as of April 20:

1. Demolition of existing building at 273 Lakeshore Blvd.

2. Excavation of foundation footings for the building and for the
   surrounding wall.

3. Installation of steel reinforcing rods in building pad and wall.

4. Pouring of concrete foundation.

The contractor indicated that the project was one week behind schedule for the following reasons. The building inspectors required additional
steel reinforcement not shown on the architect's blueprints. Further,
excavation of the footings required more time than the contractor anticipated because the Number 4 footings were all below grade.

This report was
written for an
audience familiar
with the project;
therefore, it needn't
be as thorough as
some reports
might be.

Future Schedule

Despite some time lost in Phase 3, we are substantially on target for
the completion of this office building by August 1. Phase 4 includes fram-
ing, drywalling, and plumbing.

FIGURE 11.5   Analytical Report—Inductive Organization

TO: Ken Ogata, Director   DATE: June 3, 199x
           Human Resources

FROM: Judy Gray, Manager
           Information Services

SUBJECT: DEVELOPING PROCEDURES FOR USING TEMPORARY
           EMPLOYEES

At your request, I am submitting this report detailing my recommendations for improving the use of temporary employees in all departments within DataCom. My recommendations are based on my own experience with hundreds of temporary employees in my department and on my interviews with other department managers.

Background

DataCom has increased its number of service accounts from 58 to 97 over the past three years. During that same period, the number of permanent employees has increased only 12 percent. Because we have not been able to find qualified individuals to hire as full-time employees, we have been forced to rely on temporary employees more heavily than ever before. During the past year DataCom has required the services of 189 temporary employees, an increase of 76 over the previous year.

Joe Hernandez in Human Resources reports that he does not expect the employment picture to improve in the future. He feels that DataCom will probably continue to hire large numbers of temporary employees for at least the next two years.

Functional headings, like these, help the reader understand the overall organization of the report but offer little specific information.

Problem

Temporary employees are hired by department managers who have little experience in acquiring temps, planning their work, or supervising them. As a result, the productivity of the temps is not always as great as it could be. Moreover, we sometimes hire expensive, highly skilled individuals for routine tasks. These workers are bored with their assigned tasks and dissatisfied with their experience at DataCom; hence they refuse to return.

Findings

A survey of department managers and supervisors revealed a unanimous desire for the establishment of a standardized set of procedures relating to the use of temporary employees.

With respect to the hiring of temps, Judith Norton[1] advocates the use of prepared forms to facilitate this process. Prepared forms resulted in a more effective hiring process in 70 percent of the companies Norton studied (245). This finding is supported by informal discussions with relevant personnel at Comdex, which experienced a dramatic improvement in the area of hiring following its introduction of prepared forms two years ago.

With respect to the management of temps, Don Swerski[2] maintains that the productivity of new employees increases when their supervisors are provided with guidelines to follow when managing these individuals. Comdex has experienced a 62 percent decline in its new-employee turnover rate since introducing temp-management guidelines last year.

Conclusions

DataCom could improve the productivity and effectiveness of its temporary employees by instituting changes in two areas: (1) establishing and communicating standardized procedures to be followed by all department managers hiring temps, and (2) introducing guidelines for supervisors to follow when managing temps.

Recommendations

1. **System for Hiring Temps**. I recommend that Human Resources prepare a form that department managers complete before they hire temporary employees. The form will require department managers to indicate precisely what skills are required for the tasks to be completed. Requests for temps should then be channelled through one office, such as Human Resources.

2. **Guidelines for Managing Temps**. I further recommend that Human Resources, in consultation with the supervisors most directly involved, develop temp-management guidelines that will incorporate the following:

   - Organizing of work to be completed.
   - Simplifying tasks
   - Ensuring that supplies and operating equipment are available.
   - Providing clear directions.
   - Encouraging the temp to ask questions clarifying tasks.

[1]Judith Norton, "Using Prepared Forms in Hiring Process," Human Resource Specialist 35 (1996), pp. 244–54.
[2]Don Swerski, "Checklist—Why Use Them?" *The Resource Magazine*, February 1996, pp. 19–35.

FIGURE 11.6 Analytical Report—Deductive Organization

MEMORANDUM

TO: Orene Harder, Vice-President   DATE: June 11, 199x
           Operations Division

FROM: Jack Harris, Office Manager, Accounting Department ᴶᴴ

SUBJECT: UPDATING OF CURRENT WIRING SYSTEM

As you requested, I have prepared a report on the option that will best
meet the Accounting Department's need for a flexible, economical wiring
system that can accommodate our ever-changing electrical, communication, and data-processing requirements.

Conclusion

Installation of flat, undercarpet wiring is the most flexible and cost-effective way to update our current wiring system.

Recommendation

I recommend that we contract AMP Products Corporation of Toronto to
install the proposed system.

Findings

Present System

   At present our department has an outdated system of floor ducts and
power poles and a network of surface wiring that is overwhelmed by the
demands we are now placing on it. The operation of 27 pieces of electrical
equipment and 34 telephones requires extensive electrical circuits and
cabling. In addition, our overhead lighting, consisting of fluorescent
fixtures in a suspended egg-crate structure, has resulted in excessive
wiring above the drop ceiling.

   We have outgrown our present wiring system, and future growth is
contingent upon the availability of power. Since Hershey's goal is to have
a computer terminal at every workstation, we must find a better way to
serve our power needs than through conventional methods.

Advantages of Proposed System

   1. Power, telephone, and data cables are now available in a flat form
      only 0.1 cm thick. This flat, flexible cable can be installed under-
      neath existing carpeting, thus preventing costly and disruptive
      renovation necessary for installing additional round cables. Because
      flat cables can be moved easily, an undercarpet system would

provide great flexibility. Whenever we move a computer terminal or add a printer, we can easily make necessary changes in the wiring.

2. Undercarpet wiring would allow us to eliminate all power poles. These poles break up the office landscape and create distracting shadows about which employees complain.

3. Installation of an undercarpet wiring system in the Accounting Department would enable Hershey to evaluate the system's effectiveness before considering it for other areas, such as sales, customer services, and field warehousing.

4. The AMP Products Corporation of Toronto estimates that undercarpet wiring for the Accounting Department would cost about $29,000. If we were to use conventional methods to install round wiring, we would have to renovate our entire department, which would cost over $200,000. Undercarpet wiring, then, saves Hershey over $170,000. Equally important, however, are the effects on productivity and employee satisfaction, which would deteriorate if renovation were required.

Other Options

Drop Ceiling System. Installing traditional wiring in the drop ceiling would be advantageous in that it would not require the disruption of workers while the carpet was lifted to install the undercarpet wiring. It is also a traditional method of wiring and thus has proven itself over many years in service.

The cost of increasing our wiring in the drop ceiling includes the rationalization of the existing wiring, which is conservatively estimated at $50,000 (Susan Terrel, Manager of Building Maintenance). This would be on top of the cost the expected increase in wiring that will result as we move toward "a computer terminal at every workstation."

Outlet System. Installing an outlet system where all wiring (telephone and power) is run through the walls to outlets. This system would require significant disruption as walls would have to be opened and resealed.

The cost of moving to a complete outlet system is estimated at $75,000 (Susan Terrel, Manger of Building Maintenance). This also would be on top of the considerable disruption and costs for opening the walls and running wiring inside the walls.

Wireless System. This system is currently in development. The technology is not considered completely reliable as described by Kaufmann in Electrical Monthly (December, 1996, p. 43). As well, it is considerably more expensive than other systems.

Summary

Informal reports are relatively short (under ten pages) and are usually written in memo, letter, or report format or on prepared forms. Reports that provide data are informational; reports that draw conclusions and make recommendations are analytical. Begin a report by formulating a statement of purpose explaining why you are writing the report.

The facts for reports are often obtained from company records, the Internet, observation, interviews, and research.

Analytical reports can be organized either deductively, with conclusions and recommendations appearing close to the beginning, or inductively, with conclusions and recommendations at the end. As with correspondence, an analysis of your audience will help determine the best organizational strategy.

To preserve credibility, your reports should be impartial. Separate fact from opinion, use moderate language, and cite sources. Use functional heads to show the outline of a report and talking heads to provide more information. Informational reports usually contain three sections: introduction, findings, and summary. Analytical reports include these sections as well as conclusions and recommendations.

APPLICATION AND PRACTICE—11

Discussion

1. How are business reports different from business letters?

2. Compare and contrast informational reports and analytical reports.

3. Define inductive organization and deductive organization. Under what circumstances should each approach be used?

4. How are the reports that you write for your courses similar to those presented in this chapter? How are they different?

Short Answers

5. List four formats suitable for reports. Be prepared to discuss each format.

6. Name five sources of information for reports.

7. List four ways to achieve objectivity in your reports.

8. List three organizational methods for informational reports.

9. Suggest two or more sources of information for the reports described in each of the following situations.

    a. As a student representative on the Curriculum Review Committee, you have been asked to report on the course requirements in your major and make recommendations for change.

    b. As department manager, you must write a report on the pros and cons of establishing job descriptions for employees in your department.

    c. You want to propose to management that the defective copier in your department be replaced.

d. You must document the progress of a 12-month campaign to alter the image of a jeans' manufacturer.

10. How do problem and purpose statements facilitate the planning of reports?

11. What is the purpose of (a) functional heads, and (b) talking heads? Give an example of each type of heading.

12. The citation of sources adds what to your report?

CASE 11–1

Information Report

The owner of your company has decided that she wants to make greater use of the E-mail system that you have been developing over the last few years. She feels that in the late 20th century, a leading-edge company such as yours should use E-mail entirely for its internal messaging. Your supervisor, John Morissey, manager of the Information Technology (IT) department, has been given the job of determining how this will occur. He asks you to prepare an information report that describes the readiness of the organization to remove paper messaging entirely. At this early stage, John is most concerned about whether the company has the hardware and software required to make the switch. You begin your task by analyzing the problem and developing a clear statement of purpose. You realize that equipment requirements are only part of the problem. If employees have the equipment but don't use it, then the equipment isn't much good. You mention this to John and he agrees. You begin with a visit to each department to take inventory of computers and software. While you are there, you survey employees about their current and expected use of E-mail. Your search provides the following information:

Department (number of staff)	Platform and Hardware	% of employees who have a personal computer	% of machines on network	% of machines in department that have company E-mail package	% of employees in department who use E-mail now	% of employees in department who plan to use E-mail in the future
Front Office (100)	Desktop PCs	90	60	60	50	65
Engineering (50)	PC/MAC	95	100	100	100	100
Sales (50)	Laptop PCs/ Desktop PCs	65	30	20	20	50
Human Resources (40)	Desktop PCs	85	40	40	40	60
Production (510)	Desktop PCs	10	100	100	0	5
Field Service (100)	Laptop PCs	65	20	10	10	50
Quality Control (50)	Desktop PCs	99	99	99	80	100
Shipping/Receiving (100)	Desktop PCs	20	100	100	10	15

Once you have compiled the information, you realize that there are going to be problems. You notice that in the areas where employees work "on the floor," computer use generally is low and current use of E-mail is nonexistent. You also notice that in many departments a variety of computers are used. This variety may cause problems with linking to the network and compatibility—both issues for IT to be concerned about. You notice several other issues that you are sure will be important to your supervisor. Write an information report, memo-style, to John Morissey, Manager of Information Technology, summarizing your findings from the table above. Fill in any details you may require.

CASE 11–2

Information Report

Gather information about a position for which you might be interested in applying. Learn about the job. Discover whether certification, licenses, or experience is required. Describe the working conditions in this profession. Collection information regarding typical entry-level salaries and potential for advancement.

If your instructor wishes to make this an extended report, collect information about two companies to which you might apply. Investigate each company's history, products and/or services, size, earnings, reputation, and number of employees. Describe the functions of an employee working in the position you have investigated. To do this, interview one or more individuals who are working in that position. Devote several sections of your report to the specific tasks, functions, duties, and opinions of these individuals.

CASE 11–3

Analytical Report

In your work or your training, identify equipment that needs to be purchased or replaced (computer, printer, VCR, copier, camera, etc.). Write a report comparing two or more brands and recommending a choice based on cost-effectiveness.

CASE 11-4

Analytical Report

Your supervisor from Case 11–1, John Morissey, reads your information report and realizes that the owner's dream of an electronic organization may be more difficult than was first expected. John needs something to take to the owner that will provide a plan for how the electronic organization will occur. John asks you to develop an analytical report that recommends the best way to implement the owner's dream. You can use information collected from the original report to set the stage, but you will have to find options for how the electronic organization might happen.

You contact Ken Morris, Chief Engineer, to ask how his department developed its computer literacy. Ken indicates that all of his people work on computers as part of their job. Employees come to the job trained to operate computers, so it is easy to extend their skills to the use of E-mail. You realize that this might be a problem for production and shipping/receiving. You contact several other organizations to inquire about their E-mail systems and find that training is a major part of moving to an electronic organization. You also find that other organizations developed realistic time frames (usually in excess of 2 years), chose and consistently used an easy E-mail package (you are given a couple of suggestions), and planned to use existing equipment as much as possible (this is a very technical matter that probably should be considered at greater length by John and other Information Technology (IT) experts).

You are concerned that you were unable to talk with a manufacturing company like yours and so do not have information regarding the problem with production and shipping/receiving. You do know that for other companies that you talked with, getting non-users to use E-mail was consistently the most difficult part. Since this issue was a major hurdle for other companies, it should be considered in greater detail—perhaps in a report dealing specifically with that issue. In addition, you quickly check several secondary sources that confirm the importance of realistic time frames but also suggest the following ideas:

- use outside trainers to help with initial training;

- use cross-training—those who know E-mail train those who don't;

▧ develop employee rewards for using E-mail over paper during the switch-
over time;

▧ plan practice "E-days" where E-mail is used primarily, but paper is still there
to act as a support;

▧ choose a specific, future "E-day" that is recognized as the day that the organization switches permanently; and

▧ send important employee information regarding time off or other benefits by
E-mail during the transition period.

Now that you have collected this information, you feel you are in a position
to combine conclusions arising from the first study with this information to
produce useful recommendations. Write the analytical report to John Morissey
using memo-style. Fill in any details you may require.

Case 11-5

Analytical Report

Identify a problem in a business or organization with which you are familiar,
such as mediocre quality, indifferent service, poor attendance at organization
meetings, uninspired cafeteria food, antique office equipment, arrogant
management, lack of communication, underappreciated employees, wasteful
procedures, and so forth. Describe the problem in detail. Assume you are to
report to management (or to the leadership of an organization) about the nature
and scope of the problem. Decide on the organization of your report (inductive
or deductive). How would you gather information to lend authority to your
conclusions and recommendations? Determine the exact topic and report
length after consultation with your instructor.

GRAMMAR/MECHANICS CHECKUP—11

Other Punctuation

Although this checkup concentrates on Sections 2.23 through 2.29 of the
Grammar/Mechanics Handbook, you may also refer to other punctuation principles. Insert any necessary punctuation in the following statements. Use the
delete sign (⌒) to remove any unnecessary punctuation. In the space provided
for each statement, indicate the number of changes you make. Count each mark
separately; for example, a set of parentheses counts as 2. When you finish,
compare your responses with those shown below. If your responses differ,
study carefully the specific sections shown in parentheses.

2 (2.27)

Example: (De-emphasize.) The consumption of Mexican food products is highest in certain provinces (Ontario and British Columbia), but this food trend is spreading to other parts of the country.

1. (Emphasize.) The convention-planning committee has invited three managers Jim Lowey, Frank Beyer, and Carolyn Wong to make presentations.

2. Would you please Miss Sanchez use your computer to recalculate these totals?

3. (De-emphasize.) A second set of demographic variables see Figure 13.9 on page 432 includes nationality, religion, and race.

4. Because the word recommendation is frequently misspelled we are adding it to our company style book.

5. Recruiting, hiring, and training: these are three important functions of a human resources officer.

6. The office manager said, "Who placed an order for 15 dozen ribbon cartridges

7. Have any of the research assistants been able to locate the article entitled How the GST Will Affect You

8. (Emphasize.) The biggest grain-producing provinces Manitoba, Saskatchewan, and Alberta are experiencing severe budget deficits.

9. Have you sent invitations to Mr Ronald E Harris, Miss Michelle Hale, and Ms Sylvia Kraicer

10. Dr. Y.W. Yellin wrote the chapter entitled Trading on the Options Market that appeared in a book called Securities Markets.

11. Rafael said, "I'll be right over" however he has not appeared yet.

12. In business the word liability may be defined as any legal obligation requiring payment in the future.

13. Because the work was scheduled to be completed June 10; we found it necessary to hire temporary workers to work June 8 and 9.

14. Did any c o d shipments arrive today

15. Hooray I have finished this checkup haven't I

---

1. (2) managers—Wong—(2.26a, 2.27) 3. (2) (see page 432) (2.27) 5. (1) training—(2.26c) 7. (3) "How You"? (2.28e, 2.28f) 9. (4) Mr. E. Ms. Mason? (2.23b, 2.24) 11. (2) over"; however, (2.16, 2.28f) 13. (1) June 10, (2.06) 15. (3) Hooray! checkup, I? (2.24, 2.25)

GRAMMAR/MECHANICS CHALLENGE—11

Document for Revision

The following progress report is wordy and contains faults in grammar, punctuation, spelling, and number form. Drawing upon the guidelines provided in the Grammar/Mechanics Handbook and what you learned in this chapter, revise the report.

Poor Report

TO: Jon Peterson   DATE: August 10, 199x
             Executive Producer

FROM: Vicki Schmolka
             Location Manager

SUBJECT SITE FOR FILMING OF "REDWOOD BAY"

This memo describes the progress of my exploration for an appropriate rustic home to be used in connection with the fishing village sequences in the film "Cedar Bay".

Work Completed: To prepare for this assignment several sites in the Rushing River area were visited. Possible locations include a town complete with turn of the century homes, victorian shops and rustic rooming houses. One acceptional cite is the sea shanty inn a 97 year old hotel situated close to the wharf and with a breathtaking view of the ocean.

Work to Be Completed: In the next 5 days I'll search the coast north of the Rushing River area including the villages of Deep Bay, Cabot Cove, and Hidden Bay. Hidden Bay is abandoned. Many of the old villages contain charming structures that may present exactly the degree of atmosphere and mystery we seek, these villages have the added advantage of easy acess.

My final report in regards to the 3 most promising locations are nearly completed. You will in all probability be able to visit these cites August 21st.

12

Formal Reports

In this chapter, you will learn to do the following:

- Write a meaningful statement of purpose for a formal report.
- Collect information from both primary and secondary sources.
- Research topics from books, periodicals, and computer databases.
- Recognize three methods for documenting information sources.

- Distinguish among five organizational strategies.
- Outline topics and use appropriate heading format.
- Illustrate data, using tables, charts, and graphs.
- Sequence 12 parts of a long report.

The primary differences between formal and informal reports are tone, structure, and length.

Formal reports, whether they offer only information or whether they also analyze that information and make recommendations, typically have three characteristics: formal tone, traditional structure, and lengthiness. They provide management with vital information for decision-making. In this chapter, we will consider the entire process of writing a formal report: planning the report, collecting and documenting information, organizing and illustrating data, and presenting the final report.

Planning the Report

Like informal reports, formal reports begin with a thorough definition of the project including an analysis of the audience and the research problem. For formal reports, you must also consider the scope and limitations of the project.

It would be impossible to research and evaluate all aspects of a given topic. You should determine the scope of your report at the outset. If you are writing about low morale among night-shift employees, how many of your 475 employees should you interview? Should you limit your research to company-related morale factors, or should you consider external factors over which the company has no control? By answering these questions, you are determining the precise boundaries of the topic.

Both the scope and quality of your report will inevitably be affected by such factors as time constraints, scarcity of information, or lack of access to information. These limitations should be clearly acknowledged in your report.

Once you have determined the scope of the project, write a purpose statement. The purpose statement should describe the goal, significance, and scope of the report. Notice how the following statement pinpoints the research needed for the report:

The planning of every report begins with a statement of purpose explaining the goal, scope, and limitations of the project.

> The purpose of this report is to explore employment possibilities for entry-level paralegal workers in the city of St. John's. It will consider typical salaries, skills required, opportunities, and working conditions. This research is significant because of the increasing number of job openings in the paralegal profession. This report will not consider legal secretarial employment, which represents a different employment focus.

Collecting and Documenting Information

Effective reports, whether formal or informal, are founded on accurate information. Information collected for a report may be grouped into two categories, primary and secondary. Primary information is obtained from firsthand observation and experience, while secondary information comes from reading what others have observed or experienced.

Primary Sources

Five logical sources of information for a report are company records, observation, interviews, surveys, and experiments.

Company Records.   Information for reports regarding company operations often originates in company records. Accounting and marketing reports would include information on previous performance taken from existing records.

Primary information are facts that have not already been collected and recorded by someone else.

Observation.   In business reports, personal observation often provides essential information. For example, if Alima Sodiri, a marketing manager, were writing a report recommending changes in sales territories, she would probably begin by carefully observing the current territories and analyzing sales coverage. If Samantha Jones, a student, were reporting on employment possibilities, she might begin by observing classified ads in a local newspaper.

Interviews.   Collecting information by talking with individuals gives the researcher immediate feedback and provides a chance for explanation of questions if necessary. If the information collected is to be used scientifically or systematically, the interviewer should follow an interview schedule—that is, the same questions, stated identically, should be addressed to all interviewees.

Surveys.   If many questions need to be asked of a large group of individuals and if costs must be kept down, then surveys may be used to collect data. Good surveys, however, cannot be conducted casually. Questions should be carefully written and tested on sample groups before actually being administered. Thought should be given to how the results will be tabulated and interpreted.

Experiments.   Although experimentation is more common in the physical and social sciences, decision-makers in business may also use this technique to gather information. In promoting a new product, for example, a business might experiment with an ad in two different newspapers and compare the results.

Secondary Sources

Many formal business reports require library research to provide background information.

Secondary information for business reports can come from published sources held in libraries or from databases available through computer networks. Many formal reports begin with extensive library research to provide an overview of the problem being investigated. In fact, for any problem about which you are unfamiliar, your school or public library is a good place to begin seeking information. Nearly always you will find that someone else has studied the same or a similar problem and has written something helpful. Begin your library research by talking with the reference librarian about your project. Most libraries also provide brochures or other printed material to help you locate reference materials on their shelves and in other libraries. Here are several major sources of library information for you to consult.

Computer Databases.   Most libraries provide computer bibliography search help at little or no cost. CD-ROM databases contain references to a wide variety of business information. Many libraries offer additional on-line search resources such as the Internet or ERIC. Reference librarians will help you decide on appropriate databases and key words to describe your topic.

Databases on CD-ROM include electronic versions of the more traditional paper indexes, encyclopedias, dictionaries, directories, and handbooks. The *Canadian Business and Current Affairs* (*CBCA*) index includes 7 Canadian daily newspapers and about 200 Canadian business magazines and journals. *Academic Abstracts* is an index of about 500 periodicals, including popular magazines as well as technical and professional journals. This index also contains full-text reviews of about 2000 books. The *Applied Science and Technology Index* (*ASTI*) lists articles from more than 350 journals covering such fields as aeronautics, chemistry, computer science, construction, food industry, and engineering. The *Auditor General of Canada Reports* database contains the full text of all annual reports issued by the office of the Auditor General of Canada. The *Canadian Encyclopedia* database contains the full text of all four volumes of the encyclopedia, as well as the full text of the *Gage Canadian Dictionary*. *Canadian Media Resources*, *Canadian Periodical Index*, and *Social Science Source* are also useful databases for students as well as professionals. Canadian On-line Inquiry makes a number of Canadian and international databases available to researchers. INFOGLOBE gives researchers access to *The Globe and Mail*; *Maclean's* and *The Financial Post* are also available through FP ONLINE. Availability of these databases varies depending on the library.

On-line Services.   As mentioned in Chapter 11, the Internet and other on-line services allow users to access vast amounts of information. The Internet's World Wide Web contains millions of home pages, or Web sites, which provide useful information as well as hypertext links to related home pages. A graphical user interface (GUI) such as NCSA Mosaic, Netscape Navigator, or Microsoft Explorer allows researchers access to global resources with the click of a mouse button. There is a potential downside to Internet use. As noted in the previous chapter, on-line searching can be a time-consuming process. It can also be expensive if you subscribe to a private service provider. Finally, there is no guarantee that information obtained from the Internet will be accurate or reliable. Remember that the Internet isn't the only source for useful secondary information. A search of available Web sites should be considered part of a larger, more comprehensive research plan.

Periodicals.   Periodicals are magazines, journals, and pamphlets. They often provide the most current information on a topic. To locate articles in general-interest magazines such as *Time*, *Maclean's*, *Harrowsmith*, and *Saturday Night*, consult the *Canadian Periodical Index*. To locate articles in business, industrial, and trade publications, such as *Canadian Business* and *Canadian Consumer*, consult the *Canadian Business Periodicals Index*. Other indexes include the *Canadian News Index*, the *Canadian Index*, *CNI Clips* (microform), and the *Canadian Press Newsfile*. Most professions also publish their own periodicals that cover the major issues facing those professions.

Encyclopedias, Dictionaries, Handbooks.   The reference section of a library holds special collections of helpful material. General encyclopedias include *The Canadian Encyclopedia* and *Encyclopedia Canadiana*. Specialized encyclopedias include *Encyclopedia of the Social Sciences*, *Encyclopedia of Science and Technology*, *Exporter's Encyclopedia*, *Accountant's Encyclopedia*, and *The Financial Post Moneywise Magazine Directory of Personal Finance*. The reference section may also house useful dictionaries that function as encyclopedias, such as *Associations Canada 1991: An Encyclopedic Dictionary*, the *ITP Nelson Canadian Dictionary*, the *Dictionary of Canadian Biography*, the *Dictionary of Canadian Law*, and Prentice-Hall's *Encyclopedic Dictionary of Business*. Handbooks provide current information in specialized professions. These include the *Canadian News Release Handbook*, the *Canadian Small Business Handbook*, and the *Canadian Writers Handbook*.

Directories.   Canadian business directories include *The Blue Book of Canadian Business*, which lists and ranks thousands of Canadian companies, and the *Canadian Key Business Directory*, which lists companies by name, location, product, and Dun and Bradstreet number. Other directories include the *Canadian Trade Index*, the *Canadian Index*, the *Financial Post Directory of Directors*, and *Fraser's Canadian Trade Directory*.

Government Publications.   Statistics Canada offers several yearly publications, including the *Canada Handbook*, which provides information on the economy; the *Canada Yearbook*, which offers statistical information on the economy, trade, and finance; and the *Market Research Handbook*, which provides statistical information on Canadian markets. Statistics Canada also produces a database called E-STAT. The federal government catalogues its publications in the *Government of Canada Publications List*. Provincial government publications are also available in most libraries.

Newspapers. Newspapers from around the country and the world not only are fascinating to read but also supply current information. Locating articles on your topic, however, is difficult unless you limit yourself to the newspapers that index their articles. General newspaper indexes (aside from those available on CD-ROM) include the *Canadian News Index*, *CNI Clips* (microform), and the *Canadian Press Newsfile*. Some indexes to consider for American newspapers are *The Los Angeles Times Index*, *National Observer Index*, *The New York Times Index*, and *The Wall Street Journal Index*.

Holdings Catalogues. Computerized holdings catalogues allow users to conduct keyword searches of the library's resources. Librarians are usually happy to show readers how to find information in the catalogues and how then to locate the books on the shelves. Books provide excellent historical, in-depth information on a subject. However, more current information is generally available in magazines listed in periodical guides.

Library Research

To document a formal report with secondary sources, you must take good library notes, include source notes in the report, and list all references in a bibliography.

Here are tips on conducting library research.

- Take a good supply of coins with you to the library so that you can make photocopies of promising pages.

- Before you begin working with listings of periodicals, find out what magazines your library has on-shelf. It's most disappointing to find fascinating titles for articles in magazines that your library doesn't carry.

- Don't allow yourself to become a victim of information overload. You can't read everything that's been written about your subject. Look up only relevant and current references. Be selective.

- Be resourceful and persevering when searching for information. For example, if you're looking for a background report about speaking skills for businesspeople, you might look under such descriptors as *speech*, *communication*, *language*, *public relations*, and *conversation*.

- Take effective notes. Place each reference on a separate card or sheet of paper. Record the author's name, title of the article or book, and complete publication information, in addition to your notes regarding the content of the references.

- Use only a few quotations in your report. Good writers use direct quotes only (1) to emphasize opinions because of the author's status as an expert, (2) to duplicate the exact wording before criticizing, or (3) to repeat identical phrasing because of its precision, clarity, or pertinence.

Internet Research

If you are conducting a search of the World Wide Web using Netscape Navigator, you will begin with a screen like the one shown in Figure 12.1. You can choose one of six "hot buttons": What's New, What's Hot, Handbook, Net Search, Net Directory, and Software. Because you want to search, you would select Net Search. The screen depicted in Figure 12.2 shows five search engines (Infoseek Guide, Lycos, Magellan, Excite, and Yahoo), each with its own special features. In this figure, you can see that Infoseek Guide has been selected. Choosing a keyword related to your topic, typing it in the box under *Search for*, and clicking on *seek now*, will limit your search to sites that deal with the keyword topic.

Searching the Internet can be done using general search methods or keyword search methods.

Figure 12.1   Netscape Navigator Screen

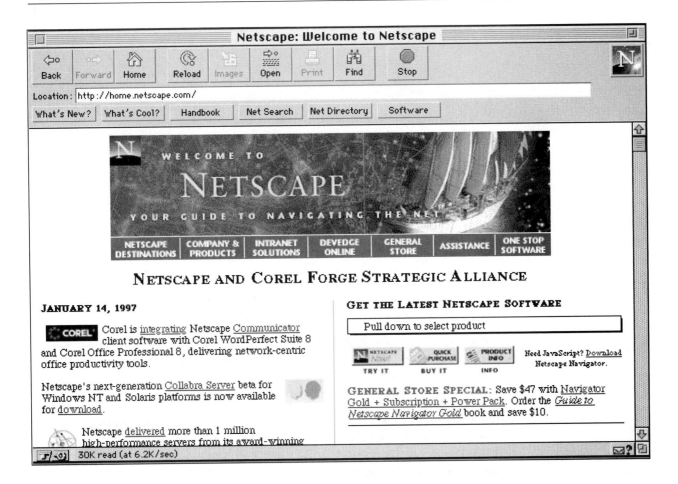

Figure 12.3 shows the next screen in Infoseek Guide. Here you can further specify your topic by typing a keyword or phrase in the box under *Search for information about*. (Note that you can select locations other than the World Wide

Figure 12.2   Net Search Screen

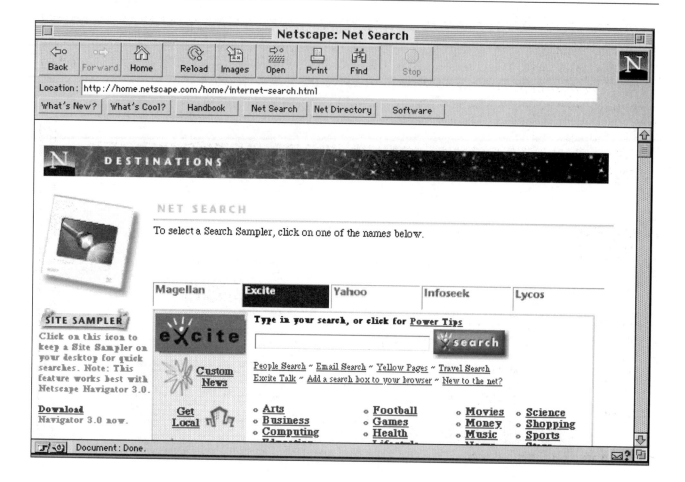

Web by using the dropdown button just below the search box.) If you wish to conduct a general search, you can choose one of the topics listed on the left of the screen. Clicking on *Business* would give you the screen depicted in Figure 12.4. Here you are presented with a choice between continuing your search by typing a keyword or phrase in the *Search for information about*, scrolling down to see the sources available on this screen, or browsing the *Related topics* section.

Documentation Methods

Citations.   If you use information from secondary sources (including the Internet), you must indicate where the information originated. Even if you paraphrase, the ideas must be documented. In Appendix 2, you will find three methods of documentation: (1) the footnote method, (2) the endnote method, and (3) the parenthetic or MLA method. You will also find guidelines for citing electronic sources.

Figure 12.3   Infoseek Guide Screen

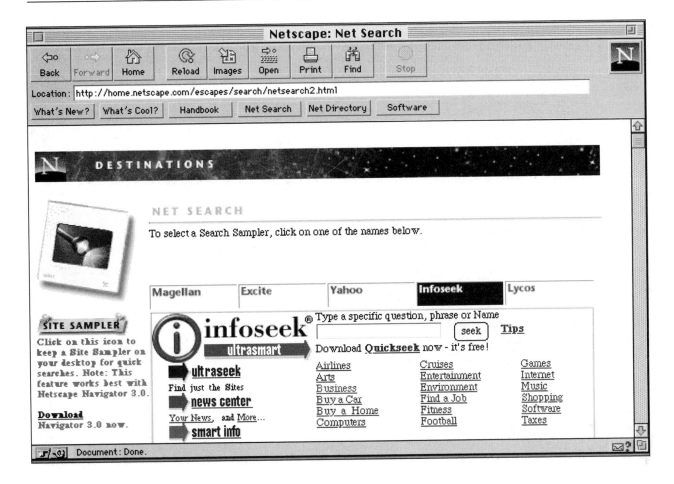

Bibliography.   A bibliography is an alphabetic list of all books, articles, and other sources of information cited or consulted in preparing a formal report. This list is useful to readers and a necessary component in a long, formal report. Instructions for preparing a bibliography are also given in Appendix 2.

Organizing Information

The readability of a report is greatly enhanced by skilful organization of the facts presented. Organizational strategies for formal reports are essentially the same as those used for informal reports. Here is a brief overview of the methods of organization used in formal reports.

Figure 12.4   Business Screen

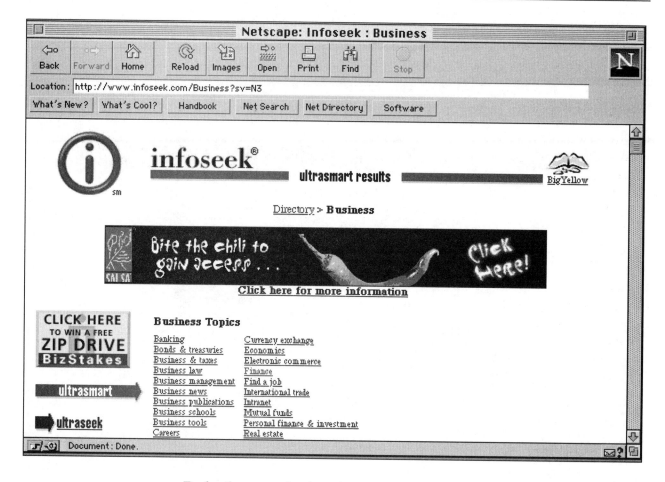

- **Deductive organization**. As you recall from Chapter 11, the deductive strategy presents big ideas first. In formal reports, that would mean beginning with recommendations or findings. For example, if you were studying five possible locations for a proposed shopping centre, you would begin by recommending the site you judge to be best and follow with discussion of other sites. Use this strategy when the reader is supportive and knowledgeable.

- **Inductive organization**. Inductive reasoning presents facts and discussion first, followed by conclusions and recommendations. Since formal reports generally seek to educate the reader, this order of presentation is often most effective. Following this sequence, a study of possible locations for a shopping centre would begin with information regarding all proposed sites followed by analysis of the information and conclusions drawn from that analysis.

- **Chronological organization**. Information sequenced along a time frame is arranged chronologically. This plan is effective for presenting historical information or for describing a procedure. A description of the development of a multinational company, for example, would be chronological. A report explaining how to obtain federal funding for a project might be organized chronologically, in the order of the steps to be taken. Often topics are arranged in a past-to-present or present-to-past sequence.

■ **Geographical or spatial organization**. Information arranged geographically or spatially is organized by physical location. For instance, a report analyzing a company's national sales might be divided into sections representing different geographical areas such as the Maritimes, Southern Ontario, the Prairies, and the West Coast.

■ **Topical or functional organization**. Some subjects lend themselves to arrangement by topic or function. A report analyzing changes in the management hierarchy of an organization might be arranged in this manner. The report would first consider the duties of the CEO, followed by the functions of the general manager, business manager, marketing manager, and so forth.

In organizing a long, formal report, you may find that you combine some of the preceding plans. However it's done, you must break your topic into major divisions, usually three to six. These major divisions then must be partitioned into smaller subdivisions. To identify these divisions, you may use functional heads (such as *introduction, findings, discussion, conclusions*, and *recommendations*) or more descriptive or talking heads, which explain the contents of the text. You may wish to review the suggestions for writing effective headings that appeared in Chapter 11, page 265.

> The overall presentation of a topic may be inductive or deductive, while parts of the report are chronological (such as the background) or topical (such as discussion of findings).

Outlining

The best way to organize a report is to record its divisions in an outline. This outline is a tool of the writer; it is not part of the final report. The purpose of an outline is to show at a glance the overall plan of the report. Figure 12.5 shows an abbreviated outline of a report about forms of business ownership.

Figure 12.6 illustrates the format for levels of headings in reports. Notice that the title represents a first-degree heading and appears in capital letters centred on a line. Other headings reveal their importance and their relevance to the outline by their position and their format. Second-degree headings are centred and underlined. Third-degree headings start at the left margin and are underlined. Fourth-degree headings (sometimes called paragraph headings) are indented; text immediately follows the heading.

Illustrating Information

Tables, charts, graphs, illustrations, and other visual aids can play an important role in clarifying, summarizing, and emphasizing information. Numerical data become meaningful, complex ideas are simplified, and visual interest is provided by the appropriate use of graphics. Here are general tips on making the most effective use of visual aids:

> The tips presented here for generating and implementing graphs in formal reports are useful in other presentations as well.

■ Use visual aids to reinforce the text, not replace it.

Figure 12.5 Outline Format

FORMS OF BUSINESS OWNERSHIP

I. Sole proprietorship (*first main topic*)

   A. Advantages of sole proprietorship (*first subdivision of Topic I*)

      1. Minimal capital requirements (*first subdivision of Topic A*)

      2. Control by owner (*second subdivision of Topic A*)

      3. Tax savings (*third subdivision of Topic A*)

   B. Disadvantages of sole proprietorship (*second subdivision of Topic I*)

      1. Unlimited liability (*first subdivision of Topic B*)

      2. Limited management talent (*second subdivision of Topic B*)

      3. Restricted credit availability (*third subdivision of Topic 1*)

II. Partnership (*second main topic*)

   A. Advantages of partnership (*first subdivision of Topic II*)

      1. Access to capital (*first subdivision of Topic A*)

      2. Management talent (*second subdivision of Topic A*)

      3. Ease of formation (*third subdivision of Topic A*)

   B. Disadvantages of partnership (*second subdivision of Topic II*)

      1. Unlimited liability (*first subdivision of Topic B*)

      2. Personality conflicts (*second subdivision of Topic B*)

The tips presented here for generating and implementing graphs in formal reports are useful in other presentations as well.

▦ Clearly identify the contents of the visual aid with meaningful titles and headings.

▦ Refer the reader to the visual aid by discussing it in the text and mentioning its location and figure or table number.

▦ Locate the table as close as possible to its reference in the text.

▦ Strive for vertical placement of visual aids. Readers are disoriented by horizontal pages in reports.

▦ Give credit to the source if appropriate.

Tables

Probably the most frequently used visual aid in reports is the table. A table presents quantitative information in a systematic order of columns and rows.

FIGURE 12.6 Format of Headings

↓ 13 lines

FORMS OF BUSINESS OWNERSHIP   **First-degree heading**

↓ 2 lines

Sole Proprietorship   **Second-degree**
                                                                                    heading
↓ 3 lines

Advantages of Sole Proprietorship   **Third-degree**
                                                                                    heading
↓ 2 lines
                                                                                    Fourth-degree
Minimal capital requirements. _____   **heading**

_____

Control by owner. _____

_____

Tax savings. _____

_____
↓ 3 lines

Disadvantages of Sole Proprietorship
↓ 2 lines

Unlimited liability. _____

_____

Limited management talent._____

_____

Restricted credit availability. _____

_____
↓ 3 lines

Partnership
↓ 2 lines

Advantages of Partnership
↓ 2 lines

Access to capital._____

_____

Management talent. _____

_____

Ease of formation. _____

_____
↓ 3 lines

Disadvantages of Partnership
↓ 2 lines

Unlimited liability._____

_____

Personality conflicts. _____

_____

FIGURE 12.7 Table

Table 1

MANITOBA'S MAJOR FOREIGN EXPORTS, 1992

Commodity Group	$ Millions	Percent
Cereal Grains	911.2	24.0
Nickel*	510.3	13.4
Machinery and Appliances	229.7	6.0
Motor Vehicles and Parts	226.7	6.0
Live Animals	222.3	5.9
Oilseeds	170.9	4.5
Aircraft Components	152.3	4.0
Electrical Equipment	110.3	2.9
Paper and Printed Products	101.5	2.7
Fats and Oils	84.1	2.2
Wood and Wood Articles	74.8	2.0
Vegetables and Tubers	66.0	1.7
Inorganic Chemicals	62.2	1.6
Furniture and Fixtures	49.5	1.3
Plastic and Plastic Articles	48.5	1.3
Top Commodity Groups	3020.3	79.5
Total 1992 Exports	3799.9	100.0

* Most of Manitoba's nickel is exported via Ontario, so exact quantities and destination are unknown. Manitoba's foreign nickel exports are estimated at 90% of total production.

Source: *The 1993 Manitoba Budget,* Province of Manitoba (Winnipeg: Department of Finance, Province of Manitoba, 1993), p. 5.

Be sure to identify columns and rows clearly. In Figure 12.7, *Commodity Group* represents the row heading; *$ Millions* and *Percent* represent column headings.

Charts and Graphs

A chart or graph clarifies data by showing the relationship between one variable and another. Computer software can make professional-looking charts and graphs easy to produce.

Pie Charts.   Pie, or circle, charts help readers visualize a whole and the proportions of its components, as shown in Figure 12.8. Pie charts are particularly useful in showing percentages. In preparing pie charts, begin dividing the pie at the 12 o'clock position. It's helpful to include both a description and the actual percentage of the total with each segment. Group a number of small components into one segment. The segments should total 100 percent. Labels

Figure 12.8   Pie Chart

Distribution of Job Separators by the Number of Weeks
of Joblessness, 1986

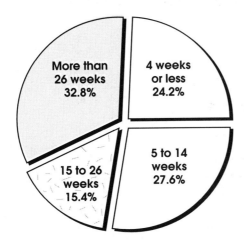

Source: Estimates by the Economic Council of Canada, based on data from Statistics Canada.
A Lot to Learn: Education and Training Canada, Economic Council of Canada (Ottawa: Minister of
Supply and Services Canada, 1992), p. 23.

are easiest to read when typed horizontally. When the segments are large
enough, labels may be placed inside, as in Figure 12.8. If the segments are
smaller, place the labels outside.

Line Charts.   Line charts are useful in showing changes in quantitative data
over time. Like many visual aids, line charts cannot show precise data; instead,
they give an impression of a trend or movement. Notice in Figure 12.9 that the
time variable (years) is shown horizontally and the quantitative variable
(*Percent, Billions of Dollars,* etc.) is shown vertically.

Bar Charts.   A bar chart uses horizontal bars or vertical columns to compare
data. Figure 12.10 shows the importance of training in Canada. Could this
information have been meaningfully expressed in a pie chart?

Organization Charts.   An organization chart shows management structure
and lines of authority. The chart in Figure 12.11 defines the hierarchy of authority from the board of directors to individual managers.

Other Visual Aids

You can add icons, clip art, or scanned images to your reports by using word-
processing programs, such as Microsoft Word, WordPerfect, and MacWrite, or
presentation programs such as Powerpoint or Harvard Graphics. Desktop

Figure 12.9 Line Chart

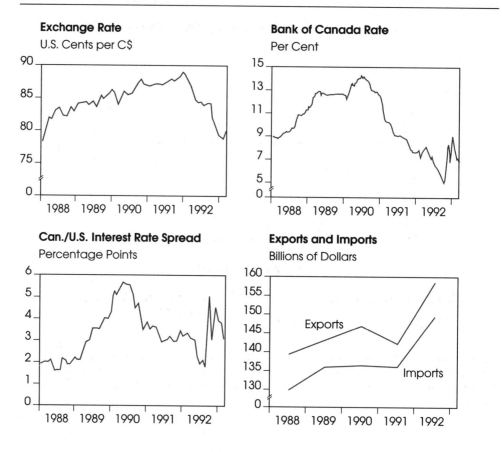

Source: *The 1993 Manitoba Budget*, Province of Manitoba (Winnipeg: Department of Finance, Province of Manitoba, 1993), p. 5.

Professional graphic effects can be created with readily available commercial products.

publishing programs such as PageMaker can produce even more sophisticated graphics. Some enterprising report writers are developing multimedia presentations that combine video, audio, and animation. Although multimedia presentations are appropriate for certain kinds of reports, they go well beyond the presentation needs of most report writers.

Presenting the Final Report

Overall Organization

Long reports generally are organized into three major divisions and a number of subdivisions. The order of three divisions in a formal report is outlined here.

Figure 12.10 Bar Chart

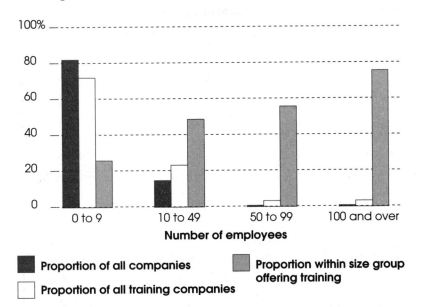

Importance of Training by Company Size, Canada, 1987

Why does this chart use vertical columns instead of horizontal bars?

Source: *Good Jobs, Bad Jobs: Employment in the Service Economy*, The Economic Council of Canada (Ottawa: Minister of Supply and Services Canada, 1990), p. 16. Based on data from Statistics Canada, *Distribution Report, Human Resource Training and Development Survey* (Ottawa, 1990).

Prefatory Parts (parts preceding the body)

Title fly*

Title page

Letter of authorization*

Letter of transmittal

Table of contents

Abstract, synopsis, or executive summary

Long formal reports contain three major sections: prefatory parts, body, and supplementary parts.

Body

Introduction or background

Discussion of findings

Summary, conclusion, recommendations

Figure 12.11   Organization Chart

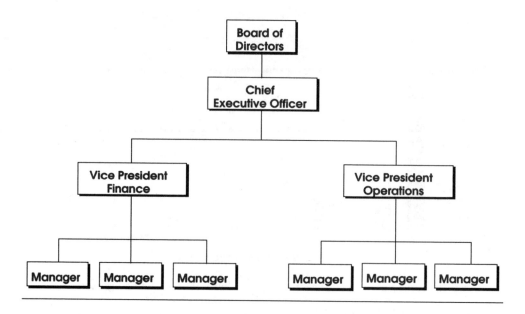

Supplementary Parts

Endnotes or Works Cited

Bibliography

Appendix*

---

* Not illustrated in our model formal report.

Parts

Now let's look more carefully at the individual parts of a long, formal report. Refer to Figure 12.12 for illustration of most of these parts.

- **Title fly.** A single page with the title begins a formal report. The title fly is no more than a plain sheet of paper with only the title on it. In less formal reports, the title fly is omitted. Compose the title of your report carefully so that it shows immediately what the report covers and what it does not cover.

- **Title page.** In addition to the title, the title page shows the author, the individual or organization who authorized the report, as well as the recipient of the report, and the date.

- **Letter of authorization.** If a letter or memo authorizes the report, it may be included in the prefatory material. This optional part is omitted from the model in Figure 12.12.

- **Letter of transmittal.** This is the first impression the reader receives of the report; as such, it should be given serious consideration. Use the direct strategy and include some or all of the suggestions here:

1. Deliver the report ("Here is the report you authorized").

2. Present an overview of the report.

3. Suggest how to read or interpret it.

4. Describe limitations, if they exist.

5. Acknowledge those who assisted you.

6. Suggest follow-up studies, if appropriate.

7. Express appreciation for the assignment.

8. Offer to discuss the report personally.

- **Table of contents.** Identify the name and location of every part of the report except the title fly, title page, and table of contents itself. Use spaced periods (leaders) to join the part with its page number.

- **Abstract, synopsis, or executive summary.** A summary condensing the entire report may carry any of these names. This time-saving device, which should be kept under one page, summarizes the purpose, findings, and conclusions.

- **Introduction or background.** After the prefatory parts, begin the body of the report with an introduction that includes any or all of the following items:

  1. Explanation of how the report originated and why it was authorized.

  2. Description of the problem that prompted the report and the specific research questions to be answered.

  3. Purpose of the report.

  4. Scope (boundaries) and limitations or restrictions of the research.

  5. Sources and methods of collecting information.

  6. Summary of findings, if the report is written deductively.

  7. Preview of the major sections of the report to follow, thus providing coherence and transition for the reader.

- **Discussion of findings.** This is the main section of the report, and it contains numerous headings and subheadings. It is unnecessary to use the title *Discussion of Findings*; many business report writers prefer to begin immediately with the major headings into which the body of the report is divided. As with short reports, you may organize the body deductively, inductively, chronologically, geographically, or topically. Present your findings objectively, avoiding the use of first-person pronouns (*I*, *we*). Include tables, charts, and graphs, if necessary, to illustrate findings. Analytical and scientific reports may include another section entitled *Implications of Findings*, in which the findings are analyzed and related to the problem. Less formal reports contain the author's analysis of the research findings within the *Discussion* section.

- **Summary, conclusions, recommendations.** If the report has been largely informational, it ends with a summary of the information presented. If the report analyzes research findings, then the report ends with conclusions drawn from the analyses. An analytical report frequently poses research questions. The conclusion to such a report reviews the major findings and answers the research questions.

If a report seeks to determine a course of action, it may end with conclusions and recommendations. The recommendations regarding a course of action may be placed in a separate section or incorporated in the conclusions.

■ **Footnotes, endnotes, or works cited.** See Appendix 2 for details on how to document sources. In the footnote method, the source notes appear at the foot of each page. In the endnote method, they are displayed immediately after the text on a page called Notes. In the parenthetic or MLA method of documentation, the notes are listed on a page called *Works Cited* or *Works Consulted*.

■ **Bibliography.** Most formal reports include a bibliography that lists all sources—including those not actually cited in notes—consulted in the report research. Guidelines for preparing a bibliography are provided in Appendix 3.

■ **Appendix.** The appendix contains any supplementary information needed to clarify the report. Charts and graphs illustrating significant data are generally part of the body of the report. An appendix might include such items as a sample questionnaire, a questionnaire cover letter, correspondence relating to the report, maps, other reports, and optional tables.

Figure 12.12   Model Long Report

(Letter of Transmittal)

BRG Research Consultants
1926-5th Street North
Calgary, AB T2B K3L
(403) 467-1290

June 15, 199x

Randall Stewart, Vice-President
Severin Industries Canada
3514-42nd Street
Calgary, AB T1A 07P

Dear Mr. Stewart:

The attached report, requested by your office April 10, describes the
results of our comparative study of business costs in various sites in
North America. We believe you will find the results of this study useful in
selecting a location for your new production facility.

The study compares 15 sites across North America using seven location-
sensitive cost factors ranging from industrial land costs to taxation rates.
Both the sites and the cost factors were selected in consultation with
experts in the fields of location and cost analysis. Our research indicates
that Moncton, New Brunswick, would be the most cost-effective location
for the proposed facility.

Please note the following limitations of the study:

1. It is based on current tax rates and cost factors, all of which are subject
   to change.

2. It does not consider situation-specific cost factors, including costs arising from seasonal change or additional costs such as local licensing and
   other fees.

3. It does not consider noncost related factors, including workforce availability, quality of life, transportation infrastructure, education, and
   medical care.

We would be pleased to discuss this report and its findings at your
convenience.

Sincerely,

Caitlin Pescatelli

Caitlin Pescatelli
Research Associate

Figure 12.12   Continued

A Comparative Study of Business Costs in
Selected North American Sites

Prepared for

Severin Industries Canada
Calgary, Alberta

Prepared by

Caitlin Pescatelli
Research Associate
BRG Research Consultants

June 13, 199x

Figure 12.12 Continued

CONTENTS

Figure 12.12 Continued

Background

This study was designed to determine the most cost-effective location for Severin Industries' new production facility. At the recommendation of industry and location experts, the scope of the report has been limited to the 15 locations indicated in Figure 1. The eight Canadian cities and seven U.S. cities were analyzed and compared on the basis of the following cost factors[1]:

- Industrial land costs

- Construction costs

- Labour costs

- Electricity costs

- Transportation costs

- Federal, regional, and local taxation rates

The relative importance of each cost factor is indicated in Figure 2.

Figure 1 Sites Included in Study

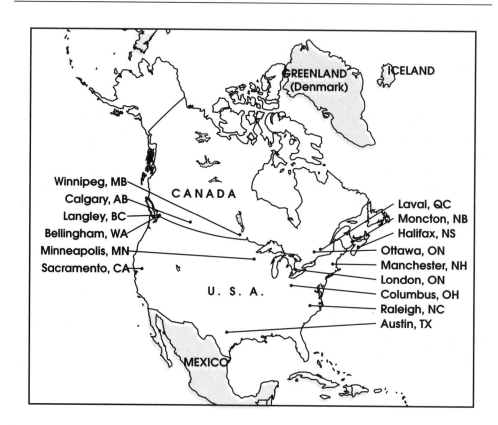

Figure 12.12   Continued

Figure 2   Relative Importance of Key Location-Sensitive Costs

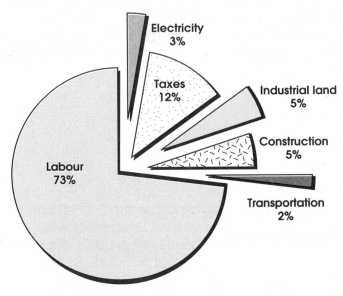

(% of total location-sensitive costs)

*Labour costs break down as follows: wages (54%), employee-sponsored benefits (13%), and statutory benefits and taxes (6%).

A business model was designed that would represent Severin's new facility and the software industry generally. The model facility was assumed to have sales in excess of $10 million and a minimum of 100 employees. It was to be built on 5-acre sites in suburban areas zoned for light-to-medium industrial uses. Data for this report came from an examination of 105 business operations located in the 15 target cities and sharing these characteristics.

•

•

•

The research findings presented in the Discussion of Findings section fall into the cost-factor categories listed above.

Figure 12.12   Continued

Location Profiles[2]

1. **Austin, Texas.** Austin is located 400 kilometres north of the US–Mexico border and 380 kilometres south of Dallas. Its population in 1995 was 1,016,400. Since the mid-1950s, Austin has become a significant centre for technology-based industries. The city's largest private-sector employers are computer and technology manufacturers.

> •
> •
> •

15. **Winnipeg, Manitoba.** Winnipeg is at the geographic centre of North America, located approximately 100 kilometres north of the Canada–U.S. (Minnesota–North Dakota) border and 800 kilometres northwest of Minneapolis. Winnipeg's population stood at 659,361 in 1995 and is expected to reach 676,800 by the year 2001. Transportation, food processing, primary metals, and printing and publishing are among the city's primary industry sectors. The technology sector is playing an increasingly significant role in the local economy.

Figure 12.12 Continued

Discussion of Findings

All figures presented in this section are in Canadian dollars.

Industrial Land Costs

The analysis focused on the costs of establishing facilities in suburban areas zoned for light-to-medium industrial uses. Land-cost data were gathered through interviews with representatives of the economic development offices and realty firms in each location. Land costs quoted were for a 5-acre site of fully serviced industrial land in a light-to-medium industrial park.

The lowest industrial land costs were found in Moncton, and the highest costs in Langley. Land costs in Langley are more than five times those in Moncton. Costs for all locations under examination are shown in Figure 3.

Figure 3 Industrial Land Costs in Selected Locations

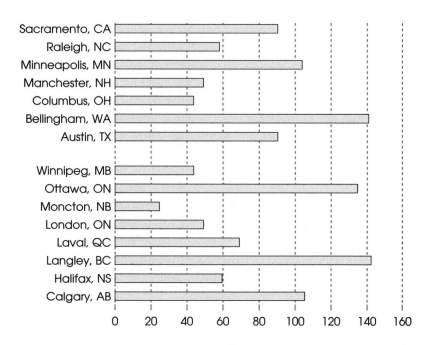

Thousands of Dollars per Acre

Figure 12.12   Continued

Construction Costs

Figure 4 shows average construction costs for a one-storey factory with 60,000 square feet in floor space. Of the 15 cities examined, Halifax had the lowest construction costs, at $38 per square foot. The highest costs were found in Manchester, at $60 per square foot.

Figure 4   Construction Costs in Selected Locations

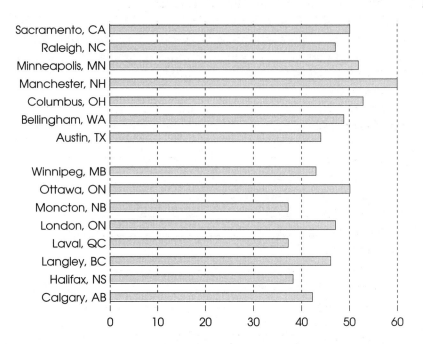

Dollar Cost per Square Foot

Figure 12.12   Continued

Labour Costs

In the business operations examined, labour costs represented 14–31 percent of total operating costs. For the purposes of this report, labour costs were broken down into the following: (1) wages, (2) employer-sponsored benefits, and (3) statutory benefits and taxes.

Wages. Annual wage costs for selected manufacturing positions are shown in Figure 5. Lowest wage costs were found in Moncton.

Figure 5   Annual Wages in Selected Locations[3]

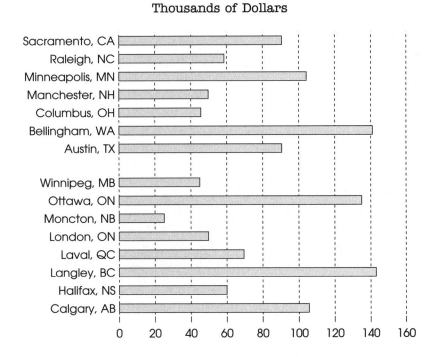

Thousands of Dollars

Employer-sponsored benefits. A comparison of employer-sponsored benefit costs in Canada and the United States was undertaken. Table 1 shows that these costs represented 27.9 percent of annual payroll in the United States, compared with 19.3 percent in Canada. Much of this difference is attributable to higher medical insurance premiums in the United States. These premiums represented 8.2 percent of annual payroll in the U.S. operations studied, compared with 1 percent in the Canadian operations.

Figure 12.12   Continued

Table 1   Employer-Sponsored Benefit Costs as a Percentage of Annual Payroll, Canada versus the United States

	United States %	Canada (%)
Payments for or in lieu of vacation	5.6	3.2
Payments for or in lieu of holidays	3.3	1.5
Self-insured short-term disability/sick-leave pay	1.2	0.8
Other	0.4	0.9
Payments for Time Not Worked	**10.5**	**6.4**
Retirement and pension plan payments	6.1	6.3
Life insurance and death benefits	0.5	0.4
Medical insurance premiums	8.2	1.0
Short-term disability, sickness, or accident insurance and long-term disability or wage continuation	0.6	1.6
Dental insurance premiums	0.5	1.0
Other (vision, physical and mental fitness, etc.)	0.5	—
Other	1.0	2.6
Employer-Sponsored Plans	**17.4**	**12.9**
TOTAL	**27.9**	**19.3**

Statutory benefits and taxes. Statutory benefits and taxes include employment insurance premiums; medicare (U.S.) and medical plan premiums (Canada); Social Security and Canada Pension Plan payments; workers' compensation; and other payroll taxes. A Department of Foreign Affairs and International Trade study of employee benefit costs in Canada and the United States found that statutory plans represent 9.2 percent of annual payroll in the United States, compared with 11.2 percent in Canada.

Figure 12.12   Continued

Electricity Costs

Electricity costs for industrial users are significantly lower in Canada
than the United States. The monthly costs shown in Figure 6 are based on
consumption of 250,000 kilowatt hours (KwH) per month and a demand
load of 400 kilo-volt-amperes (KvA). Lowest costs were found in Moncton.

Figure 6   Monthly Electricity Costs in Selected Locations

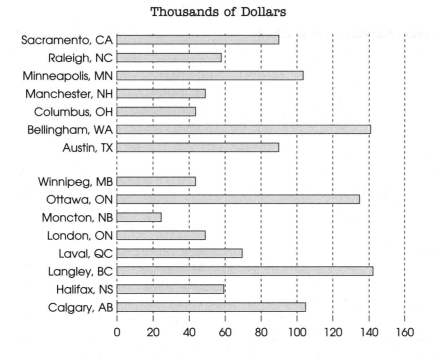

Figure 12.12   Continued

Transportation Costs

Truck transportation costs per tonne in Canada are considerably lower than those in the United States, because of the effect of the exchange rate and also because legal vehicle weight limits are higher in Canada than in the United States. As Figure 7 illustrates, lowest costs were found in Laval. It is important to note that as a result of differences in operating regulations, rates, and fuel taxes, transportation costs can vary significantly for any given shipment depending upon the states or provinces being traversed.[4]

Figure 7   Intra-State/Provincial Transportation Cost Factors*

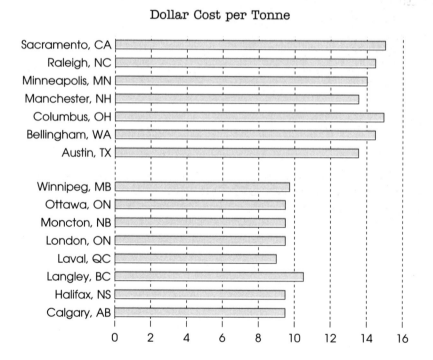

*Data are based on transportation of a single shipment of goods 400 km within represented state or province.

Figure 12.12   Continued

Federal, Regional, and Local Taxation Rates

Federal, regional, and local taxation rates vary significantly among the locations examined.

The federal tax rate for Canadian manufacturers is 22 percent of taxable income. In the United States, a graduated scale provides a rate of 34 percent for taxable income between $335,000 and $10 million. In the United States, state taxes are deductible from federal taxable income.

Various states and provinces offer differing tax incentives for start-up businesses. Canada allows a 100 percent deduction for eligible research and development (R&D) expenditures, in addition to a 20 percent federal investment tax credit. Nova Scotia, New Brunswick, Quebec, Ontario, and Manitoba provide additional tax credits for R&D expenditures. In the United States, the general tax treatment for similar R&D expenditures is a 20 percent credit at the federal level.

Nominal taxation rates should not be used as the sole measure of the impact of taxation in each location. Other factors such as depreciation rates and the availability of investment incentives have a significant impact on the amount of taxes paid.[5]

Location Rankings

Table 2 shows cost-specific as well as overall rankings for each selected location. In Table 3 rankings are rated by percentage of relative importance (see Figure 2 for percentages). Moncton and Winnipeg are ranked first and second respectively in both overall and weighted rankings.

Figure 12.12 Continued

Table 2 Ranking of Selected Locations by Cost Factor

Location	Industrial Land	Construction	Labour	Electricity	Transportation	Overall Ranking
Calgary, AB	11	4	11	1	6	5
Halifax, NS	7	1	7	8	2	4
Langley, BC	15	7	10	3	8	8
Laval, QC	8	2	9	4	1	3
London, ON	4	8	11	11	3	6
Moncton, NB	1	3	1	6	5	1
Ottawa, ON	13	12	8	10	4	11
Winnipeg, MB	2	5	2	2	7	2
Austin, TX	9	6	5	12	10	7
Bellingham, WA	14	10	6	5	12	12
Columbus, OH	3	14	3	9	14	9
Manchester, NH	5	15	13	15	9	13
Minneapolis, MN	12	13	14	7	11	14
Raleigh, NC	6	9	4	13	13	10
Sacramento, CA	10	11	15	14	15	15

Figure 12.12 Continued

Table 3 Rankings Weighted by Percentage of Relative Importance

Location	Overall Ranking	Weighted Results	Weighted Ranking
Calgary, AB	5	267.96	11
Halifax, NS	4	177.80	6
Langley, BC	8	262.06	10
Laval, QC	3	218.44	8
London, ON	6	273.32	12
Moncton, NB	1	36.65	1
Ottawa, ON	11	226.34	9
Winnipeg, MB	2	57.86	2
Austin, TX	7	150.28	5
Bellingham, WA	12	180.89	7
Columbus, OH	9	108.74	3
Manchester, NH	13	336.94	13
Minneapolis, MN	14	360.61	14
Raleigh, NC	10	130.88	4
Sacramento, CA	15	385.43	15

Conclusion and Recommendation

Comparison of the 15 selected North American sites on the basis of industrial land costs, construction costs, labour costs, electricity costs, transportation costs, and taxation rates leads to the conclusion that Moncton, New Brunswick, would be the most cost-effective location for Severin's new production facility.

On the basis of this finding, we recommend that Severin undertake a follow-up study comparing the first- and second-ranked sites—Moncton and Winnipeg—with respect to the following:

1. Situation-specific cost factors, including costs arising from seasonal change
2. Additional costs such as local licensing or other fees
3. Noncost related factors, including workforce availability, quality of life, transportation infrastructure, education, and medical care.

Figure 12.12   Continued

Notes

1. The cost factors selected for the purposes of this report are based on William Wedler, *Location-Sensitive Cost Factors in Industrial Locations* (Toronto: University of Toronto Press, 1996) p. 256.

2. Information in this section is derived from Jane Hathoway, *Places in America* (New York: Dryden Press, 1996), pp. 10–15; and Sarah Laufman, *Canadian Cities* (Montreal: New Canadian Press, 1996), pp. 18–28.

3. The data presented in this section is taken from Government of Canada, Department of Foreign Affairs and International Trade, *Annual Wages and Salaries in Canada and the United States, 1996* (Ottawa: Supply and Services Canada, 1996), pp. 3–8, 18–25.

4. Norbert Girardin. "Cross-Border Trucking Costs: A Comparative Study," *Transportation Review* 14 (June 1994), p. 24.

5. Heintz Kreutzer, "Taxation Rates and Their Impact on Business Location," *Industrial Development* 116 (May 1994), p. 25.

Bibliography

Canada. Department of Foreign Affairs and International Trade. *Annual Wages and Salaries in Canada and the United States, 1996*. Ottawa: Supply and Services Canada, 1996.

Girardin, Norbert. "Cross-Border Trucking Costs: A Comparative Study." *Transportation Review* 14. June 1994.

Gladu, Brenda. "Financing Major Construction Projects." *The Journal of the Association of Structural Engineers*. August 1995.

Hathoway, Jane. *Places in America*. New York: Dryden Press, 1996.

Kaufman, Richard. *Economic Analysis Models*. Winnipeg: University of Manitoba Press, 1994.

Kreutzer, Heintz. "Taxation Rates and Their Impact on Business Location." *Industrial Development* 116. May 1994.

Laufman, Sara. *Canadian Cities*. Montreal: New Canadian Press, 1996.

Smith, Shannon. *Cost Factors in Industrial Location*. Toronto: Storyville Publishing, 1995.

Soding, Blain. "Site Selection, Plant Locations and Local Communities." *Industrial Development* 120. May 1995.

Wedler, William. *Location-Sensitive Cost Factors in Industrial Location*. Toronto: University of Toronto Press, 1996.

Summary

Formal reports differ from informal reports in tone, structure, and length. The planning of every report begins with a purpose statement explaining the goal, significance, and scope of the project. Reports include primary information and secondary information gained through research. Formal reports require a careful citation of information taken from secondary sources in the form of footnotes, or endnotes, and a list of references in a bibliography.

The overall presentation of the report may be deductive or inductive and the individual parts may be arranged chronologically, geographically, spatially, or topically. Formal reports often use visual aids to emphasize, summarize, or clarify information. Some general guidelines apply to the use of visual aids: they must have meaningful titles and headings; they must be identified and discussed in the text; they must be located close to their reference in the text; they should be vertical on the page; and the source must be credited if appropriate. Professional-looking visuals can be created by using graphics software packages.

Final presentation of the formal report includes three major sections: prefatory parts such as the title page, table of contents, letter of authorization, letter of transmittal, and an abstract or summary; the body, which includes an introduction, discussion of findings, and summary, conclusions, and recommendations; and supplementary parts such as the endnotes or works cited, a bibliography, and the appendix.

APPLICATION AND PRACTICE—12

Discussion

1. If formal reports are seldom written in business, why study them?

2. How is the process of writing a formal report similar to that of writing an informal report?

3. How could a report be organized inductively and topically at the same time?

4. Should every long, formal report have graphic aids? Explain.

5. Distinguish between primary and secondary information. Which is more likely to be useful in a business report?

Short Answers

6. Name five plans for organizing information in a formal report. Be prepared to explain each.

7. What is the first step in writing a formal report?

8. If you were writing a formal report on computerizing your company's accounting functions, what primary sources of data would you seek? Be prepared to explain.

9. List four sources of secondary information, and be prepared to discuss how each might be useful in writing a formal report on computerizing your company's accounting functions.

10. List four degrees of headings and explain how they are different.

11. Pie charts are most helpful in showing what?

12. Line charts are most effective in showing what?

13. If you've never used a library before, where should you probably begin?

14. List the parts of a formal report. Be prepared to discuss each.

15. Should business reports be single- or double-spaced?

Writing Improvement Exercises

Outlining.   Construct an outline using the following information gathered initially to write a report. Include a title. Assume that you would collect more information later. After you complete the outline, indicate what level of heading each line of the outline would require.

16. The operation of a business would be very risky without some form of property insurance. Most fire insurance policies protect against loss to buildings and their contents. Wooden buildings, of course, would cost more than brick buildings to insure. The contents of buildings are valued separately. Insurance experts believe that nearly one-third of all business-related fires may be caused by arson. Another form of property insurance is marine insurance. Ocean marine insurance is the oldest form of insurance in the country. It protects the ship and its cargo. Inland marine insurance, strangely enough, protects against damage to property being transported in three areas: goods transported by ship, truck, or train. That is, goods being moved by any of these three means may be covered with inland marine insurance.

   Nearly 3 million automobile accidents occur each year in Canada. Automobile insurance is a form of property insurance. It covers many areas, including additional personal injury coverage (to protect policyholders, their family members, and any passengers in the car), third-party liability coverage, and uninsured motorist coverage. Auto insurance also includes property damage. This pays the cost of damage to other people's property (such as buildings and cars). Collision insurance is different. It pays for damage to the policyholder's car. You can have full coverage or deductible ($100 to $500).

Organizing.   Assume that you are a research consultant with Search, Inc. Your firm has been asked to find a sales and distribution site in the Winnipeg area for Farrell Electrical Components, 345 Hastings St., Vancouver, British Columbia V8N 1L2. Farrell seeks suitable office space, including a reception area (where three office employees could work), one private office, and a conference/display area. Farrell also wants 700 m^2 of heated warehouse space. It should be equipped with a sprinkler system and have 5 m ceilings. If sales are successful, Farrell may need an additional 500 m² of warehouse space in the future. Farrell needs to locate near Winnipeg International Airport; moreover, it must be close to trucking terminals and main thoroughfares in an area zoned for light industry. It also seeks an impressive-looking building with a modern executive image. Farrell wants to lease for at least two years with possible renewal. It needs to make a decision within three weeks. If no space is available, it will delay until next year.

You have been assigned the task of researching this assignment and then writing a report that includes a recommendation for Farrell based upon your findings.

17. Who is the audience for this long report? Should you include extensive background information explaining why the report is being written? Explain.

18. Would you rely on primary or secondary research? How would you gather information for this report?

19. What constraints would limit your research?

20. What visual aids would enhance this report?

21. On a separate sheet write a purpose statement that could become part of the introduction to your report. Include Farrell's requirements.

22. You have narrowed the choices to five locations near Winnipeg International Airport. On a separate sheet make a table from your rough notes. Include a title and subtitle, as well as appropriate columnar headings.

23. Compose a lead-in sentence that introduces the table you have inserted in your report.

24. What strategy would you follow in organizing this report? Why?

Activities

25. **Visual aids.** From *Maclean's*, *Canadian Business*, a textbook, your local newspaper or some other publication, locate one example of a table, a pie chart, a line chart, a bar chart, and an organization chart. Bring copies of these visual aids to class. How effectively could the data have been expressed in words, without the graphics? Is the appropriate graphic form used? How is the graphic introduced in the text? Your instructor may wish you to submit a memo discussing visual aids.

26. **Bibliography.** Select a topic that interests you. Prepare a bibliography of at least five current magazine articles, three books, and five other references that contain relevant information regarding the topic. Your instructor may ask you to divide your bibliography into sections: *Books, Periodicals, Other Resources.*

27. **Computer databases.** Compose a list of computer information sources available through a library in your area. What are the charges for receiving information? What is the procedure for using the services? Write a memo describing your findings. Include one or more visual aids to illustrate your information.

28. **Interview report.** Collect information regarding communication skills used by individuals in a particular career (accounting, management, marketing, office administration, paralegal, and so forth). Interview three or more individuals in a specific occupation in that profession. Determine how much and what kind of writing they do. Do they make oral presentations? How much time do they spend in telephone communication? What recommendations do they have for training for this position? What conclusions can you draw from your research? What recommendations would you make for individuals entering this profession? Write a report of about five single-spaced or ten double-spaced pages. Include at least one visual aid. Your instructor may wish you to include a section requiring library research into the perception of businesspeople over the past ten years regarding the communication skills of employees.

GRAMMAR/MECHANICS CHECKUP—12

Capitalization

Review Sections 3.01 through 3.16 of the Grammar/Mechanics Handbook. Then study each of the following statements. Circle any lowercase letter that should be capitalized. Draw a slash (/) through any capital letter that you wish to change to lowercase. In the space provided for each statement, indicate the number of changes you made and record the number of the G/M principle illustrated. If you made no changes, write *0*. When you finish, compare your responses with those shown below. If your responses differ, study carefully the principle in parentheses.

<u>4</u>   <u>(3.01, 3.06a)</u>   **Example:** After consulting our ~~A~~ttorneys for ~~L~~egal advice, Vice-~~p~~resident Mills signed the ~~C~~ontract.

_____

1. All canadian passengers from Flight 402 must pass through Customs Inspection at Gate 17 upon arrival at Pearson international airport.

_____

2. Personal tax rates for japanese citizens are low by International standards; rates for Japanese corporations are high, according to Iwao Nakatani, an Economics Professor at Osaka university.

_____

3. In the end, Business passes on most of the burden to the Consumer: What looks like a tax on Business is really a tax on Consumption.

_____

4. Jean-Claude enrolled in courses in History, Sociology, Spanish, and Computer Science.

_____

5. Did you see the article entitled "Careers in horticulture are nothing to sneeze at"?

_____

6. Although I recommend the Minex Diskettes sold under the brand-name Maxidisk, you may purchase any Diskettes you choose.

_____

7. According to a Federal Government report, any development of Provincial and Municipal waterways must receive an environmental assessment.

_____

8. The prime minister of canada said, "this country continues to encourage Foreign investments."

_____

9. The Comptroller of Ramjet International reported to the President and the Board of Directors that revenue canada was beginning an investigation of their Company.

_____

10. My Mother, who lives near St. John's, reports that protection from the Sun's rays is particularly important in the East.

_____

11. Our Managing Editor met with Leslie Hawkins, Manager of the Advertising Sales Department, to plan an Ad Campaign for our special issue.

_____

12. In the fall, Editor in Chief Ramirez plans an article detailing the astounding performance of the austrian, german, and italian currencies.

13. To reach Mount Royal park, which is located on an Island in the St. Lawrence river, tourists may pass over the Jacques Cartier bridge.   _____

14. On page 6 of the catalogue, you will see that the computer science department is offering a number of courses in programming.   _____

15. Please consult figure 3.2 in chapter 5 for statistics canada figures regarding non-english-speaking residents.   _____

1. (5) Canadian, customs inspection, International Airport (3.01, 3.02, 3.07)   **3. (4)** business, consumer, business, consumption (3.01, 3.13)   **5. (5)** Horticulture, Are, Nothing, Sneeze, At (3.12)   **7. (4)** federal government, provincial, municipal (3.10)   **9. (5)** comptroller, president, Revenue Canada, company (3.01, 3.04, 3.06e)   **11. (5)** managing editor, manager, ad campaign (3.01, 3.06d, 3.06e, 3.09)   **13. (4)** Park, island, River, Bridge (3.01, 3.03)   **15. (5)** Figure, Chapter, Statistics Canada, English (3.02, 3.04, 3.07)

GRAMMAR/MECHANICS CHALLENGE—12

Document for Revision

The following report abstract is wordy and contains faults in grammar, punctuation, spelling, and number form. Drawing upon the guidelines provided in the Grammar/Mechanics Handbook and what you learned in this chapter, revise the abstract.

Poor Document

Abstract

On the date of November 10th Dennis W. Wilbur, Director, Human Resources development authorized a study to ascertain whether or not the human resources department was following the CEO's directive to move toward equal representation of men and women at Globex.

A research program was developed to make inquiry into each divisions hiring practices. Data in regard to the employment of 23,102 past and present employees was searched by the program to make a determination of the dates of all new hiring in the last 5 years, and the division. Each division was also polled for the number of men and women employed their. Statistics Canada information were also examined in way of comparison.

The following findings in regard to the aforementioned study, resulted;

Vancouver is 5% above the company average in its hiring of women in the last 5 year period
Toronto is 7% below the company average in its hiring of women in the last 5 year period

On the basis of these findings the Diversity Committee (1) recommends the development of an intensive recruiting program to search for and bring qualified females into the Toronto division and (2) the development of a training program to train female employees for drafting and design positions in Toronto.

Communication for Employment

In this chapter, you will learn to do the following:

- Analyze your employment qualifications.
- Locate job market information.
- Write an effective résumé.

- Compose solicited and unsolicited letters of application.
- Prepare for and participate in a job interview.

Regarding your future career, the most important document you may ever write is your résumé. In this chapter, you will learn to write an effective résumé, as well as an application letter and other messages related to employment. Before you begin to create documents that will help you win the position you want, you should analyze your qualifications and the job market.

Your résumé may be the most important document you ever write.

Preparation for Employment

Analyzing Your Interests and Skills

Begin to develop your employment portfolio by considering the kinds of work in which you are interested and the skills you have to offer. Think about successful past or current life experiences. These experiences may be paid work or other life experiences such as your last job, playing ringette, learning the guitar, or volunteering at a local hospital. Then, ask yourself the following questions.

Analyze your interests and skills by considering successful current or past life experiences.

1. **What have I enjoyed most about these situations**? Have I enjoyed working with people, equipment, information; being inside or outside; being in a 9–5 office setting or in a position with more flexible hours?

2. **What have I disliked most about these situations**? Was it the boss, the money, the hours, the tasks that I never seemed to do correctly, the demands put on my abilities?

3. **When I was particularly successful, what did I contribute to those successes?** Was I successful because I followed directions well or made an independent decision? Was it extra work I did because I wanted to see the job done correctly? Was it my contribution to an overall team effort?

4. **Of all the experience I have had where I have had to accept responsibility, which four or five do I consider the most rewarding and why?** Was it the money, the responsibility, the opportunity to learn, the ability to show my knowledge, the stable environment, or the constantly changing environment that I found rewarding?

5. **If I could design my own job, what would it require of me, and what would I be able to do in it?** This needn't be an actual job with a title. It can be a list of the descriptions from the previous questions.

In describing your success stories, you are producing an inventory of your interests. As well, you are choosing the skills and abilities you most enjoy using. You enjoy certain activities because you have the ability to do those activities successfully.

Analyzing Your Qualifications

The composition of your résumé begins with a thorough analysis of your background, experience, and qualifications.

Like many students writing their résumé, you may think that you have little experience that will qualify you for a permanent profession. To help you analyze and organize information for your résumé, review your experience and achievements by filling out inventory lists. Focus on employment, course work, special training and skills, and relevant extracurricular activities. If you don't have much employment experience, focus on volunteer situations and interests. Your lists should look like this:

Employment Inventory

Employer _____ Dates _____

Job Titles _____

Duties, responsibilities (list three to five):

_____

_____

Special Skills Inventory

List three to five special aptitudes or skills.

_____

_____

The verbs and adjectives you use to describe your skills and accomplishments should be precise and vivid. Using action words and providing sufficient information will make your résumé come alive. Which of the following résumé statements is more helpful:

Kept books for Sunset Avionics, or *Performed all bookkeeping functions including quarterly inventory count and valuation*? Here are some words to help you describe yourself.

Effective Adjectives for Successful Résumés

adaptable	efficient	painstaking
aggressive	enthusiastic	proficient
alert	flexible	reliable
ambitious	hardworking	resourceful
competent	logical	responsible
conscientious	loyal	serious
creative	objective	thoughtful

Effective Action Verbs for Successful Résumés

analyzed	discovered	organized
arranged	distributed	originated
assembled	edited	oversaw
assisted	evaluated	participated
calculated	expedited	planned
charted	formulated	prepared
composed	generated	presented
consolidated	hired	provided
coordinated	identified	recorded
created	instituted	reorganized
delegated	learned	researched
demonstrated	maintained	revised
designed	managed	solved
developed	obtained	streamlined
directed	operated	

Ideas for Using Action Verbs

Reduced delivery delays.

Improved inventory procedures.

Devised streamlined stocking techniques.

Ordered medical supplies for Surgery, Cardiac Surgery, and Nursing.

Supervised mailing of monthly statements.

Collected payments from 125 accounts.

Oversaw installation of automated record keeping.

Expedited repairs on company-owned vehicles.

Followed up overdue shipments.

Trained and supervised counter clerks.

Advised supervisor regarding purchase of microcomputer.

Increased productivity in word processing centre.

Scheduled use of conference rooms.

Saved money on supplies through comparative shopping.

Identified key factors in sales decline.

Arranged travel accommodations for four executives.

Analyzing the Job Market

The next step is to gather employment information and analyze the job market. A résumé and application letter will be most successful if they are written to respond to the employment requirements and expectations in your profession. To learn about employment specifications in your profession, consider the following sources of information:

- **Employment/counselling service.** Your school career centre or counselling office may offer career profiles, career and education directories, and testing services.

- **Reference librarian.** Ask your school or local public library reference librarian for employment information relating to your profession (e.g., newsletters, journals, and magazines).

- **Interviews.** Talk with people in your profession. Ask questions about qualifications and preparation for positions that interest you. Interviews will provide you not only with useful information but also with a potentially valuable contact.

- **Government services and publications.** Federal and provincial governments may offer services such as career hotlines. Public service commissions (which recruit for government positions) and individual government departments print career-related literature and sponsor career development and training initiatives. Your local Human Resources Development Canada (HRDC) office carries career directories, fact sheets, labour market data, and information on training strategies; it also provides on-line services and computerized interest inventories.

- **Professional organizations.** Many professional organizations answer requests for information by handing out profiles of their career fields. Examples are the Insurance Institute of Canada, the Society of Engineering Technicians and Technologists, the Canadian Council of Pharmacists, and chambers of commerce. You may also wish to join a professional organization in your area of interest and subscribe to its publications.

- **Part-time job.** Seek a summer or part-time job in your career area. Part-time employment in your field is probably the best way to gather information, make contacts, and get started in a career.

- **Instructors.** Ask for advice from teachers in your profession, especially those who work with employers through advisory committees or by offering consulting services.

- **The Internet.** Use the search engines discussed in Chapter 12. Several HRDC offices have Web sites that are maintained regularly and offer job search advice.

Résumé

The résumé is a summary of your experience, skills, and qualifications. The principal purpose of the résumé is to help you get an interview. The résumé also serves as a reminder of your qualifications after the interview.

Your goal in sending a résumé is to secure an interview.

The appearance of your résumé is important. Use good-quality white bond paper and sharp, black type. Leave ample white space in the margins and between headings. Your résumé is your "picture," so make sure that it looks good. Robert Half, who runs a large recruiting firm, says that he reads résumés in this way: "I always begin by gaining a general impression of the résumé. Is it neat and obviously prepared with care? Typos? Sloppy sentences, bad grammar? Job applicants who turn out a sloppy, careless résumé for themselves (they've had all the time they need to do it right) can pretty much be counted on to do the same in their job."[1]

Use a computer to prepare your résumé. Word processing or desktop publishing allows you to experiment with headings, placement, and spacing to fit everything on the page attractively. Moreover, you can update and tailor your résumé to specific job advertisements with ease in the future. Don't show off your software capabilities by using humorous cartoons or flashy borders as part of your résumé design. Such gimmicks detract from your credentials.

Try to fit your résumé on one or two pages. Résumés that run longer run the risk of being passed over. If, however, you've had plenty of experience and you're applying for a high-level position, a longer résumé may be appropriate.

Résumés usually begin with a main heading. The remaining categories—education, work experience, and activities and achievements—should be arranged in order of effectiveness in getting you the job. Put your most important qualifications first. De-emphasize any weaknesses. For example, if you have obvious gaps in your work record, avoid putting employment dates in a conspicuous position.

A winning résumé contains some or all of the following categories: main heading, career objective, education, work experience, special skills or achievements, and references.

Main Heading

Keep the main heading uncluttered and simple. List your name, address, and telephone number where messages can be left. (Prospective employers tend to call the next applicant when no one answers.) Some enterprising job searchers include an E-mail address if they subscribe to a private Internet service provider. You may omit the word *Résumé*, particularly if you have little extra space. If you must show a temporary address, place it on one side of the heading and your permanent address on the other.

DONNA H. JENKINS

Address Until June 15, 1997:
171 Green Street
Winnipeg, MB R3G 1W5
(204) 372-3944
(204) 368-8922 (messages)

Permanent Address:
176 Hapnot Drive
Flin Flon, MB R4L 2T4
(204) 555-3290

Career Objective

Including a career or employment objective in your résumé shows that you have considered short- and long-term goals and have made a commitment to a career. The danger of such a statement is that it can disqualify you from consideration if it does not appear to be compatible with the demands of the available position. When writing a career objective, you should decide whether you prefer a narrow career objective aimed at a specific job or a general objective that will make you employable in a number of job categories. Compare the following specific and general objectives:

Specific employment objectives.

To obtain a position as an administrative secretary in a large insurance organization that offers advancement leading to a management position in administrative support.

To become a junior paralegal in a law firm specializing in litigation, with the long-range goal of attending law school and becoming an attorney.

Entry-level position with a progressive firm that provides an opportunity to work with people as well as products in developing and selling effective information systems. Long-range goal is to become a product development manager.

General employment objectives.

To begin a career in personnel with exposure to recruiting, training, benefit administration, and contract negotiation. Long-range goal is to become a personnel manager.

If you have two separate employment areas in which you plan to apply, make separate résumés with different objectives.

Education

Place your education next if it is more impressive and more closely related to the position sought than your work experience. Begin with the school you attended most recently. Employers are most interested in postsecondary schooling, but your high school may be listed if you have not completed a college or university program. Include the name and location of the school, dates of attendance, major and minor areas of study, and degrees, diplomas, or certificates received. Your grade-point average is important to prospective employers. One way to enhance your GPA is to calculate it in your major courses only (for example, *3.6 GPA in major*).

A list of completed courses makes dull reading; use such a list only if you can relate the courses to the position sought. Include special certificates earned, seminars attended, and workshops completed. Indicate the percentage of your education that you financed, if appropriate. If your education is incomplete, include such statements as *B.A. degree expected September 1997* or *72 credits completed in 120-credit program*. Entitle this section *Education, Academic Preparation*, or *Professional Training*.

Emphasize your education if it's more impressive than your experience.

Work Experience

Put this section first if your work experience is significant and relevant to the position you are seeking. List your most recent employment first and work backwards, including only those jobs that you think will help you get this position. Include the following information:

1. Employer's name and address (city and province)

2. Dates of employment (month and year)

3. Job title (most important position)

4. Significant duties, activities, accomplishments, and promotions

Describe your employment accomplishments concisely but concretely. Avoid generalities, such as *Interacted with customers*. Be more specific, such as *Greeted customers cheerfully, Successfully resolved problems regarding custom drapery orders*, or *Acted as intermediary between customers and drapery workroom*. Include forceful verbs, omit the personal pronoun *I*, and use balanced, parallel constructions.

In listing your work experience, you can achieve emphasis through the format you choose for presenting your information. Notice how the following examples emphasize the information shown first.

Your résumé does not require a complete history of your previous employment. Some job applications may ask for a full employment history, but your résumé may be selective.

Select and emphasize work experiences that qualify you for the particular job in which you are interested.

Emphasizes Job Title

Secretary
Teletech Controls, Inc. Toronto, ON
June 1992–August 1994 (half-time)

- Accurately transcribed dictated letters, memos, and software documentation.

- Used word processing and database programs on IBM PC.

- Promoted from typist to secretary after nine months.

- Received praise from manager for ability to work under pressure.

Don't be modest about selling yourself.

Emphasizes Employer and Location

Royal Bank of Canada, Calgary, AB
Teller, Aug. 1992 to Jan. 1997

- Recorded accurately over $100,000 worth of deposits and withdrawals daily.

- Reconciled day's cash and cheque totals consistently with computer journal scan.

- Handled customer inquiries and complaints resourcefully and cheerfully.

Emphasizes Dates

June 1990 to Dec. 1995
The R.T. French Company, Halifax, NS
Supervisor of Inventory Control

- Promoted from accounting assistant in cost control to assistant supervisor after nine months.

- Became supervisor after 18 months, overseeing the work of nine employees and a budget of $430,000.

- Devised and introduced new inventory-tracking procedures that saved over $25,000 annually.

Strive to illustrate and quantify examples of your strong character traits.

Try to select work experiences and achievements that illustrate your initiative, dependability, responsibility, resourcefulness, economy, and interpersonal skills. If possible, quantify them: *Keyboarded all the production models for a 215-page employee procedures manual; Handled over $2000 in counter sales daily;* or *Missed only two days of work in the past 24 months.* Employers are interested in concrete examples of your qualifications.

Special Skills, Achievements, and Characteristics

Your work experience and education may not portray a complete picture of your potential for employment. Evaluate your special attributes, skills, and extracurricular activities. Select characteristics or accomplishments that demonstrate writing and speaking skills, leadership, organizational skills, and cooperation. Include awards, scholarships, honours, recognition, commendations, certificates, and licences. Show special skills, such as your ability to use specific computer programs, office equipment, sign language, or languages other than English. Highlight exceptional aptitudes, such as learning computer programs quickly without instruction and working well under stress.

Emphasize items in this category, particularly if you have little work experience. You may list your special skills or use action statements to demonstrate them. Strive for parallel (balanced) constructions in these statements.

- Knowledge of FDDI, ATM, Ethernet, and LANs.

- Excellent grammar, language, and writing skills developed in business English and business communication courses.

- Tutored Sheridan College students by helping them revise term papers and reports.

- Collected dues, kept financial records, and paid bills while serving as treasurer of 35-member York Bowling Club.

- Awarded Royal Trust Company's $200 prize as outstanding student in finance.

- Served as member of championship soccer team.

References

Opinion is divided about listing the names and addresses of your references on your résumé. Such a list takes up valuable space and generally is not instrumental in securing an interview. After an interview, however, a list of individuals willing to discuss your qualifications becomes important. A prospective employer may at that time want to check your background by calling those individuals you suggest.

Whether or not you decide to include references as part of your résumé, you should have their names available when you begin your job search. Ask three to five previous employers, instructors, or other people in the community (other than family members or friends) who have seen you work (volunteer organization board members, local club directors) if they would be willing to answer inquiries regarding your qualifications. Choose references that can say something substantive about your work. Be sure to provide them with an opportunity to refuse. No reference is better than a negative one.

Traditional (Chronological) Résumé

In the traditional résumé, items that appear in the work experience and education categories are listed in reverse chronological order. The traditional résumé highlights job titles, company names, and dates of employment, and may also include sections enumerating skills and achievements. This format is excellent for individuals who have experience in their profession and who show steady career growth. (See Figure 13.1 for an example of a model traditional résumé.)

> Provide a picture of a well-rounded individual.

> Traditional chronological résumés include the headings *Education*, *Work Experience*, and so forth.

Figure 13.1   Résumé in Traditional (Chronological) Format

MONICA ONG
32 Gurnett Drive
Hamilton, Ontario L9C 7K1
(905) 345-1901

Objective   Responsible and challenging position in accounting department of large corporation in Toronto area.

Employment   Staff Accountant, Micom Systems, Hamilton, Ontario
Experience   June 1995 to present

Responsibilities
- Reviewed and analyzed journal entries, labour records, and material and cost reports.
- Estimated departmental revenue and expenses totalling approximately $225,000 annually.
- Interpreted contracts and related provincial and federal regulations to determine accounting treatment.

Accomplishments
- Devised and implemented improved system estimating material costs.
- Promoted from tax assistant to staff accountant after six months.
- Received commendation for superior service to company.

Bookkeeper, General Motor Inns, Toronto, Ontario
April 1991 to June 1995

Responsibilities
- Processed invoices for data entry.
- Reconciled daily income and expense reports from 12 Holiday Inns.
- Assisted in preparing payroll for over 60 employees.

Accomplishments
- Compiled departmental manual containing detailed job descriptions for all employees.
- Administered office in absence of manager.
- Received 110 percent salary increase in four years.

Bookkeeper, First Canadian Bank, Toronto, Ontario
November 1989 to April 1991

Responsibilities
- Operated cheque sorter.
- Reconciled computer printouts to incoming statements.

Accomplishments
- Became fastest and most accurate operator of cheque sorter.

Education   Mohawk College, Hamilton, Ontario. Working toward a diploma in accounting. 25 of 40 credits completed.
Humber College, Toronto, Ontario. Certificate in bookkeeping and accounting, 1990.

References   Provided on request.

Functional Résumé

The functional résumé format focuses attention on a candidate's skills rather than on the candidate's past employment. Like the traditional résumé, the functional résumé includes the candidate's name, address, telephone number, job objective, and education. Instead of listing jobs, however, the functional résumé shows skills and accomplishments. The skills section is the largest, typically including two or three headings, such as *Communication Skills, Supervisory and Management Skills*, or *Retailing and Marketing Experience*.

The functional résumé format is effective both for highlighting accomplishments and for de-emphasizing a negative employment history. People who have changed jobs frequently, who have gaps in their employment record, who have little employment experience, or who are changing careers may prefer this format. A drawback of the functional résumé is that prospective employers are more accustomed to seeing the traditional résumé and may reject the former approach simply because it is different. To be safe, you should include a short employment history in a functional résumé (see Figure 13.2).

A résumé that combines the traditional and functional formats is shown in Figure 13.3.

Analyzing Résumés

Now let's consider the reasoning behind the two types of résumés in more detail. In the traditional résumé shown in Figure 13.4, notice the placement of *Employment Experience* after *Career Objective*. By choosing this placement, the applicant, Ilona Perov, emphasizes the similarities between her last job and the one to which she is now applying. She also lists different responsibilities and accomplishments for each of the positions she has held even though the job duties were probably quite similar. Her selection of duties underscores the logical progression of her career path.

Ilona also makes some interesting formatting decisions. She emphasizes job titles and diplomas by bolding them and dates by isolating them in the left margin. Should she get an interview, she is well prepared to explain the gap in her employment record (June 1992 to June 1993).

Now examine the résumé shown in Figure 13.5. Tammy has chosen a functional résumé because it would be more difficult to emphasize the work-related experience she gained at school using a traditional résumé format. The functional résumé format allows her to highlight accomplishments from both work and school.

Tammy has researched her chosen field and sales, and she knows how important communication and management skills are in this area. She therefore lists her work-related accomplishments under the categories *Communication Skills* and *Organizational and Management Skills*. At the same time, she de-emphasizes her relatively short employment history by positioning it last on her résumé and by omitting job titles.

Faxing and Scanning

Some prospective employers may ask you to send your résumé by fax. In addition, once received, your résumé may be scanned and stored in the company's

A functional résumé may emphasize skills and potential rather than experience and job titles.

Even on a functional résumé, it's wise to include a short employment history.

Emphasize the similarities between your last job and the one to which you are applying.

Functional résumés highlight accomplishments from both work and school.

Figure 13.2 Résumé in Functional Format

David Penner
225 Whitehall Rd.
Winnipeg, MB
R4L 2H7
(204) 458-3214

Education

Red River Community College, Winnipeg, MB, Business Administration diploma, June 1996. Grade-point average in major (Accounting): 3.25.

Accounting Skills

- Interviewed and collected tax information from 50 small-business owners.
- Posted to general ledger, prepared trial balances, and detected discrepancies with 98 percent accuracy.

Computer Skills

- Used Lotus 1-2-3 and Microsoft Word to complete and report on month- and year-end finances of company with $25,000 in sales per year.
- Used Powerpoint to develop 15-minute promotional presentation.
- Produced newsletter for Entrepreneurs' Club using Adobe PageMaker.
- Developed Web site for Club and linked to College site.

Communication Skills

- Developed and produced successful presentation to college Board of Governors requesting financial support.
- Wrote all copy for 500-member club newsletter.
- Developed long-term plans for two volunteer organizations.

Experience

1996, 1997 Tax preparer, One Stop Tax Services, Winnipeg, MB.

1991–95 Volunteer, Junior Achievement Regional Office, Winnipeg, MB.

1996–97 Vice-president, Entrepreneurs' Club, Red River Community College.

Figure 13.3   Résumé in Combined Traditional and Functional Format

Kevin James Becker
334 Queen Street West
Toronto, Ontario
M5R 3Y2
(416) 438-8871

Objective
Responsible management trainee position in retail with long-range goal of becoming a senior retail manager.

Skills
- Communicated effectively with customers in both retail and service setting.
- Trained and supervised novice sales personnel.
- Demonstrated sound decision-making as independent small-business owner.
- Interacted well with employees both as assistant manager and as owner/employer.
- Organized and maintained stock inventories efficiently.
- Operated database, word processing, and other computer programs.

Experience
Assistant Sales Manager
Image Men's Wear, Scarborough, Ontario
Sept. 1992 to present
- Promoted from salesperson to assistant sales manager after six months.
- Designed and arranged point-of-purchase displays.
- Assembled toys and children's furniture.
- Maintained a clean and safe sales floor.
- Trained new salespeople, teaching them merchandise, sales techniques, and customer courtesy.
- Completed inventories needed for maintaining correct stock levels.

Owner
Becker's Landscaping, Toronto, Ontario
Summers, 1990–1992
- Managed own gardening and landscaping service.

Education
University of Toronto, Bachelor of Business Administration degree, 1992.
- Acquired theoretical and practical knowledge of management, marketing, and merchandising by successfully completing courses in small-business management, human relations, principles of selling, sales management, and retail merchandising.
- Developed communication skills in public speaking and business writing.
- Grade-point average in major: 3.6 (4 = A).
- Financed 100 percent of educational expenses.

References
Available on request

Figure 13.4   Résumé in Traditional (Chronological) Format

ILONA PEROV
552 Fairfield Rd.
Victoria, BC
V1L 2W3
(604) 340-1190

Career Objective

To be employed as a paralegal in a law office where I may assist lawyers specializing in probate or family law.

Employment Experience

June 1993 to present

Administrative Assistant
Hirshfield, Cohen, & Yellin, Victoria, BC
- Promoted from file clerk to calendaring position after seven months.
- Scheduled court reporters for 28 busy lawyers.
- Mastered the Barrister computer program in 25 hours with little instruction.

May 1990 to June 1992

Area Office Clerk
- Visiting Nurse Association, Victoria, BC
- Admitted and discharged patients in absence of R.N.
- Typed and mailed doctors' orders.
- Answered all incoming telephone calls on Horizon telephone system.
- Learned office computer software with only 20 hours of training.

June 1988 to May 1990

Secretary
Maynard, Rothman, & Farrell, Saanich, BC
- Produced 50 to 70 financial statements and other legal documents weekly using Microsoft Word Version 6 and Excel.
- Composed selected letters from dictated outline.
- Answered clients' questions on busy telephone system.

Education

1995

Paralegal diploma
University of Victoria, Victoria, BC
- Now attending evening classes in paralegal training. Expected completion date June 1998.

1988

Administrative Assistant diploma
Camosun College, Victoria, BC
- Secretarial Science major.
- Dean's List, two semesters.

Skills and Abilities

Typing: 85 wpm
Shorthand: 70–80 wpm
Software: Microsoft Word Version 6, Excel, Lotus 1-2-3
Ability to learn computer programs and telephone systems quickly.

References

Provided on request.

Figure 13.5 Résumé in Functional Format

TAMMY R. McKAY

590 Oxford St.
Halifax, NS
B3L 2R5
(902) 608-8555

Objective

Entry-level position in sales with progressive firm. Desire opportunity for advancement into management. Willing to travel.

Communication Skills

- Demonstrated barbecue products and accessories in central and northern Nova Scotia retail outlets, achieving sales amounting to 120 percent of forecast.
- Conducted telephone survey of selected businesses in two counties to determine users of farm equipment and to promote company services.
- Took part in President's task force to solicit donations to Dalhousie Alumni Foundation.
- Generated over $15,000 in telephone subscriptions to Dalhousie Alumni Foundation.
- Helped conduct survey, analyzed results, and wrote a 20-page report regarding the need for developing a cultural events program at Dalhousie University.
- Presented talks before selected campus classes and organizations encouraging students to vote in coming elections.

Organizational and Management Skills

- Helped organize highly successful campus campaign to register student voters.
- Set up schedule of events and made arrangements for Newman Club weekend student retreat.
- Trained and supervised two counter employees at Pizza Bob's.
- Organized courses, extracurricular activities, and part-time employment to graduate in two years.
- Earned 3.2 grade point average (A = 4.0) while financing 70 percent of my education.

Education

1995	Dalhousie University, Halifax, NS, B.A.
	Major: Political Science. Minor: Psychology

Employment

1994–95	Pizza Bob's, Dartmouth, NS
1993	Bovay & Associates Manufacturers' Representatives, Halifax, NS
1992	Market Research, Inc., Lunenburg, NS

References

Available on request

database. When formatting, allow sufficient space between lines to ensure that your résumé faxes or scans effectively. You should also choose a font that works well with scanners and fax machines. Avoid ornate fonts or those that mimic handwriting (italics can be a problem). The point size you select for your chosen font should be large enough to allow for effective faxing or scanning.

Application Letter

Written to introduce the résumé and to secure an interview, the letter of application (or cover letter) follows the persuasive strategy discussed in Chapter 9. The letter should include three parts: (1) an opening that obtains the interest of the reader, (2) a body that explains and convinces, and (3) a closing that asks for a particular action.

Obtaining Interest

The first step in gaining the interest of your reader is addressing that individual by name. Rather than sending your letter to the "Personnel Manager" or "Personnel Department," make an effort to identify the name of the appropriate individual. Inquire at the organization for the correct spelling and for the complete address. This personal touch distinguishes your letter and demonstrates your serious interest in employment.

The opening of a cover letter depends on whether the application is solicited or unsolicited. If an employment position has been announced and applicants are being solicited, then the beginning of your letter of application may be more direct. If you do not know whether a position is open and you are prospecting for a job, use an indirect approach. Whether direct or indirect, the opening should attract the attention of the reader. Avoid overworked and unimaginative openings such as *Please consider this letter an application for the position of ...* or *This is an application for ...*

For solicited jobs, consider the following techniques and examples for opening your letter:

1. Refer to the source of your information precisely. If an employee told you of the position mention his or her name.

   At the suggestion of Mr. Ruben Juarez of your Personnel Department, I submit my qualifications for the position of personnel assistant.

2. If you are answering an advertisement, mention the exact position advertised and the name and date of the publication.

   Your advertisement in the May 10 *Vancouver Sun* for an entry-level technical writer greatly appeals to me.

   The May 15 issue of the *Herald Examiner* reports that you are seeking a mature, organized, and reliable administrative assistant.

3. Refer to the job title and describe how your qualifications fit the requirements.

> With an honours degree in recreation studies and two years of part-time experience organizing social activities for a personal-care hospital, I believe I am qualified for your advertised position of activity director.

> Because of my specialized training in computerized accounting from Simon Fraser University, I feel confident that I have the qualifications you described in your advertisement for an accountant.

If your letter of application is unsolicited, try one of these techniques in your opening:

1. Demonstrate interest in and knowledge of the reader's business.

> Since the Canadian Automobile Association is organizing a new information management team for its recently established group insurance division, could you use the services of a well-trained business administration graduate who seeks to become a successful data-processing professional?

Do research in *Standard & Poor's Corporation Records* and other publications to learn about a company before you apply.

2. Show how your special talents and experience will benefit the company.

> Could your company use a college-trained individual with excellent communication skills, self-starting personality, and recent experience in word processing?

> Do you have an opening for an energetic, aggressive individual with successful sales experience?

3. Use a catchy phrase or quote, particularly if you are seeking a position in an industry that values creativity.

> "Out, out bright candle" may be exclaimed on the stage, but your production lighting need never be in jeopardy. As an experienced theatrical technician with a strong background in analog/digital electronics, I would be able to provide lighting and sound to meet the exact specifications of both your local and your travelling productions.

Explaining and Convincing

Once you have captured the attention of the reader, use the body of the letter to explain your purpose and to present convincing evidence of your qualifications.

Use persuasive techniques to convince the reader that you are qualified.

If you are responding to an advertisement, show how your preparation and experience fill the stated requirements. If you are prospecting for a job, you may not know the exact requirements. Your employment research and knowledge of your profession, however, should give you a reasonably good idea of what is expected for this position.

Emphasize reader benefits. Describe your strong points in relation to the needs of the employer.

Instead of	Try This
I have completed courses in communications, report writing, and technical writing.	Courses in business communications, report writing, and technical writing have helped me develop the research and writing skills required of your technical writers.

Use the application letter to explain, amplify, and interpret selected facts from the three sections of your résumé: education, experience, and skills and accomplishments. Choose your strongest qualifications and show how they fit this job. Students with little experience will probably emphasize their education and its practical applications, as this candidate did:

> Because you need an architect's apprentice with proven ability, I submit a drawing of mine that won second place in the Algonquin College drafting contest last year.

In this part of your letter, discuss relevant personal traits. Employers are looking for candidates who get along well with others, take responsibility, show initiative, and learn easily. Notice how the following paragraph treats interpersonal skills.

> In addition to developing valuable technical and academic skills at St. Francis Xavier, during my tenure as vice-president of the business students' organization, U.B.S.O., I planned and supervised two successful fund-raising events. These activities involved motivating and coordinating the efforts of 35 students. To your company I offer the same organizational and interpersonal skills.

Use this section or the next to refer the reader to your résumé. Do so incidentally as part of another statement or directly. Here are two examples:

> As you will notice from my résumé, I will graduate in June with a bachelor's degree in business administration.

> Please refer to the attached résumé for additional information regarding my education, experience, and references.

In writing the body of your letter of application, keep these points in mind:

1. Emphasize only those skills, accomplishments, and qualities that are related directly to the job. If you try to cover everything, your letter will be too long and too general.

2. Use concrete examples in place of generalities. Instead of *I have supervisory experience*, write *I supervised five employees*. Instead of *I am responsible*, write *I was responsible for scheduling all conventions*.

3. Be confident. Instead of *It is my belief that I could be an effective manager*, write *I can be an effective manager*. Follow such assertions with evidence of your potential.

Show how your strongest qualifications fulfill the requirements of the position.

Include illustrations of your ability to work well with others.

Here are tips for writing a successful letter of application.

4. Suggest reader benefits. Instead of *I have developed good interpersonal skills,* write *Being able to work well with others will help me serve your clients effectively.*

5. Avoid obvious flattery, such as *I am extremely interested in your fine company.*

6. Don't mention specifics regarding salary. It's better to save this subject for the interview.

Asking for Action

After presenting your case, suggest an action in your last paragraph. Ask for an interview. If you live in another city, you may ask for an employment application or an opportunity to be interviewed by the organization's nearest representative. Never ask for the job. To do so would be presumptuous and naive. In requesting an interview, try to suggest reader benefits. Sound sincere and appreciative. Make it easy for the reader to agree—supply your telephone number and optimum times to call you. Consider these examples:

> I hope that this brief description of my qualifications and the additional information on my résumé indicate to you my genuine desire to put my skills as an architect's apprentice to work for you. Please call me at (416) 388-9012 before 10 a.m. or after 3 p.m. to arrange an interview.

> If you need an industrious, well-trained word processing specialist with proven communication skills, call me at (506) 228-3221 to arrange an interview. I can meet with you at any time convenient to your schedule.

Conclude your letter by asking for an interview—not for a job.

Putting It All Together

In Figure 13.6, a recent graduate writes a solicited letter of application in response to a newspaper advertisement. Notice how the example puts together the three parts of the application letter to produce a convincing selling tool. The goal here is to obtain an interview.

In Figure 13.7, a young applicant seeks a job where none is known to be available. The writer emphasizes work experience because it is directly related to the position. Notice how often specific examples are used to illustrate the writer's qualifications.

Other Employment Documents

Application Follow-up Letter

If your letter or your application generates no response within a reasonable time, you may decide to send a short follow-up letter like the one shown in Figure 13.8. Doing so (1) jogs the memory of the personnel officer, (2) demonstrates your serious interest, and (3) allows you to emphasize your significant qualifications or to add new information.

A follow-up letter reminds the prospective employer of your sincere interest and enables you to emphasize your strongest qualifications or to add new information.

Figure 13.6   Solicited Letter of Application

342 Richmond Rd.
Calgary, Alberta
T8N 1E4
June 2, 199x

Ms. Maria S. Morales
Office Manager
Granger Insurance Company
100 Bowness Rd.
Calgary, Alberta
T7L 1R5

Dear Ms. Morales:

Begins strongly by showing how the writer's background matches the job description.

With two years of part-time office experience and a soon-to-be-completed diploma in office administration, I feel that I could be the "well-trained" administrative assistant for which you advertised in the April 26 issue of the <u>Calgary Herald</u>.

Highlights information from the three most important parts of the résumé: education, experience, and personal activities.

Seven full courses in office administration have provided me with training in microcomputer-based word processing and database programs, such as those used in your office. Composing and revising business letters and reports in my business communications class, as well as transcribing over 100 dictated letters and memorandums in my transcription class, helped me perfect my communication skills.

Two years of part-time employment in the law office of James D. Turner taught me how to work under pressure and how to organize my activities for maximum productivity. I enjoyed the team effort required by big projects, and I was commended for my professional attitude.

As you will see from my résumé, I have actively participated in college activities. These activities have provided me with interpersonal and leadership experiences that should enhance my effectiveness as an employee in your business.

Closes confidently by connecting the request for an interview with a statement of reader benefit.

If you want a well-prepared administrative assistant who could be immediately productive in your office, please leave a message for me at (403) 630-2204 so that I may return your call and arrange an interview.

Sincerely,

Cham Musan

Cham Musan

Enclosure

Figure 13.7   Unsolicited Letter of Application

290 Emery St.
London, Ontario
N3R 2T6
May 25, 199x

Mr. Jaroslav Morozov
Vice-President, Personnel
Resorts International, Inc.
257 Yonge St.
Toronto, Ontario
M4R 2E3

Dear Mr. Morozov:

Is there an opening in your junior management trainee program for an energetic individual with both practical experience and formal training in hotel/restaurant management?

> Gains attention by spotlighting the applicant's qualifications for the position.

For the past two years, I have worked as part-time clerk and now as desk manager of a 100-unit resort complex in Grand Bend, on Lake Huron. In this position, I am responsible for custodial and room-service staff scheduling, convention planning, and customer relations. The supervisory, organizational, and communication skills that I have developed in this capacity will enable me to function successfully as a trainee at one of your resorts.

> Relates applicant's experiences directly to the position being sought.

As a result of this job and others, I realized that I enjoy serving customers and meeting the challenges that public service demands. I decided to enter the hospitality field, and in June I will be receiving a two-year diploma in hotel management from the University of Western Ontario. Complementing my work experience and studies are personal qualities that will make me a successful manager. Supervising six employees, I learned to make decisions, to take responsibility for them, and to work well with others. In supporting myself while completing my degree, I learned to manage my time and to persevere despite adversity. Most importantly, I discovered a career that is ideally suited to my talents and goals.

> Uses concrete examples to demonstrate personal qualities.

Professor Jerome Mitchell, chairman of the hotel/restaurant management program at Western, as well as other individuals listed as references on the enclosed résumé, will confirm my potential as a management trainee.

> Calls attention to résumé and to references.

At a time convenient for you, I would appreciate the opportunity to discuss my qualifications for beginning a career with your company. I will call you early next Monday to see if we can arrange a meeting.

> Because the writer cannot be reached by telephone, he takes the initiative for making contact.

Sincerely,

Michael W. Weston

Michael W. Weston
Enclosure

Figure 13.8   Application Follow-up Letter

Dear Ms. Morales:

Please be assured that I am still interested in becoming an administrative assistant with your organization.

Since I wrote to you in May, I have completed my diploma and have been employed as a summer replacement for office workers in several downtown offices. This experience has sharpened my word processing and communication skills; it has also introduced me to a wide range of office procedures.

Please keep my application in your active file and let me know when I may put my formal training, technical skills, and practical experience to work for you.

Sincerely,

Interview Follow-up Letter

After you have been interviewed, send a brief letter of thanks. This courteous gesture will distinguish you from other applicants (most will not bother), and it will remind the interviewer of your visit.

Send a follow-up letter immediately after the interview.

Follow-up letters are most effective if sent immediately following the interview. In your letter, refer to specific topics discussed in the interview. Avoid worn-out phrases, such as *Thank you for taking the time to interview me* or *I appreciate the time that you took from your busy schedule to interview me*. Notice in the follow-up letter in Figure 13.9 how the writer expresses appreciation without using stereotyped expressions.

Figure 13.9   Interview Follow-up Letter

Dear Ms. Marquardt:

In our conversation last week, I appreciated learning about the products and the departmental operations of Datatech.

The writer expresses thanks while at the same time reinforcing the application.

Thanks for providing a tour of your information processing centre and introducing me to the supervisor and the trainer. After meeting them and observing the equipment and procedures used to turn out documents in the centre, I remain confident that I could be a productive member of your staff. To give me an opportunity to prove my abilities, call me at 322-4891.

Sincerely,

Application Form

Many organizations require that applicants complete an application form in place of or in addition to submitting a résumé. An application form permits them to gather and store standard information about each applicant. Here are some tips on filling out such forms:

1. Carry a card summarizing vital statistics such as: social insurance number; graduation dates; beginning and ending dates of all employment; salary history; full names, occupational titles, occupational addresses, and telephone numbers of persons who have agreed to serve as references; and your present telephone number (if you have a new one and may forget it).

2. Fill out the form neatly. Print your answers if your handwriting is poor.

3. Answer all questions. Write *Not Applicable* if appropriate.

4. Be prepared for a salary question. Unless you know what comparable employees are earning in this company, the best strategy is to suggest a salary range or to write in *Negotiable* or *Open*.

5. Ask if you may submit your résumé in addition to the application form.

Job application forms require detailed information. Be prepared by following these suggestions.

Interview

Job interviews can be stressful. In an interview, the employer is comparing your qualifications with those of other candidates. You can greatly enhance your chances for success at an interview if you prepare carefully. The way you conduct yourself during and after the interview is also critical in determining whether or not you will get the job.

Proper preparation can make interviews less stressful.

Before the Interview

The amount of preparation you bring to an interview can spell the difference between failure and success. Here are some tips on preparing for an interview.

1. **Research the organization you are seeking employment with**. Read annual reports, catalogues, and brochures for information on the company's service or product, as well as its history and future directions. If you need more information, consider a call or a visit to the company.

2. **Learn about the position**. Find out as much as you can about the position regarding duties, typical salary range, and opportunities for advancement.

3. **Identify your major selling points**. A selling point can be a skill or personal characteristic that is of particular importance to the sought-after

position. Be prepared to discuss three to five of your own selling points, as well as occasions on which you have applied them with success.

4. **Prepare answers to possible questions**. You can expect questions about how your education, skills, and experience relate to this specific position. Be prepared to discuss how your qualifications meet the organization's needs. Also prepare some questions of your own. Prospective employers often end an interview with *Do you have any questions?* Ask about training for new employees, travel requirements, promotion policies, shift work, or on-call arrangements.

5. **Prepare for the salary question**. Ideally, you should know the position's typical salary range. The more experience you have, the more room there will be for negotiations. If your experience is minimal, you will probably be offered a salary somewhere between the low point and the midpoint in the typical salary range.

6. **Be prepared for illegal or inappropriate questions**. Suggestions for responding to these kinds of questions are provided at the end of this chapter.

7. **Be on time and appropriately dressed**. Arrive five or ten minutes early. Don't overdo perfume, after-shave lotion, and jewellery. Your apparel should be a shade more formal than that expected in the position.

During the Interview

When you first meet the interviewer, shake hands firmly and address him or her by name. Most interviewers will use the opening moments of the interview to engage the applicant in small talk. Don't dismiss this phase of the interview as being unimportant. First impressions can colour an interviewer's perceptions of your performance later on in the interview. Throughout the interview, you should maintain eye contact and be aware of your body language.

During the formal phase of the interview, focus on your strengths. Provide brief responses to questions that relate to your weaknesses, or else try to turn a negative into a positive with such comments as: *I have not had extensive paid work experience in that area, but I have completed a 50-hour training program that provided hands-on experience using the latest technology and methods. My recent training taught me to be open to new ideas and showed me how I can continue learning on my own. I was commended for being a quick learner.* Never say anything negative about a previous employer. If asked why you left your last position, say that you learned all you could from that job, not that you were unhappy. No one wants to hire a complainer.

Conclude the interview on a positive note. Summarize your strongest qualifications, show your enthusiasm for the position, and thank the interviewer for his or her time.

After the Interview

Your responsibilities don't end when you leave the interview room. To benefit further from the interview experience, spend some time considering your performance afterward. While the events are still fresh in your mind, make notes on what went well and what could be improved next time.

Don't delay in writing a letter thanking the interviewer for a constructive interview (Figure 13.9).

How to Respond to Ten Frequently Asked Interview Questions

1. **Why do you want to work for us?** This is your chance to put your research of the organization to use. Describe your desire to work for them not only from *your* perspective but also from *their* point of view. What have you to offer them?

2. **Why should we hire you?** Talk about your selling points in relation to the demands of the position. Describe your skills, academic preparation, and relevant experience. If you have little experience, don't apologize—the interviewer has read your résumé. Emphasize strengths as demonstrated by your education, such as initiative and persistence in completing assignments, ability to learn quickly, self-sufficiency, and excellent attendance.

3. **What can you tell me about yourself?** Use this chance to promote yourself. Stick to professional or business-related strengths; avoid personal or humorous references. Be ready with at least three success stories illustrating characteristics important to this job. Demonstrate responsibility you have been given; describe how you contributed as a team player.

4. **What are your strongest (or weakest) personal qualities?** Stress your strengths, such as "I believe I am conscientious, reliable, tolerant, patient, and thorough." Add examples that illustrate these qualities: "My supervisor said that my research was exceptionally thorough." If pressed for a weakness, give a strength disguised as a weakness: "Perhaps my greatest fault is being too painstaking with details"; or "I am impatient when tasks are not completed on time." Don't admit weaknesses, not even to sound human. You'll be hired for your strengths, not your weaknesses.

5. **What do you expect to be doing ten years from now?** Formulate a realistic plan that takes into account your present age and situation. The important thing is to be prepared for this question.

6. **Do you prefer working with others or by yourself?** This question can be tricky. Provide an answer that not only suggests your interpersonal qualities but also reflects an ability to make independent decisions and work without supervision.

7. **Have you ever changed your major area of interest during your education? Why?** Another tricky question. Don't admit weaknesses or failures. In explaining changes, suggest career potential and new aspirations awakened by your expanding education, experience, or maturity.

8. **What have been your most rewarding or disappointing work (or school) experiences?** If possible, concentrate on positive experi-

ences such as technical and interpersonal skills you acquired. Avoid dwelling on negative or unhappy topics. Never criticize former employers.

9. **Have you established any new goals lately?** Watch out here. If you reveal new goals, you may inadvertently admit deficiencies. Instead of "I've resolved to finally learn how to operate a computer," try "Although I'm familiar with basic computer applications, I'm now reading and studying more about computer applications in ..."

10. **What are your long- and short-term goals?** Suggest realistic goals that you have consciously worked out before the interview. Know what you want to do with your future. To admit to an interviewer that you're not sure what you want to do is a sign of immaturity, weakness, and indecision.

How to Respond to Illegal Questions

In Canada, job applicants are protected by human-rights legislation that states that an employer cannot dismiss or discriminate against a person in employment because of such factors as race, colour, ancestry, place of origin, political belief, religion, marital status, sexual orientation, physical or mental disability, age, gender (including pregnancy), or conviction for a criminal charge that is unrelated to the employment. Sexual harassment is also considered to be illegal discrimination. It is also contrary to human-rights legislation for an employer to pay less to one sex for work that is similar to work performed by the other sex.

If you are asked an illegal question, how do you answer? If it is an employer for whom you want to work, it is up to you to indicate your suitability for the job without compromising your rights. You must decide whether to ask a counterquestion or whether to answer even though the question contravenes human-rights legislation. Consider the following examples suggested by Human Resource Development Canada:

1. **Respond with a counterquestion.** "Could you tell me how my (age, marital status, place of birth, religion, etc.) might have a bearing on the job I am applying for?" or "That's a very interesting question. I'd be happy to answer it if you could tell me the reason for asking it."

2. **Choose to answer.** *How old are you?* If you are an older worker, mention experience, fitness, knowledge, maturity, stability, and business contacts. Often, there may be an objection that you are overqualified or probably expect a higher salary. You may mention (if it is true) that you are more interested in job satisfaction at this point in your career. If you are a younger worker, you might mention

flexibility, pride in punctuality and work performance, energy, eagerness to learn, and any references you may have.

Are you married? If yes and you have children, assure the employer that you have reliable child care and that you pride yourself on punctuality. You may also mention that you plan to stay in the area. If you aren't married, assure the employer of your reliability and indicate some community involvement. Emphasize that you are free to do overtime and travel, if that is true for you.

How long have you been in Canada? Relate your answer to current Canadian markets and the employer's immediate needs. Mention Canadian work experience or training, ideally in your community. If your experience is from elsewhere in Canada or the United States, mention it. Show the employer your current knowledge of the job. Include any codes, bylaws, acts, or government regulations that may pertain and your knowledge of the product or service and trends in the industry. Also, mention transferable skills such as the ability to learn quickly, and the work challenges you have successfully met that would be likely to occur in Canada.

Summary

Your résumé may be the most important document you ever write. Before you write, gather employment information, and analyze the job market through newspapers, interviews, Canada Employment Centres, or seeking a part-time job in your profession. Begin with a thorough analysis and summary of your background, experience, and qualifications. Your goal in sending a résumé is to get an interview.

Try to fit your résumé on one or two pages and avoid gimmicks unless you are applying to a profession that values creativity. Résumés begin with a main heading and include education, experience, activities, and achievements. Organization can be either traditional (chronological), or functional, depending on your background. Your résumé does not require a complete history of your previous employment; emphasize work experiences that qualify you for the job in which you are interested. Illustrate and quantify examples of your strong character traits. Provide a picture of a well-rounded individual.

The application letter is written to introduce the résumé and to secure an interview. Use the direct strategy for solicited applications and the indirect for unsolicited applications. The first paragraph should include the position advertised and the name and date of the publication in which it was found. It should also create interest in your qualifications. Include information about the company to which you are applying where appropriate. Use persuasive techniques to show how your strongest qualifications fulfil the requirements of the position. Include illustrations of your ability to work well with others. Use concrete examples and write confidently. Suggest reader benefits and avoid obvious flattery. Conclude your letter by asking for an interview.

Prepare yourself for the interview by researching the company and developing answers to expected questions. During the interview, highlight your strengths and be yourself. Avoid sending negative nonverbal messages. After the interview, analyze your performance and send a follow-up letter to remind the prospective employer of your sincere interest, to reiterate your strongest qualifications, or to add new information.

APPLICATION AND PRACTICE—13

Discussion

1. Why is the résumé the most important document you may ever write?

2. How can inventory lists help you write a résumé?

3. A résumé should include the names of references. Discuss.

4. If prospective employers are most interested in the résumé, why bother to write a letter of application?

5. Discuss four or more personal characteristics that employers are seeking in applicants.

Short Answers

6. Name six sources of job information.

7. List six headings you might use in your résumé.

8. How is a traditional résumé different from a functional résumé?

9. What are the advantages of using the traditional résumé format?

10. What are the advantages of using the functional résumé format?

11. What are two functions of the letter of application?

12. Describe the three parts of the letter of application.

13. List three techniques for opening a solicited letter of application.

14. List three techniques for opening an unsolicited letter of application.

15. Name at least five things to avoid in a letter of application.

16. List three reasons for sending a follow-up letter if you have had no response to an application letter or an employment application.

17. If an application form requests a salary figure, how should you respond?

Writing Improvement Exercise

18. Analyze each section of the following letter of application.

Dear Personnel Manager:

(1) Please consider this letter as an application for the position of staff accountant that I saw advertised in the Saskatoon *Star-Phoenix* on April 27. Accounting has been my major in college, and although I have had no paid work experience in this profession, I believe that I could be an asset to Meyers & Jacoby.

(2) For four years I have studied accounting, and I am fully trained for full-charge bookkeeping as well as computer accounting. I have taken 36 credits in college accounting and courses in electronic data processing. I have also taken other courses that may help me in business, including

business communications, human relations, report writing, and economics.

(3) In addition to my course work, during the tax season I have been a student volunteer for VITA. This is a project to help individuals in the community prepare their income tax returns, and I learned a lot from this experience. I have also received some experience in office work and working with figures when I was employed as an office assistant for Copy Quick, Inc.

(4) I am a competent and responsible person who gets along pretty well with others. I have been a member of some college and social organizations and have even held elective office.

(5) I feel that I have a strong foundation in accounting as a result of my course work and my experience. Along with my personal qualities and my desire to succeed, I hope that you will agree that I qualify for the position of staff accountant with Meyers & Jacoby.

Sincerely,

Make specific suggestions to the writer of this letter for improving each of the five paragraphs.

Activities

19. Learn about employment in your profession. Visit your local library or campus employment office. Find a description of a position for which you could apply in two to five years. From the library, employment office, or a local association, find information that describes employment in the area in which you are interested. Save this information to attach to your letter of application.

20. Clip a job advertisement from the classified section of a local newspaper. Select an ad describing the kind of employment you will seek in two to five years. (If you can find no advertisement, write one. Construct an advertisement for a legitimate position that could possibly have been advertised.) Save this advertisement to attach to your résumé when you submit it.

21. Using information you have gathered from your research and from other sources, describe the successful candidate for the position in Activity No. 21. What education will this individual have? Experience? Skills? Personal qualities? Physical abilities? Appearance?

22. In preparation for writing your résumé, write two career objectives for yourself. Write one that is broad, encompassing both short- and long-term goals, and another that is narrow and aimed at a specific job.

23. Make inventory lists for these areas: course-work achievements, employment and internships, activities and achievements, and personal qualities. Use active verbs. Review the examples and résumés in this chapter.

   ▪ **Course-work achievements.** List degrees, diplomas, certificates, and training accomplishments. List courses, seminars, or skills that are relevant to the job you seek.

   ▪ **Employment and internships.** Begin with your most recent job. For each position, list the following information: employer; your job title; dates of employment; and three to five duties, activities, or accomplishments. Emphasize activities related to the job you seek.

   ▪ **Activities and achievements.** List three to five personal activities that you enjoy, and any extracurricular achievements. Analyze your items. Do any of them demonstrate personal and character traits that employers value? Write action statements using these items.

   ▪ **Personal qualities.** List three to five of your strongest personal characteristics relevant to employment. Write statements that demonstrate these characteristics.

24. Using the information you have just developed, write your résumé. Use a word processor if possible. Revise until it is perfect. Attach a copy of the advertisement from Activity No. 20.

25. Write a letter of application delivering your résumé. Attach the information you assembled in Activity No. 19.

26. Assume that you were interviewed for this position. Write a follow-up letter.

27. Write an unsolicited letter seeking a part-time or summer position with an actual firm in your area.

28. Fill in the sample application blank shown in Figure 13.10. Take the time to find all the necessary information. This filled-in form can then be removed and carried with you to serve as a reference when applying for employment.

29. Practise employment interviewing. Choose a partner in your class. Make a list of five employment questions from those shown on pages 349 to 351. Prepare answers to those questions. Before the class you and your partner will role-play an interview. One acts as interviewer; the other is the candidate. Prior to the interview, the candidate tells the interviewer what job and company he or she is applying to. For the interview, the interviewer and candidate should dress appropriately and sit in chairs facing each other before the class. The interviewer greets the candidate and makes the candidate comfortable. The candidate gives the interviewer a copy of his or her résumé. The interviewer asks two (or more, depending upon your instructor's schedule) questions from the candidate's list. The interviewer may also ask follow-up questions if appropriate. When finished, the interviewer ends the meeting graciously. After one interview, reverse roles and repeat.

Figure 13.10 Sample Employment Application

TO OUR APPLICANTS: Please answer all questions completely. If you need help in completing this application, please request assistance from a member of this office. We will be pleased to serve you.	

NAME: Last	First	Middle	TODAY'S DATE

PRESENT ADDRESS: No. Street	City	Province	Postal Code

HOME TELEPHONE: ( )	WORK TELEPHONE: ( )	SOCIAL INSURANCE NUMBER:

POSITION APPLIED FOR:	SALARY EXPECTED	DATE OPEN FOR HIRE

WOULD YOU WORK – ☐ Full-time? ☐ Part-time?   REFERRED BY:

WERE YOU PREVIOUSLY EMPLOYED BY US? ☐ Yes? ☐ No?   IF "YES," WHEN?

DO YOU HAVE THE LEGAL RIGHT TO BE EMPLOYED IN CANADA? ☐ Yes? ☐ No?

PERSONS TO BE NOTIFIED IN CASE OF ACCIDENT OR EMERGENCY: NAME

ADDRESS:	TELEPHONE NUMBER: ( )

NAME:

ADDRESS:	TELEPHONE NUMBER: ( )

ON THE LINES BELOW, PLEASE LIST ANY FRIENDS OR RELATIVES WHO ARE WORKING FOR US.

Name   Relationship

1.

2.

EDUCATION

NAME AND LOCATION OF HIGH SCHOOL: DID YOU GRADUATE ☐ Yes   ☐ No

Name of College, University, Trade or Vocational School	Location	Major Subjects	Degrees or Certificates

SKILLS/ABILITIES

Please list any skills or abilities you have which you think may be used in your employment here. Any craft, trade, office, clerical, professional or administrative skills or abilities may be included. Also list any skills or abilities you gained doing volunteer work, household duties or while pursuing a hobby.

Skill/Ability	Duration of Training	Length of Experience

TYPING SPEED: Manual	Electric	SHORTHAND SPEED:	WORD PROCESSING OR DATA ENTRY?	NAME MACHINES OPERATED:

OTHER MACHINES OPERATED:

Figure 13.10 Continued

EMPLOYMENT / EXPERIENCE				
Please list all jobs and activities for the past ten years or since attending school as a full-time student. Include part-time employment and self-employment. Include experience gained doing volunteer work or community service work. Begin with the most recent employment and activities first.				
NAME OF EMPLOYER				YOUR JOB TITLE
ADDRESS OF EMPLOYER				DESCRIBE WORK YOU PERFORMED
SUPERVISOR'S NAME, JOB TITLE AND TELEPHONE NUMBER				
DATE STARTED	DATE ENDED	DURATION	PAY	REASON FOR LEAVING
NAME OF EMPLOYER				YOUR JOB TITLE
ADDRESS OF EMPLOYER				DESCRIBE WORK YOU PERFORMED
SUPERVISOR'S NAME, JOB TITLE AND TELEPHONE NUMBER				
DATE STARTED	DATE ENDED	DURATION	PAY	REASON FOR LEAVING
NAME OF EMPLOYER				YOUR JOB TITLE
ADDRESS OF EMPLOYER				DESCRIBE WORK YOU PERFORMED
SUPERVISOR'S NAME, JOB TITLE AND TELEPHONE NUMBER				
DATE STARTED	DATE ENDED	DURATION	PAY	REASON FOR LEAVING
NAME OF EMPLOYER				YOUR JOB TITLE
ADDRESS OF EMPLOYER				DESCRIBE WORK YOU PERFORMED
SUPERVISOR'S NAME, JOB TITLE AND TELEPHONE NUMBER				
DATE STARTED	DATE ENDED	DURATION	PAY	REASON FOR LEAVING

REFERENCE CHECKS	
MAY WE ASK YOUR PRESENT OR PREVIOUS EMPLOYERS ABOUT YOU? ☐ Yes ☐ No	NOT UNTIL I GIVE NOTICE ON (date)

DRIVER'S LICENCE NUMBER:	CLASS	PROVINCE WHERE ISSUED:

SIGNATURE: X	DATE:

By my signature above, I certify that all answers and statements on this application are true and complete to the best of my knowledge. I understand that should an investigation disclose untruthful or misleading answers, my application may be rejected, my name removed from consideration, or my employment terminated.

GRAMMAR/MECHANICS CHECKUP—13

Number Style

Review Sections 4.01 through 4.13 of the Grammar/Mechanics Handbook. Then study each of the following pairs. Assume that these expressions appear in the context of letters, reports, or memos. In the space provided for each pair, write *a* or *b* to indicate the preferred number style and record the number of the G/M principle illustrated. When you finish, compare your responses with the following. If your responses differ, study carefully the principles in parentheses.

___a___ (4.01a)

Example: (a) six investments   (b) 6 investments

1. (a) sixteen credit cards	(b) 16 credit cards
2. (a) Fifth Avenue	(b) 5th Avenue
3. (a) 34 newspapers	(b) thirty-four newspapers
4. (a) July eighth	(b) July 8
5. (a) twenty dollars	(b) $20
6. (a) on the 15th of June	(b) on the fifteenth of June
7. (a) at 4:00 p.m.	(b) at 4 p.m.
8. (a) 8 sixty-four page books	(b) eight 64-page books
9. (a) over 18 years ago	(b) over eighteen years ago
10. (a) 2,000,000 residents	(b) 2 million residents
11. (a) fifteen cents	(b) 15 cents
12. (a) a thirty-day warranty	(b) a 30-day warranty
13. (a) 2/3 of the books	(b) two-thirds of the books
14. (a) two telephones for 15 employees	(b) 2 telephones for 15 employees
15. (a) 6 of the 130 letters	(b) six of the 130 letters

---

1. b (4.0la)   3. a (4.01a)   5. b (4.02)   7. b (4.04)   9. b (4.08)   11. b (4.02)   13. b (4.12)   15. a (4.06)

GRAMMAR MECHANICS CHALLENGE—13

Document for Revision

The following résumé (shortened for this exercise) is wordy and contains faults in grammar, punctuation, spelling, number form, and verb form. Drawing upon the guidelines provided in the Grammar/Mechanics Handbook and what you learned in this chapter, revise the résumé.

Poor Résumé

Megan A. Kozlov
623 Topsail Road
St. John's, Newfoundland
A1B 3Z4

Education
    Memorial University, St. John's, Newfoundland. Degree expected in June 1997. Major Arts
Experience:
    Office Assistant. Host Systems, St. John's, 1994 to present Responsible for entering data on Macintosh computer. I had to insure accuracy and completness of data that was to be entered. Another duty was maintaining a clean and well-organized office. I also served as Office Courier.
    Lechter's Housewares. Outlook Newfoundland. 2nd asst. Mgr I managed store in absence of mgr. And asst. Mgr. I open and close registers. Ballanced daily reciepts. Ordered some mds. I also had to supervise 2 employees, earning rapid promotion.
    Clerk typist. Sunshine Travel Outlook Nfld. 1992-93. (Part time) Entered travel information on IBM PC. Did personalized followup letters to customer inquirys. Was responsible for phones. I also handled all errands as courier.
Strengths
    IBM PC, Macintosh, proofreading
    Can type 50 words/per/minute
    I am a fast learner, and very accurate
    Word-perfect, Lotus 123.

Note

1. Robert Half, "Managing Your Career: How Do You Read a Résumé?" *Management Accounting*, May 1988, p. 20.

14

Listening and Speaking

In this chapter, you will learn to do the following:

- Identify barriers to effective listening.
- Suggest techniques for becoming an active and effective listener.
- Analyze the audience, organize the content, and prepare visual aids for an oral presentation.
- Select the best method for delivering an oral report.
- Discuss techniques for reducing stage fright.

- Implement techniques of effective speaking.
- Participate in productive and enjoyable meetings.
- Use the telephone as an efficient business tool.
- Recognize efficient dictation techniques.

Adults spend 45 percent of their communicating time listening and 30 percent speaking.

Successful people, in both their business and their private lives, require a variety of communication skills. Some estimates suggest that adults spend 45 percent of their communicating time listening, 30 percent speaking, 16 percent reading, and 9 percent writing. Writing skills demand the most attention because they are most difficult to develop and because written documents record the most significant events in our lives. However, you should also develop other communication skills that are often taken for granted, such as listening and speaking.

Improving Listening Skills

Do you ever pretend to be listening when you're not? Do you know how to look attentive in class when your mind wanders? Do you ever "tune out" people when their ideas are boring or complex? Do you find it difficult to concentrate on ideas when a speaker's appearance or mannerisms are strange?

Most of us would answer "yes" to one or more of these questions because we have developed poor listening habits. In fact, some researchers suggest that we listen at only 25 percent efficiency. Such poor listening habits are costly in business. Letters must be retyped, shipments reshipped, appointments rescheduled, and directions restated. Some business organizations have decided that they cannot afford to pay the price of poor listening. These companies have instituted programs to improve listening habits among their personnel.

For most of us, listening is a passive, unconscious activity. We don't give much thought to whether or not we're really listening. Only when a message is urgent do we try to listen more carefully. Then we become more involved in the communication process. We reduce competing environmental sounds; we concentrate on the speaker's words; we anticipate what's coming; we ask questions. Good listeners are active listeners.

To improve listening skills, we first need to recognize barriers that prevent effective listening. Then we need to focus on specific techniques that are effective in improving listening skills.

Barriers to Effective Listening

As we learned in Chapter 1, barriers can interfere with the communication process. Some of the barriers and distractions that prevent good listening are discussed here.

- **Physical barriers**. You cannot listen if you cannot hear what is being said. Physical impediments include hearing disabilities, poor acoustics, and noisy surroundings. It's also difficult to listen if you're ill, tired, uncomfortable, or worried.

- **Psychological barriers**. As noted in Chapter 1, every person brings to the communication process a different set of cultural, ethical, and personal values. Each of us has an idea of what is right and what is important. If messages run counter to our preconceived thoughts, we tend to "tune out" or ignore the speaker and thus fail to hear. For example, if Carolyn Dee thinks that her work is satisfactory, she might filter out criticism from her supervisor. Such selective listening results in poor communication and is unproductive both for the listener and for the speaker.

- **Word-choice problems**. We've already learned that jargon and unfamiliar words can negatively affect the communication process because such words lack meaning for the receiver. In addition, emotion-laden or "charged" words can adversely affect listening. If the mention of words like *abortion* or *overdose* has had an intense emotional impact, a listener may be unable to concentrate on the words that follow.

- **Nonverbal distractions**. Many of us find it difficult to listen if the speaker is different from what we consider normal. Unusual clothing, mannerisms, or perhaps even an unusual hairstyle could cause sufficient distraction to prevent us from hearing what the speaker has to say.

- **Thought speed**. Because thought speed is over three times as great as speech speed, listener concentration may break down. Our minds are able to process thoughts much faster than speakers can enunciate them. Therefore, we become bored and our minds wander.

Most individuals listen at only 25 percent efficiency.

Passive listeners don't get involved; active listeners make a physical and mental effort to hear.

Barriers to listening may be physical, psychological, verbal, or nonverbal.

Most North Americans speak about 125 words per minute. The human brain can process information at least three times as fast.

- **Faking attention**. Most of us have learned to look as if we are listening even when we're not. Such behaviour was perhaps necessary as part of our socialization. Faked attention, however, threatens effective listening because it allows the listener to daydream. Those who practise faked attention often find it difficult to concentrate even when necessary.

- **Grandstanding**. Since our own experiences and thoughts are most important to us, we often wish to monopolize conversations. We sometimes fail to listen carefully because we're just waiting politely for the next pause so that we can have our turn to speak.

How to Become an Active Listener

You can reverse the harmful effects of poor listening habits by making a conscious effort to become an active listener. Listening actively means becoming involved. You can't sit back and hear whatever an unattentive mind happens to receive. These techniques will help you become an active and effective listener.

- **Stop talking**. The first step in becoming a good listener is to stop talking. Let others explain their views. Learn to concentrate on what the speaker is saying, not on what your next comment will be.

- **Control your surroundings**. Whenever possible, remove competing sounds. Turn off radios, close windows or doors, turn off noisy appliances, or move away from loud people or engines. Choose a quiet time and place for listening.

To become a good listener, control your surroundings and your mind-set.

- **Establish a receptive attitude**. Expect to learn something by listening. Develop a positive and receptive frame of mind. If the message is complex, consider it mental gymnastics. It's hard work but good exercise for the mind to stretch and expand its limits.

- **Keep an open mind**. We all sift and filter information through our own prejudices and values. For improved listening, discipline yourself to listen objectively. Be fair to the speaker. Hear what is really being said, not what you want to hear.

- **Listen for main points**. Concentration is enhanced and satisfaction is heightened when you look for and recognize the speaker's central themes.

- **Capitalize on delay time**. Make use of the quickness of your mind by reviewing the speaker's points. Anticipate what's coming next. Evaluate evidence the speaker has presented. Don't allow yourself to daydream.

- **Listen between the lines**. Focus on both what is spoken and what is unspoken. Listen for feelings as well as for facts.

- **Judge ideas, not appearances**. Concentrate on the content of the message, not on its delivery.

- **Don't respond immediately**. Force yourself to listen to the speaker's entire argument or message before reacting. Such restraint may enable you to understand the speaker's reasons and logic before you jump to unwarranted conclusions.

■ **Take selective notes.** For some situations, thoughtful note taking may be necessary to record important facts that must be recalled later. Select only the most important points so that the note-taking process does not interfere with your concentration on the speaker's entire message.

■ **Provide feedback.** Let the speaker know that you are listening. Nod your head; maintain eye contact. Ask relevant questions at appropriate times. Getting involved improves the communication process for both the speaker and the listener.

Improving Speaking Skills

Listening and speaking make up a large part of the time you spend communicating. How much time you devote to speaking—and, more particularly, to making speeches and oral presentations—depends on your occupation and on the level you reach in your career. Few businesspeople regularly deliver formal speeches. Instead, most of us communicate orally in informal conversations and small-group discussions.

Yet, any individual aspiring to a business career is well advised to develop speaking skills. A computer-equipment sales representative may have to sell his or her products before a group of potential customers. An accountant must explain the financial position of an organization to management. A travel agent must describe an excursion package to a single client or to a group. Just as the need for writing skills increases as you rise in your profession, so does the need for speaking skills. It is no coincidence that those individuals who are promoted in organizations are effective writers and speakers.

Preparing an Oral Report

One of the most common speaking functions for businesspeople is the presentation of ideas in an oral report. Such a presentation is most frequently made informally to a superior or to a small group of colleagues. Only occasionally do businesspeople make formal speeches before large groups.

Planning an oral report is similar in many ways to preparing for a written report. You need to analyze the audience, organize the content, and plan visual aids.

Analyzing the Audience

Knowing about your audience will help you decide how to structure your report. The size of the audience influences the formality of your presentation: a large audience generally requires a more formal and less personalized approach. Other factors, such as age, sex, education, experience, and attitude

Listening actively may mean taking notes and providing feedback.

As you advance in your career, the ability to express your ideas orally takes on greater significance.

Before you make an oral presentation, you should (1) analyze the audience, (2) organize your topic, and (3) plan visual aids, if appropriate.

toward the subject, also affect your presentation. Analyze these factors to determine your strategy, vocabulary, illustrations, and level of detail. Your answers to specific questions will guide you in adapting the topic to your audience:

- How will this topic appeal to this audience?
- What do I want the audience to believe?
- What action do I want the audience to take?
- What aspects of the topic will be most interesting to the audience?
- Which of the following will be most effective in making my point: statistics? graphic illustrations? demonstrations? case histories? analogies? cost figures?

Organizing Content

A precise statement of purpose helps you organize the content of your presentation.

Begin to organize your oral report by defining its purpose. Is your goal to inform? To persuade? To recommend? In describing your goal, write a statement of purpose by completing the following sentence: The goal of this report is

- To inform all staff members of the benefits and options in the new dental program.
- To persuade the vice-president of marketing that a consolidation of the Alberta and British Columbia sales territories would reduce costs and increase efficiency.
- To recommend to the Board of Directors the establishment of a members' advisory committee that would encourage input from the employees of the organization.

After you have a firm statement of purpose, organize your report to reach your goal. Like business letters and written reports, oral reports may follow either a direct or an indirect strategy. It seems most logical, though, to organize a report indirectly. Since listeners are generally unfamiliar with a problem, they typically need some explanation or introductory comment to ease them into the topic. Whether you use a direct or an indirect approach, make an outline to guide the organization of your report. Concentrate on two to four main points only. Follow an outline form similar to that shown in Chapter 12 for a long report.

Most presentations should focus on only two to four principal points.

Like long reports, oral presentations often contain three parts: introduction, body, and conclusion. Experienced speakers explain the organization of speeches as follows: *(1) tell them what you're going to tell them, (2) tell them what you have to say, and then (3) tell them what you've just told them.* Such a scheme may seem redundant, but repetition helps the audience retain information.

The audience for oral reports, unlike readers, cannot control the rate of presentation or reread main points. Therefore, knowledgeable speakers help their listeners recognize the organization and main points in an oral report by emphasizing and reiterating them. Good speakers also keep the audience on track by including helpful transitions, reviews, and previews.

Help the listener follow your presentation by describing its organization (introduction, body, and conclusion).

- **Introduction.** At the beginning of your report, identify yourself (if necessary) and your topic. Describe the goal of your report, how it is organized, and what main points you will cover. Also in your introduction make an effort to capture the attention of the audience with a question, startling fact, joke, story, quotation, or some other device. Make sure, of course, that your attention-getter is relevant to your topic.

- **Body**. Follow your outline in presenting the two to four main points of your topic. Develop each with adequate, but not excessive, support and detail. Keep your presentation simple and logical—listeners have no pages to review if they become confused.

The best devices you can use to ensure comprehension are verbal indicators that tell where you've been and point out where you're going. Summarize a segment of your report with a summary statement like

> We see, then, that the two major problems facing management are raw material and labour costs.

or combine a review with a preview, such as

> Now that we've learned how sole proprietorships are different from partnerships, let's turn to corporations.

> I've described two good reasons for consolidating sales territories, but the final reason is most important.

Repeat main ideas as you progress. Indicate new topics or shifts in direction with helpful transitional expressions, such as *first, second, next, then, therefore, moreover, on the other hand, on the contrary,* and *in conclusion.*

- **Conclusion**. You may end a presentation by reviewing the main themes of the talk, or you may complete the presentation by referring to your opening. Concentrate on the information that achieves your purpose. What do you want your listeners to believe? What action do you want them to take? When you finish, ask if audience members have any questions. If silence ensues, remark that you'll be happy to answer questions individually after the program is completed.

Include verbal signposts so that listeners know where you've been and where you're heading in your presentation.

Conclude your presentation by emphasizing the information that you want your listeners to remember.

Planning Visual Aids

Some authorities suggest that we learn and remember 85 percent of all our knowledge visually. The oral report that incorporates visual aids is twice as likely to be understood and retained as a report lacking visual supplements. By appealing to both the senses of sight and sound, a message can double its impact.

When you incorporate visual aids into an oral report, keep a few points in mind:

Oral reports are most successful when they show and tell.

1. Use visual aids only for major points or for information that requires clarification.

2. Keep the visual aids simple.

3. Make sure the necessary equipment works properly. Have a backup ready.

4. Ensure that everyone can see the visual aids.

5. Talk to the audience, not to the visual aids.

In selecting ways to illustrate your oral report, you have a number of options, each with its particular uses, advantages, and disadvantages.

Transparencies.   Transparencies are popular in business and education because they are easy and inexpensive. Transparencies emphasize points for the viewers and can serve to prompt the speaker. They are popular in business and education because they can be prepared in advance.

Computer-based Slide Presentations.   Traditional transparency presentations are increasingly being replaced by computer-based presentations. Presentation software such as Powerpoint allows you to add colour, pictures, and movement to your slides. Here are some tips on creating computer-based presentations:

1. **Use high-contrast colours.** Using dark backgrounds and font colours can produce dramatic images on your computer screen. When projected, however, these same images can be hard to see in a lighted room.

2. **Choose graphic elements carefully.** Choose a few elements that enhance your presentation but don't distract the viewer from your message. Be especially careful with background lines and colours; these should frame your message, not overwhelm it.

3. **Be consistent with all your choices.** Position information and art in the same relative location on each slide and include a title for each slide. Be consistent in your use of fonts. This is easy to do if you use a master slide for your presentation.

4. **Test your presentation and hardware.** As part of your preparation, test the timing of your presentation as well as the hardware required to show and project your files. Something as simple as the wrong connecting cable between your computer and the colour palate (LCD panel) or projector can scuttle an otherwise flawless presentation.

Flip Charts.   Like a giant pad of paper, a flip chart consists of large sheets attached at the top. You may prepare the sheets in advance or write on them as you speak and flip through the pad. Flip charts are usually less visible than transparencies because they are placed on an easel on a level with the speaker and because the sheets are smaller than the images projected on a screen. However, flip charts require no special equipment, and they can be quite colourful if you use felt-tip markers.

Slides.   For picturesque, nonverbal messages, slides can be colourful and entertaining. Verbal messages on slides are more difficult to achieve unless you use a graphic-design service. Slides, of course, require a slide projector and a screen, as well as an operator. One possible drawback is that when you project slides in a darkened room, you lose eye contact with the audience and you run the risk of putting the audience to sleep.

Handouts. Speakers often use handouts, such as a sheet of paper or a packet, to supplement the presentation. Handouts may consist of an outline, list of selected main points, illustration, flow chart, table, or any other material that helps clarify the report. Members of the audience appreciate handouts because they have ready-made notes to take with them to remind them of the report. The major disadvantage of handouts is that audience members may read the handouts instead of listening to the speaker. For this reason, some speakers distribute handouts only at the end of their presentations.

Experienced speakers distribute handouts when they conclude their presentations.

Delivering the Oral Report

Delivery Methods

Once you have prepared your report, how will you present it? If you are like most speakers, you will use one of four delivery methods: (1) memorized delivery, (2) reading delivery, (3) extemporaneous delivery, or (4) impromptu delivery.

■ **Memorized delivery.** Inexperienced speakers often feel that they must memorize an entire report to be effective. Actually, unless you're a trained actor, a memorized delivery can sound unnatural. Also, forgetting your place can be disastrous. Therefore, memorizing an entire oral presentation is not recommended. However, memorizing significant parts—the introduction, the conclusion, or a significant quotation—can be an effective way to begin or end a presentation.

Don't try to memorize an entire oral presentation. It sounds artificial and is a catastrophe if you become confused.

■ **Reading delivery.** Reading a report to an audience creates a negative impression. It suggests that you don't know your topic very well. The audience may lose confidence in your expertise. Reading also prevents you from maintaining eye contact with the audience. If you can't see their reactions, you can't benefit from feedback. Worst of all, reading is simply boring. If you must read your report, practise it thoroughly enough so that you can look up occasionally as you present familiar sections.

If you read an oral presentation, you may put your audience to sleep.

■ **Extemporaneous delivery.** The most effective method for presenting oral reports is the extemporaneous delivery. In this method, you plan the report carefully and talk from notes containing key sentences. By practising with your notes, you can talk to your audience in a conversational manner. Your notes should not consist of entire paragraphs, nor should they be single words. Instead, use complete sentences based on the major ideas in your outline. These key ideas will keep you focused and will help your memory, but only if you have thoroughly practised the presentation.

Write out complete sentences for the key ideas in your talk.

■ **Impromptu delivery.** An impromptu, or unprepared, delivery is necessary if you are asked to give a spontaneous report. For example, you might be asked to report on the progress of a fund-raising drive of which you are coordinator. Many activities in business require impromptu oral reports. Usually, you are very familiar with your topic, but you have little time to prepare your thoughts. Presenting accurate, coherent, persuasive, and well-organized information without adequate preparation is very difficult for even the most professional speaker. If you are asked to give an impromptu report, take a few moments to compose your thoughts and to write down your main points.

Delivery Techniques

Nearly everyone experiences some degree of nervousness when speaking before a group. This is a natural reaction which, when controlled, can add positive energy to your presentation. You can learn to control nervousness as well as to incorporate techniques of effective speaking by studying suggestions from experts. Successful speakers use the following suggestions before, during, and after their reports:

Here are techniques that experts use before, during, and after delivering oral presentations.

Before You Speak

- **Prepare thoroughly.** One of the most effective ways to remain confident is to know your topic well and to prepare a careful sentence outline. Speakers who are unprepared usually suffer the worst anxiety.

- **Rehearse repeatedly.** Practise your presentation from beginning to end. Place your outline sentences on separate cards. You may also wish to include transitional sentences to help you move to the next topic. Use these cards as you practise, and include your visual aids in your rehearsal. Record your rehearsal on tape so that you can hear how you sound.

- **Time yourself.** Make your presentation fit the time allotted to you. If there are no time guidelines, try to make it no more than 20 minutes. Most audiences tend to get restless during longer talks. Set a timer during your rehearsal to measure your speaking time.

- **Arrange for necessary props.** Many beginning speakers like the security of a high desk or lectern from which to deliver a presentation. It serves as a note holder and a convenient place to rest your hands and arms.

- **Check the room.** Before you talk, make sure that the lectern or desk you requested has been provided. If you are using sound equipment or a projector, make sure they are operational. Check electrical outlets and the position of the viewing screen. Ensure that the seating arrangement is appropriate to your needs.

Deep-breathing exercises can significantly reduce stress.

- **Practise stress reduction.** You can alleviate stage fright by engaging in deep-breathing exercises or by creating a mental image of yourself delivering the speech in your practice location. Concentrate on your breathing or your imaging, not on the audience awaiting you.

During Your Presentation

- **Begin with a pause**. When you first approach the audience, take a moment to adjust your notes and make yourself comfortable. Establish your control of the situation.

- **Present your first sentence from memory**. By memorizing your opening, you can immediately establish rapport with the audience through eye contact. You'll also sound confident and knowledgeable.

- **Maintain eye contact**. Look at your audience. If the size of the audience frightens you, pick out two individuals on the right and two on the left. Talk directly to these people.

- **Control your voice and vocabulary**. Speak in moderated tones but loudly enough to be heard. Eliminate verbal extras, such as *eh, ah, er,* and *uh.* Silence is preferable to meaningless fillers when you are thinking of your next idea. Silences always seem longer to the speaker than to the audience.

- **Put the brakes on**. Many novice speakers talk too rapidly, displaying their nervousness and making it very difficult for audience members to understand their ideas. Slow down and listen to what you're saying.

- **Move naturally**. Use the lectern to hold your notes so that you are free to move about casually and naturally. Avoid fidgeting with your notes, your clothing, or items in your pockets. Learn to use your body to express a point.

- **Use visual aids effectively**. Discuss and interpret each visual aid for the audience. Move aside as you describe it so that it can be seen fully. Use a pointer if necessary and face the audience as you point to items—don't turn to face the visual.

- **Avoid digressions**. Stick to your outline and notes. If it's not part of your rehearsed material, leave it out so that you can finish on time. Remember, too, that your audience may not be as enthralled with your topic as you are.

- **Summarize your main points**. Conclude your presentation by reiterating your main points or by emphasizing what you want the audience to think or do. Once you have announced your conclusion, proceed to it directly. Don't irritate the audience by talking for five or ten more minutes.

After Your Presentation

- **Distribute handouts**. If you have prepared handouts with information the audience will need to have after the presentation, pass them out when you finish.

- **Encourage questions**. If the situation permits a question-and-answer period, announce it at the beginning of your presentation. Then,

Don't let a question-and-answer period dissolve into numerous individual conversations. Keep control by repeating questions for the entire audience to hear.

when you finish, ask for questions. Set a time limit for questions and answers.

- **Repeat questions**. Although the speaker may hear the question, some people in the audience often do not. Begin each answer with a repetition of the question. This also gives you thinking time.

- **Answer questions directly**. Avoid becoming defensive or debating the questioner.

- **Keep control**. Don't allow one individual to take over. Keep the entire audience involved.

- **End gracefully**. To signal the end of the session before you take the last question, say something like "We have time for just one more question." After you answer the last question, express appreciation to the audience for the opportunity to talk with them.

Diversity Check—Nonwritten Communication

Nonwritten communication practices that are the norm in the Canadian business world may be inappropriate in other cultural contexts. When communicating orally, choose your words carefully and avoid jargon just as you would in written communication. Speak slowly and clearly, but not to the point of patronizing the listener. Keep in mind that your tone of voice will also determine how your message is received. Your idea of an emphatic tone of voice may be experienced by others as overbearing loudness.

When communicating with people from other cultural contexts, you should also consider how they might respond to nonverbal messages.

- **Body language**. Particular aspects of body language can mean different things to different cultures. Facial expressions and gestures that are an integral part of business communication in Canada may bemuse or even offend contacts from other cultures. In Japan, for example, vivid facial expressions are considered a sign of immaturity.

- **Personal appearance**. Our clothing and other aspects of our personal appearance play a part in the messages we send. Some cultures find specific items of jewellery offensive; others impose stringent dress codes, particularly for women.

- **Proxemics**. Proxemics is the study of spatial separation individuals maintain. Different cultures have different ideas of what constitutes an acceptable degree of separation in various social and interpersonal situations. Misunderstandings or discomfort can result when a businessperson violates the personal space of a contact from another culture.

Developing Successful Meetings

Whether you like attending them or not, meetings are a necessary part of business today. These meetings can be more successful—and even enjoyable—if leaders and participants use their listening, speaking, and planning skills.

Meetings are called to gather information, clarify policy, seek consensus, and solve problems. Meetings are different from speeches, where one person talks *to* an audience; in meetings participants *exchange* ideas. Meetings can be occasions for successful exchange of information, or they can be boring failures and time-wasters.

Why Meetings Fail

Many failed meetings are the result of poor planning. Perhaps the meeting was unnecessary. Alternatives—such as personal conversation, memos, or telephone calls—might have served the purpose as well.

Poor leadership dooms some meetings. The leader fails to announce the planned agenda or to keep the group discussing target items. The discussion digresses or flounders on trivia, and no resolution is reached. Then the group must meet again—and no one enjoys additional meetings.

Poor meetings are usually the result of poor planning or ineffective leadership.

Planning Meetings

Successful meetings begin with planning. Decide first on a goal or an objective, and then determine whether a meeting is the best way to achieve the goal. If the goal is to announce a new policy regarding the scheduling of vacations, is a meeting the best way to inform employees? Perhaps a memo would be better.

If a meeting is necessary, prepare an agenda of items to be discussed. As shown in Figure 14.1, the best agendas list topics, an estimate of time for each item, and an ending time. They also include the names of participants who are responsible for presenting topics or for performing some action. Send the agenda (and perhaps the minutes of the last meeting) at least two days prior to the meeting. Notify only those people directly concerned with the business of this meeting. Plan to serve refreshments if you think the participants need them.

Agendas help prepare participants for meetings.

Conducting Meetings

Conducting good meetings requires real skill, which not every leader comes prepared with. Such skill comes with practice and with knowledge of the following suggestions. To avoid wasting time and irritating the attendees, always start meetings on time—even if some participants are missing. Delaying sets a poor example. Individuals who come on time resent waiting for latecomers. Moreover, latecomers may fail to be on time for future meetings, knowing that the leader doesn't always start punctually.

Begin with a three- to five-minute introduction that includes the following: (1) goal and length of the meeting, (2) background of the problem, (3) possible solutions and constraints, (4) tentative agenda, and (5) procedures to be followed. At this point ask if participants agree with you thus far.

Some experts say that the most important part of a meeting is the first five to ten minutes when the leader introduces the topic and sets the tone.

FIGURE 14.1   Sample Agenda

Sales Department Restructuring Committee
Monthly Information Meeting
Tuesday, August 21, 19xx
9 a.m. to 11 a.m.
Executive Conference Room

Agenda

1. Approval of agenda/additions Rahib (Chair)	10 min.
2. Review and approval of previous minutes Rahib (Chair)	10 min.
3. Report on current timelines and senior management expectations for restructuring Susan	20 min.
4. Committee Reports a. Territories Nathan	15 min.
b. Product Assignments Joan	15 min.
c. Commission Structure André	15 min.
5. Report on comparisons with other companies Thelma	10 min.
6. Other issues	25 min.
7. Adjournment Rahib	11 a.m.

Then assign one attendee to take minutes. It's impossible for the leader to direct a meeting and record its proceedings at the same time. Open the discussion, and from that point forward, say as little as possible. Adhere to the agenda and the time schedule. Keep the discussion on topic by tactfully guiding speakers back to the main idea. Encourage all individuals to participate. You can do this by occasionally asking for the opinions of the smart but silent participants. Try not to let one or two people monopolize the discussion. When the group seems to have reached a consensus, summarize it in your own words and look to see if everyone agrees. Finally, end the meeting at the agreed time. Announce that a report of the proceedings will be sent to all.

Participating in Meetings

As a participant, you can get the most out of a meeting and contribute to its success by coming prepared. Read the agenda and gather any information

How to Conduct an Effective Meeting

Although the traditional Rules of Order are too formal for most small-group business meetings, the following guidelines and procedures will help you keep the meeting on target and on time.

1. **Be fair**. Allow full participation and don't try to steer the meeting toward what you believe to be the best conclusion. Your role as leader is to facilitate interaction between meeting participants.

2. **Know the purpose of the meeting**. Having a clear idea of the goal of the meeting will allow you to facilitate effectively and to keep the discussion on track.

3. **Decide on a method of decision-making**. If you are running a meeting where decisions are made democratically, then you can introduce motions as a way of arriving at decisions on particular matters. If there is insufficient information on a specific issue, you should defer the decision until the needed information becomes available. Debate on important nonvoting issues can also be deferred to future meetings if the agenda does not permit adequate discussion time.

necessary for your knowledgeable participation. Know the problem, its causes, possible solutions, alternatives, and how others have dealt with it. One way to make yourself visible in an organization is to take part successfully in meetings. Careful preparation and wise contribution at meetings often signal to management that you are prepared to take on new responsibilities.

Arrive at the meeting on time. Be ready to speak on an issue, but consider your timing. It may be useful to wait for others to speak first so that you can shape your remarks to best advantage. Productive, enjoyable meetings result from good planning, skilful leadership, and active participation.

Employees looking for ways to recommend themselves to their superior consider meetings to be opportunities for showing their stuff.

Writing the Minutes

Minutes provide a summary of the proceedings of meetings. Minutes may be formal or informal, according to the group and the purpose of the minutes.

Traditional minutes, as illustrated in Figure 14.2, are written for large groups. The following items are usually included in the order shown here:

1. Name of group, date, time, place, name of meeting

2. Names of people present; names of absentees, if appropriate

3. Disposition of previous minutes

4. Old business

5. Announcements, reports

6. Summary of discussion

7. Motions presented in exact wording, vote, action taken

8. Name and signature of individual recording minutes

FIGURE 14.2   Minutes of Meeting, Traditional

PROFESSIONAL SOCIAL WORKERS ASSOCIATION

199x International Convention
Planning Committee Meeting

October 23, 199x, 10 a.m.
Conference Room A, Century Towers

Present: Marilyn Andrews, June Gonzales, Brendan Miller, Nakina
             Sakami, Margaret Zappa, Martha Zebulski

Absent: Amy Costello

The meeting was called to order by Chair Margaret Zappa at
10:05 a.m. Minutes from the June 22 meeting were read and approved.

Announcements

1. Margaret Zappa announced that the time and location of the
   committee's next meeting have been changed to January 4 at the
   Winnipeg Holiday Inn, Sunset Room.
2. Nakina Sakami encouraged committee members to attend a PSA
   issues conference scheduled for February 10.

Reports—Seminars/Workshops

June Gonzales reported that she was working on the development of
five professional workshops for the convention. These major workshops
would be conducted by leaders in office automation, human-resources
management, and personal development. By the next meeting June
expects to have specific individuals committed to presentations.

Conference Hotel Options

Large organizations and legislative bodies require traditional or formal minutes to record their proceedings.

Brendan Miller and Martha Zebulski said that they hoped the
committee members had had time to study the information distributed
earlier regarding the three hotels being considered for the Vancouver
conference: Sheraton Plaza, Hilton Regency, and Embassy Suites
Vancouver. Brendan reported that the Hilton has superior banquet facilities, ample conference rooms, and recently remodelled interiors.
However, the best rate possible for rooms is $95 per night. Martha said
that the Embassy Suites Vancouver also has excellent banquet facilities,
adequate meeting rooms, and will offer us rooms at $82 per night. No one

spoke in favour of the Sheraton Plaza. Following considerable discussion, Nakina Sakami moved that we hold the 199x PSA International Convention at the Embassy Suites Vancouver. Brendan Miller seconded the motion. The motion passed 5–1.

Conference Theme

Margaret Zappa reviewed themes of three previous conventions, all of which focused on technology and the changing role of the secretary. June Gonzales suggested the following possibility: "The New, the Tried and True, and the Unusual." Martha Zebulski suggested a communication theme but had no specific ideas. Several other possibilities were discussed. The chair appointed a subcommittee of June and Martha to bring to the next committee meeting two or three concrete theme ideas.

Exhibits

Brendan Miller suggested that the number of exhibits be expanded at the Vancouver convention. At past conventions, exhibits of new publications, software for keeping client files, and industry products were adequate. For this convention, however, Brendan felt that we should try to involve more companies and products. Discussion followed regarding how this might be accomplished. Brendan Miller moved that the PSA office staff develop a list of possible exhibitors. These potential exhibitors should be sent flyers promoting the convention and encouraging them to be represented. Marilyn Andrews seconded the motion. It passed 6–0.

The meeting was adjourned at 11:46 by Margaret Zappa.

Respectfully submitted,

Nakina Sakami

Nakina Sakami, Secretary

Informal minutes, illustrated in Figure 14.3, are shorter and easier to read. They place less emphasis on the conventions of reporting. Informal minutes concentrate on decisions, action, and responsibility. For these reasons, the minutes of smaller organizations and business meetings may follow this format.

Improving Telephone Techniques

Telephones can be used to increase productivity and generate good will. Most of us, however, give little conscious attention to the impression our telephone personality conveys or to how we could transform the telephone into a

FIGURE 14.3   Minutes of Meeting, Informal

Grand Beach Homeowners' Association
Board of Directors Meeting
April 12, 199x

MINUTES

Directors Present: J. Weinstein, A. McGraw, J. Carson, C. Stefanko,
                     A. Pettus
Directors Absent: P. Hook

Summary of Topics Discussed

1. Report from Architectural Review Committee. Copy attached.

2. Landscaping of centre divider on P.T.H. 59. Three options considered: hiring private landscape designer, seeking volunteers from community, assigning association custodian to complete work.

3. Collection of outstanding assessments. Discussion of delinquent accounts and possible actions.

4. Use of beach club by film companies. Pros: considerable income. Cons: damage to furnishings, loss of facility to homeowners.

5. Nomination of directors to replace those with two-year appointments.

Decisions Reached

1. Hire private landscaper to renovate and plant centre divider on P.T.H. 59.

2. Attach liens to homes of members with delinquent assessments.

3. Submit to general membership vote the question of renting the beach club to film companies.

Action Items

Item	Responsibility	Due Date
1. Landscaping bid	J. Carson	May 1
2. Attorney for liens	P. Hook	April 20
3. Creation of nominating committee	A. Pettus	May 1

Smaller, less formal organizations may use streamlined, more efficient minutes like these.

valuable business tool. To make the most of this form of communication, follow these suggestions.

Making Telephone Calls

1. **Decide whether the call is really necessary.** In some cases, it may be more efficient to deliver the information by memo.

2. **Prepare a mini-agenda.** If the call is necessary, write down notes regarding all the topics you need to discuss. You don't want to call a second time because you forgot an important item the first time.

3. **Use a three-point introduction.** Introduce yourself by giving (a) your name, (b) your affiliation, and (c) your reason for calling. For example, "May I speak to Sara Price? This is Diego Serrano of Datatech, and I'm interested in the location of the March convention." This introduction enables the other individual to respond immediately without asking further questions.

4. **Be cheerful and responsive.** Let your voice show the same kind of animation that you radiate when you greet people in person. In your mind try to envision the individual answering the telephone. Smile at that person. Some companies urge employees to use a mirror to ensure that they smile. A smile affects the tone of voice.

5. **Bring it to a close.** When your business is transacted, it is your responsibility as caller to end the call. This can be difficult. Use closing language, such as "I've certainly enjoyed talking with you," "Thanks for your help," or "I must go now, but may I call you again in the future if I need ...?"

6. **Avoid telephone tag.** If the person you call isn't in, ask the secretary or receptionist when it would be best for you to call again. Leave word that you will call at a specific time—and do it. If you ask an individual to call you, give a time when you can be reached—and be in.

7. **Be prepared to leave a message.** Decide on what message you will leave should you encounter an answering machine or voice-mail system.

Leaving Messages

1. **Identify yourself.** Provide your name, affiliation, and telephone number (include your area code if the call is long distance). Speak slowly and clearly when leaving your message.

2. **Leave the time and date of the telephone call.** Not all answering systems record the date or time a message was received.

3. **Be brief and to the point.** Many answering systems have time limits and will cut you off if your message runs too long. Get to the point quickly. If you would like your call returned, indicate when you will be available to take the call.

Frequent telephone calls interrupt workers and reduce productivity. Consider writing a memo instead of calling.

The three-point intro consists of your name, your business, and a brief description of the subject of your call.

Leave a brief but concise message when responding to voice mail or answering machine.

Receiving Telephone Calls

1. **Identify yourself immediately**. In answering your telephone or someone else's, provide your company name, then your name and other identification, if appropriate. Remember that the caller may not be familiar with your name or your department. Say it clearly and slowly, so that you can be understood.

2. **In answering calls for others, be courteous and helpful**. Don't, however, give out confidential information. It's better to say, "She's away from her desk" or "He's out of the office" than to report a colleague's exact whereabouts.

3. **Take messages carefully**. Repeat the spelling of names and verify telephone numbers. Write the message legibly and record the time and date.

4. **In transferring calls, explain what you're doing**. Explain why you are transferring, and identify the extension to which you are transferring the call in case the caller is disconnected.

Summary

Listening and speaking skills are used extensively in the business world. Listening can be either active or passive. Barriers to listening may be physical, psychological, verbal, or nonverbal, and often arise from passive listening. To become an active listener, try to control your surroundings and your attitude toward the message, stop talking, keep an open mind, listen for main points, take notes, and provide feedback.

As you advance in your career, the ability to express your ideas orally takes on greater significance. Before you make an oral presentation, (1) analyze your audience by considering how you will appeal to them, deciding what you want the audience to believe, what action you want to occur, and what information will most effectively get the message across; (2) organize your topic by creating a purpose statement, focusing on two to four main points, providing a description of the organization of your presentation using verbal signposts, and creating a conclusion that emphasizes what should be remembered; (3) plan simple, readable visual aids that clarify or strengthen your major points.

Delivering an oral presentation takes practice. Don't try to memorize the entire presentation or read from a prepared text. An extemporaneous delivery including prepared notes and key ideas written out in full is most effective. Prepare by timing your presentation. Check the room to ensure that the set-up and equipment are appropriate for your needs. When speaking, begin with a pause and speak your first sentence from memory. Maintain eye contact and control your voice speed, loudness, and vocabulary. Try to move naturally and avoid digressions. After your presentation, control the question-and-answer period by repeating questions for the audience to hear and answering questions directly.

Meetings, a necessary part of business life, can fail because of poor planning. Begin your planning by setting a goal or objective. Prepare an agenda for participants and distribute it two to three days in advance. Begin the meeting with a brief introduction. As a participant, come prepared to contribute.

Your telephone personality is an important part of communicating at work. When making a call, prepare by jotting down a mini-agenda. Use a three-point introduction, be cheerful and responsive, and bring the conversation to a close when your business is transacted. Try to avoid telephone tag. When leaving a message, identify yourself and make sure your message is clear and to the point. When receiving calls, identify yourself and take messages carefully and courteously.

APPLICATION AND PRACTICE—14

Discussion

1. Discuss seven barriers to effective listening and give an example of each from the business world.

2. Discuss the advantages and disadvantages of taking notes while you are listening. When would note taking be most effective?

3. Compare and contrast the development of oral and written reports.

4. Why is it necessary to keep the audience informed of the organization of an oral report?

5. Discuss the duties of a leader and the functions of a participant at business meetings.

Short Answers

6. According to some estimates, adults spend what percent of their communicating time
   a. listening
   b. speaking
   c. reading
   d. writing

7. List 11 ways to improve your listening skills. Be prepared to discuss each.

8. Name five characteristics that you should identify about your audience before preparing an oral report.

9. On how many main points should an oral report concentrate?

10. What is the first step in developing an oral report?

11. List the three parts of an oral report. Be prepared to discuss what goes in each part.

12. List five kinds of visual aids for oral reports. Be prepared to discuss each.

13. List five techniques that are helpful in overcoming stage fright.

14. Notes for an oral report should consist of what?

15. What is an agenda, and what should it include?

16. Who takes the minutes of a meeting, and what are done with them?

17. Give an example of an efficient three-point opening to a telephone call. Use your own name and information.

18. What is telephone tag, and how can it be avoided?

Activities

19. Observe the listening habits in one of your classes for a week. Write a memo report to your instructor describing your observations.

20. Analyze your own listening habits. What are your strengths and weaknesses? Decide on a plan for improving your listening skills. Write a memo to your instructor including your analysis and your improvement plan.

21. You are a student in a business management or other class. Your instructor notices that you have good listening habits. Disturbed by the poor listening skills of some other class members, your instructor asks you to do research and to present a program (for extra credit) to help students improve their listening skills. For this presentation:

a. Write a specific statement of purpose.
b. Prepare a complete outline.
c. Write the introduction.
d. List visual aids that would be appropriate. Describe their content.

22. If you are now employed or have been employed, adapt the assignment in Activity No. 21 to your work. Assume that your supervisor has asked you to present an in-service training workshop that helps employees improve listening skills. Respond to the instructions in items (a) through (d).

23. Visit your library and select a speech from *Vital Speeches of Our Day* or some other source. Write a memo report to your instructor in which you analyze the speech based on the following items:

    a. Effectiveness of the introduction, body, conclusion
    b. Evidence of effective overall organization
    c. Use of verbal indicators to create coherence
    d. Emphasis of two to four main points
    e. Effectiveness of supporting facts (use of examples, statistics, quotations, and so forth)

24. Adapt a newspaper or magazine article to an oral report format. Assume that you are to present this report before your business communications class. Submit the outline, introduction, and conclusion to your instructor, or present the report to your class.

25. Write a memo to your instructor describing the fears or anxieties that you have experienced when presenting a speech. Suggest ways to reduce your fears.

26. Interview two or three individuals in your profession. How is oral communication important in this profession? Does the need for oral skills change as one advances? What suggestions can this individual make for developing proficient oral communication skills among newcomers to the profession? Discuss your findings with your class.

27. Present an impromptu report. Submit to your instructor a list of three to four business or nonbusiness topics you know well. These topics may include a range of interests, from "How to Choose a Used Car" to "The Canadian Trade Outlook." Your instructor will select one topic from this list. Take ten minutes in class to organize an oral presentation that concentrates on an aspect of your topic that can be covered in three minutes. Make notes that include an introduction, body, and conclusion. Your instructor will divide your class into groups of four to six students. Present your report before your group. (All groups will be reporting simultaneously.) As a listening exercise, evaluate each student's report and delivery. Make note of at least three facts you learned from each report. Your instructor may ask you to prepare a short evaluation form for the impromptu reports.

28. If you prepared a business report in Chapter 11, deliver it as an extemporaneous report before your class. Your instructor will determine how much time you have. Use visual aids, if appropriate, and be sure to leave enough time for questions and answers.

29. Plan a meeting. Assume that the next meeting of your students' organization will discuss preparations for a career day in the spring. The group will hear reports from committees working on speakers, business recruiters, publicity, reservations of campus space, set-up of booths, and any other matters you can think of. As president, prepare an agenda for the meeting. Compose your introductory remarks to open the meeting. Your instructor may ask you to submit these two documents or use them in staging an actual meeting in class.

30. Listen for instructions. Your instructor will "talk" or explain the facts from one of the letter or memo assignments in an earlier exercise. The instructor may add extraneous information or omit something vital. Take notes from your instructor's presentation. Ask questions, if necessary. Do not look at a written version of the information. Then write the document prescribed.

31. Practise making and taking telephone calls. Your instructor will divide the class into pairs. Read the scenario for (a), which follows. Take a moment to rehearse your role silently. Then play the role with your partner. If there is time, repeat the scenarios, changing roles, and work through (b) to (f).

Partner 1	**Partner 2**
a. Use your own name. You are the personnel manager of Datatronics, Inc. Call Elizabeth Franklin, office manager at Whispering Pines Resort. Inquire about a job applicant, Lisa Lee, who listed Ms. Franklin as a reference. Place the call.	You are the receptionist for Whispering Pines. The caller asks for Elizabeth Franklin, who is having a root canal done at her dentist's today. Answer the call appropriately.
b. Call Ms. Franklin again the following day to inquire about the same job applicant, Lisa Lee. Ms. Franklin answers today, but she talks on and on, describing the applicant in great detail. Tactfully close the conversation.	Play the role of Ms. Franklin, office manager. Describe Lisa Lee, an imaginary employee (think of someone with whom you've worked). Include many details, such as how well she worked with others, her appearance, her habits, etc.
c. Play the role of receptionist for Fran Morris, of Morris Enterprises. Answer a call for Ms. Morris, who is working in another office, at Ext. 245, where she will accept calls.	Use your own name as legal assistant for Bernard Roget. Call Fran Morris to verify a meeting date Mr. Roget has with Ms. Morris.
d. You are now Fran Morris, president of Morris Enterprises. Call your attorney, Bernard Roget, about a legal problem.	You are the receptionist for the attorney, Bernard Roget. Mr. Roget is skiing in Banff and will return in two days, but he doesn't want his clients to know where he is. Take a message.
e. Call Mr. Roget again.	Take a message again.
f. Call Mr. Roget again, but this time leave a message that will ensure communication.	Take a message.

32. Make a five-minute oral presentation. Select a challenging business-related magazine article of at least 1000 words. Prepare a well-organized presentation that includes the following: (a) an attention-getting opening plus an introduction to the major ideas, (b) three to four main points that are easy for the audience to identify, and (c) a conclusion that reviews the main points and ends by asking for questions. Avoid self-conscious remarks such as "My report is about ..." or "The article says ..." or "I guess that ends it." Use one visual aid. Allow no more than three minutes for questions and answers. Your instructor may ask you to distribute copies of your article to the class one or two days prior to your presentation so that they may ask informed questions. Turn in an outline to your instructor before your presentation.

33. Prepare a five- to ten-minute oral report. Use one of the following topics or a topic that you and your instructor agree on. You are an expert who has been called in to explain some aspects of the topic before a group of interested individuals. Since your time is limited, prepare a concise yet forceful report with effective visual aids.

 a. How and why are some companies (such as Apple Computer) building recreation and parties into the corporate culture?

 b. What kinds of employment advertisements are legal, and what kinds are potentially illegal?

 c. How should one dress for an employment interview?

 d. What is the economic outlook for a given product (shoes, women's apparel, domestic cars, TV sets, etc.) this year?

 e. What franchise would offer the best opportunities for investment for an entrepreneur in your area?

 f. What brand and model of computer and printer represent the best buys for home use today?

 g. What is the current employment outlook in three career areas of interest to you?

 h. Why should you be hired for a position that you have applied for?

 i. For its sales personnel, should your company rent automobiles, own them, or pay mileage costs on employee-owned vehicles?

 j. Where should your professional organization hold its next convention?

 k. What local plant or animal is endangered, and how can it be protected?

 l. What evidence supports the view that computer terminals are dangerous to users?

 m. How can your school (or company) improve its image?

 n. Why should individuals invest in a company or scheme of your choice?

 o. What are some common and uncommon ways in which fax messages are being used today?

GRAMMAR/MECHANICS CHECKUP—14

Punctuation Review

Review Sections 1.17 and 2.01 to 2.29 of the Grammar/Mechanics Handbook. Study each of the following statements and insert any necessary punctuation. In the space provided for each statement, indicate the number of marks that you added. When you finish, compare your responses with those shown below. If your responses differ, study carefully the specific principles shown in parentheses.

Example: Regina has never been much of a financial mecca, but suddenly it has attracted some new insurance companies.

                      1 (2.05)

 1. A Toronto based law firm Sanders & Dempsey has been promoting Regina's location.

 2. Saskatchewan may have fewer restrictions therefore many smaller insurance companies are rushing to apply for full service and limited service privileges.

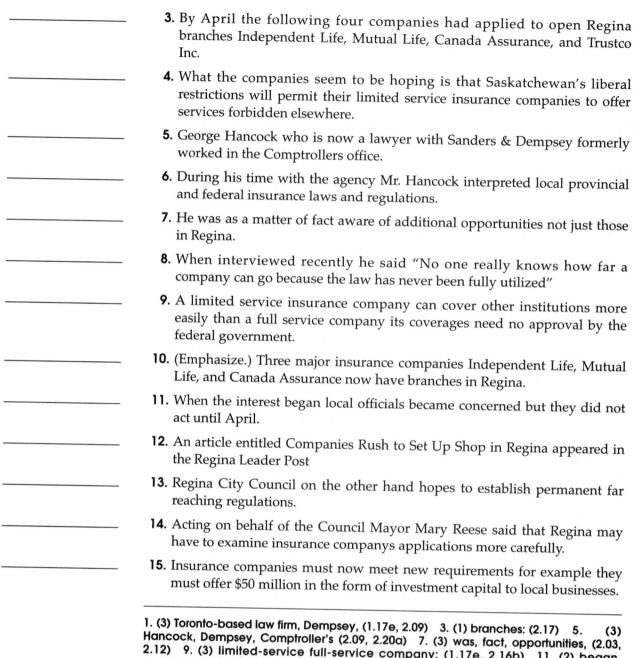

3. By April the following four companies had applied to open Regina branches Independent Life, Mutual Life, Canada Assurance, and Trustco Inc.

4. What the companies seem to be hoping is that Saskatchewan's liberal restrictions will permit their limited service insurance companies to offer services forbidden elsewhere.

5. George Hancock who is now a lawyer with Sanders & Dempsey formerly worked in the Comptrollers office.

6. During his time with the agency Mr. Hancock interpreted local provincial and federal insurance laws and regulations.

7. He was as a matter of fact aware of additional opportunities not just those in Regina.

8. When interviewed recently he said "No one really knows how far a company can go because the law has never been fully utilized"

9. A limited service insurance company can cover other institutions more easily than a full service company its coverages need no approval by the federal government.

10. (Emphasize.) Three major insurance companies Independent Life, Mutual Life, and Canada Assurance now have branches in Regina.

11. When the interest began local officials became concerned but they did not act until April.

12. An article entitled Companies Rush to Set Up Shop in Regina appeared in the Regina Leader Post

13. Regina City Council on the other hand hopes to establish permanent far reaching regulations.

14. Acting on behalf of the Council Mayor Mary Reese said that Regina may have to examine insurance companys applications more carefully.

15. Insurance companies must now meet new requirements for example they must offer $50 million in the form of investment capital to local businesses.

1. (3) Toronto-based law firm, Dempsey, (1.17e, 2.09) 3. (1) branches: (2.17)   5.   (3) Hancock, Dempsey, Comptroller's (2.09, 2.20a)   7. (3) was, fact, opportunities, (2.03, 2.12)   9. (3) limited-service full-service company; (1.17e, 2.16b)   11. (2) began, concerned; (2.06a, 2.16c) 13. (4) Council, hand, permanent, far-reaching (1.17e, 2.03, 2.08)   15. (2) requirements; example, (2.16)

GRAMMAR/MECHANICS CHALLENGE—14

Document for Revision

The following short presentation is wordy and contains faults in grammar, punctuation, spelling, and number form. Drawing upon the guidelines provided in the Grammar/Mechanics Handbook, revise the document.

Poor Document

Visual Aids

Before making a business prsentation consider this proverb, "Tell me, I forget. Show me; I remember, Involve me; I understand." Owing to the fact that your goals as a speaker are to make the listeners understand remember and act on your ideas; include visuals to get them interested and involved. 3 or the most popular visuals are: overhead transparencys, slides, and handouts.

Overhead transparencies. Student and professional speakers alike rely in large measure on the overhead projecter for a great many reasons. Most meeting areas ore equiped with projectors and screens. Moreover acetate transparencys for the overhead are cheap, they are easily prepared on a computer or copier; and they are simple to use.

Slides. Slides deliver excellent resolution, creates an impression of professionalism, and they can be seen by large groups. Yet, their cost, inflexibility, and fairly difficult preparation off-set there advantages. Moreover, because they must be projected in a darkened room; speakers loose eye contact with the audience. He runs the risk of of the problem of putting the viewers to sleep.

Handouts. You can enhance and compliment your presentations by distributing pictures, outlines and brochures, articals, charts, summarys, or other supplements. You should, however, hold in abeyance the distribution of handouts until such time as you are finished.

Note

1. Based on "Chats," Day-Timers, Inc., Allentown, PA.

1 Formatting Letters and Memorandums

The first impression a letter or memo makes on its reader often determines whether that document will actually be read. The appearance of a document also affects the reader's reaction to its contents. A neatly typed letter on good paper, arranged in proper form and centred, is inviting to read. It carries a nonverbal message indicating that the writer cares about this document and its effect on the reader. An attractive letter or memo suggests that the writer is a caring and careful individual. It suggests that the business he or she represents is successful and well managed.

To send a positive, nonverbal message along with the words of your letters and memos, pay attention to form and appearance. Make your documents neat, correct, and inviting. So that you may become familiar with customary format and placement, here is a description of the parts and styles for business letters and memorandums.

Letter Parts

Letterhead. Most business organizations use 8½-by-11-inch paper printed with a letterhead displaying their official name, address, and telephone number (see Figure A1.1). Sometimes the letterhead also includes a logo and an advertising message (such as *Great Western Insurance: A new brand of insurance).*

Return address. If you type a letter on paper without a printed letterhead, place your address immediately above the date (see Figure A1.2, Letter 4). Do not include your name here; you will type your name at the end of your letter. In typing your return address, avoid abbreviations except for the province, which appears as a two-letter code (see Table A1.1).

TABLE A1.1 Two-Letter Provincial, Territorial, and U.S. State Abbreviations

State/Prov./Terr.	Code	State/Prov./Terr.	Code	State/Prov./Terr.	Code	State/Prov./Terr.	Code
Alabama	AL	Indiana	IN	**New Brunswick**	**NB**	Puerto Rico	PR
Alaska	AK	Iowa	IA	**Newfoundland**	**NF**	**Quebec**	**QC**
Alberta	**AB**	Kansas	KS	New Hampshire	NH	Rhode Island	RI
Arizona	AZ	Kentucky	KY	New Jersey	NJ	**Saskatchewan**	**SK**
Arkansas	AR	Louisiana	LA	New Mexico	NM	South Carolina	SC
British Columbia	**BC**	Maine	ME	New York	NY	South Dakota	SD
California	CA	**Manitoba**	**MB**	North Carolina	NC	Tennessee	TN
Colorado	CO	Maryland	MD	North Dakota	ND	Texas	TX
Connecticut	CT	Massachusetts	MA	**Northwest Territories**	**NT**	Utah	UT
Delaware	DE	Michigan	MI	**Nova Scotia**	**NS**	Vermont	VT
District of Columbia	DC	Minnesota	MN	Ohio	OH	Virginia	VA
Florida	FL	Mississippi	MS	Oklahoma	OK	Washington	WA
Georgia	GA	Missouri	MO	**Ontario**	**ON**	Wisconsin	WI
Hawaii	HI	Montana	MT	Oregon	OR	Wyoming	WY
Idaho	ID	Nebraska	NE	Pennsylvania	PA	**Yukon Territory**	**YT**
Illinois	IL	Nevada	NV	**Prince Edward Island**	**PE**		

Dateline. On letterhead paper, type the date two line spaces below the last line of the letterhead or 5 cm from the top edge of the paper (line 13). On plain paper place the date immediately below your return address. Since the date goes on line 13, start the return address an appropriate number of lines above it. The most common dateline format is as follows:

June 9, 1993

For European or military correspondence, use the following dateline format:

9 June 1993

Inside address. Type the inside address—that is, the address of the organization receiving the letter—single-spaced, starting at the left margin. The number of lines between the dateline and the inside address depends on the size of the body of the letter, the size of type (the pitch) used, and the length of the typing lines. Generally, two to ten lines are appropriate.

Be careful to duplicate the exact wording and spelling of the recipient's name and address on your documents. Copy this information from the letterhead of the correspondence you are answering. If, for example, you are responding to *Jackson & Perkins Co.*, don't address your letter to *Jackson and Perkins Corp.*

For inside (letter and envelope) addresses, use a courtesy title, such as *Mr., Ms., Mrs., Dr., Professor,* or *Reverend*, whenever possible. If you are unsure of a woman's title, *Ms.* is appropriate. If an individual's name does not indicate gender (for example, *Leslie* or *Pat*), omit the title.

Remember, the inside address is there not for readers who already know who and where they are, but for the writers so that they may accurately file a copy.

In general, avoid abbreviations unless they appear in the printed letterhead of the document being answered.

Letters may be addressed to an organization, to an individual within an organization, or to the attention of an individual within an organization. Study the following examples and the salutations appropriate for each.

Letter Addressed to an Organization	Letter Addressed to an Individual Within an Organization
Canadian Metals, Inc. 236 Sunset Avenue Toronto, ON M4W 3W2	Mr. Arnold M. Hansen Canadian Metals, Inc. 236 Sunset Avenue Toronto, ON M4W 3W2
Ladies and Gentlemen:	Dear Mr. Hansen:

Letter Addressed to the Attention of an Individual Within an Organization

Canadian Metals, Inc. Attention Mr. Arnold M. Hansen **OR** 236 Sunset Avenue Toronto, ON M4W 3W2	Canadian Metals, Inc. 236 Sunset Avenue Toronto, ON M4W 3W2
Ladies and Gentlemen:	Attention Mr. Arnold M. Hansen Ladies and Gentlemen:

Attention line.   An attention line, as shown in the preceding example as well as in Figure A1.2, Letter 2, allows you to send your message officially to an organization but for the attention of a specific individual, officer, or department. Notice that the appropriate salutation for a letter addressed to an organization (despite its attention line) is *Ladies and Gentlemen.*

Attention lines are useful because they let you direct your message to a specific individual. However, if the addressed individual is no longer with the organization, your letter will be processed by an appropriate successor. It would not be forwarded as a private letter to the individual addressed on the envelope.

Place the attention line two lines below the inside address, or type it immediately below the organization name within the inside address (see Figure A1.2, Letter 2). The latter position is preferable for word processing equipment since the address can then be automatically copied to the envelope and the attention line will not interfere with the last-line placement of the postal code. (Mail can be sorted automatically by optical character scanners at the post office if the postal code appears in the last line of a typed address.) A colon following the word *Attention* is optional.

Salutation.   Place the letter greeting, or salutation, two lines below the last line of the inside address or the attention line (if used). The letter may be addressed to an individual (*Dear Scott* or *Dear Mr. Waters*) or to an organization (*Ladies and Gentlemen*). Even if you are on a first-name basis, the appropriate punctuation following the salutation is a colon, not a comma. Do not use an individual's full name in the salutation (not *Dear Mr. Scott Waters*) unless you are unsure of the addressee's gender. If you do not know whether to use *Mr.* or *Ms.*, then you may include both the given and surnames without a courtesy title: *Dear Leslie Jones.*

Subject line. A brief indication of the subject of the document may be typed two lines below the salutation (see Figure A1.1). The subject line is often entirely in capitals with a colon following the word *SUBJECT.*

Body. Most business letters are typed single-spaced, with double spacing between paragraphs.

Complimentary close. Typed two lines below the last line of the letter, the complimentary close may be formal (*Very truly yours*) or informal (*Sincerely yours* or *Cordially*).

Author, title, department. Three to four blank lines should be left after the complimentary close so that the author has space to sign. The author's name should be typed, in addition to the signature, so that it's legible. The title, department, or division identification may be included if desired.

Reference initials. If used, the initials of the typist and author are typed two lines below the author's name and title.

Enclosure notation. When an enclosure or attachment accompanies the letter, a notation to that effect is typed two lines below the reference initials. This notation reminds the typist to insert the enclosure in the envelope, and it reminds the recipient to look for the enclosure or attachment. The notation may be spelled out (*Enclosure, Attachment*), or it may be abbreviated (*Enc., Att.*). It may indicate the number of enclosures or attachments, and it may also identify an enclosure specifically (*Enclosure: Brochure No. 213*).

Copy notation. If you make copies of correspondence for other individuals, you may use *cc* to indicate carbon copy, *pc* to indicate photocopy, or merely *c* for any kind of copy (see Figure A1.2, Letter 3). A colon following the initial(s) is optional.

Letter Styles

You should be familiar with at least four letter styles.

Block Style. The letter shown in Figure A1.2, Letter 1, is arranged in block style. This means that all lines begin at the left margin. Since this style is easy to format, it's quite popular.

Figure A1.1 Parts of Business Letters

Letterhead

CENTRAL BELL

···

Serving all your communication needs

···

13590 Viceroy Boulevard
Whitby, ON L1N 3R6

↓ line 13

Dateline

September 22, 19xx

↓ 3 to 10 lines

Inside Address

Software Services, Inc.
Attention Telecommunications Manager
19533 Bertrand Boulevard
Burlington, ON L6V 2M3

↓ 2 lines

Salutation

Ladies and Gentlemen:

↓ 2 lines

SUBJECT: CHANGES IN TELEPHONE SERVICE

↓ 2 lines

Body

As part of our plan to expand and improve telephone service provided to Ontario customers, we will be making some changes in the central office equipment serving your area. This will enable us to offer you a variety of new services.

The new equipment we are installing may affect some customers' telephone equipment. Please contact your dealer prior to December 1, which is our change date. We plan to have our new equipment in operation approximately January 1.

Your equipment dealer will need to know these facts:

1. Central Bell is installing DMS-100 equipment in the Reseda 01 Central Office.

2. Installation is planned for December 15.

The new switching equipment will offer many electronic services such as Call Waiting, Call Forwarding, Speed Calling, and other features. Enclosed is a brochure describing these services. Requests for changes or additions to your existing telephone service should be directed to your Central Bell business office representative at (905) 430-1902.

↓ 2 lines

Complimentary
Close

Sincerely,

↓ 2 lines

Organization Name

CENTRAL BELL

Jerry C. Tuffeland

↓ 4 lines

Author

Jerry C. Tuffeland
Vice President, Services

2882 Rodeo Road
Calgary, AB
T2N 6C5

November 17, 19xx

Mr. Mark S. Stevenson
Office Manager
Galaxy Enterprises
17690 Venture Boulevard
Edmonton, AB T5L 9R4

Dear Mr. Stevenson

SUBJECT: BLOCK LETTER FORMAT

This letter illustrates full block style. All typed lines begin at the left margin. The date is usually typed two inches from the top or two lines below the last line of the letterhead, whichever is lower.

This letter also shows open punctuation. No colon follows the salutation, and no comma follows the complimentary close. Although this punctuation style is quite efficient, we find that most of our customers prefer to include punctuation after the salutation and the complimentary close.

If a subject line is included, it is typed two lines below the salutation. The word *SUBJECT* is optional. Most readers will recognize a statement in this position as the subject without an identifying label.

The complimentary close appears two lines below the end of the last paragraph. Four lines below the complimentary close appear the typed name and identification of the letter author.

The full block style is quite popular among word processing specialists because it requires fewer keystrokes than other letter styles.

Sincerely

Rochelle Davis

Rochelle Davis
Graphic Designer

wts

Letter 1
Block Letter Style, Open Punctuation

PACIFIC
WESTERN
COLLEGE
885 Big Tree Highway
Vancouver, BC V6N 3H6

May 12, 19xx

First Federal Banking Services
Attention Office Manager
220 Oceanview Avenue
Victoria, BC V4C 9L2

Ladies and Gentlemen:

Here is the information you requested regarding modified block letter style.

The modified block style letter is different from the full block style in two respects: (1) the date may be centred or may appear flush with the right margin, as shown here, and (2) the closing lines begin five spaces to the left of the page centre.

In the modified block style letter, paragraphs may be indented five spaces or blocked at the left margin. Either style is acceptable in business offices.

If a letter contains an attention line, it may appear in one of two positions: on the second line of the inside address (as shown here) or two lines below the last line of the inside address block. We recommend that it appear as shown in this letter because it may be copied to the envelope easily with word processing equipment.

Many business organizations prefer the modified block letter style because of its traditional appearance. Enclosed is additional information regarding letter styles.

Cordially yours,

Darlene McClure

Darlene McClure, Professor
Office Technologies Department

trt
Enclosure

Letter 2
Modified Block Style, Mixed Punctuation

❖ *UNITED INSURANCE SERVICES*

128 Fifth Street South, Winnipeg, MB R3T 5X4

November 12, 19xx

Professor Karen Butts
Department of Business
Prairieview Community College
Brandon, MB R2T 9B1

SIMPLIFIED LETTER FORMAT

This letter, Professor Butts, illustrates the simplified letter format that our office prefers. This format has the following distinctive features:

1. All lines begin at the left margin.
2. The salutation and complimentary close are omitted.
3. A subject line in all caps appears three lines below the inside address and three lines above the first paragraph.
4. The author's name and identification appear five lines below the last paragraph.

We enjoy this letter style because it's efficient. It's also useful because we no longer must worry about the property of salutation, complimentary closes, and individuals' titles. Moreover, this letter style is effective in writing to businesses when we have no individual to address.

James D. Clark

JAMES D. CLARK, VICE PRESIDENT

wer

c Victoria Munoz

Letter 3
Simplified Letter Style

3420 Concord Lane
Prince Albert, SK S4T 3T1
March 30, 19xx

Ms. Marilyn Theissman, President
Rockaway Health Care Specialists
1045 Blue Duck Drive
Saskatoon, SK S7K 5L3

Dear Ms. Theissman:

At your request I am sending you this message in illustration of the personal business letter style.

This letter style is appropriate for people writing letters as individuals instead of writing as representatives of business organizations.

The heading includes the writer's street and city address, along with the date. These lines begin on line 11 at the centre of the page, or they may be blocked to and at the right margin. The inside address appears about four to eight lines below the date, depending upon the length of the letter.

The letter may be typed in block or modified block style with open or mixed punctuation. The paragraphs may be indented or blocked.

The writer signs the letter between the complimentary close and the typed signature. Normally no reference initials are included since the writer has prepared the letter.

Sincerely,

Melanie Grable

Melanie Grable

Letter 4
Personal Business Letter Style

Modified block style. The letters shown in Figures A1.1 and A1.2, Letter 2, illustrate modified block style. The date may be centred, begun at the centre of the page, or backspaced from the right margin. The closing lines—including the complimentary close, author's name, and author's title—begin at the centre. The first line of each paragraph may begin at the left margin or may be indented five or ten spaces. All other lines begin at the left margin.

Simplified style. Many organizations today prefer the simplified letter style shown in Figure A1.2, Letter 3. All lines begin at the left margin. A subject line appears in capital letters four blank lines below the inside address. The salutation and complimentary close are omitted. The signer's name and identification appear in capital letters four blank lines below the last paragraph. Although seldom seen in business, this letter style is efficient and avoids the problem of appropriate salutations and courtesy titles.

Personal business style. Individuals preparing their own personal letters on plain paper should follow the style shown in Figure A1.2, Letter 4. The writer's street and city address appear on lines 11 and 12. The date immediately follows on line 13. The writer may choose block or modified block formatting.

Memorandum Parts

Printed forms. For intra-office correspondence, many offices use memorandum forms imprinted with the organization name. This stationery is different from letterhead paper intended for external correspondence. Memorandum stationery generally displays only the company name, division, or department; it does not include the company address or descriptive advertising.

Headings. Memorandum forms typically have the following printed guide words: *To, From, Date,* and *Subject.* The position of the guide word *Date* may vary. In filling in information following the guide words, align the bottom of the print with the bottom of the guide words. Leave two spaces after the guide words before beginning the text.

Body. The message of a memo begins three lines beneath the last guide word. Leave 1¼-inch side margins, and single-space the body of a memo.

Signature. Unlike business letters, memos are not signed. Instead, authors may sign their initials after their typed names following *From* in the heading.

Memorandum Styles

Memorandums are generally typed on printed memo stationery. However, if no printed forms are available, memos may be typed on plain paper or on paper printed with the company letterhead. On a full sheet of paper, start on line seven. Double-space and type in capitals the guide words: *TO:, FROM:, DATE:, SUBJECT:*. Align all the fill-in information two spaces after the longest guide word (*SUBJECT:*). Leave three lines after the last line of the heading and begin typing the body of the memo. Like business letters, memos are single-spaced.

Memos are generally formatted with side margins of about 3 cm, or they may conform to the printed memo form, as shown in Figure A1.3.

Formatting and Spacing

Business letters should be typed so that they are framed by white space. By setting proper margins and by controlling the number of line spaces between the date and the inside address, you can arrange your letters so that they are attractively balanced on the page. Here are typical settings for 10- or 12-pitch machines. Reduce the number of lines following the date if your letter has special parts such as a subject line, attention line, or company name in the closing.

	Letters with 150 Words or Fewer in the Body	Letters with 150 to 250 Words in the Body	Letters with 250 to 350 Words in the Body
Side margins:	5 cm	4 cm	3 cm
Lines after the date:	7 to 11 (12 pitch)	5 to 9 (12 pitch)	4 to 6 (10 pitch)
	6 to 8 (10 pitch)	3 to 5 (12 pitch)	3 to 4 (10 pitch)

In preparing documents on a typewriter, follow accepted spacing conventions. Space twice after a period, question mark, or exclamation point at the end of a sentence. Generally space once after periods following abbreviations (such as *Mr. J. A. Jones*). Space twice after a colon, except in the expression of time (3:15 p.m.). Space once after semicolons. In preparing documents with a computer word-processing program, never double-space.

FIGURE A1.3 Memorandum

↓ line 7

TO: Almeda Wilmarth, Supervisor   DATE: January 24, 19xx
            Legal Division

FROM: Judy Leusink, Director J.L.
            Personnel Services

SUBJECT: DENTAL-CARE BENEFITS SEMINAR

↓ 3 lines

Please plan to attend a seminar February 8 at 4 p.m. in the Main
Conference Room to learn about options in our new dental-care plan.

At that meeting a representative from Fidelity Mutual will describe the
"Denti-Care" program. This plan is designed to provide the most cost-
effective form of dental care for you and your family. If you or one of
your dependents requires dental care, you will be able to choose from a
variety of options. The representative from Fidelity Mutual will discuss
the options available. At this meeting you will learn more about the
following:

   1. How "Denti-Care" works for Data General employees

   2. Options for major dental coverage

   3. Your responsibilities

   4. Our contract benefits

If you are unable to attend, please call Sherri Jones at Ext. 255.

Documenting Information

Long reports typically include information from other sources. You can quote this information directly, using the exact words of the original author, or you can paraphrase, putting the author's ideas into your own words. In both cases, credit must be given to the original author. To do this, use the conventions of documentation—that is, follow accepted procedures for showing where information originated. Although many methods of documenting reports are currently in practice, we will discuss only three: (1) the footnote method, (2) the endnote method, and (3) the parenthetic, or MLA, method. The footnote method was commonly used for research papers because readers could easily see references. However, it was difficult for typists to judge the position of these references at the bottoms of pages. For that reason, some writers began using endnotes. The parenthetic method simplifies the documentation process even further. But we may see a return to footnote and endnote use, now that many computerized programs make the process so easy.

In this discussion, we shall be concerned only with suggestions for the writers of long business reports. We shall not try to present a comprehensive treatment of documentation, including all the exceptions and procedures appropriate for authors of books, doctoral dissertations, and masters' theses. For more detailed treatments of documentation techniques, see *The Chicago Manual of Style*, Fourteenth Edition, University of Chicago Press; *The MLA Handbook for Writers of Research Papers*, Third Edition, Modern Language Association of America; *A Manual for Writers of Term Papers, Theses, and Dissertations* by Kate L. Turabian; or *HOW 6: Handbook for Office Workers*, Sixth Edition, by Clark and Clark.

Footnote Method

The traditional method of citing sources is footnoting. As the name suggests, references appear at the foot or bottom of each page. Refer to Figure A2.1 for illustration of some of the following suggestions regarding footnotes in a long report.

1. Place a superscript (raised number) at the end of the sentence or clause that contains information to be acknowledged, regardless of where the quoted or paraphrased data appears in the sentence or clause.

2. Number footnotes consecutively throughout the report.

3. Indent and single-space quoted material of four or more typewritten lines as shown in Footnote 2 of Figure A2.1.

4. At the bottom of the page, use a 1-½-inch (4 cm) line to separate the footnotes from the text.

5. Single-space footnote entries and double-space between them.

6. For book entries include author (first name first); name of book in capital letters, in italics, or underscored (the underscore represents italics); edition; publishing information in parentheses (city, province or state abbreviation if city is not commonly recognizable, name of publisher, date); and page or pages cited.

7. For periodical entries include author (if given), article title in quotation marks, periodical title underscored, date, volume, and page or pages cited.

8. For newspaper entries include author or description of article (such as "editorial"), main heading of article in quotation marks, newspaper name underscored, date, page or pages cited, and columns (optional).

Here are some of the most frequently used footnote forms.

Book, One Author

[1]Mara Brown, *Landing on Your Feet: A Canadian Guide to Surviving, Coping, and Prospering from Job Loss* (Toronto: McGraw Publishing, 1992), p. 18.

Book, Many Authors

[2]Marinn Collins, David Studd, and John Wallace, *Making Career Decisions* (Scarborough, ON: Nelson Canada, 1984), pp. 138–45.

Academic Journal Article

[3]Alan C. Cairns, "The Governments and Societies of Canadian Federalism," *Canadian Journal of Political Science* 10, no. 4 (1987), pp. 48–51.

Monthly Magazine Article

[4]Mark Snyder, "Self-Fulfilling Stereotypes," *Psychology Today*, July 1982, p. 68.

Newspaper Article

[5]Jane Turner, "Finding Work in the 90's," *Winnipeg Free Press*, 22 August 1993: p. A1.

Government Publication

[6]Canada Employment and Immigration, *How to Find a Job* (Ottawa: Supply and Services Canada, 1991), p. 20.

Encyclopedia Article Without Author

[7]"Great Lakes," *Encyclopaedia Britannica*, 15th ed. (1985).

Interview

[8]Maude Barlow (National Chairperson, Council of Canadians), personal interview, 21 May 1993.

In referring to a previously mentioned footnote, cite the page number along with the author's last name or a shortened form of the title if no author is given (see Footnote 3 in Figure A2.1). The Latin forms *ibid.*, *op. cit.*, *loc. cit.*, and *et al.* are rarely seen in business reports today.

Endnote Method

A second method of documenting reports is the endnote method. As with the footnote method, superscript numerals within the text identify data to be cited. However, instead of appearing at the bottom of each page, source notes are located at the end of the report on a separate page. The title starts on line 13. Figure A2.2 illustrates endnotes. Notice that no superscripts are used in note numbering.

The endnote method is easier for the author than the footnote method because notes do not have to be placed on the same page where they are cited. Word processing further simplifies the task. As the author keys each reference, the computer software automatically numbers references and renumbers if changes are made. When the text is completed, the system prints a numbered list of all references.

Parenthetic, or MLA, Method

The third method of documentation, recommended by the Modern Language Association (MLA), uses parenthetical information to identify references. Within the text a brief reference to identify a source is inserted. This parenthetical comment usually consists of the author's last name and the page on which the reference is found. If the work is anonymous or the author's name is unavailable, an abbreviated title is used to identify the reference. The following excerpt illustrates the parenthetic documentation method.

> Several private studies on the subject of occupational health are now being conducted (Peters 127). In addition, the Department of Health plans to develop its own study at a cost of $600,000 ("Uneasy Silence" 54).

When the author is mentioned in the textual material, it is unnecessary to include the name again in the parenthetical reference. Just insert the page reference, as shown here.

Peter also notes that stress could be a contributing factor in the health problems reported thus far (135)

At the end of the report, all references are included on a page entitled "Works Cited," as illustrated in Figure A2.3

FIGURE A2.1   Portion of Report Page Showing Footnoting

In our own day, satirical magazines have flourished only in French-speaking Quebec where *Croc* celebrated its tenth anniversary in 1989, and an upstart competitor *Safarir* (derived from "Cela me fait rire," or "that makes me laugh") has achieved a monthly circulation of 45,000 in little more than two years.[1] In the early years of this century, humorous publications such as Bob Edward's *Calgary Eye-Opener*, a newspaper, and *The Goblin*, a magazine launched by University of Toronto students after the First World War, were immensely popular. *The Goblin* claimed to have a circulation of more than 10,500 copies and the biggest newsstand sale in Canada after its first year of publication,[2] but English-speaking Canadians seemed to lose their sense of humour after that. One of the *The Goblin*'s best cartoonists, Richard Taylor, subsequently moved to the United States and became a regular contributor to *The New Yorker*;[3] about sixty years later, Graydon Carter abandoned a failing magazine in Ottawa to achieve a huge success in New York where, in 1985, he cofounded the monthly satirical scandal magazine *Spy*.[4]

---

[1] "Safarir's Laughing All the Way to the Bank," Marketing 12 (1990), p. 26.

[2] Peter Desbarats and Terry Mosher, The Hecklers (Toronto: McClelland & Stewart, 1979), p. 83.

[3] Desbarats and Mosher, p. 83.

[4] Fraser Sutherland, The Monthly Epic—A History of Canadian Magazines (Toronto: Fitzhenry & Whiteside, 1989), p. 34.

FIGURE A2.2 Portion of Report Page Showing Endnotes

NOTES

1. "Safarir's Laughing All the Way to the Bank," <u>Marketing</u> 12 (1990), p. 26.

2. Peter Desbarats and Terry Mosher, <u>The Hecklers</u> (Toronto: McClelland & Stewart, 1979), p. 83.

3. Desbarats and Mosher, p. 83.

4. Fraser Sutherland, <u>The Monthly Epic—A History of Canadian Magazines</u> (Toronto: Fitzhenry & Whiteside, 1989), p. 34.

FIGURE A2.3 Works Cited, MLA Method

WORKS CITED

Desbarats, Peter. *Guide to Canadian News Media*. Toronto: Harcourt Brace Jovanovich, 1990.
Ontario. Special Senate Committee on the Mass Media. *Report*. Ottawa: Queen's Printer, 1970.
"Safarir's Laughing All the Way to the Bank." *Marketing* 12 (1990): 26.
Walsh, Doris. "Who Will Your Readers Be in the Next Decade?" *Folio* 1 (15 Mar. 1990): 84–89.

The Bibliography

A bibliography is an alphabetic list of materials on a topic. If used, it appears after appendix items. Although it looks similar to footnotes or endnotes, the bibliography is different in these ways:

1. The bibliography is optional. It is often included in a long report as an added resource to the reader. It may be omitted if the total number of footnotes is fewer than ten.

2. Its entries are arranged alphabetically by author for easy reference.

3. It may include all the works consulted as well as those actually cited.

4. For readability, entries are displayed in hanging indented form—that is, the second and succeeding lines are indented five spaces from the left margin.

5. The arrangement and punctuation of each entry is somewhat different from footnote form.

Study the following entries to note their differences from footnote form. See page 301 for an example of a complete bibliography as part of a long report.

Book, One Author

Brown, Mara. *Landing on Your Feet: A Canadian Guide to Surviving, Coping, and Prospering from Job Loss.* Toronto: McGraw Publishing, 1992.

Book, Same Author

———. *Life After Your Career.* Winnipeg: Cargo Press, 1990.

Book, Many Authors

Collins, Marinn, David Studd, and John Wallace. *Making Career Decisions.* Scarborough, ON: Nelson Canada, 1984.

Magazine or Journal Article

Cairns, Alan C. "The Governments and Societies of Canadian Federalism." *Canadian Journal of Political Science* 10, no. 4 (1987), pp. 48–51.

Newspaper Article

Turner, Jane. "Finding Work in the 90's." *Winnipeg Free Press.* 22 August 1993, p. A1.

Government Publication

Canada Employment and Immigration. *How to Find a Job.* Ottawa: Supply and Services Canada, 1991.

Encyclopedia Article Without Author

"Great Lakes." *Encyclopaedia Britannica.* 15th ed., 1985.

Interview

Maude Barlow. Personal interview. 21 May 1993.

Electronic Sources

A general rule of thumb for documenting electronic sources is to cite as much information as is available. When documenting CD-ROM databases, simply add the publication medium to the citation.

CD-ROM

The Oxford English Dictionary. 2nd ed. CD-ROM. Oxford: Oxford University Press, 1992.

Citations of CD-ROM databases that are regularly updated and provide text of books, articles, and other publications should include bibliographic information for the print version (if available), title of database, publication medium, producer of database (if relevant), and date of latest revision.

CD-ROM Update

Garfield, Terrance. "Life in the Nova Scotia Coal Mines." *The Globe and Mail* 24 April 1996. *Canadian Business and Current Affairs (CBCA)* CD-ROM. October 1996.

To document information retrieved from an on-line source, include print version information (if applicable), publication medium (on-line), network or service used to retrieve the information (Internet, CompuServe, Canadian On-line Enquiry, INFOGLOBE), and date of retrieval.

On-line Source

Garfield, Terrance. "Life in the Nova Scotia Coal Mines." *The Globe and Mail* 24 April 1996. INFOGLOBE. On-line. 15 May 1996.

You may add the electronic address you used to retrieve the document.

Sweeny, Richard. "Of Bits and Bytes." *Electronic Computer Magazine* 16 (Sept. 1996): 10 pp. On-line. Internet. 12 Oct. 1996. Available: ecmag.mb.ca

Treat E-mail memos and letters as you would nonelectronic messages.

E-mail

Moody, Sheila. "Parking Passes." E-mail to the author. 12 March 1996.

Citations of information retrieved from public electronic bulletin boards or Usenet newsgroups should include date of posting (followed by description *On-line posting*), electronic address, network, and date of retrieval.

On-line Posting

Singh, Harbinder. "Re: Technical writing and Intercultural Communication." 15 June 1996. On-line posting. Newsgroup tech.edu.communica. Usenet. 23 June 1996.

Grammar/Mechanics Handbook

The Grammar/Mechanics Handbook consists of

1. Grammar/Mechanics Diagnostic Test

- To assess students' strengths and weaknesses in eight areas of grammar and mechanics.

2. Grammar/Mechanics Profile

- To pinpoint specific areas in which students need remedial instruction or review.

3. Grammar Review with Review Exercises

- To review basic principles of grammar, punctuation, capitalization, and number style.

- To provide reinforcement exercises allowing students to interact with the principles of grammar and test their comprehension.

- To serve as a systematic reference to grammar and mechanics throughout the writing course.

- To be used for classroom-centred instruction or self-guided learning.

Grammar/Mechanics Diagnostic Test

Name: _____

This diagnostic test is intended to reveal your strengths and weaknesses in using the following:

plural nouns	adjectives	punctuation
possessive nouns	adverbs	capitalization style
pronouns	prepositions	number style
verbs	conjunctions	

The test is organized into sections corresponding to these categories. In sections A through G, each sentence is either correct or has one error related to the category under which it is listed. If a sentence is correct, write C. If it has an error, underline the error and write the correct form in the space provided. Use ink to record your answers. When you finish, check your answers with your instructor and fill out the Grammar/Mechanics Profile on page 410.

A. Plural Nouns

_____branches_____

Example: The newspaper named editors in chief for both <u>branchs</u>.

_____

1. Three of the attornies representing the defendants were from cities in other states.

_____

2. Four students discussed the positives and negatives of attending colleges or universities.

_____

3. Since the 1970s, most companys have begun to send bills of lading with shipments.

_____

4. Neither the Johnsons nor the Morris's knew about the changes in beneficiaries.

_____

5. The manager asked all secretaries to work on the next four Saturday's.

B. Possessive Nouns

_____

6. We sincerely hope that the jurys' judgment reflects the stories of all the witnesses.

_____

7. In a little over two months time, the secretaries had finished three reports for the president.

_____

8. Mr. Franklins staff is responsible for all accounts receivable contracted by customers purchasing electronics parts.

_____

9. At the next stockholders meeting, we will discuss benefits for employees and dividends for shareholders.

_____

10. Three months ago several employees in the sales department complained of Mrs. Smiths smoking.

C. Pronouns

_____me_____

Example: Whom did you ask to replace Tom and <u>I</u>?

_____

11. My manager and myself were willing to send the copies to whoever needed them.

12. Some of the work for Mr. Gagné and I had to be reassigned to Mark and him. _____

13. Although it's motor was damaged, the car started for the mechanic and me. _____

14. Just between you and me, only you and I know that she will be transferred. _____

15. My friend and I applied for employment at Reynolds, Inc., because of their excellent employee benefits. _____

D. Verb Agreement

Example: The list of arrangements <u>have</u> to be approved by Tim and her. _____**has**_____

16. The keyboard, printer, and monitor costs less than I expected. _____

17. A description of the property, together with several other legal documents, were submitted by my attorney. _____

18. There was only two enclosures and the letter in the envelope. _____

19. Neither the manager nor the employees in the office think the solution is fair. _____

20. Because of the holiday, our committee prefer to delay its action. _____

E. Verb Mood, Voice, and Tense

21. If I was able to fill your order immediately, I certainly would. _____

22. To operate the machine, first open the disk drive door and then you insert the diskette. _____

23. If I could chose any city, I would select Yellowknife. _____

24. Those papers have laid on his desk for more than two weeks. _____

25. The auditors have went over these accounts carefully, and they have found no discrepancies. _____

F. Adjectives and Adverbs

26. Until we have a more clearer picture of the entire episode, we shall proceed cautiously. _____

27. For about a week their newly repaired copier worked just beautiful. _____

28. The recently elected official benefited from his coast to coast campaign. _____

29. Mr. Snyder only has two days before he must complete the end-of-the-year report. _____

30. The architects submitted there drawings in a last-minute attempt to beat the deadline. _____

G. Prepositions and Conjunctions

_____ 31. Can you tell me where the meeting is scheduled at?

_____ 32. It seems like we have been taking this test forever.

_____ 33. Our investigation shows that the distribution department is more efficient then the sales department.

_____ 34. My courses this semester are totally different than last semester's.

_____ 35. Both of the managers were aware of and interested in the proposal.

H. Commas

For each of the following sentences, insert any necessary commas. Count the number of commas that you added. Write that number in the space provided. All punctuation must be correct to receive credit for the sentence. If a sentence requires no punctuation, write *0*.

_____2_____ **Example:** However, because of developments in theory and computer applications, management is becoming more of a science.

_____ 36. For example management determines how orders assignments and responsibilities are delegated to employees.

_____ 37. Your order Mrs. Tahan will be sent from Toronto Ontario on July 10.

_____ 38. When you need service on any of your pieces of equipment we will be happy to help you Mr. Hamel.

_____ 39. Kevin Long who is the project manager at Datatech suggested that I call you.

_____ 40. You have purchased from us often and your payments in the past have always been prompt.

I. Commas and Semicolons

Add commas and semicolons to the following sentences. In the space provided, write the number of punctuation marks that you added.

_____ 41. The salesperson turned in her report however she did not indicate what time period it covered.

_____ 42. Dividend payments are tax deductible interest payments on bonds are not.

_____ 43. We are opening a branch office in Kelowna and hope to be able to serve all your needs from that office by the middle of January.

_____ 44. As suggested by the committee we must first secure adequate funding then we may consider expansion.

_____ 45. When you begin to conduct research for a report consider the many library sources available namely books, periodicals, government publications, and newspapers.

J. Commas and Semicolons

46. After our office manager had the printer repaired it jammed again within the first week although we treated it carefully.

47. Our experienced courteous staff has been trained to anticipate your every need.

48. In view of the new law that went into effect April 1 our current liability insurance must be increased however we cannot immediately afford it.

49. As stipulated in our contract your agency will supervise our graphic arts and purchase our media time.

50. As you know Mrs. Laurendeau we aim for long-term business relationships not quick profits.

K. Other Punctuation

Each of the following sentences may require dashes, colons, question marks, quotation marks, periods, and underscores (to indicate italics), as well as commas and semicolons. Add the appropriate punctuation to each sentence. Then, in the space provided, write the total number of marks that you added.

Example: Price͵service͵ and reliability͵ these are our prime considerations.   3

51. The following members of the department volunteered to help on Saturday Kim, Carlos, Dan, and Sylvia.

52. Mr Danner, Miss Reed, and Mrs Garcia usually arrived at the office by 8 30 a m.

53. Three of our top managers Tim, Marcy, and Asad received cash bonuses.

54. Did the vice-president really say "All employees may take Friday off "

55. We are trying to locate an edition of Maclean's that carried an article entitled Microcomputers Beat the Office Crunch

L. Capitalization

For each of the following sentences, circle any letter that should be capitalized. In the space provided, write the number of circles that you marked.

Example: Ⓥice Ⓟresident Ⓓaniels devised a procedure for expediting purchase orders from Ⓐrea 4 warehouses.   4

56. although English was his first language, he also spoke spanish and could read french.

57. on a trip to the east coast, uncle henry visited the bay of fundy.

58. karen enrolled in classes in history, german, and sociology.

59. the business manager and the vice-president each received a new apple computer.

60. jane lee, the president of kendrick, inc., will speak to our conference in the spring.

M. Number Style

Decide whether the numbers in the following sentences should be written as words or as figures. Each sentence either is correct or has one error. If it is correct, write C. If it has an error, underline it and write the correct form in the space provided.

_____**five**_____ **Example:** The bank had <u>5</u> branches in three suburbs.

_____ **61.** More than 2,000,000 people have visited the Parliament Buildings in the past nine years.

_____ **62.** Of the 35 letters sent out, only three were returned.

_____ **63.** We set aside forty dollars for petty cash, but by December 1 our fund was depleted.

_____ **64.** The meeting is scheduled for May 5th at 3 p.m.

_____ **65.** In the past 20 years, nearly 15 percent of the population changed residences at least once.

Grammar/Mechanics Profile

In the spaces at the right, place a check mark to indicate the number of correct answers you had in each category of the Grammar/Mechanics Diagnostic Test.

		Number Correct*				
		5	4	3	2	1
1–5	Plural Nouns	_____	_____	_____	_____	_____
6–10	Possessive Nouns	_____	_____	_____	_____	_____
11–15	Pronouns	_____	_____	_____	_____	_____
16–20	Verb Agreement	_____	_____	_____	_____	_____
21–25	Verb Mood, Voice, and Tense	_____	_____	_____	_____	_____
26–30	Adjectives and Adverbs	_____	_____	_____	_____	_____
31–35	Prepositions and Conjunctions	_____	_____	_____	_____	_____
36–40	Commas	_____	_____	_____	_____	_____
41–45	Commas and Semicolons	_____	_____	_____	_____	_____
46–50	Commas and Semicolons	_____	_____	_____	_____	_____
51–55	Other Punctuation	_____	_____	_____	_____	_____
56–60	Capitalization	_____	_____	_____	_____	_____
61–65	Number Style	_____	_____	_____	_____	_____

*Note: 5 = have excellent skills; 4 = need light review; 3 = need careful review; 2 = need to study rules; 1 = need serious study and follow-up reinforcement.

Grammar Review

Parts of Speech (1.01)

1.01 Functions.   English has eight parts of speech. Knowing the functions of the parts of speech helps writers better understand how words are used and how sentences are formed.

a. Nouns name persons, places, things, qualities, concepts, and activities (for example, *Kevin, Montreal, computer, joy, work, banking*).

b. Pronouns substitute for nouns (for example, *he, she, it, they*).

c. Verbs show the action of a subject or join to the subject words that describe it (for example, *walk, heard, is, was jumping*).

d. Adjectives describe or limit nouns and pronouns and often answer the questions *what kind? how many?* and *which one?* (for example, *fast* sale, *ten* items, *good* manager).

e. Adverbs describe or limit verbs, adjectives, or other adverbs and frequently answer the questions *when? how? where?* and *to what extent?* (for example, *tomorrow, rapidly, here, very*).

f. Prepositions join nouns or pronouns to other words in sentences (for example, desk *in* the office, ticket *for* me, letter *to* you).

g. Conjunctions connect words or groups of words (for example, you *and* I, Andras *or* Jill).

h. Interjections express strong feelings (for example, *Wow!, Oh!*).

Nouns (1.02–1.06)

Nouns name persons, places, things, qualities, concepts, and activities. Nouns may be classified into a number of categories.

1.02 Concrete and Abstract.   Concrete nouns name specific objects that can be seen, heard, felt, tasted, or smelled. Examples of concrete nouns are *telephone, dollar, IBM, apple*. Abstract nouns name generalized ideas such as qualities or concepts that are not easily pictured. *Emotion, power,* and *tension* are typical examples of abstract nouns. Business writing is most effective when concrete words predominate. It's clearer to write "We need 16-pound bond paper" than to write "We need office supplies." Chapter 2 provides practice in developing skill in the use of concrete words.

1.03 Proper and Common.   Proper nouns name specific persons, places, or things and are always capitalized (*General Electric, Winnipeg, Jennifer*). All other nouns are common nouns and begin with lowercase letters (*company, city, student*). Rules for capitalization are presented in Section 3.01 through Section 3.16.

1.04 Singular and Plural.   Singular nouns name one item; plural nouns name more than one. From a practical view, writers seldom have difficulty with singular nouns. They may need help, however, with the formation and spelling of plural nouns.

1.05 Guidelines for Forming Noun Plurals

a. Add *s* to most nouns (*chair, chairs; mortgage, mortgages; Monday, Mondays*).

b. Add *es* to nouns ending in *s, x, z, ch*, or *sh* (*bench, benches; boss, bosses; box, boxes; Lopez, Lopezes*).

c. Change the spelling in irregular noun plurals (*man, men; foot, feet; mouse, mice; child, children*).

d. Add *s* to nouns that end in *y* when *y* is preceded by a vowel (*attorney, attorneys; valley, valleys; journey, journeys*).

e. Drop the *y* and add *ies* to nouns ending in *y* when *y* is preceded by a consonant (*company, companies; city, cities; secretary, secretaries*).

f. Add *s* to the principal word in most compound expressions (*editors-in-chief, fathers-in-law, bills of lading, runners-up*).

g. Add *s* to most numerals, letters of the alphabet, words referred to as words, degrees, and abbreviations (*5s, 1990s, Bs, ands, CPAs.*) Note that metric abbreviations take neither a period nor an *s* to make the plural (*1g, 2g*).

h. Add *'s* only to clarify letters of the alphabet that might be misread, both uppercase (*A's, I's, M's, U's*) and lowercase (*i's, p's,* and *q's*). An expression like *c.o.d.s* requires no apostrophe because it would not easily be misread.

1.06 Collective Nouns.   Nouns such as *staff, faculty, committee, group,* and *herd* refer to a collection of people, animals, or objects. Collective nouns may be considered singular or plural depending upon their action. See Section 1.10i for a discussion of collective nouns and their agreement with verbs.

Review Exercise A—Nouns

In the space provided for each item, write *a* or *b* to complete the following statements accurately. When you finish, compare your responses with those shown below. For each item on which you need review, consult the numbered principle shown in parentheses.

(1.05f)	**1.** Nearly all (a) *editor-in-chiefs,* (b) *editors-in-chief* demand observance of standard punctuation.
(1.05d)	**2.** Several (a) *attorneys,* (b) *attornies* worked on the case together.
(1.05b)	**3.** Please write to the (a) *Davis's,* (b) *Davises* about the missing contract.
(1.05e)	**4.** The industrial complex has space for nine additional (a) *companys,* (b) *companies.*
(1.05e)	**5.** That accounting firm employs two (a) *secretaries,* (b) *secretarys* for five CPAs.
(1.05d)	**6.** Four of the wooden (a) *benches,* (b) *benchs* must be repaired.

7. The home was constructed with numerous (a) *chimneys,* (b) *chimnies.*   (1.05d)

8. Tours of the production facility are made only on (a) *Tuesdays,* (b) *Tuesday's.*   (1.05a)

9. We asked the (a) *Lopez's,* (b) *Lopezes* to contribute to the fund-raising drive.   (1.05b)

10. Both my (a) *sister-in-laws,* (b) *sisters-in-law* agreed to the settlement.   (1.05f)

11. The stock market is experiencing abnormal (a) *ups and downs,* (b) *up's and down's.*   (1.05g)

12. Is it possible that the two (a) *foremans,* (b) *foremen* both misunderstood the time of the meeting?   (1.05c)

13. This office is unusually quiet on (a) *Sundays,* (b) *Sunday's.*   (1.05a)

14. Several news (a) *dispatchs,* (b) *dispatches* were released during the strike.   (1.05b)

15. Two major (a) *countries,* (b) *countrys* will participate in trade negotiations.   (1.05e)

16. Some young children have difficulty writing their (a) *bs and ds,* (b) *b's and d's.*   (1.05h)

17. The (a) *board of directors,* (b) *boards of directors* of all the major companies participated in the survey.   (1.05f)

18. In their letter the (a) *Metzes,* (b) *Metzs* said they intended to purchase the property.   (1.05b)

19. In shipping we are careful to include all (a) *bill of sales,* (b) *bills of sale.*   (1.05f)

20. Over the holidays many (a) *turkies,* (b) *turkeys* were consumed.   (1.05d)

---

1. b   3. b   5. a   7. a   9. b   11. a   13. a   15. a   17. b   19. b

Pronouns (1.07–1.09)

Pronouns substitute for nouns. They are classified by case.

1.07 Case. Pronouns function in three cases, as shown in the following chart.

Nominative Case (Used for subjects of verbs and subject complements)	Objective Case (Used for objects of prepositions and objects of verbs)	Possessive Case (Used to show possession)
I	me	my, mine
we	us	our, ours
you	you	your, yours
he	him	his
she	her	her, hers
it	it	its
they	them	their, theirs
who, whoever	whom, whomever	whose

1.08 Guidelines for Selecting Pronoun Case

a. Pronouns that serve as subjects of verbs must be in the nominative case.

He and *I* (not *Him* and *me*) decided to apply for the jobs.

b. Pronouns that follow linking verbs (such as *am, is, are, was, were, be, being, been*) and rename the words to which they refer must be in the nominative case.

It must have been *she* (not *her*) who placed the order. (The nominative-case pronoun *she* follows the linking verb *been* and renames *It*.)

If it was *he* (not *him*) who called, I have his number. (The nominative-case pronoun *he* follows the linking verb *was* and renames *It*.)

c. Pronouns that serve as objects of verbs or objects of prepositions must be in the objective case.

Mr. Laporte asked *them* to complete the proposal. (The pronoun *them* is the object of the verb *asked*.)

All computer printouts are sent to *him*. (The pronoun *him* is the object of the preposition *to*.)

Just between you and *me*, profits are falling. (The pronoun *me* is one of the objects of the preposition *between*.)

d. Pronouns that show ownership must be in the possessive case. Possessive pronouns (such as *hers, yours, ours, theirs,* and *its*) require no apostrophes.

We found my diskette, but *yours* (not *your's*) may be lost.

All parts of the machine, including *its* (not *it's*) motor, were examined.

The house and *its* (not *it's*) contents will be auctioned.

Don't confuse possessive pronouns and contractions. Contractions are shortened forms of subject–verb phrases (such as *it's* for *it is*, *there's* for *there is*, and *they're* for *they are*).

e. When a pronoun appears in combination with a noun or another pronoun, ignore the extra noun or pronoun and its conjunction. In this way, pronoun case becomes more obvious.

The manager promoted Jeff and *me* (not *I*). (Ignore *Jeff and*.)

f. In statements of comparison, mentally finish the comparative by adding the implied missing words.

Next year I hope to earn as much as *she*. (The verb *earns* is implied here: ... *as much as she earns*.)

g. Pronouns must be in the same case as the words they replace or rename. When pronouns are used with appositives, ignore the appositive.

A new contract was signed by *us* (not *we*) employees. (Temporarily ignore the appositive *employees* in selecting the pronoun.)

We (not *us*) citizens have formed our own organization. (Temporarily ignore the appositive *citizens* in selecting the pronoun.)

h. Pronouns ending in *self* should be used only when they refer to previously mentioned nouns or pronouns.

Robert and *I* (not *myself*) are in charge of the campaign.

i. Use objective-case pronouns as objects of the prepositions *between, but, like,* and *except.*

Everyone but John and *him* (not *he*) qualified for the bonus.

Employees like Miss Gallucci and *her* (not *she*) are hard to replace.

j. Use *who* or *whoever* for nominative-case constructions and *whom* or *whomever* for objective-case constructions. In making the correct choice, it's sometimes helpful to substitute *he* for *who* or *whoever* and *him* for *whom* or *whomever.*

For *whom* was this book ordered? (This book was ordered for *him/ whom?*)

Who did you say would drop by? (*Who/he* ... would drop by?)

Deliver the package to *whoever* opens the door. (In this sentence the clause *whoever opens the door* functions as the object of the preposition *to.* Within the clause itself *whoever* is the subject of the verb *opens.* Again, substitution of *he* might be helpful: *He/Whoever* opens the door.)

1.09 Guidelines for Making Pronouns Agree with Their Antecedents.
Pronouns must agree with the words to which they refer (their antecedents) in gender and in number.

a. Use masculine pronouns to refer to masculine antecedents, feminine pronouns to refer to feminine antecedents, and neuter pronouns to refer to antecedents without gender.

The man opened *his* office door. (Masculine gender applies.)

A woman sat at *her* desk. (Feminine gender applies.)

This computer and *its* programs fit our needs. (Neuter gender applies.)

b. Use singular pronouns to refer to singular antecedents.

Any customer who writes us should have *his* (not *their*) letter answered promptly. (The singular pronoun *his* refers to the singular subject *customer.*)

Common-gender (masculine) pronouns traditionally have been used when the gender of the antecedent is unknown. Sensitive writers today, however, prefer to recast such constructions to avoid the need for common-gender pronouns. Study these examples for alternatives to the use of common-gender pronouns.[1]

Customers' letters should be answered promptly.

Customers who write us should have their letters answered promptly.

Any customer who writes us should have *his or her* letter answered promptly. (This alternative is the least acceptable since it is wordy and calls attention to itself.)

c. Use singular pronouns to refer to singular indefinite subjects and plural pronouns for plural indefinite subjects. Words such as *anyone, something,* and *anybody* are considered indefinite because they refer to no specific person or object. Some indefinite pronouns are always singular; others are always plural.

Always Singular		Always Plural
anybody	everything	both
anyone	neither	few
anything	nobody	many
each	no one	several
either	somebody	
everyone	someone	

Somebody in the group of touring women left *her* (not *their*) purse in the museum.

Either of the companies has the right to exercise *its* (not *their*) option to sell stock.

d. Use singular pronouns to refer to collective nouns and organization names.

The engineering staff is moving *its* (not *their*) facilities on Friday. (The singular pronoun *its* agrees with the collective noun *staff* because the members of *staff* function as a single unit.)

Jones, Cohen, & James, Inc., *has* (not *have*) cancelled *its* (not *their*) contract with us. (The singular pronoun *its* agrees with Jones, Cohen, & James, Inc. because the members of the organization are operating as a single unit.)

e. Use a plural pronoun to refer to two antecedents joined by *and*, whether the antecedents are singular or plural.

---

[1]Note: See Chapter 3, p. 46 for additional discussion of common-gender pronouns.

Our company president and our vice-president will be submitting *their* expenses shortly.

f. Ignore intervening phrases—introduced by expressions like *together with*, *as well as*, and *in addition to*—that separate a pronoun from its antecedent.

One of our managers, along with several salespeople, is planning *his* retirement. (If you wish to emphasize both subjects equally, join them with *and*: "One of our managers and several salespeople are planning *their* retirements.")

g. When antecedents are joined by *or* or *nor*, make the pronoun agree with the antecedent closest to it.

Neither Zohra nor Kim wanted *her* (not *their*) desk moved.

Review Exercise B—Pronouns

In the space provided for each item, write *a*, *b*, or *c* to complete the statement accurately. When you finish, compare your responses with those shown below. For each item on which you need review, consult the numbered principle shown in parentheses.

1. Mr. Behrens and (a) *I*, (b) *myself* will be visiting sales personnel in the New Brunswick district next week. _____ (1.08h)

2. James promised that he would call; was it (a) *him*, (b) *he* who left the message? _____ (1.08b)

3. Much preparation for the seminar was made by Mrs. Washington and (a) *I*, (b) *me* before the brochures were sent out. _____ (1.08c)

4. The Employee Benefits Committee can be justly proud of (a) *its*, (b) *their* achievements. _____ (1.09d)

5. A number of inquiries were addressed to Jeff and (a) *I*, (b) *me*, (c) *myself*. _____ (1.08c 1.08e, 1.08h)

6. (a) *Who*, (b) *Whom* did you say the letter was addressed to? _____ (1.08j)

7. When you visit Mutual Trust, inquire about (a) *its*, (b) *their* certificates. _____ (1.09d)

8. Copies of all reports are to be reviewed by Mr. Khan and (a) *I*, (b) *me*, (c) *myself*. _____ (1.08c, 1.08e, 1.08h)

9. Apparently one of the female applicants forgot to sign (a) *her*, (b) *their* application. _____ (1.09b)

10. Both the diskette and (a) *it's*, (b) *its* cover are missing. _____ (1.08d)

11. I've never known any man who could work as fast as (a) *him*, (b) *he*. _____ (1.08f)

12. Just between you and (a) *I*, (b) *me*, the stock price will fall by afternoon. _____ (1.08j)

13. Give the supplies to (a) *whoever*, (b) *whomever* ordered them. _____ (1.08j)

14. (a) *Us*, (b) *We* employees have been given an unusual voice in choosing benefits. _____ (1.08g)

15. On her return from Mexico, Mrs. Hamilton, along with many other passengers, had to open (a) *her*, (b) *their* luggage for inspection. _____ (1.09f)

16. Either James or Robert will have (a) *his,* (b) *their* work reviewed next week.

17. Any woman who becomes a charter member of this organization will be able to have (a) *her,* (b) *their* name inscribed on a commemorative plaque.

18. We are certain that (a) *our's,* (b) *ours* is the smallest wristwatch available.

19. Everyone has completed the reports except Inez and (a) *he,* (b) *him.*

20. Lack of work disturbs Mr. Thomas as much as (a) *I,* (b) *me.*

1.a   3.b   5.b   7.a   9.a   11.b   13.a   15.a   17.a   19.b

Verbs (1.10–1.15)

Verbs show the action of a subject or join to the subject words that describe it.

1.10 Guidelines for Agreement with Subjects. One of the most troublesome areas in English is subject–verb agreement. Consider the following guidelines for making verbs agree with subjects.

a. A singular subject requires a singular verb.

The stock market *opens* at 10 a.m. (The singular verb *opens* agrees with the singular subject *market.*)

He *doesn't* (not *don't*) work on Saturday.

b. A plural subject requires a plural verb.

On the packing slip several items *seem* (not *seems*) to be missing.

c. A verb agrees with its subject regardless of prepositional phrases that may intervene.

This list of management objectives *is* extensive. (The singular verb *is* agrees with the singular subject *list.*)

Every one of the letters *shows* (not *show*) proper form.

d. A verb agrees with its subject regardless of intervening phrases introduced by *as well as, in addition to, such as, including, together with,* and similar expressions.

An important memo, together with several letters, *was* misplaced. (The singular verb *was* agrees with the singular subject *memo.*)

The president as well as several other top-level executives *approves* of our proposal. (The singular verb *approves* agrees with the subject *president.*)

e. A verb agrees with its subject regardless of the location of the subject.

Here *is* one of the letters about which you asked. (The verb *is* agrees with its subject *one,* even though it precedes *one.* The adverb *here* cannot function as a subject.)

There *are* many problems yet to be resolved. (The verb *are* agrees with the subject *problems*. The adverb *there* cannot function as a subject.)

In the next office *are* several word processing machines. (In this inverted sentence, the verb *are* must agree with the subject *machines*.)

f. Subjects joined by *and* require a plural verb.

Analyzing the reader and organizing a strategy *are* the first steps in letter writing. (The plural verb *are* agrees with the two subjects, *analyzing* and *organizing*.)

The tone and the wording of the letter *were* persuasive. (The plural verb *were* agrees with the two subjects, *tone* and *wording*.)

g. Subjects joined by *or* or *nor* may require singular or plural verbs. Make the verb agree with the closer subject.

Neither the memo nor the report *is* ready. (The singular verb *is* agrees with *report*, the closer of the two subjects.)

h. The following indefinite pronouns are singular and require singular verbs: *anyone, anybody, anything, each, either, every, everyone, everybody, everything, many a, neither, nobody, nothing, someone, somebody,* and *something.*

Either of the alternatives that you present *is* acceptable. (The verb *is* agrees with the singular subject *either*.)

i. Collective nouns may take singular or plural verbs, depending on whether the members of the group are operating as a unit or individually.

Our management team *is* united in its goal.

The faculty *are* sharply *divided* on the tuition issue. (Although acceptable, this sentence sounds better recast: The faculty *members* are sharply divided on the tuition issue.)

j. Organization names and titles of publications, although they may appear to be plural, are singular and require singular verbs.

Clark, Anderson, and Home, Inc., *has* (not *have*) hired an automation consultant.

Thousands of Investment Tips is (not *are*) again on the bestseller list.

1.11 Voice. Voice is that property of verbs that shows whether the subject of the verb acts or is acted upon. Active-voice verbs direct action from the subject toward the object of the verb. Passive-voice verbs direct action toward the subject.

Active voice: Our employees *write* excellent letters.

Passive voice: Excellent letters *are written* by our employees.

Business writing that emphasizes active-voice verbs is generally preferred because it is specific and forceful. However, passive-voice constructions can help a writer be tactful. Strategies for effective use of active- and passive-voice verbs are presented in Chapter 4.

1.12 Mood. Three verb moods express the attitude or thought of the speaker or writer toward a subject: (1) the indicative mood expresses a fact; (2) the imperative mood expresses a command; and (3) the subjunctive mood expresses a doubt, a conjecture, or a suggestion.

Indicative: I *am looking* for a job.

Imperative: *Begin* your job search with the want ads.

Subjunctive: I wish I *were* working.

Only the subjunctive mood creates problems for most speakers and writers. The most common use of subjunctive mood occurs in clauses including *if* or *wish*. In such clauses, substitute the subjunctive verb *were* for the indicative verb *was*.

If he *were* (not *was*) in my position, he would understand.

Mr. Dwarka acts as if he *were* (not *was*) the boss.

I wish I *were* (not *was*) able to ship your order.

The subjunctive mood may be used to maintain good will while conveying negative information. The sentence "I wish I *were* able to ship your order" sounds more pleasing to a customer than "I cannot ship your order," although, for all practical purposes, both sentences convey the same negative message.

1.13 Tense. Verbs show the time of an action by their tense. Speakers and writers can use six tenses to show the time of sentence action; for example:

Present tense:	I *work*; he *works*.
Past tense:	I *worked*; she *worked*.
Future tense:	I *will work*; he *will work*.
Present perfect tense:	I *have worked*; he *has worked*.
Past perfect tense:	I *had worked*; she *had worked*.
Future perfect tense	I *will have worked*; he *will have worked*.

1.14 Guidelines for Verb Tense

a. Use present tense for statements that, although they may be introduced by past-tense verbs, continue to be true.

What did you say his name *is*? (Use the present tense *is* if his name has not changed.)

b. Avoid unnecessary shifts in verb tenses.

The manager *saw* (not *sees*) a great deal of work yet to be completed and remained to do it herself.

Although unnecessary shifts in verb tense are to be avoided, not all the verbs within one sentence have to be in the same tense; for example:

She *said* (past tense) that she *likes* (present tense) to work late.

1.15 Irregular Verbs. Irregular verbs cause difficulty for some writers and speakers. Unlike regular verbs, irregular verbs do not form the past tense and past participle by adding *-ed* to the present form. Here is a partial list of selected troublesome irregular verbs. Consult a dictionary if you are in doubt about a verb form.

Troublesome Irregular Verbs

Present	Past	Past Participle (Always use helping verbs.)
begin	began	begun
break	broke	broken
choose	chose	chosen
come	came	come
drink	drank	drunk
go	went	gone
lay (to place)	laid	laid
lie (to rest)	lay	lain
ring	rang	rung
see	saw	seen
write	wrote	written

a. Use only past-tense verbs to express past tense. Notice that no helping verbs are used to indicate simple past tense.

The auditors *went* (not *have went*) over our books carefully.

He *came* (not *come*) to see us yesterday.

b. Use past participle forms for actions completed before the present time. Notice that past participle forms require helping verbs.

Steve *had gone* (not *went*) before we called. (The past participle *gone* is used with the helping verb *had*.)

c. Avoid inconsistent shifts in subject, voice, and mood. Pay particular attention to this problem area, for undesirable shifts are often characteristic of student writing.

Inconsistent: When Mrs. Moscovitch read the report, the error was found. (The first clause is in the active voice; the second, passive.)

Improved: When Mrs. Moscovitch read the report, she found the error. (Both clauses are in the active voice.)

Inconsistent: The clerk should first conduct an inventory. Then supplies should be requisitioned. (The first sentence is in the active voice; the second, passive.)

Improved: The clerk should first conduct an inventory. Then he or she should requisition supplies. (Both sentences are in the active voice.)

Inconsistent: All workers must wear security badges, and you must also sign a daily time card. (This sentence contains an inconsistent shift in subject from all workers in the first clause to you in the second clause.)

Improved: All workers must wear security badges, and they must also sign a daily time card.

Inconsistent: Begin the transaction by opening an account; then you enter the customer's name. (This sentence contains an inconsistent shift from the imperative mood in the first clause to the indicative mood in the second clause.)

Improved: Begin the transaction by opening an account; then enter the customer's name. (Both clauses are now in the indicative mood.)

Review Exercise C—Verbs

In the space provided for each item, write *a* or *b* to complete the statement accurately. When you finish, compare your responses with those shown below. For each item on which you need review, consult the numbered principle shown in parentheses.

_____ (1.10c)

1. A list of payroll deductions for our employees (a) *was*, (b) *were* sent to the personnel manager.

_____ (1.10e, 1.10f)

2. There (a) *is*, (b) *are* a customer service engineer and two salespeople waiting to see you.

_____ (1.10f)

3. Increased computer use and more complex automated systems (a) *is*, (b) *are* found in business today.

_____ (1.10j)

4. Crews, Meliotes, and Bove, Inc., (a) *has*, (b) *have* opened an office in St. John's.

_____ (1.15a)

5. Yesterday Mrs. Phillips (a) *choose*, (b) *chose* a new office on the second floor.

_____ (1.14a)

6. The man who called said that his name (a) *is*, (b) *was* Johnson.

7. *Modern Office Procedures* (a) *is*, (b) *are* beginning a campaign to increase readership.   _____(1.10j)_____

8. Either of the flight times (a) *appears*, (b) *appear* to fit my proposed itinerary.   _____(1.10h)_____

9. If you had (a) *saw*, (b) *seen* the rough draft, you would better appreciate the final copy.   _____(1.15b)_____

10. Across from our office (a) *is*, (b) *are* the parking structure and the information office.   _____(1.10e, 1.10f)_____

11. Although we have (a) *began*, (b) *begun* to replace outmoded equipment, the pace is slow.   _____(1.15b)_____

12. Specific training as well as ample experience (a) *is*, (b) *are* important for that position.   _____(1.10d)_____

13. Inflation and increased job opportunities (a) *is*, (b) *are* resulting in increased numbers of working women.   _____(1.10f)_____

14. Neither the organizing nor the staffing of the program (a) *has been*, (b) *have been* completed.   _____(1.10g)_____

15. If I (a) *was*, (b) *were* you, I would ask for a raise.   _____(1.12)_____

16. If you had (a) *wrote*, (b) *written* last week, we could have sent a brochure.   _____(1.15b)_____

17. The hydraulic equipment that you ordered (a) *is*, (b) *are* packed and will be shipped Friday.   _____(1.10a)_____

18. One of the reasons that sales have declined in recent years (a) *is*, (b) *are* lack of effective advertising.   _____(1.10c)_____

19. Either of the proposed laws (a) *is*, (b) *are* going to affect our business negatively.   _____(1.10h)_____

20. Bankruptcy statutes (a) *requires*, (b) *require* that a failing company disclose its financial situation to its creditors.   _____(1.10b)_____

---

1. a   3. b   5. b   7. a   9. b   11. b   13. b   15. b   17. a   19. a

Review Exercise D—Verbs

In the following sentence pairs, choose the one that illustrates consistency in use of subject, voice, and mood. Write *a* or *b* in the spaces provided. When you finish, compare your responses with those shown below. For each item on which you need review, consult the numbered principle shown in parentheses.

1. (a) You need more than a knowledge of equipment; one also must be able to interact well with people.   _____(1.15c)_____

   (b) You need more than a knowledge of equipment; you also must be able to interact well with people.

2. (a) Tim and Maurice were eager to continue, but Bob wanted to quit.   _____(1.14b)_____

   (b) Tim and Maurice were eager to continue, but Bob wants to quit.   _____(1.15c)_____

3. (a) The salesperson should consult the price list; then you can give an accurate quote to a customer.

(b) The salesperson should consult the price list; then he or she can give an accurate quote to a customer.

(1.15c)

4. (a) Read all the instructions first; then you install the printer program.

(b) Read all the instructions first, and then install the printer program.

(1.14b)

5. (a) She was an enthusiastic manager who always had a smile for everyone.

(b) She was an enthusiastic manager who always has a smile for everyone.

---

1. b   3. b   5. a

Adjectives and Adverbs (1.16–1.17)

Adjectives describe or limit nouns and pronouns. They often answer the questions *what kind? how many?* or *which one?* Adverbs describe or limit verbs, adjectives, or other adverbs. They often answer the questions *when? how? where?* or *to what extent?*

1.16 Forms. Most adjectives and adverbs have three forms, or degrees: positive, comparative, and superlative.

	Positive	Comparative	Superlative
Adjective:	clear	clearer	clearest
Adverb:	clearly	more clearly	most clearly

Some adjectives and adverbs have irregular forms.

	Positive	Comparative	Superlative
Adjective:	good	better	best
	bad	worse	worst
Adverb:	well	better	best

Adjectives and adverbs composed of two or more syllables are usually compared by the use of *more* and *most;* for example:

The Payroll Department is *more efficient* than the Shipping Department.

Payroll is the *most efficient* department in our organization.

1.17 Guidelines for Use

a. Use the comparative degree of the adjective or adverb to compare two persons or things; use the superlative degree to compare three or more.

Of the two letters, which is *better* (not *best*)?

Of all the plans, we like this one *best* (not *better*).

b. Do not create a double comparative or superlative by using *-er* with *more* or *-est* with *most*.

His explanation couldn't have been *clearer* (not *more clearer*).

c. A linking verb (*is, are, look, seem, feel, sound, appear,* and so forth) may introduce a word that describes the verb's subject. In this case, be certain to use an adjective, not an adverb.

The characters on the monitor look *bright* (not *brightly*). (Use the adjective *bright* because it follows the linking verb *look* and modifies the noun characters. It answers the question *What kind of characters?*)

The company's letter made the customer feel *bad* (not *badly*). (The adjective *bad* follows the linking verb *feel* and describes the noun *customer.*)

d. Use adverbs, not adjectives, to describe or limit the action of verbs.

The business is running *smoothly* (not *smooth*). (Use the adverb *smoothly* to describe the action of the verb *is running. Smoothly* tells how the business is running.)

Don't take his remark *personally* (not *personal*). (The adverb *personally* describes the action of the verb *take.*)

e. Two or more adjectives that are joined to create a compound modifier before a noun should be hyphenated.

The *four-year-old* child was tired.

Our agency is planning a *coast-to-coast* campaign.

Hyphenate a compound modifier following a noun only if your dictionary shows the hyphen(s).

The study she submitted was *all-inclusive.* (Include the hyphen because most dictionaries do.)

The tired child was four years old. (Omit the hyphens because the expression follows the word it describes, *child*, and because dictionaries do not indicate hyphens.)

f. Keep adjectives and adverbs close to the words that they modify.

She asked for a cup of *hot* coffee (not a *hot cup of coffee*).

Claudette had *only* two days of vacation left (not *Patty only had two days*).

Students may sit in the *first* five rows (not *in the five first rows*).

He has saved *almost* enough money for the trip (not *He has almost saved*).

g. Don't confuse the adverb *there* with the possessive pronoun *their* or the contraction *they're*.

Put the documents *there*. (The adverb *there* means "at that place or at that point.")

There are two reasons for the change. (The adverb *there* is used as an expletive or filler preceding a linking verb.)

We already have *their* specifications. (The possessive pronoun *their* shows ownership.)

They're coming to inspect today. (The contraction *they're* is a shortened form of *they are*.)

Review Exercise E—Adjectives and Adverbs

In the space provided for each item, write *a* or *b* to complete the statement accurately. If two sentences are shown, select *a* or *b* to indicate the one expressed more effectively. When you finish, compare your responses with those shown below. For each item on which you need review, consult the numbered principle shown in parentheses.

(1.17c)   **1.** After the interview, Krishnan looked (a) *calm*, (b) *calmly*.

(1.17b)   **2.** If you had been more (a) *careful*, (b) *carefuler* the box might not have broken.

(1.17d)   **3.** Because a new manager was appointed, the advertising campaign is running very (a) *smooth*, (b) *smoothly*.

(1.17e)   **4.** To avoid a (a) *face to face*, (b) *face-to-face* confrontation, she wrote a letter.

(1.17d)   **5.** Darren completed the employment test (a) *satisfactorily*, (b) *satisfactory*.

(1.17c)   **6.** I felt (a) *bad*, (b) *badly* that he was not promoted.

(1.17a)   **7.** Which is the (a) *more*, (b) *most* dependable of the two models?

(1.17g)   **8.** Can you determine exactly what (a) *there*, (b) *their*, (c) *they're* company wants us to do?

(1.17a)   **9.** Of all the copiers we tested, this one is the (a) *easier*, (b) *easiest* to operate.

(1.17f)   **10.** (a) Mr. Aldron almost was ready to accept the offer.

            (b) Mr. Aldron was almost ready to accept the offer.

(1.17f)   **11.** (a) We only thought that it would take two hours for the test.

            (b) We thought that it would take only two hours for the test.

(1.17f)   **12.** (a) Please bring me a glass of cold water.

            (b) Please bring me a cold glass of water.

(1.17f)   **13.** (a) The committee decided to retain the last ten tickets.

            (b) The committee decided to retain the ten last tickets.

(1.17e)   **14.** New owners will receive a (a) *60-day*, (b) *60 day* trial period.

(1.17d)   **15.** The time passed (a) *quicker*, (b) *more quickly* than we expected.

(1.17e)   **16.** We offer a (a) *money back*, (b) *money-back* guarantee.

17. Today the financial news is (a) *worse*, (b) *worst* than yesterday.   <u>(1.17a)</u>

18. Please don't take his comments (a) *personal*, (b) *personally*.   <u>(1.17d)</u>

19. You must check the document (a) *page by page*, (b) *page-by-page*.   <u>(1.17e)</u>

20. (a) We try to file only necessary paperwork.   <u>(1.17f)</u>

    (b) We only try to file necessary paperwork.

---

1. a   3. b   5. a   7. a   9. b   11. b   13. a   15. b   17. a   19. a

Prepositions (1.18)

Prepositions are connecting words that join nouns or pronouns to other words in a sentence. The words *about, at, from, in,* and *to* are examples of prepositions.

1.18 Guidelines for Use

a. Include necessary prepositions.

What type *of* software do you need (not *what type software*)?

I graduated *from* high school two years ago (not *I graduated high school*).

b. Omit unnecessary prepositions.

Where is the meeting? (Not *Where is the meeting at?*)

Both printers work well. (Not *Both of the printers.*)

Where are you going? (Not *Where are you going to?*)

c. Avoid the overuse of prepositional phrases.

Your Halifax credit application is before me. (Not *Your application for credit at our branch in the Halifax area is before me.*)

d. Repeat the preposition before the second of two related elements.

Applicants use the résumé effectively *by* summarizing their most important experiences and *by* relating their education to the jobs sought.

e. Include the second preposition when two prepositions modify a single object.

George's appreciation *of* and aptitude *for* computers led to a promising career.

(The use of prepositions in idiomatic expressions is discussed in Chapter 2, p. 27.)

Conjunctions (1.19)

Conjunctions connect words, phrases, and clauses. They act as signals, indicating when a thought is being added, contrasted, or altered. Coordinate conjunctions (such as *and, or,* and *but*) and other words that act as connectors (such as *however, therefore, when,* and *as*) tell the reader or listener in what direction a thought is heading. They're like road signs signalling what's ahead.

1.19 Guidelines for Use

a. Use coordinating conjunctions to connect only sentence elements that are parallel or balanced.

Weak: His report was correct and written in a concise manner.

Improved: His report was correct and concise.

Weak: Management has the capacity to increase fraud, or reduction can be achieved through the policies it adopts.

Improved: Management has the capacity to increase fraud or to reduce it through the policies it adopts.

b. Do not use the word *like* as a conjunction.

It seems *as if* (not *like*) this day will never end.

c. Avoid using *when* or *where* inappropriately. A common writing fault occurs in sentences with clauses introduced by *is when* and *is where*. Written English ordinarily requires a noun (or a group of words functioning as a noun) following the linking verb *is*. Instead of acting as conjunctions in these constructions, the words *where* and *when* function as adverbs, creating faulty grammatical equations (adverbs cannot complete equations set up by linking verbs). To avoid the problem, revise the sentence, eliminating *is when* or *is where*.

Weak: A bullish market is when prices are rising in the stock market.

Improved: A bullish market is created when prices are rising in the stock market.

Weak: A flowchart is when you make a diagram showing the step-by-step progression of a procedure.

Improved: A flowchart is a diagram showing the step-by-step progression of a procedure.

Weak: Word processing is where you use a computer and software to write.

Improved: Word processing involves the use of a computer and software to write.

A similar faulty construction occurs in the expression *I hate when*. English requires nouns, noun clauses, or pronouns to act as objects of verbs, not adverbs.

Weak: I hate when we're asked to work overtime.

Improved: I hate it when we're asked to work overtime.   OR

Improved: I hate being asked to work overtime.

d. Don't confuse the adverb *then* with the conjunction *than*. *Then* means "at that time"; *than* indicates the second element in a comparison.

We would rather remodel *than* (not *then*) move.

First, the equipment is turned on; *then* (not *than*) the program is loaded.

Review Exercise F—Prepositions and Conjunctions

In the space provided for each item, write *a* or *b* to indicate the sentence that is expressed more effectively. When you finish, compare your responses with those shown below. For each item on which you need review, consult the numbered principle shown in parentheses.

1. (a) Do you know where this shipment is being sent?   (1.18b)
   (b) Do you know where this shipment is being sent to?

2. (a) She was not aware of nor interested in the company insurance plan.   (1.18e)
   (b) She was not aware nor interested in the company insurance plan.

3. (a) Mr. Samuels graduated college last June.   (1.18a)
   (b) Mr. Samuels graduated from college last June.

4. (a) "Flextime" is when employees arrive and depart at varying times.   (1.19c)
   (b) "Flextime" is a method of scheduling worktime in which employees
       arrive and depart at varying times.

5. (a) Both employees enjoyed setting their own hours.   (1.18b)
   (b) Both of the employees enjoyed setting their own hours.

6. (a) I hate when the tape sticks in my VCR.   (1.19c)
   (b) I hate it when the tape sticks in my VCR.

7. (a) What style of typeface should we use?   (1.18a)
   (b) What style typeface should we use?

8. (a) Business letters should be concise, correct, and written clearly.   (1.19a)
   (b) Business letters should be concise, correct, and clear.

9. (a) Mediation in a labour dispute occurs when a neutral person helps   (1.19c)
       union and management reach an agreement.
   (b) Mediation in a labour dispute is where a neutral person helps union
       and management reach an agreement.

10. (a) It looks as if the plant will open in early January.   (1.19b)
    (b) It looks like the plant will open in early January.

11. (a) We expect to finish up the work soon.   (1.18b)
    (b) We expect to finish the work soon.

12. (a) At the beginning of the program in the fall of the year at the central   (1.18c)
        office, we experienced staffing difficulties.
    (b) When the program began last fall, the central office experienced
        staffing difficulties.

13. (a) Your client may respond by letter or a telephone call may be made.   (1.19a)

(b) Your client may respond by letter or by telephone.

(1.19c)

14. (a) A résumé is when you make a written presentation of your education and experience for a prospective employer.
    (b) A résumé is a written presentation of your education and experience for a prospective employer.

(1.18e)

15. (a) Stacy exhibited both an awareness of and talent for developing innovations.
    (b) Stacy exhibited both an awareness and talent for developing innovations.

(1.19d)

16. (a) This course is harder then I expected.
    (b) This course is harder than I expected.

(1.19c)

17. (a) An ombudsman is an individual hired by management to investigate and resolve employee complaints.
    (b) An ombudsman is when management hires an individual to investigate and resolve employee complaints.

(1.18b)

18. (a) I'm not certain where to take this document to.
    (b) I'm not certain where to take this document.

(1.18d)

19. (a) By including accurate information and by writing clearly, you will produce effective memos.
    (b) By including accurate information and writing clearly, you will produce effective memos.

(1.19a)

20. (a) We need computer operators who can load software, monitor networks, and files must be duplicated.
    (b) We need computer operators who can load software, monitor networks, and duplicate files.

---

1. a   3. b   5. a   7. a   9. a   11. b   13. b   15. a   17. a   19. a

Punctuation Review

Comma (Part 1) (2.01–2.04)

2.01 Series.   Commas are used to separate three or more equal elements (words, phrases, or short clauses) in a series. To ensure separation of the last two elements, careful writers always use a comma before the conjunction in a series.

> Business letters usually contain a dateline, address, salutation, body, and closing. (This series contains words.)

> The job of an ombudsman is to examine employee complaints, resolve disagreements between management and employees, and ensure fair treatment. (This series contains phrases.)

Trainees complete basic keyboarding tasks, technicians revise complex documents, and editors proofread completed projects. (This series contains short clauses.)

2.02 Direct Address.   Commas are used to set off the names of individuals being addressed.

Your inquiry, *Mrs. Johnson,* has been referred to me.

We genuinely hope that we may serve you, *Mr. Lee.*

2.03 Parenthetical Expressions.   Skilled writers use parenthetical words, phrases, and clauses to guide the reader from one thought to the next. When these expressions interrupt the flow of a sentence and are unnecessary for its grammatical completeness, they should be set off with commas. Examples of commonly used parenthetical expressions follow:

all things considered	however	needless to say
as a matter of fact	in addition	nevertheless
as a result	incidentally	no doubt
as a rule	in fact	of course
at the same time	in my opinion	on the contrary
consequently	in the first place	on the other hand
for example	in the meantime	therefore
furthermore	moreover	under the circumstances

As a matter of fact, I wrote to you just yesterday. (Phrase used at the beginning of a sentence.)

We will, *in the meantime,* send you a replacement order. (Phrase used in the middle of a sentence.)

Your satisfaction is our first concern, *needless to say.* (Phrase used at the end of a sentence.)

Do not use commas if the expression is necessary for the completeness of the sentence.

Tamara had *no doubt* that she would finish the report. (Omit commas because the expression is necessary for the completeness of the sentence.)

2.04 Dates, Addresses, and Geographical Items.   When dates, addresses, and geographical items contain more than one element, the second and succeeding elements are normally set off by commas.

a. Dates

The conference was held February 2 at our home office. (No comma is needed for one element.)

The conference was held February 2, 1986, at our home office. (Two commas set off the second element.)

The conference was held Tuesday, February 2, 1986, at our home office. (Commas set off the second and third elements.)

In February 1986 the conference was held. (This alternative style, omitting commas, is acceptable if the month and year only are written.)

b. Addresses

The letter addressed to Mr. Jim W. Ekman, 600 Novella St., Winnipeg, Manitoba R2H 1R4, should be sent today. (Commas are used between all elements except the province and postal code, which in this special instance are considered a single unit.)

c. Geographical items

She moved from Windsor, Ontario, to Truro, Nova Scotia. (Commas set off the province unless it appears at the end of the sentence, in which case only one comma is used.)

In separating cities from provinces and days from years, many writers remember the initial comma but forget the final one, as in the examples that follow:

The package from Edmonton, Alberta{,} was lost.

"We opened June 1, 1985 {,} and have grown steadily since."

Review Exercise G—Comma (Part 1)

Insert necessary commas in the following sentences. In the space provided write the number of commas that you add. Write C if no commas are needed. When you finish, compare your responses with those shown below. For each item on which you need review, consult the numbered principle shown in parentheses.

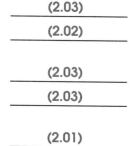

(2.03)   1. As a rule we do not provide complimentary tickets.

(2.02)   2. You may be certain Mr. Martinez that your policy will be issued immediately.

(2.03)   3. I have no doubt that your calculations are correct.

(2.03)   4. The safety hazard on the contrary can be greatly reduced if workers wear rubber gloves.

(2.01)   5. Every accredited TV newscaster radio broadcaster and newspaper reporter had access to the media room.

6. Deltech's main offices are located in Vancouver British Columbia and Regina Saskatchewan   _____ (2.04c)

7. The employees who are eligible for promotions are Terry Evelyn Maneesh Rosanna and Yves.   _____ (2.01)

8. During the warranty period of course you are protected from any parts or service charges.   _____ (2.03)

9. Many of our customers include architects engineers attorneys and others who are interested in data-base management programs.   _____ (2.01)

10. I wonder Mrs. Stevens if you would send my letter of recommendation as soon as possible.   _____ (2.02)

11. The new book explains how to choose appropriate legal protection for ideas trade secrets copyrights patents and restrictive covenants.   _____ (2.01)

12. The factory is scheduled to be moved to 2250 North Main Street Belleville Ontario L4A 1T2 within two years.   _____ (2.04b)

13. You may however prefer to correspond directly with the manufacturer in Hong Kong.   _____ (2.03)

14. Are there any alternatives in addition to those that we have already considered?   _____ (2.03)

15. The rally has been scheduled for Monday January 12 in the football stadium.   _____ (2.04a)

16. A cheque for the full amount will be sent directly to your home Mr. Sanchez.   _____ (2.02)

17. Goodstone Tire & Rubber for example recalled 400,000 steel-belted radial tires because some tires failed their rigid tests.   _____ (2.03)

18. Alex agreed to unlock the office open the mail and check all the equipment in my absence.   _____ 2.01)

19. In the meantime thank you for whatever assistance you are able to furnish.   _____ (2.03)

20. Research facilities were moved from Montreal Quebec to Fredericton New Brunswick.   _____ (2.04c)

---

1. rule,   3. C   5. newscaster, radio broadcaster,   7. Terry, Evelyn, Maneesh, Rosanna,
9. architects, engineers, attorneys,   11. ideas, trade secrets, copyrights, patents,
13. may, however,   15. Monday, January 12,   17. Rubber, for example,   19. meantime,

Comma (Part 2) (2.05–2.09)

2.05 Independent Clauses. An independent clause is a group of words that has a subject and a verb and that could stand as a complete sentence. When two such clauses are joined by *and, or, nor,* or *but,* use a comma before the conjunction.

> We can ship your merchandise July 12, *but* we must have your payment first.

Net income before taxes is calculated, *and* this total is then combined with income from operations.

Notice that each independent clause in the preceding two examples could stand alone as a complete sentence. Do not use a comma unless each group of words is a complete thought (that is, has its own subject and verb).

Net income before taxes is calculated *and* is then combined with income from operations. (No comma is needed because no subject follows *and*.)

2.06 Dependent Clauses. Dependent clauses do not make sense by themselves; for their meaning they depend upon independent clauses.

a. Introductory clauses. When a dependent clause precedes an independent clause, it is followed by a comma. Such clauses are often introduced by *when*, *if*, and *as*.

When your request came, we immediately responded.

As I mentioned earlier, Mrs. James is the manager.

b. Terminal clauses. If a dependent clause falls at the end of a sentence, use a comma only if the dependent clause is an afterthought.

The meeting has been rescheduled for October 23, *if this date meets with your approval.* (Comma used because dependent clause is an afterthought.)

We responded immediately *when we received your request.* (No comma is needed.)

c. Essential and nonessential clauses. If a dependent clause provides information that is unneeded for the grammatical completeness of a sentence, use commas to set it off. In determining whether such a clause is essential or nonessential, ask yourself whether the reader needs the information contained in the clause to identify the word it explains.

Our district sales manager, *who just returned from a trip to the Western District,* prepared this report. (This construction assumes that there is only one district sales manager. Since the sales manager is clearly identified, the dependent clause is not essential and requires commas.)

The salesperson *who just returned from a trip to the Western District* prepared this report. (The dependent clause in this sentence is necessary to identify which salesperson prepared the report. Therefore, use no commas.)

The position of assistant sales manager, *which we discussed with you last week,* is still open. (Careful writers use *which* to introduce nonessential clauses. Commas are also necessary.)

The position *that we discussed with you last week* is still open. (Careful writers use *that* to introduce essential clauses. No commas are used.)

2.07 Phrases.   A phrase is a group of related words that lacks both a subject and a verb. A phrase that precedes a main clause is followed by a comma only if the phrase contains a verb form or has five or more words.

> *Beginning November 1*, Mutual Savings will offer two new combination chequing/savings plans. (A comma follows this introductory phrase because the phrase contains the verb form *beginning*.)

> *To promote their plan*, we will conduct an extensive direct-mail advertising campaign. (A comma follows this introductory phrase because the phrase contains the verb form *to promote*.)

> *In a period of only one year*, we were able to improve our market share by 30 percent. (A comma follows the introductory phrase—actually two prepositional phrases—because its total length exceeds five words.)

> *In 1985* our organization installed a multi-user system that could transfer programs easily. (No comma needed after the short introductory phrase.)

2.08 Two or More Adjectives.   Use a comma to separate two or more adjectives that equally describe a noun. A good way to test the need for a comma is this: mentally insert the word *and* between the adjectives. If the resulting phrase sounds natural, a comma is used to show the omission of *and*.

> We're looking for a versatile, programmable calculator. (Use a comma to separate *versatile* and *programmable* because they independently describe *calculator*. *And* has been omitted.)

> Our experienced, courteous staff is ready to serve you. (Use a comma to separate *experienced* and *courteous* because they independently describe *staff*. *And* has been omitted.)

> It was difficult to refuse the sincere young telephone caller. (No commas are needed between *sincere* and *young* because *and* has not been omitted.)

2.09 Appositives.   Words that rename or explain preceding nouns or pronouns are called *appositives*. An appositive that provides information not essential to the identification of the word it describes should be set off by commas.

> Rozmin Kamani, *the project director for Sperling's*, worked with our architect. (The appositive, *the project director for Sperling's*, adds nonessential information. Commas set it off.)

Review Exercise H—Comma (Part 2)

Insert only necessary commas in the following sentences. In the space provided, indicate the number of commas that you add for each sentence. If a sentence requires no commas, write *C*. When you finish, compare your responses with those shown below. For each item on which you need review, consult the numbered principle shown in parentheses.

_____(2.05)_____   1. A corporation must be registered in the province in which it does business and it must operate within the laws of that province.

_____(2.05)_____   2. The manager made a point-by-point explanation of the distribution dilemma and then presented a plan to solve the problem.

_____(2.06a)_____   3. If you will study the cost analysis you will see that our company offers the best system at the lowest price.

_____(206.c)_____   4. Molly Epperson who amassed the greatest number of sales points was awarded the bonus trip to Hawaii.

_____(206.c)_____   5. The salesperson who amasses the greatest number of sales points will be awarded the bonus trip to Hawaii.

_____(2.07)_____   6. To promote good will and to generate international trade we are opening offices in the Far East and in Europe.

_____(2.07)_____   7. On the basis of these findings I recommend that we retain Jane Rada as our counsel.

_____(2.08)_____   8. Mary Lam is a dedicated hard-working employee for our company.

_____(2.08)_____   9. The bright young student who worked for us last summer will be able to return this summer.

_____(2.06a)_____   10. When you return the completed form we will be able to process your application.

_____(2.06b)_____   11. We will be able to process your application when you return the completed form.

_____(2.06c)_____   12. The employees who have been with us over ten years automatically receive additional insurance benefits.

_____(2.07)_____   13. Knowing that you wanted this merchandise immediately I took the liberty of sending it by Express Parcel Services.

_____(2.05)_____   14. The central processing unit requires no scheduled maintenance and has a self-test function for reliable performance.

_____(2.05)_____   15. International competition nearly ruined the Canadian shoe industry but the textile industry remains strong.

_____(2.09)_____   16. Joyce D'Agostino our newly promoted office manager has made a number of worthwhile suggestions.

_____(2.07)_____   17. For the benefit of employees recently hired we are offering a two-hour seminar regarding employee benefit programs.

_____(2.06b)_____   18. Please bring your suggestions and those of Mr. Mason when you attend our meeting next month.

_____(2.06b)_____   19. The meeting has been rescheduled for September 30 if this date meets with your approval.

_____(2.06c)_____   20. Some of the problems that you outline in your recent memo could be rectified through more stringent purchasing procedures.

---

1. business,   3. analysis,   5. C   7. findings,   9. C   11. C   13. immediately,
15. industry,   17. hired,   19. September 30,

Comma (Part 3) (2.10–2.15)

2.10 Degrees and Abbreviations. Degrees following individuals' names are set off by commas. Abbreviations such as *Jr.* and *Sr.* are also set off by commas unless the individual referred to prefers to omit the commas.

> Anne G. Turner, *M.B.A.*, joined the firm.
>
> Michael Migliano, *Jr.*, and Michael Migliano, *Sr.*, work as a team.
>
> Anthony A. Gensler *Jr.* wrote the report. (The individual referred to prefers to omit commas.)

The abbreviations *Inc.* and *Ltd.* are set off by commas only if a company's legal name has a comma just before this kind of abbreviation. To determine a company's practice, consult its stationery or a directory listing.

> Firestone and Blythe, *Inc.*, is based in Canada. (Notice that two commas are used.)
>
> Computers *Inc.* is extending its franchise system. (The company's legal name does not include a comma just before *Inc.*)

2.11 Omitted Words. A comma is used to show the omission of words that are understood.

> On Monday we received 15 applications; on Friday, only 3. (Comma shows the omission of *we received.*)

2.12 Contrasting Statements. Commas are used to set off contrasting or opposing expressions. These expressions are often introduced by such words as *not, never, but,* and *yet.*

> The consultant recommended hard-disk storage, *not* floppy-disk storage, for our operations.
>
> Our budget for the year is reduced, *yet* adequate.
>
> The greater the effort, the greater the reward.

If increased emphasis is desired, use dashes instead of commas, as in "Only the sum of $100—not $1000—was paid on this account."

2.13 Clarity. Commas are used to separate words repeated for emphasis. Commas are also used to separate words that may be misread if not separated.

> The building is a long, long way from completion.
>
> Whatever is, is right.
>
> No matter what, you know we support you.

2.14 Quotations and Appended Questions

a. A comma is used to separate a short quotation from the rest of a sentence. If the quotation is divided into two parts, two commas are used.

The manager asked, "Shouldn't the managers control the specialists?"

"Not if the specialists," replied Chen, "have unique information."

b. A comma is used to separate a question appended (added) to a statement.

You will confirm the shipment, won't you?

2.15 Comma Overuse.
Do not use commas needlessly. For example, commas should not be inserted merely because you might drop your voice if you were speaking the sentence.

One of the reasons for expanding our East Coast operations is {,} that we anticipate increased sales in that area. (Do not insert a needless comma before a clause.)

I am looking for an article entitled {,} "State-of-the-Art Communications." (Do not insert a needless comma after the word *entitled*.)

A number of food and nonfood items are carried in convenience stores such as {,} 7-Eleven and Mac's. (Do not insert a needless comma after *such as*.)

We have {,} at this time {,} an adequate supply of parts. (Do not insert needless commas around prepositional phrases.)

Review Exercise 1—Comma (Part 3)

Insert only necessary commas in the following sentences. Remove unnecessary commas with the delete sign (ℐ-). In the space provided, indicate the number of commas inserted or deleted in each sentence. If a sentence requires no changes, write C. When you finish, compare your responses with those shown below. For each item on which you need review, consult the numbered principle shown in parentheses.

_____ (2.12)	**1.** We expected Charles Bedford not Krystana Rudko to conduct the audit.
_____ (2.14a)	**2.** Brian said "We simply must have a bigger budget to start this project."
_____ (2.14a)	**3.** "We simply must have " said Brian "a bigger budget to start this project."
_____ (2.11)	**4.** In August customers opened at least 50 new accounts; in September only about 20.
_____ (2.14b)	**5.** You returned the merchandise last month didn't you?
_____ (2.13)	**6.** In short employees will now be expected to contribute more to their own retirement funds.
_____ (2.12)	**7.** The better our advertising and recruiting the stronger our personnel pool will be.

8. Mrs. Delgado investigated selling her stocks not her real estate to raise the necessary cash.   _(2.12)_

9. "On the contrary" said Mrs. Mercer "we will continue our present marketing strategies."   _(2.14a)_

10. Our company will expand into surprising new areas such as, women's apparel and fast foods.   _(2.15)_

11. What we need is more not fewer suggestions for improvement.   _(2.12)_

12. Randall Clark Esq. and Jonathan Georges M.B.A. joined the firm.   _(2.10)_

13. "The world is now entering" said President Saunders "the Age of Information."   _(2.14a)_

14. One of the reasons that we are inquiring about the publisher of the software is, that we are concerned about whether that publisher will be in the market five years from now.   _(2.15)_

15. The speech by D. A. Spindler Ph.D. was particularly difficult to follow because of its technical and abstract vocabulary.   _(2.10)_

16. The month before a similar disruption occurred in distribution.   _(2.13)_

17. We are very fortunate to have, at our disposal, the services of excellent professionals.   _(2.15)_

18. No matter what you can count on us for support.   _(2.13)_

19. Mrs. Sandoval was named legislative counsel; Mr. Freeman executive advisor.   _(2.11)_

20. The information you are seeking can be found in an article entitled, "The Fastest Growing Game in Computers."   _(2.15)_

---

1. Bedford, Rudko,   **3.** have," said Brian,   **5.** month,   **7.** recruiting,   **9.** contrary," Mercer,   **11.** more, not fewer,   **13.** entering," Saunders,   **15.** speech, Spindler, Ph.D.,   **17.** have at our disposal,   **19.** Freeman,

Semicolon (2.16)

2.16 Independent Clauses, Series, Introductory Expressions

a. Independent clauses with conjunctive adverbs. Use a semicolon before a conjunctive adverb that separates two independent clauses. Some of the most common conjunctive adverbs are *therefore, consequently, however,* and *moreover.*

> Business letters should sound conversational; *therefore,* familiar words and contractions are often used.

> The bank closes its doors at 3 p.m.; *however,* the automatic bank machine is open all the time.

> Notice that the word following a semicolon is *not* capitalized (unless, of course, that word is a proper noun).

b. Independent clauses without conjunctive adverbs. Use a semicolon to separate closely related independent clauses when no conjunctive adverb is used.

Bond interest payments are tax deductible; dividend payments are not.

Ambient lighting fills the room; task lighting illuminates each workstation.

Use a semicolon in *compound* sentences, not in *complex* sentences.

After one week the paper feeder jammed; we tried different kinds of paper. (Use a semicolon in a compound sentence.)

After one week the paper feeder jammed, although we tried different kinds of paper. (Use a comma in a complex sentence. Do not use a semicolon after *jammed*.)

The semicolon is very effective for joining two closely related thoughts. Don't use it, however, unless the ideas are truly related.

c. Independent clauses with other commas. Normally, a comma precedes *and, or,* and *but* when those conjunctions join independent clauses. However, if either clause contains commas, change the comma preceding the conjunction to a semicolon to ensure correct reading.

If you arrive in time, you may be able to purchase a ticket; but ticket sales close promptly at 8 p.m.

Our primary concern is financing; and we have discovered, as you warned us, that money sources are quite scarce.

d. Series with internal commas. Use semicolons to separate items in a series when one or more of the items contain internal commas.

Delegates from Brandon, Manitoba; Lethbridge, Alberta; and North Bay, Ontario, attended the conference.

The speakers were Katherine Lang, manager, Riko Enterprises; Henry Holtz, vice-president, Trendex, Inc.; and Margaret Slater, personnel director, West Coast Productions.

e. Introductory expressions. Use a semicolon when an introductory expression such as *namely, for instance, that is,* or *for example* introduces a list following an independent clause.

Switching to computerized billing are several local companies; namely, Ryson Electronics, Miller Vending Services, and Black Advertising.

The author of a report should consider many sources; for example, books, periodicals, government publications, and newspapers.

Colon (2.17–2.19)

2.17 Listed Items

a. With colon. Use a colon after a complete thought that introduces a formal list of items. A formal list is often preceded by such words and phrases as *these, thus, the following,* and *as follows.* A colon is also used when words and phrases like these are implied but not stated.

> Additional costs in selling a house involve *the following:* title examination fee, title insurance costs, and closing fee. (Use a colon when a complete thought introduces a formal list.)

> Collective bargaining focuses on several key issues: cost-of-living adjustments, fringe benefits, job security, and hours of work. (The introduction of the list is implied in the preceding clause.)

b. Without colons. Do not use a colon when the list immediately follows a *to be* verb or a preposition.

> The employees who should receive the preliminary plan *are* James Sears, Monica Spears, and Rose Mendez. (No colon is used after the verb *are.*)

> We expect to consider equipment *from* IBM, Wang, Exxon, and Apple. (No colon is used after the preposition *from.*)

2.18 Quotations.   Use a colon to introduce long one-sentence quotations and quotations of two or more sentences.

> Our consultant said: "This system can support up to 32 users. It can be used for decision support, computer-aided design, and software development operations at the same time."

2.19 Salutations.   Use a colon after the salutation of a business letter.

> Ladies and Gentlemen: Dear Mrs. Tsang: Dear Jamie:

Review Exercise J—Semicolons, Colons

In the following sentences, add semicolons, colons, and necessary commas. For each sentence indicate the number of punctuation marks that you add. If a sentence requires no punctuation, write C. When you finish, compare your responses with those shown below. For each item on which you need review, consult the numbered principle shown in parentheses.

1. A strike in Montreal has delayed shipments of parts consequently our production has fallen behind schedule.   (2.16a) _____

2. Our branch in Sherman Oaks specializes in industrial real estate our branch in Island Lakes concentrates on residential real estate.   (2.16b) _____

3. The sedan version of the automobile is available in these colours Olympic red metallic silver and Aztec gold.   (2.01, 2.17a) _____

(2.06a, 2.16a)

(2.01, 2.17b)

(2.03, 2.16c)

(2.16a)

(2.01, 2.07, 2.17b)

(2.01, 2.17a)

(2.05)

(2.16b)

(2.16a)

(2.06a, 2.16a)

(2.01, 2.17a)

(2.01, 2.17b)

(2.06a, 2.16a)

(2.16d)

(2.01, 2.16e)

(2.16b)

(2.05)

4. If I can assist the new manager please call me however I will be gone from June 10 through June 15.

5. The individuals who should receive copies of this announcement are Henry Doogan Alicia Green and Kim Wong.

6. We would hope of course to send personal letters to all prospective buyers but we have not yet decided just how to do this.

7. Many of our potential customers are in southern British Columbia therefore our promotional effort will be strongest in that area.

8. Since the first of the year we have received inquiries from one attorney two accountants and one information systems analyst.

9. Three dates have been reserved for initial interviews January 15 February 1 and February 12.

10. Several staff members are near the top of their salary ranges and we must reclassify their jobs.

11. Several staff members are near the top of their salary ranges we must reclassify their jobs.

12. Several staff members are near the top of their salary ranges therefore we must reclassify their jobs.

13. If you open an account within two weeks you will receive a free chequebook moreover your first 500 cheques will be imprinted at no cost to you.

14. Monthly reports from the following departments are missing Legal Department Personnel Department and Engineering Department.

15. Monthly reports are missing from the Legal Department Personnel Department and Engineering Department.

16. Since you became director of that division sales have tripled therefore I am recommending you for a bonus.

17. The convention committee is considering Dartmouth Nova Scotia Moncton New Brunswick and Charlottetown Prince Edward Island.

18. Several large companies allow employees access to their personnel files namely General Electric Eastman Kodak and Infodata.

19. Sylvie first asked about salary next she inquired about benefits.

20. Sylvie first asked about the salary and she next inquired about benefits.

---

1. parts; consequently,   3. colours: Olympic red, metallic silver,   5. Doogan, Alicia Green,   7. British Columbia; therefore,   9. interviews: January 15, February 1,   11. ranges;   13. weeks, chequebook; moreover,   15. Legal Department, Personnel Department,   17. Dartmouth, Nova Scotia; Moncton, New Brunswick; Charlottetown,   19. salary;

Apostrophe (2.20-2.29)

2.20 Basic Rule.   The apostrophe is used to show ownership, origin, authorship, or measurement.

Ownership: We are looking for *Brian's* keys.

Origin: At the *president's* suggestion, we doubled the order.

Authorship: The *accountant's* annual report was questioned.

Measurement: In two *years'* time we expect to reach our goal.

a. **Ownership word does not end in** *s*. To place the apostrophe correctly, you must first determine whether the ownership word ends in an *s* sound. If it does not, add an apostrophe and an *s* to the ownership word. The following examples show ownership words that do not end in an *s* sound:

the employee's file	(the file of a single employee)
a member's address	(the address of a single member)
a year's time	(the time of a single year)
a month's notice	(notice of a single month)
the company's building	(the building of a single company)

b. **Ownership word ends in** *s*. If the ownership word does end in an *s* sound, usually add only an apostrophe.

several employees' files	(files of several employees)
ten members' addresses	(addresses of ten members)
five years' time	(time of five years)
several months' notice	(notice of several months)
many companies' buildings	(buildings of many companies)

A few singular nouns that end in *s* are pronounced with an extra syllable when they become possessive. To these words, add *'s*.

my boss's desk

the waitress's table

the actress's costume

Use no apostrophe if a noun is merely plural, not possessive.

All the sales representatives, as well as the secretaries and managers, had their names and telephone numbers listed in the directory.

2.21 Names. The writer may choose either traditional or popular style in making singular names that end in an *s* sound possessive. The traditional style uses the apostrophe plus an *s*, while the popular style uses just the apostrophe. Note that only with singular names ending in an *s* sound does this option exist.

Traditional Style	Popular Style
Russ's computer	Russ' computer
Mr. Jones's car	Mr. Jones' car
Mrs. Morris's desk	Mrs. Morris' desk
Ms. Horowitz's job	Ms. Horowitz' job

The possessive form of plural names is consistent: the Joneses' car, the Horowitzes' home, the Polvoroses' daughter.

2.22 Gerunds. Use 's to make a noun possessive when it precedes a gerund, a verb form used as a noun.

> Mr. Smith's smoking prompted a new office policy. (*Mr. Smith* is possessive because it modifies the gerund *smoking*.)

> It was Ms. Lincoln's careful proofreading that revealed the discrepancy.

Review Exercise K—Apostrophes

Insert necessary apostrophes in the following sentences. In the space provided for each sentence, indicate the number of apostrophes that you added. If none were added, write *C*. When you finish, compare your responses with those shown below. For each item on which you need review, consult the numbered principle shown in parentheses.

(2.20b) _____ 1. Your account should have been credited with six months interest.

(2.21) _____ 2. If you go to the third floor, you will find Mr. Londons office.

(2.20b) _____ 3. All the employees personnel folders must be updated.

(2.20a) _____ 4. In a little over a years time, that firm was able to double its sales.

(2.21) _____ 5. The Harrises daughter lived in Whitehorse for two years.

(2.20a) _____ 6. An inventors patent protects his or her patent for seventeen years.

(2.20b) _____ 7. Both companies headquarters will be moved within the next six months.

(2.20b) _____ 8. That position requires at least two years experience.

(2.20b) _____ 9. Some of their assets could be liquidated; therefore, a few of the creditors were satisfied.

(2.20b) _____ 10. All secretaries workstations were equipped with terminals.

(2.20b) _____ 11. The package of electronics parts arrived safely despite two weeks delay.

(2.20b) _____ 12. Many nurses believe that nurses notes are not admissible evidence.

(2.21) _____ 13. According to Mr. Cortez [or Cortezs] latest proposal, all employees would receive an additional holiday.

(2.20b) _____ 14. Many of our members names and addresses must be checked.

(2.21) _____ 15. His supervisor frequently had to correct Jacks financial reports.

(2.20a) _____ 16. We believe that this firms service is much better than that firms.

(2.20a) _____ 17. Mr. Jackson estimated that he spent a years profits in reorganizing his staff.

(2.20b) _____ 18. After paying six months rent, we were given a receipt.

(2.21) _____ 19. The contract is not valid without Mrs. Harris [or Harriss] signature.

(2.22) _____ 20. It was Mr. Smiths signing of the contract that made us happy.

---

1. months'   3. employees   5. Harrises'   7. companies'   9. C   11. weeks'
13. Cortez' or Cortez's   15. Jack's   17. year's   19. Harris' or Harris's

Other Punctuation (2.23–2.29)

2.23 Period

a. **Ends of sentences.** Use a period at the end of a statement, command, indirect question, or polite request. Although a polite request may have the same structure as a question, it ends with a period.

> Corporate legal departments demand precise skills from their workforce. (End a statement with a period.)

> Get the latest information by reading current periodicals. (End a command with a period.)

> Mr. Rand wondered if we had sent any follow-up literature. (End an indirect question with a period.)

> Would you please re-examine my account and determine the current balance. (A polite request suggests an action rather than a verbal response.)

b. **Abbreviations and initials.** Use periods after initials and after many abbreviations.

R. M. Johnson	c.o.d.	Ms.
M.D.	a.m.	Mr.
Inc.	i.e.	Mrs.

Use just one period when an abbreviation falls at the end of a sentence.

> Guests began arriving at 5:30 p.m.

2.24 Question Mark.   Direct questions are followed by question marks.

> Did you send your proposal to Datatronix, Inc.?

Statements with questions added are punctuated with question marks.

> We have completed the proposal, haven't we?

2.25 Exclamation Point.   Use an exclamation point after a word, phrase, or clause expressing strong emotion. In business writing, however, exclamation points should be used sparingly.

> Incredible! Every terminal is down.

2.26 Dash.   The dash (constructed at a keyboard by striking the hyphen key twice in succession) is a legitimate and effective mark of punctuation when used according to accepted conventions. As an emphatic punctuation mark, however, the dash loses effectiveness when overused.

a. **Parenthetical elements.** Within a sentence a parenthetical element is usually set off by commas. If, however, the parenthetical element itself contains internal commas, use dashes (or parentheses) to set it off.

Three top salespeople—Tom Judkins, Morgan Templeton, and Mary Yashimoto—received bonuses.

b. Sentence interruption. Use a dash to show an interruption or abrupt change of thought.

News of the dramatic merger—no one believed it at first—shook the financial world.

Ship the materials Monday—no, we must have them sooner.

Sentences with abrupt changes of thought or with appended afterthoughts can usually be improved through rewriting.

c. Summarizing statement. Use a dash (not a colon) to separate an introductory list from a summarizing statement.

Sorting, merging, and computing—these are tasks that our data processing programs must perform.

2.27 Parentheses. One means of setting off nonessential sentence elements involves the use of parentheses. Nonessential sentence elements may be punctuated in one of three ways: (1) with commas, to make the lightest possible break in the normal flow of a sentence; (2) with dashes, to emphasize the enclosed material; and (3) with parentheses, to de-emphasize the enclosed material. Parentheses are frequently used to punctuate sentences with interpolated directions, explanations, questions, and references.

The cost analysis (which appears on page 8 of the report) indicates that the copy machine should be leased.

Units are lightweight (approximately 500 g) and come with a leather case and operating instructions.

The IBM laser printer (have you heard about it?) will be demonstrated for us next week.

A parenthetical sentence that is not imbedded within another sentence should be capitalized and punctuated with end punctuation.

The Model 20 has stronger construction. (You may order a Model 20 brochure by circling 304 on the reader service card.)

2.28 Quotation Marks

a. Direct quotations. Use double quotation marks to enclose the exact words of a speaker or writer.

"Keep in mind," Mrs. Yellowquill said, "that you'll have to justify the cost of automating our office."

The boss said that automation was inevitable. (No quotation marks are needed because the exact words are not quoted.)

b. Quotations within quotations. Use single quotation marks (apostrophes on the typewriter) to enclose quoted passages within quoted passages.

> In her speech Mrs. Deckman remarked, "I believe it was the poet Robert Frost who said, 'All the fun's in how you say a thing.' "

c. Short expressions. Slang, words used in a special sense, and words following *stamped* or *marked* are often enclosed within quotation marks.

> Rafael described the damaged shipment as "gross." (Use quotation marks for slang words.)

> Students often have trouble spelling the word "separate." (Quote words used in a special sense.)

> Jobs were divided into two categories: most stressful and least stressful. The jobs in the "most stressful" list involved high risk or responsibility. (Quote words used in a special sense.)

> The envelope marked "Confidential" was put aside. (Words following *marked* are often enclosed in quotation marks.)

In the four preceding sentences, the words enclosed within quotation marks can be set in italics, if italics are available.

d. Definitions. Double quotation marks are used to enclose definitions. The word or expression being defined should be underscored or set in italics.

> The term *penetration pricing* is defined as "the practice of introducing a product to the market at a low price."

e. Titles. Use double quotation marks to enclose titles of literary and artistic works, such as magazine and newspaper articles, chapters of books, movies, television shows, poems, lectures, and songs. Names of major publications—such as books, magazines, pamphlets, and newspapers—are set in italics (underscored) or typed in capital letters.

> Particularly helpful was the chapter in Smith's EFFECTIVE WRITING TECHNIQUES entitled "Right Brain, Write On!"

> John's article, "Corporate Raiders," appeared in *The Toronto Sun*; however, we could not locate it in a local library.

f. Additional considerations. Periods and commas are always placed inside closing quotation marks. Semicolons and colons, on the other hand, are always placed outside quotation marks.

> Mme Levesque said, "I could not find the article entitled 'Technology Update.' "

> The president asked for "absolute security": all written messages were to be destroyed.

Question marks and exclamation points may go inside or outside closing quotation marks, as determined by the form of the quotation.

Sales Manager Martin said, "Who placed the order?" (The quotation is a question.)

When did the sales manager say, "Who placed the order?" (Both the incorporating sentence and the quotation are questions.)

Did the sales manager say, "Randeep placed the order"? (The incorporating sentence asks the question; the quotation does not.)

"In the future," shouted Bob, "ask me first!" (The quotation is an exclamation.)

2.29 Brackets. Within quotations, brackets are used by the quoting writer to enclose his or her own inserted remarks. Such remarks may be corrective, illustrative, or explanatory.

Mrs. Lavalée said, "CRTC [Canadian Radio Television and Telecommunications Commission] has been one of the most widely criticized agencies of the federal government."

Review Exercise L—Other Punctuation

Insert necessary punctuation in the following sentences. In the space provided for each item, indicate the number of punctuation marks that you added. Count sets of parentheses and dashes as two marks. Emphasis or de-emphasis will be indicated for some parenthetical elements. When you finish, compare your responses with those shown below. For each item on which you need review, consult the numbered principle shown in parentheses.

(2.23a)

(2.26)

(2.23a, 2.23b)

(2.23b)

(2.23b)

(2.27)

(2.25)

(2.28d)

(2.27)

(2.28f)

(2.28c)

1. Will you please stop payment on my Cheque No. 233

2. (Emphasize.) Your order of October 16 will be on its way you have my word by October 20.

3. Mr Sirakides, Mrs Sylvester, and Ms Sidhu have not yet responded

4. Mrs. Penner asked if the order had been sent c o d

5. Interviews have been scheduled for 3:15 p m, 4 p m, and 4:45 p m

6. (De-emphasize.) Three knowledgeable individuals the plant manager, the construction engineer, and the construction supervisor all expressed concern about soil settlement.

7. Fantastic The value of our stock just rose 10 points on the stock market exchange

8. The expression de facto means existing in fact, regardless of the legal situation.

9. (De-emphasize.) Although the appliance now comes in limited colours brown, beige, and ivory, we expect to see new colours available in the next production run.

10. Was it the manager who said What can't be altered must be endured

11. The stock market went nuts over the news of the takeover.

12. Because the envelope was marked Personal, we did not open it.   (2.28c)

13. Price, service, and reliability these are our prime considerations in equipment selection.   (2.26c)

14. The letter carrier said Would you believe that this package was marked Fragile   (2.28b, 2.28f)

15. (Emphasize.) Three branch managers Kelly Cardinal, Stan Meyers, and Ivan Sergo will be promoted.   (2.26a)

16. (De-emphasize.) The difference between portable and transportable computers see Figure 4 for weight comparisons may be considerable.   (2.27)

17. All the folders marked Current Files should be sent to the Personnel Division.   (2.28c)

18. I am trying to find the edition of Canadian Life that carried an article entitled The Future Without Shock.   (2.28e)

19. Martha Simon M D and Ken Nemire R N were hired by Healthnet, Inc   (2.10, 2.23b)

20. The computer salesperson said This innovative, state-of-the-art computer sells for a fraction of the big-name computers' prices.   (2.28a)

---

1. 233.   3. Mr. Mrs. Ms. responded   5. p.m. p.m. p.m.   7. Fantastic! exchange!
9. (brown ivory),   11. "nuts"   13. reliability—   15. managers—Sergo—
17. "Current Files"   19. Simon, M.D., Nemire, R.N., Inc.

Style and Usage

Capitalization (3.01–3.16)

Capitalization is used to distinguish important words. However, writers are not free to capitalize all words they consider important. Rules or guidelines governing capitalization style have been established through custom and use. Mastering these guidelines will make your writing more readable and more comprehensible.

3.01 Proper Nouns.   Capitalize proper nouns, including the specific names of persons, places, schools, streets, parks, buildings, religions, holidays, months, agreements, programs, services, and so forth. Do not capitalize common nouns that make only general references.

Proper Nouns	Common Nouns
Michael DeNiro	a salesman in electronics
Germany, Japan	two countries that trade with Canada
George Brown College	a community college
Assiniboine Park	a park in the city
Phoenix Room, Delta Inn	a meeting room in the hotel

Catholic, Presbyterian	two religions
Victoria Day, New Year's Day	two holidays
Priority Post	a special package delivery service
Lion's Gate Bridge	a bridge
Consumer Product Safety Act	a law to protect consumers

When a common-noun element is used in combination with two or more proper nouns, do not capitalize the common noun. For example, "Our markets include countries across both the Pacific and the Atlantic *oceans*."

3.02 Proper Adjectives.   Capitalize most adjectives that are derived from proper nouns.

Greek symbol	British thermal unit
Roman numeral	Norwegian ship
Xerox copy	Inuit land claims

Do not capitalize the few adjectives that, although originally derived from proper nouns, have become common adjectives through usage. Consult your dictionary when in doubt.

manila folder	mimeograph copies
india ink	china dishes

3.03 Geographic Locations.   Capitalize the names of *specific* places such as cities, provinces, states, mountains, valleys, lakes, rivers, oceans, and geographic regions.

Iqaluit	Lake Ontario
Rocky Mountains	Arctic Ocean
Cape Breton Island	James Bay
the East Coast	the Pacific Northwest

3.04 Organization Names.   Capitalize the principal words in the names of all business, civic, educational, governmental, labour, military, philanthropic, political, professional, religious, and social organizations.

Inland Steel Company	Board of Directors, Teachers' Credit Union
The Globe and Mail[2]	The Rainbow Society
Toronto Stock Exchange	Securities and Exchange Commission
National Action Committee on the Status of Women	Psychological Association of Manitoba
Child and Family Services	Mennonite Brethren Bible College

---

[2]Note: Capitalize *the* only when it is part of the official name of an organization, as printed on the organization's letterhead.

3.05 Academic Courses and Degrees. Capitalize particular academic degrees and course titles. Do not capitalize references to general academic degrees and subject areas.

> Professor Bernadette Ordian, Ph.D., will teach *Accounting* 221 next fall.

> Mrs. Snyder, who holds *bachelor's* and *master's* degrees, teaches *marketing* classes.

> René enrolled in classes in *history*, *English*, and *management*.

3.06 Personal and Business Titles

a. Capitalize personal and business titles when they precede names.

Vice-President Ames	Uncle Carlos
Board Chairperson Frazier	Councillor Herbert
Member of Parliament Ronald Tantoo	Sales Manager Klein
Professor McLean	Dr. Mira Rosner

b. Capitalize titles in addresses, salutations, and closing lines.

Mr. Jacques Fontaine	Very truly yours,
Director of Purchasing	
Space Systems, Inc.	
Richmond, BC V3L 4A6	Cara J. Smith Supervisor, Marketing

c. Capitalize titles of high governmental rank or religious office, whether they precede a name, follow a name, or replace a name.

the Prime Minister of Canada	Gaston Pelletier, Senator
the Premier's office	the Speaker of the Commons
the Governor General of Manitoba	an audience with the Pope
J. W. Ross, Minister of Finance	

d. Do not capitalize more common titles following names.

> The speech was delivered by Wayne Hsu, *president*, Inter-Tel Canada.

> Lois Herndon, *chief executive officer*, signed the order.

e. Do not capitalize more common titles appearing alone.

> Please speak to the *supervisor* or the *office manager*.

> Neither the *president* nor the *vice-president* was asked.

However, when the title of an official appears in that organization's minutes, bylaws, or other official document, it may be capitalized.

f. Do not capitalize titles when they are followed by appositives naming specific individuals.

We must consult our *director of research,* Ronald E. West, before responding.

g. Do not capitalize family titles used with possessive pronouns.

my mother   our aunt   your father   his cousin

h. Capitalize titles of close relatives used without pronouns.

Both *Mother* and *Father* must sign the contract.

3.07 Numbered and Lettered Items.   Capitalize nouns followed by numbers or letters (except in page, paragraph, line, and verse references).

Flight 34, Gate 12   Plan No. 2

Part 3   Warehouse 33-A

Invoice No. 55489   Figure 8.3

Model A5673   Serial No. C22865404-2

Rural Route 10   page 6, line 5

3.08 Points of the Compass.   Capitalize north, south, east, west, and their derivatives when they represent specific geographical regions. Do not capitalize the points of the compass when they are used in directions or in general references.

Specific Regions	General References
living in the North	west of the city
Easterners, Westerner	western Ontario, southern Saskatchewan
going to the Middle East	the northern part of Canada

3.09 Departments, Divisions, and Committees.   Capitalize the names of departments, divisions, or committees within your own organization. Outside your organization capitalize only specific department, division, or committee names.

The inquiry was addressed to the *Legal Department* in our *Consumer Products Division.*

Fazil was appointed to the *Employee Benefits Committee.*

Send your résumé to their *personnel division.*

A *planning committee* will be named shortly.

3.10 Governmental Terms.   Do not capitalize the words *federal, government, nation,* or *province* unless they are part of a specific title.

Unless *federal* support can be secured, the *provincial* project will be abandoned.

The *Provincial* Employees' Pension Fund is looking for secure investments.

3.11 Product Names. Capitalize product names only when they refer to trademarked items. Except in advertising, common names following manufacturers' names are not capitalized.

Trademarked Names	Common Names
IBM Selectric	Apple computer
Toyota Tercel	Swingline stapler
BASF FlexyDisk	3M diskettes
Dictaphone Thought Tank	Sony dictation machine
DuPont Teflon	Canon camera

3.12 Literary Titles. Capitalize the principal words in the titles of books, magazines, newspapers, articles, movies, plays, songs, poems, and reports. Do *not* capitalize articles (*a, an, the*), short conjunctions (*and, but, or, nor*), and prepositions of fewer than four letters (*in, to, by, for,* etc.) unless they begin or end the title.

Jackson's *What Job Is for You?* (Capitalize book titles.)

Gant's "Software for the Executive Suite" (Capitalize principal words in article titles.)

"The Improvement of Fuel Economy with Alternative Motors" (Capitalize report titles.)

3.13 Beginning Words. In addition to capitalizing the first word of a complete sentence, capitalize the first word in a quoted sentence, independent phrase, item in an enumerated list, and formal rule or principle following a colon.

The business manager said, "*All* purchases must have requisitions." (Capitalize first word in a quoted sentence.)

Yes, if you agree. (Capitalize an independent phrase.)

Some of the duties of the position are as follows:

1. *Transcribing* dictation from recording equipment

2. *Receiving* and routing telephone calls

3. *Verifying* records, reports, and applications (Capitalize items in an enumerated list.)

One rule has been established through the company: *No* smoking is allowed in open offices. (Capitalize a rule following a colon.)

3.14 Celestial Bodies. Capitalize the names of celestial bodies such as *Mars, Saturn,* and *Neptune.* Do not capitalize the terms *earth, sun,* or *moon* unless they appear in a context with other celestial bodies.

> Where on *earth* did you find that manual typewriter?

> *Venus* and *Mars* are the closest planets to *Earth.*

3.15 Ethnic References. Capitalize terms that refer to a particular culture, language, or race.

Oriental	Hebrew
Caucasian	Indian
Latino	Judeo-Christian
Persian	Cree
African-American	*but:* anglophone, francophone

3.16 Seasons. Do not capitalize seasons.

> In the *fall* it appeared that *winter* and *spring* sales would increase.

Review Exercise M—Capitalization

In the following sentences correct any errors that you find in capitalization. Circle any lowercase letter that should be changed to a capital letter. Draw a slash (/) through a capital letter that you wish to change to a lowercase letter. In the space provided, indicate the total number of changes you have made in each sentence. If you make no changes, write *0.* When you finish, compare your responses with those shown below. For each item on which you need review, consult the numbered principle shown in parentheses.

5
_____

(3.01)
_____

(3.03)
_____
(3.01, 3.03, 3.05)
_____

(3.06e, 3.12)
_____

(3.06e, 3.06g)
_____

(3.01, 3.07)
_____

Example: Bill McAdams, currently /Assistant /Manager in our Personnel ⊙epartment, will be promoted to /Manager of the Employee Services ⊙ivision.

1. The medical care act, passed in 1966, established the present system of government medical insurance.

2. Our company will soon be moving its operations to the west coast.

3. Marilyn Hunter, m.b.a., received her bachelor's degree from McGill university in montreal.

4. The President of Datatronics, Inc., delivered a speech entitled "Taking off into the future."

5. Please ask your Aunt and your Uncle if they will come to the Lawyer's office at 5 p.m.

6. Your reservations are for flight 32 on canadian airlines leaving from gate 14 at 2:35 p.m.

7. Once we establish an organizing committee, arrangements can be made to rent holmby hall.   _(3.01)_

8. Bob was enrolled in history, spanish, business communications, and physical education courses.   _(3.05)_

9. Either the President or the Vice-President of the company will make the decision about purchasing xerox copiers.   _(3.06e, 3.11)_

10. Rules for hiring and firing Employees are given on page 7, line 24, of the Contract.   _(3.01, 3.07)_

11. Some individuals feel that canadian management does not have the sense of loyalty to its employees that japanese management has.   _(3.02)_

12. Where on Earth can we find better workers than Robots?   _(3.01, 3.14)_

13. The minister of finance said, "we must protect our domestic economy from Foreign competition."   _(3.06c, 3.10, 3.13)_

14. After crossing the sunshine skyway bridge, we drove to Southern British Columbia for our vacation.   _(3.01, 3.08)_

15. All marketing representatives of our company will meet in the empire room of the red lion motor inn.   _(3.01)_

16. Floyd Elkins, ph.d., has been named director of research for spaceage strategies, inc.   _(3.01, 3.05, 3.06e)_

17. The special keyboard for the IBM Computer must contain greek symbols for Engineering equations.   _(3.01, 3.02, 3.11)_

18. After she received a master's degree in electrical engineering, Joanne Dudley was hired to work in our product development department.   _(3.05, 3.09)_

19. In the Fall our organization will move its corporate headquarters to the franklin building in downtown vancouver.   _(3.01, 3.03, 3.16)_

20. Dean Amador has one cardinal rule: always be punctual.   _(3.13)_

---

1. Medical Care Act   **3.** M.B.A. University Montreal   **5.** aunt uncle lawyer's
7. Holmby Hall   **9.** president vice-president Xerox   **11.** Canadian Japanese
13. Minister of Finance We foreign   **15.** Empire Room Red Lion Motor Inn
17. computer Greek engineering   **19.** fall Franklin Building Vancouver

Number Style (4.01–4.13)

Usage and custom determine whether numbers are expressed in the form of figures (for example, *5, 9*) or in the form of words (for example, *five, nine*). Numbers expressed as figures are shorter and more easily understood, yet numbers expressed as words are necessary in certain instances. The following guidelines are observed in expressing numbers in written *sentences*. Numbers that appear on business forms—such as invoices, monthly statements, and purchase orders—are always expressed as figures.

4.01 General Rules

a. The numbers *one* through *ten* are generally written as words. Numbers above *ten* are written as figures.

The bank had a total of *nine* branch offices in *three* suburbs.

All *58* employees received benefits in the *three* categories shown.

A shipment of *45,000* light bulbs was sent from *two* warehouses.

b. Numbers that begin sentences are written as words. If the number involves more than two words, however, the sentence should be written so that the number does not fall at the beginning.

Fifteen different options were available in the annuity programs.

A total of *156* companies participated in the promotion (not *One hundred fifty-six companies participated in the promotion*).

4.02 Money.   Sums of money $1 or greater are expressed as figures. If a sum is a whole dollar amount, omit the decimal and zeros (whether or not the amount appears in a sentence with additional fractional dollar amounts).

We budgeted *$30* for diskettes, but the actual cost was *$37.96*.

On the invoice were items for *$6.10, $8, $33.95,* and *$75*.

Sums less than $1 are written as figures that are followed by the word *cents*.

By shopping carefully, we can save *45 cents* per diskette.

4.03 Dates.   In dates, numbers that appear after the name of the month are written as cardinal figures (*1, 2, 3,* etc.). Those that stand alone or appear before the name of a month are written as ordinal figures (*1st, 2d, 3d,* etc.).

The Personnel Practices Committee will meet *May 7*.

On the *5th* day of February and again on the *25th*, we placed orders.

In domestic business documents, dates generally take the following form: *January 4, 1994*. An alternative form, used primarily in military and foreign correspondence, begins with the day of the month and omits the comma: *4 January 1994*.

Many writers today are using the more efficient *2d* and *3d* instead of *2nd* and *3rd*.

4.04 Clock Time.   Figures are used when clock time is expressed with *a.m.* or *p.m.* Omit the colon and zeros in referring to whole hours. When exact clock time is expressed with the contraction *o'clock*, either figures or words may be used.

Mail collection is at *11 a.m.* and *3:30 p.m.*

At *four* (or *4*) *o'clock* employees begin to leave.

4.05 Addresses and Telephone Numbers

a. Except for the number *one,* house numbers are expressed as figures.

540 Elm Street	One Desmeurons Boulevard
17802 Parliament Avenue	2 Easy Street

b. Street names containing numbers *ten* or lower are written entirely as words. For street names involving numbers greater than *ten,* figures are used.

330 Third Street	3440 Seventh Avenue
6945 East 32 Avenue	4903 West 103 Street

If no compass direction *(North, South, East, West)* separates a house number from a street number, the street number is expressed in ordinal form *(-st, -d, -th).*

256 42d Street	1390 11th Avenue

c. Telephone numbers are expressed with figures. When used, the area code is placed in parentheses preceding the telephone number.

Please call us at *(204) 347-0551* to place an order.

Mr. Sui asked you to call *(619) 554-8923, Ext. 245,* after 10 a.m.

4.06 Related Numbers.   Numbers are related when they refer to similar items in a category within the same reference. All related numbers should be expressed as the largest number is expressed. Thus if the largest number is greater than *ten,* all the numbers should be expressed as figures.

Only *5* of the original *25* applicants completed the processing. (Related numbers require figures.)

The two plans affected *34* employees working in *three* sites. (Unrelated numbers use figures and words.)

Gulf Canada operated *86* rigs, of which *6* were rented. (Related numbers require figures.)

The company hired *three* accountants, *one* customer service representative, and *nine* sales representatives. (Related numbers under *ten* use words.)

4.07 Consecutive Numbers.   When two numbers appear consecutively and both modify the same following noun, words are used to express the smaller or less complex number.

We need 250 five-page coloured inserts (not *two hundred fifty 5-page* inserts).

The magazine was devoted to *two 25-page* articles (not *2 twenty-five-page* articles).

4.08 Periods of Time.   Periods of time are generally expressed in word form. However, figures may be used to emphasize business concepts such as discount rates, interest rates, warranty periods, credit terms, loan or contract periods, and payment terms.

> This business was incorporated over *fifty* years ago.

> Any purchaser may cancel a contract within *72* hours. (Use figures to explain a business concept.)

> The warranty period is *5* years. (Use figures for a business concept.)

> Cash discounts are given for payment within *30* days. (Use figures for a business concept.)

4.09 Ages.   Ages are generally expressed in word form unless the age appears immediately after a name or is expressed in exact years and months.

> At the age of *twenty-one*, Elizabeth inherited the business.

> Wanda Unger, *37*, was named acting president.

> At the age of *4* years and *7* months, the child was adopted.

4.10 Round Numbers.   Round numbers are approximations. They may be expressed in word or figure form, although figure form is shorter and easier to comprehend.

> About *600* (or *six hundred*) stock options were sold.

> It is estimated that *1000* (or *one thousand*) people will attend.

For ease of reading, round numbers in the millions or billions should be expressed with a combination of figures and words.

> At least *1.5 million* readers subscribe to the ten top magazines.

> Deposits in money market accounts totalled more than *$115 billion*.

4.11 Weights and Measurements.   Weights and measurements are expressed with figures.

> The new deposit slip measures *5* by *15* cm.

> Some desktop calculators weigh only *1.2* kg.

> Regina is *750* kilometres from Calgary.

4.12 Fractions.   Simple fractions are expressed as words. Complex fractions may be written either as figures or as a combination of figures and words. Fractions used as adjectives require hyphens.

> Over *two-thirds* of the stockholders voted.

> This microcomputer will execute the command in *1 millionth* of a second. (Combination of words and numbers is easier to comprehend.)

She purchased a *one-fifth* share in the business.

4.13 Percentages and Decimals.   Percentages are expressed with figures that are followed by the word *percent*. Percentages used as adjectives require hyphens. The percent sign (%) is used only on business forms or in statistical presentations.

> We had hoped for a *6-percent* interest rate, but we received a loan at *7 percent*.

> Over *50 percent* of the residents supported the plan.

Decimals are expressed with figures. If a decimal expression does not contain a whole number (an integer) and does not begin with a zero, a zero should be placed before the decimal point.

> The actuarial charts show that *1.74* out of 1000 people will die in any given year.

> Inspector Norris found the setting to be *.005* inch off. (Decimal begins with a zero and does not require a zero before the decimal point.)

> Considerable savings will accrue if the unit production cost is reduced by *0.1* percent. (A zero is placed before a decimal that neither contains a whole number nor begins with a zero.)

Quick Chart—Expression of Numbers

Use Words	Use Figures
Numbers *ten* and under	Numbers *11* and over
Numbers at beginning of sentence	Money
Periods of time	Dates
Ages (note exceptions in 4.09)	Addresses and telephone numbers
Fractions	Weights and measurements
	Percentages and decimals

Review Exercise N—Number Style

Circle *a* or *b* to indicate the preferred number style. Assume that these numbers appear in business correspondence. When you finish, compare your responses with those shown below. For each item on which you need review, consult the numbered principle shown in parentheses.

1. (a) 2 alternatives   (b) two alternatives   _____ **(4.01a)**
2. (a) Seventh Avenue   (b) 7th Avenue   _____ **(4.05b)**
3. (a) sixty sales reps   (b) 60 sales reps   _____ **(4.01a)**
4. (a) November ninth   (b) November 9   _____ **(4.03)**

(4.02)	
(4.03)	
(4.04)	
(4.07)	
(4.08)	
(4.10)	
(4.02)	
(4.08)	
(4.13)	
(4.12)	
(4.11)	
(4.10)	
(4.04)	
(4.05a)	
(4.06)	
(4.06)	

5. (a) forty dollars   (b) $40

6. (a) on the 23d of May   (b) on the twenty-third of May

7. (a) at 2:00 p.m.   (b) at 2 p.m.

8. (a) 4 two-hundred page books   (b) four 200-page books

9. (a) at least 15 years ago   (b) at least fifteen years ago

10. (a) 1,000,000 viewers   (b) 1 million viewers

11. (a) twelve cents   (b) 12 cents

12. (a) a sixty-day warranty   (b) a 60-day warranty

13. (a) ten-percent interest rate   (b) 10-percent interest rate

14. (a) 4/5 of the voters   (b) four-fifths of the voters

15. (a) the rug measures one by two metres   (b) the rug measures 1 by 2 m

16. (a) about five hundred people attended   (b) about 500 people attended

17. (a) at eight o'clock   (b) at 8 o'clock

18. (a) located at 1 Broadway Boulevard   (b) located at One Broadway Boulevard

19. (a) three computers for twelve people   (b) three computers for 12 people

20. (a) 4 out of every 100 licences   (b) four out of every 100 licences

1. b   3. b   5. b   7. b   9. b   11. b   13. b   15. b   17. a or b   19. b

Correction Symbols

Agr	Agreement error
Awk	Awkward
Cap	Capitalization
Chop	Choppy
Cl	Clarity
Coh	Coherence
CS	Comma splice
Emp	Emphasis
Exp	Expletive
Frag	Fragment
Jarg	Jargon
Log	Logic
MM	Misplaced or dangling modifier
Neg	Negative tone
Org	Organization
Par	Parallel construction
Pas	Passive voice
Pn	Punctuation
RB	Reader benefit
Rdn	Redundant
Ref	Reference unclear
Rep	Repetitious
Run-on	Run-together sentence
Sp	Spelling
Spec	Lacks specificity
Syx	Syntax
Tone	Tone
TR	Transition
Var	Sentence variety
W	Wordy
WW	Wrong or inappropriate word
X	Obvious error
?	Do you really mean this?

Index

NOTES

NOTES

NOTES

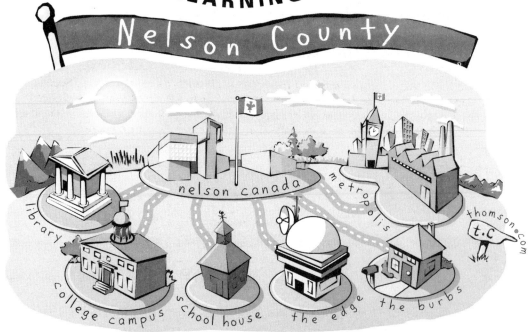

To the owner of this book

We hope that you have enjoyed *Essentials of Business Communication,* Second Canadian Edition, and we would like to know as much about your experiences with this text as you would care to offer. Only through your comments and those of others can we learn how to make this a better text for future readers.

School _____   Your instructor's name _____

Course _____   Was the text required? _____   Recommended? _____

1. What did you like the most about *Essentials of Business Communication?*

_____

_____

_____

2. How useful was this text for your course?

_____

_____

_____

3. Do you have any recommendations for ways to improve the next edition of this text?

_____

_____

_____

4. In the space below or in a separate letter, please write any other comments you have about the book. (For example, please feel free to comment on reading level, writing style, terminology, design features, and learning aids.)

_____

_____

_____

Optional

Your name _____   Date _____

May ITP Nelson quote you, either in promotion for *Essentials of Business Communication* or in future publishing ventures?

Yes _____   No _____

Thanks!

PLEASE TAPE SHUT. DO NOT STAPLE.

TAPE SHUT

TAPE SHUT

— — FOLD HERE — — —

I(T)P® Nelson
an International Thomson Publishing company

MAIL POSTE
Canada Post Corporation
Société canadienne des postes
Postage paid   Port payé
if mailed in Canada   si posté au Canada
Business Reply   Réponse d'affairess

0066102399   01

0066102399-M1K5G4-BR01

ITP NELSON
MARKET AND PRODUCT DEVELOPMENT
P.O. BOX 60223 STN BRN 8
TORONTO ON M7Y 2H1

TAPE SHUT

TAPE SHUT